THE NEW MIDDLE AGES

BONNIE WHEELER, *Series Editor*

The New Middle Ages is a series dedicated to transdisciplinary studies of medieval cultures, with particular emphasis on recuperating women's history and on femi st and gender analyses. This peer-reviewed series includes both scholarly monographs and essay collections.

PUBLISHED BY PALGRAVE:

Women in the Medieval Islamic World: Power, Patronage, and Piety
edited by Gavin R. G. Hambly

The Ethics of Nature in the Middle Ages: On Boccaccio's Poetaphysics
by Gregory B. Stone

Presence and Presentation: Women in the Chinese Literati Tradition
by Sherry J. Mou

The Lost Love Letters of Heloise and Abelard: Perceptions of Dialogue in Twelfth-Century France
by Constant J. Mews

Understanding Scholastic Thought with Foucault
by Philipp W. Rosemann

For Her Good Estate: The Life of Elizabeth de Burgh
by Frances A. Underhill

Constructions of Widowhood and Virginity in the Middle Ages
edited by Cindy L. Carlson and Angela Jane Weisl

Motherhood and Mothering in Anglo-Saxon England
by Mary Dockray-Miller

Listening to Heloise: The Voice of a Twelfth-Century Woman
edited by Bonnie Wheeler

The Postcolonial Middle Ages
edited by Jeffrey Jerome Cohen

Chaucer's Pardoner and Gender Theory: Bodies of Discourse
by Robert S. Sturges

Crossing the Bridge: Comparative Essays on Medieval European and Heian Japanese Women Writers
edited by Barbara Stevenson and Cynthia Ho

Engaging Words: The Culture of Reading in the Later Middle Ages
by Laurel Amtower

Robes and Honor: The Medieval World of Investiture
edited by Stewart Gordon

Representing Rape in Medieval and Early Modern Literature
edited by Elizabeth Robertson and Christine M. Rose

Same Sex Love and Desire Among Women in the Middle Ages
edited by Francesca Canadé Sautman and Pamela Sheingorn

Sight and Embodiment in the Middle Ages: Ocular Desires
by Suzannah Biernoff

Listen, Daughter: The Speculum Virginum and the Formation of Religious Women in the Middle Ages
edited by Constant J. Mews

Science, the Singular, and the Question of Theology
by Richard A. Lee, Jr.

Gender in Debate from the Early Middle Ages to the Renaissance
edited by Thelma S. Fenster and Clare A. Lees

Malory's Morte Darthur: Remaking Arthurian Tradition
by Catherine Batt

The Vernacular Spirit: Essays on Medieval Religious Literature
edited by Renate Blumenfeld-Kosinski, Duncan Robertson, and Nancy Warren

Popular Piety and Art in the Late Middle Ages: Image Worship and Idolatry in England 1350–1500
by Kathleen Kamerick

Absent Narratives, Manuscript Textuality, and Literary Structure in Late Medieval England
by Elizabeth Scala

Creating Community with Food and Drink in Merovingian Gaul
by Bonnie Effros

Representations of Early Byzantine Empresses: Image and Empire
by Anne McClanan

Encountering Medieval Textiles and Dress: Objects, Texts, Images
edited by Désirée G. Koslin and Janet Snyder

Eleanor of Aquitaine: Lord and Lady
edited by Bonnie Wheeler and John Carmi Parsons

Isabel La Católica, Queen of Castile: Critical Essays
edited by David A. Boruchoff

Homoeroticism and Chivalry: Discourses of Male Same-Sex Desire in the Fourteenth Century
by Richard Zeikowitz

Portraits of Medieval Women: Family, Marriage, and Politics in England 1225–1350
by Linda E. Mitchell

Eloquent Virgins: From Thecla to Joan of Arc
by Maud Burnett McInerney

HYBRIDITY, IDENTITY, AND MONSTROSITY IN MEDIEVAL BRITAIN: ON DIFFICULT MIDDLES

Jeffrey Jerome Cohen

HYBRIDITY, IDENTITY, AND MONSTROSITY IN MEDIEVAL BRITAIN: ON DIFFICULT MIDDLES
© Jeffrey Jerome Cohen, 2006.

First published in 2006 by
PALGRAVE MACMILLAN™
175 Fifth Avenue, New York, N.Y. 10010 and
Houndmills, Basingstoke, Hampshire, England RG21 6XS
Companies and representatives throughout the world.

PALGRAVE MACMILLAN is the global academic imprint of the Palgrave Macmillan division of St. Martin's Press, LLC and of Palgrave Macmillan Ltd. Macmillan® is a registered trademark in the United States, United Kingdom and other countries. Palgrave is a registered trademark in the European Union and other countries.

ISBN 13: 978–1–4039–6971–2
ISBN 10: 1–4039–6971–X

Library of Congress Cataloging-in-Publication Data

Cohen, Jeffrey Jerome.
    Hybridity, identity, and monstrosity in medieval Britain: on difficul'
    middles / Jeffrey Jerome Cohen.
        p. cm.—(New Middle Ages)
    Includes bibliographical references (p.) and index.
    ISBN 1–4039–6971–X (alk. paper)
     1. Great Britain—Ethnic relations—History—To 1500.
    2. Hybridity (Social sciences)—Great Britain—History—To 1500.
    3. Great Britain—History—Medieval period, 1066–1485. 4. Group
    identity—Great Britain—History—To 1500. 5. Great Britain—Race
    relations—History—To 1500. 6. Racism—Great Britain—History—To
    1500. 7. Monsters—History—To 1500. I. Title. II. New Middle Ages
    (Palgrave Macmillan (Firm))

DA125.A1C63 2006
305.8009′02—dc22   2005054640

A catalogue record for this book is available from the British Library.

Design by Newgen Imaging Systems (P) Ltd., Chennai, India.

First edition: May 2006

10 9 8 7 6 5 4 3 2 1

Printed in the United States of America.

CONTENTS

ACKNOWLEDGMENTS

Because the project that became this book has been with me for a long time, its contours have been shaped by far more people than I can account for in these acknowledgments. I apologize in advance for their inadequacy.

Bonnie Wheeler ensured that this book would have a home in the New Middle Ages series. I am deeply grateful for the decade of support she has given my work. Farideh Koohi-Kamali made working with Palgrave Macmillan a pleasure. Glenn Burger inspired transformation at a time of crisis. His friendship and patient insightfulness have been sustaining. Kathleen Biddick provided a helpful reading of the manuscript and engaged me in a series of catalytic discussions over enduring themes. Gail Kern Paster, my former colleague and current director of the Folger Shakespeare Library, encouraged me to take a more distant perspective on the project and to come to some grander conclusions. Her comradeship and exemplary scholarship have been a lasting gift. My thanks to these longtime supporters and recent inspirations: Larry Benson, Leah Chang, Daniel Donoghue, Rick Emmerson, Tara Foster, Noreen Giffney, Thomas Hahn, Bob Hanning, Gil Harris (with whom I look forward to a deepening friendship), Joseph Harris, Paul Hyams, Patricia Ingham, John Ganim, Ethan Knapp, Stephen Kruger, Melani McAlister, Derek Pearsall, Michael O'Rourke, Robert McRuer, Linda Salamon, Todd Ramlow, Adrian W. Randolph, Kellie Robertson, Marc Saperstein, Daniel Simmons, R. Allen Shoaf, Vance Smith, Sylvia Tomasch, Michael Uebel, Bruce Venarde, Peter Travis, Keith Ward, Gail Weiss, and Jon K. Williams.

I am grateful to Maria Teresa Chialant for inviting me to think about Jews and monsters for a symposium she organized at the Università di Salerno. The events of September 11 altered the tenor of that meeting dramatically and forced me to rethink how collective identities might change in the face of trauma. Shayne Legassie and Shirin Azizeh Khanmohamadi kindly gave me the chance to continue this investigation in New York. William Chester Jordan's invitation to compose an entry on race for a supplement to the *Dictionary of the Middle Ages* arrived at a formative time.

Audiences at the University of Alberta at Edmonton, University of Pittsburgh, Rutgers, Columbia, Cornell, Dartmouth, and the University of Leicester challenged and encouraged me as the project developed. Although the paper I presented at "Illuminations: Medieval / Modern" organized by Francisco Prado-Vilar will be part of my next book, I want to thank him and the participants in the workshop. That collegial gathering inspired a final burst of energy, ambition, and enthusiasm as the project assumed its final form.

The research and writing of this book were supported by a yearlong fellowship from the American Council of Learned Societies, a summer of research funding through the University Facilitating Fund of the George Washington University, and a year of teaching release under GW's Columbian Scholars program. I thank my beloved department chair Faye Moskowitz as well as William Frawley, dean of the Columbian College of GW, for the freedom they have given me to pursue this work, and for their unflagging confidence. I hope they will be happy with the result. A section of the third chapter of this book appeared in the edited collection *The Postcolonial Middle Ages* (Palgrave Macmillan 2000). Material in chapters four and five derives in part from my article "The Flow of Blood in Medieval Norwich," *Speculum* 78 (2004).

More personally, the book would not have been completed without the usual suspects: my parents and siblings, and especially my brother Mark; my son Alexander, who after eight years is still teaching me the proper practice of wonder; my partner in everything that matters, Wendy, who retains the ability to make the impossible likely. Finally, this book is dedicated to a life that came into the world during the most intense period of its composition: Katherine Eleanor Chave Cohen. As I finish these last words she has just turned sixteen months old, and is already a kick-ass feminist. Her father adores her.

INTRODUCTION: *IN MEDIAS RES*

When contemplating the many peoples who had inhabited their island's expanses, writers in twelfth-century Britain found themselves pulled in two divergent directions. Living in the difficult aftermath of conquest, they were powerfully attracted to a stark vision of past and present in which collective identities remained constant, retaining their elemental differences. The triumphant arrival of a new people (the Romans in the days of Caesar, the English in the fifth century, the Normans at Hastings) had led, they supposed, to a transfer of dominion, a change in power that strengthened the boundaries between communities rather than eroded them. This idea of a keenly distinct past for each insular people had been bequeathed to the twelfth century by predecessors like Gildas and Bede. One a polemicist for the native Britons and the other a partisan of the parvenu Angles, these writers arrived from opposite sides of a bitter struggle for British hegemony. Both composed narratives stressing the separateness of the peoples with whom they identified. Neither allowed some middle space to exist where the two might ally, mingle, even combine. Like the classical and patristic authors in whom they had been trained, Gildas and Bede assumed the enduring distinctiveness of the earth's populations.

Yet there also lurked the haunting knowledge that the world is combinative and complicated. Bede's immigrant ancestors may have eradicated or marginalized many of Britain's indigenes, but they are just as likely to have merged with insular populations, spurring mutual assimilations and profound transformations. The Normans may have conquered England and annexed Wales, but they also vanished in the process, assimilating to—as well as deeply altering—native ways. Between imagined or desired absolutes like "Angle" and "Briton," "English" and "Norman," "Christian" and "Jew" flourished recalcitrant impurities. In the wake of conquest as well as of less martial kinds of cultural encounter, fusions of difference inevitably arise. Postcolonial theorists label such conflictual convergence *hybridity*. As Robert J. C. Young has observed, hybridity is a concept that can carry two antithetical meanings, "contrafusion and disjunction . . . as well as fusion and assimilation."[1] Like its contemporary manifestations examined by Young, hybridity in medieval Britain tended to mix both these senses. Never synthetic in the sense of homogenizing, hybridity is a fusion *and* a disjunction, a conjoining of differences that cannot simply harmonize.

Because, for the most part, medieval historiography stressed the timeless separation of peoples, generic and linguistic constraints ensured that hybridity was not easy to express. Coincidence of the divergent was especially disquieting to writers who carried admixture in their very body, writers who labored to invent some lexicon for representing their compound composition. The historian William of Malmesbury and the ethnographer Gerald of Wales were the biological products of conquest. Their mixed descent triggered self-conflict, fostering a hesitancy evident in the sometimes uncertain texts they composed. Yet even authors who appeared to lack such postcolonial ambivalence were unable to efface completely the hybridity that permeated their worlds. Bede (who bequeathed to the twelfth century its dominating picture of the English past), Geoffrey of Monmouth (who authored a counter-history in which the Britons replaced Bede's glorious Angles), and Thomas of Monmouth (who wrote a saint's life that attempted to reintegrate a city sundered by conquest) authored narratives in which the island's peoples seem, at first glance, to form well bounded communities. These writers limned and thereby solidified the borders of collective identities by demonizing Britons, Saxons, or Jews. On deeper examination, however, all three of their texts yield glimpses of a roiling interpenetration of peoples and cultures, tempestuous intermediacies that undermine clean separations.

Hybridity, Identity, and Monstrosity in Medieval Britain maps collective identities on the twelfth-century island, concentrating upon the postcolonial expanses that I call difficult middles. Such medial spaces were difficult in a double sense: difficult to articulate, and difficult to inhabit. And yet they were everywhere. Hybrid geographies burgeoned in the wake of migration, conquest, and colonization. They proliferated at interstices, in border zones, along margins. They could also thrive within seemingly homogeneous centers. The ambit of this book therefore wanders Ireland, the Welsh march, and provincial and cosmopolitan England. Such middles, I do not doubt, erupted within many genres of twelfth-century writing. I limit myself here, however, to provocative examples from three Latin discourses: historiography, ethnography, and hagiography. William of Malmesbury's *History of the English Kings,* Geoffrey of Monmouth's *History of the Kings of Britain,* Gerald of Wales various Welsh and Irish texts, and Thomas of Monmouth's *Life and Miracles of Saint William of Norwich* betray a recurring fascination with abstruse but spectacular phenomena—prodigies, transformed persons, sorcerers, bestiality, tempests formed of blood, monsters, reveries of dismemberment, cadavers possessed of abiding life. These arresting figures embody the medialities precise language could not well express. Refusing the chaste solitude of singular categories, they intermixed and confounded all that was supposed to be held apart. Hence the monstrousness in my title, indicating that hybridity enticed identities to mutate into forms seemingly beyond the borders of the humanly possible, forms that in fact dwelled alarmingly close to home.

By the time the twelfth century drew to a close, the vigorous English community disrupted by the Norman Conquest had reconsolidated, in part by dehumanizing people who differed in religion, language, custom, descent, history. The pages of this book follow the struggles that occurred in Wales, in Ireland, and within England itself as some of their residents strained against debasing representation. The Welsh, the Irish and the Scots found themselves rendered barbarians or beasts, dwelling at a savage periphery. Likewise monsterized were the Jews, imagined to imperil the lives of Christians in the English cities where they cohabitated. Narratives of separation in the guise of ethnography, history, and hagiography helped to bring exclusive political and cultural solidities into being. Yet difficult middles proliferated at the heart or along the margins of these circumscriptive works, promising alternative histories, visions of the past and present in which difference never proves absolute, and English triumphalism becomes only one possibility among many others.

Of the peoples populating twelfth-century Britain's imagined past, some possessed a lengthy history, real or assumed (English, Irish, Scots, Welsh); some had vanished through emigration, acculturation, or eradication (Romans, Picts, Danes); one was a minority whose cultural importance far overshadowed its meager physical presence (the Jews); one was paradoxically both separate and rapidly assimilating (the Normans); and one was not a group who had ever inhabited Britain, but who were present all the same through historiography, crusade polemic, and the visual arts (Saracens). Yet all these collective identities do not, at some profound level, exist. In reviewing Marjorie Chibnall's important book *The Normans*, Leah Shopkow notes that the founding fathers of Normandy were not French-speakers but a diverse array of Scandinavians; that the Normans never constituted a majority population of any geography they made their own; that Norman invaders tended to adopt quickly local languages and customs; that their invasion forces were ethnically diverse; and that a century and a half after their unprecedented expansion the only Normans who had not vanished into other populations were those who had remained in Normandy, where they were destined to be absorbed into France. We may therefore wonder with Shopkow what exactly made all these people Normans to begin with.[2] Despite the difficulties we contemporaries might have with the collective noun, however, the Normans themselves were confident that they possessed what G. A. Loud labels a "racial distinctiveness."[3] Even while their official histories acknowledged their mixed origins, they seldom wavered in their conviction that they were a singular and united people, set apart from all others.

As part of our medieval inheritance we often speak as if groups such as the Normans, Britons, and English persisted from time immemorial, continuous and unchanged. Typically, however, the peoples in question were heterogeneous solidarities that altered over time, both in composition and self-definition.[4] Such mutable groups possess no stable or core essence. They are not reducible to genetic inheritance or biological descent. Their enduring status as a collective belongs to the realm of fantasy, where it nonetheless demonstrates a powerful ability to give substance and historical stability to what is ultimately impalpable. Community has to be imagined, to use Benedict Anderson's useful phrase, because it never arrives preformed. Such communalization is typically a process of sorting difference, establishing boundaries, and separating the world's disorder into peoples held to be patently discrete.

It used to be assumed, as the medieval sources themselves assume, that Rome dissolved when Europe was invaded by culturally homogeneous groups such as the Goths. The large-scale movements of these barbarians, it was thought, displaced aboriginal populations, either through genocide or forced relocation. Recently, however, scholars such as Walter Pohl have argued that via a process dubbed *ethnogenesis* collective identities can quickly metamorphosize. Ethnogenesis typically works when a minority elite imposes its culture upon a subjugated population. Invaded peoples are not eradicated but absorbed into a newly dominating identity. Much contemporary work on the peoples who eventually became known as the Britons, the Anglo-Saxons, and the Danes of the Danelaw stresses that the number of immigrants to the British Islands was likely to have been small. Freshly arriving warriors would have intermarried with indigenous peoples, impressing upon them their art, religion, values, culture, making it appear that what was in biological fact a mixed community constituted a fairly unified group of "Britons" or "Anglo-Saxons" or "Danes."[5] In this way a native population could be transformed at the hands of a band of conquerors. As Florin Curta points out in his summary of recent anthropological work on ethnicity, group identity may be culturally constructed through such impositions, but it is not thereby rendered insubstantial: "ethnicity is not innate, but individuals are born with it . . . it is not biologically reproduced, but individuals are linked to it through cultural constructions of biology."[6]

Collective identity is paradoxical. Although it may seem to offer at any given moment an impermeable boundary, firmly separating one people from another, over time its contours tend to be elastic, altering to adapt to changing political and cultural contexts. This dynamism can be productive, allowing a previously divided or heterogeneous group to cohere. Strategic adoption of communal nomination, the embrace of a mythic history, and the monsterization of those exterior to community can give even a newly amalgamated identity a seemingly ancient solidity. Yet enforcement of a circumscriptive boundary to demarcate the members of this ascendant identity often foists restrictive union upon those who have been excluded. Should this latter people also be politically subordinate, the reconfigured identity bestowed upon them will tend to congeal into a carceral category, locking them in alien terms. It will often seem that between those who have been "othered" (represented as inferior, bestial, monstrous) and those who belong to some dominating collective (in this book typically the English, but sometimes the Normans) exists a firm line of segregation. Yet the geography of this border space always turns out to be vast. Between belongings stretch precarious expanses inhabited by hybridities irreducible to one side or another of a bifurcated world.

In the Middle

Much of my previous scholarship has been dedicated to exploring the middle spaces of the Middle Ages: the regions between the human and the monster, the normal and the queer, woman and man, Christian and Jew or Saracen, human and animal. Much of this work has made use of psychoanalytic theory and the philosophy of Gilles Deleuze and Félix Guattari. This book continues my ongoing investigation into identity at its limits, making somewhat quieter use of contemporary critical race, feminist, and postcolonial theory. This project is intended to contribute to what a collective of fourteen medievalists have nominated the *Postcolonial Middle Ages*, where "postcolonial" stands for a diverse alliance of work that stresses the uneven structures of power that come into being when cultures meet.[7] Conquest, domination, and injustice are predictable outcomes of such clashes. Innovation, hybridity, and resistance are, however, never far behind. Postcolonial theory has explored at great lengths and within a multitude of traditions the discordant commingling of differences that produces hybridity. The utility of such work as a spur to reconceptualizing cultural admixture in the medieval period is immense.[8] Hybridity does not indicate some peaceful melding of colonizer and colonized. It does not imply the purity or homogeneity of categories such as "subaltern" prior to the advent of conquest, and it neither obliterates nor supersedes the histories it intermingles. Hybridity is so useful because it can never be an absolute category. Ashcroft, Griffiths, and Tiffin aptly call it a productive "interleaving" that engenders the new without superseding anterior cultures.[9] Homi Bhabha describes hybridity as provisional, unstable, even ludic. Incapable of calling into being some "totalizing, transcendent identity," hybridity is a space where "cultural differences 'contingently' and conflictually touch," inducing panic, resisting binarism.[10] Bhabha's work has rightfully been instrumental for medievalists engaged in postcolonial-inflected projects. Yet I have also made ample use of critical models amplified outside of English India. Analysis of Caribbean creolization by Antonio Benitez-Rojo and Edward Kamau Brathwaite are especially provocative for their emphasis on how hybridity proliferates novel forms without obliterating their incongruous histories. Gloria Anzaldúa's poetic framing of *mestizaje* at the U.S.-Mexican borderlands conjoins a somber contemplation of past violence to an exuberant exploration of future becomings. Her reverie on border identities seems at times positively medieval with its inventive deployment of marvels and monsters.[11] Although I will not explicitly engage much of this work until midway through this book, the influence of these writers should be evident throughout.

My focus is mainly upon the southeast portion of the island of Britain, an area that consolidated itself into a unified kingdom and baptized itself England. I stress, however, the dependence of that nation's self-definition upon those with whom it shared geographic and imaginative space. The book is divided into five chapters that tell a cumulative though not quite chronological story. Some of the common threads binding the analysis are an interest in the dynamics of community formation, especially in the wake of conquest; an emphasis upon exclusion and demonization as catalysts to self-delimitation; and an inquiry into what function narratives play in precipitating or revitalizing such unions. Every chapter centers upon or comes back to the impurity and heterogeneity that impossibly neat categories like "English" and "Christian" conceal. The tumultuous admixture of what was supposed to be held separate is frequently the work of the medieval monster, a defiantly intermixed figure that is in the end simply the most startling incarnation of hybridity made flesh. The monster can embody the abject, such as when the Welsh or the Jews are transfigured into bloodthirsty foes, bereft of humanity. Yet the monster can also offer a body through which can be dreamed the dangerous contours of an identity that refuses assimilation and purity.

"Acts of Separation," the first chapter, provides a succinct overview of the components from which collective identity was held to be formed in twelfth-century Britain. Many of the elements integral to status as a separate people seem at first glance to be disembodied or abstract: customs, ritual, law, language, religion. Yet each of these was understood to be a nearly congenital inheritance, the corporeal performance and fleshly expression of a shared and preexistent selfhood. The sheer embodiedness and therefore the intractability of collective identity was reinforced by theories that tied national character to ancient climatological and environmental influence. Of course, history proves that a people's laws can be changed, languages can be learned or exterminated, and a heterogeneous assortment of peoples can become a single race that believes firmly in its own individuality. Difference can be abjected onto foreigners or subalterns, people who might be represented as not in possession of full humanity; yet group status and relative prestige tend to fluctuate over time. Because of the human tendency toward mutability and admixture, collective identity was always troubled by its own fragility. Hybrid middle spaces therefore tended to be imagined as dangerous borders.

Chapter 2, "Between Belongings," examines texts by Bede, William of Malmesbury, and Geoffrey of Monmouth, three historians who turned to the past to dream collective identities essential to a troubled present. When Bede composed his *Ecclesiastical History of the English People*, no England yet existed. The southeast of the island was a battleground of small kingdoms in martial competition. These petty realms were amalgams of peoples whose ancestors had arrived from various parts of northern Europe, displacing and absorbing native Britons. By imaging that a multicultural and conflicted expanse was the natural dominion of a single race, the *gens Anglorum*, Bede bequeathed to history a powerful formulation of English singularity. When a country called England did arrive two centuries later, it was happy to embrace Bede's myth of origin. The events of 1066, however, struck a severe blow against this unity. Writing early in the twelfth century, the monk William of Malmesbury attempted to restore continuity to what seemed a disjunct past. Of dual Norman and English descent, William thought that he was well positioned to accomplish this task. Yet reconciling the two pieces of his identity proved no easier than accommodating the Normans into native history. A fascination with the monstrous, with bodies that cannot reconcile their constitutive differences, pervades William's narration of postcolonial England. As anxious as William may have been about English identity, however, he probably never felt the same defensiveness as the Welsh, a people dismissed by both the English and the Normans alike as barbarians. The last section of the chapter examines how Geoffrey of Monmouth wrote an alternative account of Britain that could challenge the Anglocentric version originated by Bede and reinvigorated by William. A mischievous and confounding text, Geoffrey's *History of the Kings of Britain* renarrated the British past, founding the island upon blood that at first glance seems remarkably pure but on closer examination turns out to be far more hybrid than even that which coursed through William of Malmesbury's veins.

"In the Borderlands," the third chapter, explores how a compound heritage haunted another famous writer of the twelfth century. At once a celibate cleric, Paris-educated intellectual, court chaplain, preacher of crusade, and the descendant of a Norman conquistador and a Welsh princess, Gerald of Wales spent his long life discovering that his multiplicitous identity could be severely circumscribed by the definitional power of others. The English elite could dismiss him as Welsh, while the Welsh could reject him as French. Gerald was never able to reconcile the multiple histories that he incarnated, the doubled blood that he bore. Early in his career he alleviated some of his uncertainty by energetically participating in the conquest of Ireland, an island distant enough for him to imagine that its population was a subhuman race, barely distinguishable from livestock. As Gerald began to sympathize and in part identify with another barbarian people, the Welsh, he became obsessed by monstrous bodies. Strangely admixed forms became his dominant mode not only for representation of hybridity but for launching an exploration of his own conflicted flesh.

The analysis moves in the fourth chapter, "City of Catastrophes," from the vastness of national and international space to the confines of a provincial city. The dominant urban center in East Anglia, Norwich, became an economic force during the period of the Viking settlement and was, at the eve of the Norman Conquest, among the most populous communities of England. Perhaps because of its associations with the family of the last English king, Norwich was profoundly reconfigured by the new wielders of insular dominion. The implantation of a massive castle, towering cathedral, and French borough radically altered urban topography. Native architectural and social structures were demolished, replaced by imported ones different from anything Norwich had previously known. "City of Catastrophes" reads these challenges to identity and community not only from surviving texts but from urban space itself, arguing that in the transformation of Norwich can be glimpsed the material consequences of the conquest, and especially its shattering effect upon indigenous ways of life. To restore harmony to this fractured, violently commingled community was going to take not only time but a miracle.

Or a whole series of miracles. The last chapter, "The Flow of Blood in Norwich," investigates the attempts by the masters of the Norman cathedral to foster a new saint's cult. In 1144, a twelve-year-old boy named William was found murdered in the woods just outside the city. His corpse bore the marks of torture. An accusation was made by his family that William had been martyred by Norwich's most recent immigrants, the Jews. The boy's bereaved family found surprising allies in the monks who staffed the city's cathedral, and William's cult enabled a city sundered by history to begin to imagine itself as a unity. This chapter explores how the

Life of St William, composed by Thomas of Monmouth, attempts to imagine this new community, but at the same time betrays the lingering differences that prevent an ultimate harmony. Thomas's text sloughs onto the Jews the alterity that once characterized the Normans arriving in Norwich, and makes the argument that should the city rid itself of these monsters dwelling amongst them, the traumatic history still evident in the city's topography will finally be surmounted. The text attempts to perform a purification, purging the city of hybridity and lasting difference by embodying all that is intolerable in the homicidal Jews.

My evidence throughout this book is gathered mainly from narratives composed by a changed island's clerical elite. These energetic and literate men, introspective and unfailingly ambitious, turned to the writing of history, hagiography, and ethnography in order to make sense of a difficult present. They lived during a time of extraordinary cultural clash and social change. Many were, as a result, of mixed heritage. William of Malmesbury was Norman on his fathers' side and English on his mother's. In the body of Gerald of Wales, the blood of Norman Marchers alloyed with that of Welsh royalty. Geoffrey and Thomas, both of whom styled themselves "of Monmouth," were of unknown descent, but traced their origin from a border town known for its commingling of Welsh, Bretons, Normans, and English. Not all of the texts examined in this book are linguistic, however, nor is the focus simply upon communal identifications as grand as the nation. My discussion of Gerald of Wales focuses upon an identity agonizingly personal. The book's fourth and fifth chapters are forays into local and urban history, reading upheavals in communal belonging through the drastically altered contours of a city. Although this book focuses upon England, my approach is oblique: England by way of the archipelago into which it was rapidly expanding, England without anglophilia. By stressing the internal heterogeneity of the inhabitants of the British Isles, my aim is to foreground the differences that had to be surmounted in order to imagine that England constituted a homogeneous unity. By stressing the importance of minority populations in general and one in particular, I also intend to counteract somewhat a limitation that Sheila Delany aptly labels inherent in "our normative training" as medievalists, a training that tends to be "profoundly eurocentric and, within that, christiancentric."[12] This book is therefore populated by the Jews, barbarians, and other human monsters who found themselves ineligible for inclusion in the burgeoning England of the twelfth century. Throughout my analysis, whether of histories that link present perturbations to a more settled past in the hopes of a stable future, or of hatred unleashed against outsiders in order to bring internal cohesion to collectives, or of the irreconcilable differences that a postcolonial society plants deep in the flesh of its members, I find in every case that medieval narratives of collective identity are bordered by and frequently enclose at their heart confounding hybridities.

It is to an examination of the construction of corporate identity that I now turn, with an eye to explaining why it is that a people can seem at once eternally stable and perpetually in flux, and what middle spaces expand between even the most solid of boundaries.

CHAPTER 1

ACTS OF SEPARATION: SHAPING
COMMUNAL BODIES

Critical race theory is an interdisciplinary approach to the study of what are (to the medievalist) recent collective identities: African American, Hispanic, white, and so on. Drawing from the analysis of law and culture as well as literature and history, this school of criticism stresses that even though race is typically assumed to be stable, enduring, and biological, in fact the contours and substance of race are subject to constant flux. Even if it is socially constructed rather than a pregiven fact, however, race is too intertwined with embodiment to be discarded or cavalierly dismissed.[1] Forces beyond the control of any particular individual circumscribe the limits of collective identities, imbuing them with their relative cultural value and engendering a paradox. Identity, whether personal or collective, is at once solid and—especially over long periods of time—mutable. Race, like gender, is susceptible to change; yet race (like gender) has an undeniable materiality.

Collective identity in twelfth-century Britain was likewise both protean and refractory. The currents of history that flowed through the British archipelago enabled some groups to congeal into self-nominated collectives, while others found themselves rigidly defined in terms they had never dreamt. When in the course of the twelfth century the category "English" proved plastic enough to accommodate the Normans, two formerly hostile groups combined into a collective identity that seemed to retain its antiquity but was in fact a novel hybrid. For a dominating group, corporate identity anchors the present to a secure past, to a shared history. For subaltern groups such as the Irish, Scots, Welsh, or (immediately after the Norman Conquest) the English, collectivization can be a process of dehumanization, locking its victims into an abject category like barbarian, beast, or monster. Because history tends to be composed by the powerful, collective identity tends to be embodied most spectacularly by those who do not choose it, by the excluded and the ostracized.[2] It is produced through the disavowal of historical similarity and the denial of those difficult and difference-ridden middles out of which purified collectives actually emerge. Perversely, however, even more of these medial spaces will proliferate as the separations necessary to maintain firm categories of communal difference are undercut by their occupants' adamant refusal to stay in their allotted places.

The historians Robert Bartlett and R. R. Davies have elaborated the taxonomies medieval peoples employed in conceptualizing their distinctiveness. Stressing process and instability over abiding group essence, these scholars have published work instrumental to medievalists pondering the emergence and solidification of European identities. Like Bartlett and Davies, I will inventory the scattered phenomena that were held to constitute collective identity in the Middle Ages, but with the intention of connecting these segregations more immediately to embodiment, communal differentiation, the abjection of difference, and the disavowal of hybridity. Medieval authors, like their classical predecessors, wrote as if peoples retain their identities unchanged over long periods of time, typically in their flesh. For Bede the Angles of Northumbria were not all that different from the Angles in their continental homeland. For Henry of Huntingdon the Picts had lived in Britain for centuries and then simply ceased to be. For Geoffrey of Monmouth the Welsh were a single and united people because they shared common descent from Trojan exiles. Yet the world seldom obeys the rules for separation described by historians and ethnographers. Angle arrivals to what became Northumbria surely intermarried with other immigrants as well as native Britons; the Picts did not vanish but amalgamated with other peoples to become part of the cultural group we know as the Scots; neither the Britons nor the Welsh were Trojans, and neither the Britons nor the Welsh typically thought of themselves as a single community, at least not until collectivity was thrust upon them. Peoples intermarry; cultures blend; collective identities alter through infection, assimilation, acculturation, métissage. Against this variability, firm boundaries are posited, unchanging pasts fantasized. Uncertainties about the coherence and continuity of identity are allayed by embodying difference in exorbitant forms, in barbarians or monsters who are imagined to imperil community—but who in fact catalyze community by circumscribing its contours. Thus by the end of the twelfth century, England envisioned itself as under siege at its borders by bellicose Welsh and Scots, and at its center by homicidal Jews.

The "acts of separation" that the chapter's title designates are the sorting processes through which collective identities emerge. My evidence is gathered mainly from authors who will return throughout this book. I have attempted as well to include the sources with which these writers would have been familiar and to indicate how others in their intellectual milieu were imagining the particularity of the world's peoples. I will also from time to time indicate the future unfoldings of these group identities, sometimes bringing their histories into the thirteenth and fourteenth centuries. In bringing together so many scattered possibilities for how collective identity might be conceptualized in a twelfth-century insular context, I do not mean to imply that these manifold elements composed some unified or uniform discourse. Rather, in identifying the particles from which collectivity was typically assembled, and in sketching the general parameters within which community could be constructed, I am very much aware that individual writers often displayed a great deal of creativity. The best readings of collective identity will therefore be text-specific, and much of the remainder of this book is given over to such smaller scale analysis. Nonetheless it seems to me useful to examine what many conceptualizations of group commonality broadly shared, what acts of separation such categorizations were built upon, and what recalcitrant impurities such taxonomies denied.

Collective identity, like personhood and gender, is substantiated through repetition and citation.[3] It is therefore best described as bodily praxis, as an interminable process of embodiment. *Natio, gens, genus, stirps* and to a lesser extent *populus, nomen, sanguis,* and *lingua* are the most frequently encountered Latin nouns for collective identities in the Middle Ages. None are incorporeal. Even a word as seemingly abstract as *natio,* destined to become the modern English word *nation,* implies in a medieval context not a geopolitical entity like the United States, with its idea of a shared geography whose diverse population nonetheless forms a single community. A medieval *natio* need be nothing more than a group of people linked by their common descent (*consaguinitas*), since *natio* and its vernacular equivalents derive ultimately from the Latin verb *nasci,* "to be born." The word thereby carries implications that we would today describe as biological. The criteria deployed in twelfth-century Britain to separate the island's peoples may at first glance seem abstract, but were in fact inextricably somatic differentiations.

The Ethiopian's Skin

An episode that unfolded in medieval Norwich well illustrates the complex and sometimes perplexing relation between community and body, especially after the boundaries that are supposed to separate identities have been traversed. In 1230, a five-year-old boy was found wandering the riverbank in the East Anglian city of Norwich.[4] He tearfully announced that he was a Jew. After a woman named Matilda de Burnham brought him to her house, some Jewish men arrived and demanded the surrender of the boy, whom they called Jurnepin. When Matilda refused, they enjoined her not to feed him pork and set off for the royal castle in search of the sheriff. The boy's father, Benedict, was summoned by a woman who recognized the child. Meanwhile the Jews complained to the sheriff and the bailiffs, demanding custody. Having at first insisted that he was indeed Jurnepin, the boy when his father arrived admitted to being Benedict's son, Odard. Abducted by a man named Jacob while playing in the streets and held captive in his house, Odard/Jurnepin had been involuntarily circumcised. Senioret, "Jew of Norwich," was outlawed for performing the act, while thirteen others were called to trial for their crimes. A series of legal starts and stops beset the case, so that it was heard in turn by the citizens and church in Norwich, by the king and the archbishop of Canterbury, by a mixed jury of Jews and Christians. In the end three Jews were hanged: Isaac le Petit, Daia, and Mosse *cum Naso* ["Nosey Moses"]. The remainder either died awaiting trial or fled abroad and became fugitives, taking their families with them. Benedict's name and occupation of physician strongly suggest that he was a converted Jew. His former coreligionists seem to have been reclaiming his son, an act that they conducted fairly openly and with confidence in royal protection through the sheriff and bailiffs, officers of the crown, and therefore the agents charged with protecting its property, the Jews.[5]

Si mutare potest Aethiops pellem suam? As the Book of Jeremiah (13:23) asks in a formulation that medieval writers were fond of quoting when thinking about collective identity, can the leopard change its spots, can the Ethiopian change his skin? The identity of the little boy found crying by the River Wensum evokes profound uncertainties about the interconnections among body, ritual, religion, and identity. Behind these questions lay an unsettled history, not just in Norwich or in England but throughout the archipelago. The conquistadors of varied ancestry who had shared the spoils of William of Normandy's newly acquired realm originally collected themselves under the umbrella designation *Franci*, differentiating themselves from the subaltern English over whom they exerted power.[6] Yet the victors at Hastings assimilated to the identity of their subjects, not vice versa. English saints, traditions, laws, and history were adopted by the kingdom's new elite, engendering a tumultuously hybrid culture that preoccupied itself with trying to imagine an unbroken past. Despite the startling plasticity that the early years of the twelfth century witnessed, moreover, the century closed with its categories of collective identity hardened into the most resistant of cultural cement. A nearly unbreachable gulf yawned between the English and the other inhabitants of the island, making it difficult to assimilate a Jew who had embraced the very faith supposed to differentiate England not only from its Jews but also from the feral peoples who encompassed its borders. The people of Scotland, Ireland, and Wales were held to be Christian in name alone, as contemptible as pagans in the degenerate practice of their creed.[7]

The collective identities that have divided the British Isles for centuries solidified during the twelfth century, with England aggressively declaring its paninsular superiority. Four non-anglophone groups were lastingly relegated to subaltern status, three finding themselves inhabiting the fringe of England's center and the fourth expelled wholesale in 1290. Yet an incident like the forced circumcision of a five-year-old boy in 1230 could shake English confidence that island identities had been permanently ordered. Is the child discovered by the river a Christian or a Jew, free citizen of Norwich or property of the crown, redeemed from ignorance or captive to an alien mode of being, Odard or Jurnepin? To which people will he be returned, the francophone Jews who demand that he not eat pig flesh, or the English-speaking Christians who claim he belongs to Norwich in a way no Jew could? Whose blood runs through his veins? Does he take his identity from his convert father, from the people his father rebuked and who have ritually reclaimed him, from the community in which he is being raised, from the community of the realm, from the universal church? The movement of the trial from local to royal to ecclesiastical arenas suggests the widening gyre of these questions, as well as their potential irresolvability. Did Christ's blood wipe the boy clean at baptism? Did the sacrament eradicate the Jewishness of his father? Whose blood must be shed in payment for the boy's physical transformation? Has the blood spilled at his circumcision changed the sanguineous flow in his body, or was that ritual of Jewish belonging a reincorporation of blood that baptism failed to alter?

Despite the incomplete nature of the archival evidence, the controversy surrounding the circumcision of Odard/Jurnepin vividly illustrates the complicated connections between communal identity and body in the Middle Ages. To speak about blood is to speak of human corporeality, of our existence as embodied creatures. As a substance and as a metonymy for bodiliness itself, blood gives being its solidity, binding personhood to flesh. Yet blood is never individual. Ancestral blood binds collective histories to individuals, ensuring that the body is never merely personal but is always shared. Medieval conceptions of collectivity are thus often familial in their vocabulary, especially as origins are traced back to mythic founders. Hengest and Horsa, great-great grandsons of Odin himself, were said by the English historian Bede to be the primal leaders of the Anglo-Saxon settlement of Britain (*Ecclesiastical History* 1.15). Just as Aeneas engendered the Romans, according to British tradition his grandson Brutus bestowed cultural and corporeal heritage upon the Britons. By the twelfth century these *Britones, Cymry*, or Welsh might have been uninterested in anything but affiliations we would today call regional. They might have fought for no single ruler, allying themselves with petty princes engaged in internecine wars. They might not even have conceptualized Wales as a geopolitical entity in the same way that the colonizing English and Normans did. Yet the trauma of vigorously renewed invasion in the twelfth century provided a rallying point. Legendary Trojan descent allowed the scattered Welsh to gather themselves into a single people. Such a community could not coalesce, moreover, without related processes of disidentification.[8] The Welsh became the Welsh relationally, through the fact that they held themselves to be utterly different from the nearby English, Flemish, Normans, Irish, and Jews. These other peoples were imagined to have their own individuating histories, their own enduring collective identities.

Consaguinitas, "communal blood," binds individual to group, shared identity to personal body. Yet despite being integral to stabilizing and substantiating identities, blood is not solid matter but restless liquid. Inherited yet susceptible to environmental influence, sustaining the body yet eager to flow from it, blood cannot solidify immutable forms. Peoples change profoundly over time. Blood's protean energy, its unceasing movement toward connection, ensures that it will commingle previously disparate categories, will confuse what it was supposed to keep discrete. Blood congeals, providing a possible stability; and blood flows, seeking any egress it can find from circumscription. As coagulant blood is the very corporeality that materializes identity and makes it real. It is history's anchor to the body. But as fluctuant blood is constant movement, a promiscuous violator of boundary. Possessed of a dual nature, acting as both inertial force and catalyst to unexpected change, blood is no mere symbol or metaphor for community. Blood is community made flesh. Alive with a detritus of inherited forms, inexhaustible in its combinatory vitality, blood is perpetually forming new admixtures, new hybrids, new monsters.

What happens when a figure like Jurnepin/Odard moves from one community to another? Is his body transformed, or does the flesh resist? The answer, of course, is *neither* and *both*. Jurnepin/Odard remains a hyphenated form, a composite. Hybridity allows neither reduction nor return.

Collective Corporeality

In delineating the components of medieval race, Robert Bartlett takes as his point of departure Regino of Prüm (d. 915), a canonist who stated that the *nationes* of the world are distinguished by customs, language, laws, and descent.[9] These constituents of collective identity are seldom as keen as

Regino's confident articulation implies, especially because the first three are subject to rapid change and might be shared across cultural boundaries or not uniformly distributed within them. Multiple and mutually exclusive myths of origin could coexist without causing much dissonance. Yet some analogue of Regino's criteria was inevitably invoked whenever medieval peoples thought about their own distinctiveness and the identities carried by their neighbors.

Although only descent explicitly anchors collective identity to body, all four of Regino's components of collective identity are corporeal, and therefore less fungible than they might seem at first glance. When dryly enumerated in the lists of ethnographers, customs [*mores*] might appear intangible. Yet customs are practices that render communal belonging visible in the flesh. They include such embodied phenomena as social comportment, table manners, bathing habits, bodily modification, clothing, armor, self-adornment, hairstyle, grooming. In the eighth century, the lack of the round Petrine tonsure among native British monks was held to be a mark of their inferiority, while the fact that they kept Easter according to the outdated Julian calendar proved they were a people of an outmoded time. When the English met the Normans at the Battle of Hastings, before a single word left either army's mouth it was obvious who belonged to which side by coiffure. Insular natives sported flowing locks and moustaches, invaders wore short hair and were freshly shaved.[10] William of Malmesbury recounts that spies sent by King Harold to reconnoiter the enemy camp reported that the Norman army was composed of priests because of their relative hairlessness: "Almost every man in William's army seemed to be a priest, all their faces including both lips being clean-shaven; for the English leave the upper lip, with its unceasing growth of hair, unshorn" (*History of the English Kings* 3.239). The sly intimation that the Normans are priestly will be echoed a bit later in the text when William of Normandy's army spends the night before battle confessing their sins and taking communion (3.242). The dissolute English meanwhile pass a sleepless evening carousing (3.241). William also suggests through grooming that the English are a latter day version of the barbaric Britons (unshaved lips had been described by Caesar, he notes, "as a national custom of the ancient Britons"). This apposition prepares the way for the changing of the guard that the conquest will effect. Although Mathew Paris maintained that Englishmen hostile to the Normans were growing their beards defiantly long even as the twelfth century was coming to a close, William's clean-cut portrait of Norman and English difference is undoubtedly simplified, performing a separation as much as describing one.[11] In both these examples, hairstyle is a custom of long history that sets bodies apart by displaying their enduring distinctiveness.

Any change in custom, then, will signify a potential change in identity. In his *Life of Wulfstan*, William of Malmesbury deploys hairstyle to make a point about the promise of hybrid futures, of bodies that (like his own) bear marks of combined English and Norman identity. The *Life* implies that Wulfstan, the most notable English bishop to survive the Norman purge of the episcopate, is said to carry a knife for personal grooming and scraping manuscripts. Should he happen to espy an English cleric with long hair, this blade flies out to snip away a lock. Wulfstan would then enjoin his victim to get a haircut:

> Anyone who thought it worth objecting he would charge with effeminacy [*mollitiem*], and openly threaten with ill: men who blushed to be what they had been born, and let their hair flow like women, would be no more use than women in the defense of their country against the foreigner [*gentes transmarinas*]. No one would deny that this was shown to be true that same year when the Normans came. (*Vita Wulfstani* 1.16.3–4)[12]

Hair demarcates in Wulfstan's harangue a racial line masquerading as a gender division. Since the English clerics resemble women, the Normans arrive to give a lesson not just in proper coiffure but in proper masculinity. What the bishop-turned-guerilla-barber could not have predicted, however, was that the dandies of William Rufus's court would adore indigenous hairstyles and grow their locks long in emulation.[13]

William's attempt to mediate Norman and English spheres through transformation of custom is unusual. Typically custom is invoked to demarcate a firm rather than traversable line. Because impeccable grooming was, to his mind, civilization incarnate, Gerald of Wales allied Irish degeneracy with their long hair and uncut beards (*History and Topography of Ireland* 3.93), allowing him a groaner of a Latin pun on beards and barbarity. Welsh civility, on the other hand, was underscored by Gerald's reference to their careful shaving and scrupulous dental hygiene (their teeth "shine like ivory," *Description of Wales* 1.11). Clothing likewise separated the civil from the wild. Barbarians wore coarse vestments, like the Irish in their rough mantles. Or they might eschew proper garb entirely, such as the Scots with their visible buttocks or the Welsh with their shockingly bare legs. Although it is difficult to know how well the injunction was enforced, the Lateran Council of 1215 had commanded that Jews living among Christians wear differentiating sartorial marks. Contemporary English manuscript illustrations record numerous versions of the *pileum cornutum*, the "horned hat," on Jewish heads.

Clothing is a strategy of distinction that makes identity visible through combinations of bodily accentuation, concealment, exaggeration, and revelation. It is meant to exhibit an inner character, to surface a corporate identity. Other customs like tattooing inscribe shared identity on the very skin. Circumcision is likewise a ritual practice that spectacularly binds *mos* to body through corporeal modification. Muslims and Jews circumcised their male children. Christians did not, and were therefore fascinated by the practice. Its assumed power to differentiate Christians from Jews is seen vividly in the Odard/Jurnepin episode, especially as the boy believes so strongly that to be circumcised is to be transformed permanently in one's flesh. Christians whose experience of Jews living in their midst was still young and who had never witnessed the eight days of prayers, feasting, and ritual that attended the circumcision of a medieval Jew might have found the event "outlandish and puzzling," perhaps even "full of menace."[14] An accusation of ritual murder made at Gloucester in 1168 arose during such a celebration attended by Jews from around England. That a connection between circumcision and race was firmly in place by the early twelfth century is also suggested by the hyperbolic descriptions of forced circumcision found in crusade propaganda. A forged letter from the Byzantine emperor that circulated widely throughout the West declared that the Turks invading the Holy Land seized Christians, cut their foreskins over baptismal fonts, and forced them to urinate into this unholy mixture. For Christian polemicists such scenes were an ultimate horror, the bloody transformation of unwilling Christian bodies into Saracen forms. The anxiety underwriting such fantasies of forced hybridity is that the other will come too close, will break the tenuous boundary that differentiates the self from all it must not be.[15]

Custom connects identity to the bearing of particular weapons and to the performance of martial codes such as chivalry. Rituals of homage likewise involve their participants bodily. When the pirate Rollo, founder of the Norman race, decides for his own security to hold newly annexed lands in fealty from the king of France, he must undergo a formalized submission. The prerequisite to this ritual is baptism, a gesture that the politically astute Rollo is happy to render. When, however, he is asked to make his public declaration of dependence, the following scene unfolds:

> [When] the bystanders suggested that Rollo should kiss the foot of his benefactor, he scorned the idea of approaching the king on his knees, and seizing the king's foot put it to his mouth as he stood there. The king fell backward, and the Northmen roared with laughter. When the Franks protested, Rollo excused his impertinence by appealing to the custom of his own country. (William of Malmesbury, *History of the English Kings* 2.127)

Baptism clearly has not changed Rollo's inner being, for William writes of his post-christening "innate and uncontrolled barbarity." The ruined ritual of submission, meanwhile, allows Rollo to assert his dominance even in a supposedly subordinate position, and to excuse the humiliation of the king by appealing to the revered traditions of the community he leads.

Sexual practice was likewise integral to the circumscription of medieval collective identities. Gerald of Wales asserted that the Welsh had inherited a sodomite identity from their Trojan forebears, even if they did not in fact engage in same-sex copulation anymore.[16] The same writer was unable to comprehend Irish marital customs because, at the advent of the English, they allowed for a polygamy that deeply challenged his own conception of marriage. Ruaidrí Ua Conchobair took six concurrent wives to solidify his political supremacy. An outraged Gerald declared the Irish an "adulterous race, an incestuous race, a race illegitimately born and begotten."[17] Difference in sexual practice was frequently linked to innate bodily difference. By the thirteenth century, it was widely believed among Christians that Jewish men bled once a month. Some connected the curse of Jewish menstruation to the Jews who declare of the death of Christ "His blood be on us, and on our children" (Matthew 27:25). Others argued that Jews, like women, suffered a humoral imbalance that rendered them melancholic and therefore susceptible to periodic bleeding. Medical texts argued that this bloody flux was caused by the detrimental changes Jewish diets wrought on their bodies. Most authorities tended to combine theological and medical explanations, and agreed that this bleeding made Jews more like women than men.[18] Muslims were long accused of sharing with women an inordinate lust and a defective ability to reason. Like the Jewish and the feminine body, Saracen corporeal imperfection was often attributed to biochemistry, in this case a humoral system thrown out of balance by blood permanently overheated by the torrid eastern sun.

Diet offers a similarly corporeal division for the segregation of peoples. For writers like William of Malmesbury and Gerald of Wales, civilized peoples ate elaborately prepared foods; savages did not. Although Ireland was more ancient in its Christianity than England, and although Ireland in the twelfth century was possessed of stunning artistic and cultural achievements, Gerald depicted the island as a primitive place in order to justify its ongoing colonization. In one particularly vivid passage he writes of hide-clad pagans living on an island in the sea of Connacht. Sailors blown off course by a storm arrive near their home, and two men sail out to greet them. These natives speak the Irish language and wear their hair long. They are also overawed by their first encounter with cheese and bread. Such labor-intensive staples of advanced civilizations are as unknown to them as the Christian religion. When last seen the ignorant pagans are gratefully departing with a loaf of bread and a chunk of cheese to bring to their people as a wonder. It is unclear whether they will devour these foods or worship them (*History and Topography of Ireland* 3.103).

Fascinated by the fact that Muslims did not drink wine, the sacramental staple of the Western diet and a beverage enmeshed in mythologies of communal blood, some Christian writers imagined that Mohammed must have been a drunkard who committed murder while inebriated.[19] Pig flesh provided a convenient boundary for Christians to separate themselves from both Muslims and Jews, who followed biblical prohibitions against its consumption. Gerald of Wales relates that a demon in Italy once confessed that he liked inhabiting the bodies of heathens and Jews because they do not eat pork, rendering that ubiquitous Christian food a strange metonymy for the Eucharist (*Jewel of the Church* 1.18).[20] In the Odard/Junepin case, the Jewish plea that the boy not be fed pork is clearly a demand that his Jewish identity be admitted. Jewish minorities were set apart from the Christians among whom they dwelled by their nonparticipation in the alimentary rhythms that structured majority life. They fasted at strange times; they ate meat during Lent; they rejected certain foods (cheese, wine, meat) not prepared in accordance with their own ritual requirements; they did not celebrate the holy days that anchored the Christian calendar and gave occasional license to communal feasting and intoxication.

In 1171, Henry II arrived in Ireland to receive the submission of the princes of the north of the country. He arranged an extravagant feast prepared *Anglicane mense*—a terminology that nicely draws attention to the fact that the Irish did not, like the English, eat at tables. The formal dinner was an act of aggression, meant to overawe the Irish royals by the copiousness of the food as well as its elegant presentation. The Irish were forcibly anglicized in the process, not just because to sit at Henry's English table was to acknowledge the superiority of his court but also because the chieftains had to eat the foreign dishes served. Among these was the flesh of crane (*carne gruina*), a bird the Irish loathed as a food.[21] Crane in their bellies and a new taste implanted on their tongues, the princes make their submission both verbally and gustatorily, exiting the repast with a little bit of Henry's England incorporated into their Irish flesh.

Custom is clearly corporeal in its expression and effects. Imagined to be an ancestral inheritance, part and parcel of biological descent, custom was central to what medieval writers called national character, the stereotyped personality a people were imagined as collectively possessing.[22] For William of Malmesbury the Danes are *barbari* whose residence among the English infects the latter with the former's native propensity to overindulge in alcohol. When Alfred secures the baptism of the Danish king, Guthrum, as part of the submission that will create the Danelaw, William writes that "the Ethiopian will not change his skin." Even after accepting Christianity, the Danes remain fundamentally unaltered in their barbarous character.[23] The biblical figure of the dark Ethiopian was a perennial favorite for conveying the inalterability of collective identities. Herbert de Losinga, the ambitious Norman bishop of Norwich (1091–1119), composed a letter to a renegade monk of British descent who had been attached to his cathedral's monastery. Herbert seizes the opportunity to impugn all the Britons as inherently untrustworthy:

> It is an awful condition, that of inability to be changed. The Ethiopian, though washed, is an Ethiopian still; nor can he, whose skin is dusky by nature, become white by Baptism. You Britons talk too much; but none of you fulfils the promises he makes. The British, methinks, are as fickle in fly- ing as they are ardent in making an assault . . . You, intoxicated with the good yield of your oats, apply yourself to copious potations . . . Fickle and most deceitful of all the Britons, come home with all speed, or prepare to receive the anathema which is being got ready for you.[24]

History does not record whether the truant Briton returned, though the contempt that the bishop's letter betrays does not encourage much hope. In Herbert's exasperated formulation (quite a common one for the eleventh and twelfth centuries) national character and collective identity are like skin color, an inalterable biological fact. Likewise the behaviors, attitudes, and historical actions—that is, the customs—through which this character manifests.

Flux

Congenital in its relation to a people's history, custom would—like the Ethiopian's unchanging skin—seem to suggest a primordial distinctiveness to collective identities.[25] Yet hairstyle, dress, and the rituals surrounding the consumption of food and drink can be adopted. Passing could and did occur, even between Muslims and Christians. To circumvent the blockade of Acre, a group of Muslims shaved their beards, donned western clothes, and placed pigs aboard their ships, distilling the visible essence of Christianity into sartorial choice, grooming, and food consumption.[26] Through accultur- ation both individuals and groups changed radically over time. Sometimes these alterations were made wholesale and by choice. More frequently they unfolded slowly, piecemeal, through an osmosis and amalgamation that mixed cultures and peoples together and formed unstable hybridities.

Tacitus, writing of the strategies his father-in-law Agricola employed to firmly anchor Britain to the Roman Empire, writes that the native Britons were convinced to adopt the toga, speak Latin, make use of public baths, and eat Roman-style feasts. "The unsuspecting Britons," Tacitus observes, "spoke of such novelties as 'civilization,' when in fact they were only a feature of their enslavement" (*Agricola* 21). Such transformation was often figured as infection. William of Malmesbury noted that during the reign of Edgar, England became so international a place that the English were contaminated by the stereotypical behaviors of a host of foreigners (*alienigenae*). They "learnt from the Saxons unalloyed ferocity, from the Flemings a spineless physical effeminacy, and from the Danes a love of drinking" (*History of the English Kings* 2.148). Although William claims that the English were previously free of such faults, he elsewhere declares that they had originally been barbaric in their appearance and comportment, bellicose in their manners, and irrational in their religion. Fortunately their embrace of Christianity ensured that their character "changed greatly with the passage of time" (3.245).

Two centuries later the English colonizers of Ireland would be accused by those still in England of going native, leading to the enactment of the Statutes of Kilkenny (1366). Ironically these laws were promulgated in French, an inheritance of England's own former subject status. They mandated that the English (*chescun Engleys*) in Ireland must speak the English language, must be named with English rather than Gaelic appellations, and must employ the "English custom, fashion, mode of riding and apparel" (*la manere guise monture et appeill Engleis*). The penalty for using the Irish language was immediate dispossession of all lands.[27] Like all legislation enacted to reverse changes long underway, however, it is unclear how effective the Statutes of Kilkenny were in separating English Ireland's mixed culture back into its constituent components. Gaelicization was probably not amenable to a legislative reversal, since it had already catalyzed vigorously mixed identities.

Through similar commingling and acculturation the people known as the Picts had long ago been absorbed into the Scots. The ancestors of the Scandinavian raiders who had settled in that area of England known as the Danelaw vanished into the native population of places like Norwich. Their Scandinavian names, saints, and language slowly faded, and within a few generations these former Danes seemed unquestionably English. The Norman Conquest seems to have hastened this assimilation. Geoffrey of Durham gives the vivid example of a boy named Tostig, born in early twelfth-century Whitby. Like Godwin, Tostig had once been an esteemed name among the English, having been carried most famously by a brother of Harold, England's king at Hastings. Tostig of Whitby, however, was so mocked by his young friends for his suddenly overly Scandinavian appellation that, sometime around 1110, he changed his name to the newly prestigious moniker *William*.[28] A name like Tostig does not necessarily indicate that its bearer was of Scandinavian descent, just as "William," "Henry," and "Stephen" quickly became as English as they were Norman. New settlers like the Danes of the Danelaw were not exactly absorbed; they did not completely vanish. Rather, the Danes became anglicized while the nearby English adopted Scandinavian ways, precipitating a hybrid culture that became even more complex with the arrival of the Normans. Likewise with post-conquest England: by the time the Normans began to self-identify as English, England was an inalterably compound expanse, a space where both groups had been profoundly transformed.

Language is a category that at first glance seems unambiguously useful in sorting peoples into collectives, especially because many medieval thinkers regarded the world's tongues as aboriginal. So much power did the encyclopedist Isidore of Seville ascribe to words that he argued that, in the wake of the confusion of tongues after Babel, distinct languages engendered the nations of the earth: "Peoples arose from languages, not languages from peoples" (*Etymologies* 9.1.14). Medieval words for language were therefore frequently the same as those used to designate a people. French and English are, in both French and English, nouns that refer to a tongue and to a collective identity. The Welsh word *iaith*, "language," implied an array of cultural differences and was therefore "one of the touchstones of Welshness."[29] As the *lingua franca* of Western Christianity, Latin enabled the Roman church to imagine itself as consisting of a single *gens*. As Bartlett points out, this articulation of religious solidarity as "race and blood . . . group identity" was the product of the Christian encounter with alien peoples, especially in the wake of the crusades.[30] Hebrew meanwhile set apart the Jews. This sacred language was treasured as a divine inheritance, a promised unity to come after long diaspora. Christians in the twelfth century read their Bible in Jerome's Latin; for them Hebrew locked the Jews into a temporality superseded and unredeemed. Mandeville would one day go so far as to describe Hebrew as a secret code that will allow the Jews to know each and join ranks when they bring about the apocalypse.[31] In England, Jewish communities continued to employ French domestically long after the Normans had self-anglicized. Jewish common names tended to be francophone to such an extent that a subset of medieval names such as Odard's new moniker Jurnepin can be described as Jewish French.

Yet speech is as permeable a boundary as custom. The languages spoken by conquered peoples might recede due to assimilation or loss of prestige. A new tongue can be mastered in order to gain social advantage. Sometimes, like Arabic in Spain, Wendish in areas occupied by German speakers, or Pictish in Britain, a language would vanish entirely as its native speakers died out, were forced to leave, or were absorbed into a dominating linguistic population. Similarly with law. Those elaborate mythologies through which medieval peoples imagined their origins typically featured a primal bestowal of a law code that would forever set the group apart. In Geoffrey of Monmouth's *History of the Kings of Britain*, Brutus, having domesticated the island of Britain and filled it with his Trojan compatriots, formulates laws for the Britons to inherit. The Welsh spoke of their *cyfraith Hywel*, "the law of Hywel," described as "one of the most cohesive forces of medieval Welsh society."[32] The Scots embraced their foundational law-givers in historical figures like Kenneth MacAlpin, Malcolm Mackenneth, and David I. The English inherited codes from Alfred the Great and Edward the Confessor. Law was held to be so integral to national character that the medieval assumption was that separate peoples were entitled to the practice of their own law, even when they cohabitated.

In actual practice, however, law was no less labile than custom or language. The ancient law of a people could be in reality a remembrance that extended back no more than a generation or two, adapted to fit current circumstances. A living, human institution, juridical power can be manipulated to constitute new communities via enfranchisement and exclusion. When Cnut ascended the English throne, he realized that a good means of keeping his new subjects from perceiving him as a tyrannical foreigner would be to order that "all the laws enacted by the ancient kings, and particularly by his predecessor Æthelred, should be observed in perpetuity" (William of Malmesbury, *History of the English Kings* 2.183). Cnut's strategy was to emphasize continuity and promote accommodation. When William of Normandy became king several decades later, on the other hand, he passed a notorious law that clearly demarcated insular natives from new elites. The *murdrum* fine was a sum of money to be paid by the English of any area in which a French-speaker was found dead by unknown hands. Such a penalty was necessary to ensure the safety of an alien minority. Its application was a potent reminder of how dramatically control of the land's governance had shifted. A century later, however, Richard fitzNigel could argue that the *murdrum* fine now applied to any unsolved homicide since intermarriage had rendered the English and French indistinguishable (*permixte*), at least at social levels higher than the peasantry. William's desire to protect his imported cohort reinforced their separateness from the country over which they now had dominion, while Richard's generalization of the law's purview envisioned a newly unified community, capable of transcending the differences engendered by conquest.

Gender, Race, and Abjection

To Regino's four-part catalogue of the components of collective identity could be added some additional constituents. Identity tends to be unevenly distributed within a hierarchical society, even when that society is otherwise united in language and culture. When Bede wrote of the *gens Anglorum*, he may only have intended to encompass the aristocracy, not the unfree or rural dwellers.[33] The poor might be imagined as having descended exclusively from a subordinate group. They might even be represented with darkened skin and other features that visually set them apart from elites.[34] In a bifurcated society where the powerful were of one culture and the subaltern of another, social status and economic class could be demarcated along sharply communal lines. Long after the descendents of the Normans in England had begun to identify themselves as English, "a tendency persisted in popular writings to describe all oppressive or wealthy rulers and administrators as Norman, and all poor and oppressed people as English."[35] The Irish and the Welsh seldom enjoyed the same standard of living as the English settlers who had built towns and castles in their midst. Gerald of Wales, perpetually hostile to the non-Norman descended English, sneeringly wrote that

> the English people [are] the most worthless of all peoples under heaven . . . In their own land the English are slaves of the Normans, the most abject slaves. In our own land [the Welsh March] there are none but Englishmen in the jobs of ploughman, shepherd, cobbler, skinner, artisan, and cleaner of the sewers.[36]

For Gerald, a historically triggered transformation in status has become for the English innate. The bodily expression of this inferiority is their association with dirt, animals, hides, and excrement. Gerald is not alone in making these equivalences. Medieval texts, authored by a literate elite, tend to represent the disenfranchised, the illiterate, and the subaltern as more *embodied* than their supposed superiors.

Associating a people with shit and other bodily effluvia is an act of abjection, an attempt to erect a vivid line of division between two groups that may in fact be uncomfortably close. Thus Lanfranc, appointed archbishop of Canterbury by William the Conqueror and overseer of the realm in the monarch's absence, declared of the defeat of Ralph Guader that the land had been cleansed of its *spurcicia Britonum*, "Breton dung."[37] Although Ralph's mother and grandmother were English, Lanfranc uses an excremental metaphor to demonize as alien a group who had in fact been instrumental to William's conquest but who now troubled the archbishop with rebellion and resistance to clerical reform.[38] Lanfranc's denigration of Ralph and his allies is therefore rather similar to Gerald's scatological vision of English laborers toiling as cleaners of latrines and as skinners (who used urine and manure to cure hides into leather). All three have a counterpart in the frequent Christian association of Jews with defecation. In his *Chronica Majora*, Matthew Paris narrated a famous story in which the Jewish moneylender Abraham of Berkhamsted places a statue of a nursing Mary at the bottom of his privy so that he can daily dishonor the image. When his wife eventually rescues the Virgin, her angry husband suffocates her. Matthew reports this as contemporary history. Abraham was a real person, jailed for strangling his wife, not some invented bogeyman like the Jews tortured in "The Prioress's Tale."[39]

Collective identity and communal embodiment nearly always involve gender boundaries. A favorite medieval slander was to label an enemy or disparaged people effeminate, as in Wulfstan's insistence that long-haired English priests are girlish. Such a charge betrays the fact that a dominating collective identity and proper masculinity were assumed to be one and the same. Outside of the mythic Amazons, women themselves tended not to be as vividly racialized as men, perhaps because they were already made to carry the burden of profound bodily differentiation. When twelfth-century authors discussed the English, the Welsh, the Irish and the Normans they were for the most part speaking of men. There are, of course, notable exceptions, such as the alluring Saracen princesses who so often become a trophy bride (and a happy convert to Christianity) in romances and chansons de geste, or the abominable Sultaness in Chaucer's *Man of Law's Tale* and its analogues. A similar monstrous inversion propels the "misfoundation" myth (as Lesley Johnson calls it) of the Greek or Syrian princesses who were supposed to have arrived on British shores long before Brutus and his Trojans.[40] Led by the imperious Albina, a female version of Brutus, this group of exiles attempts to found a matriarchical nation. Instead through intercourse with devils they bestow upon Britain its aboriginal population, a race of monsters that Brutus will one day exterminate.

Religion and Race

Figurations of medieval collectivity were inseparable from religion.[41] Creeds were imagined as monolithic, neutralizing the real differences among groups of practitioners. Jews, Muslims, and Christians each experienced heterogeneity in the practice of their faiths. The twelfth century saw the birth of the Hasidic movement, with its repudiation of more secular Jews as "the Wicked."[42] Muslims had long been split into Sunnis and Shi'is. Christians had from their earliest days been routinely riven by heretical factions, such as Britain's home-grown Pelagianism. Yet despite internal diversity Jews, Muslims and Christians alike were confident that they possessed the true knowledge of the divine, and this uniquely privileged relation, they held, set them apart. The imagined community of each religion offered a potent ideological tool. That all Christians could be supposed to constitute a single people was a sentiment useful for promulgating crusade. Internal nuance also tended to vanish whenever one of these three groups attempted to represent the others. Latin Christians classified as Saracens a diverse array of peoples who included Turks, Arabs, and non-Western Christians such as the Nestorians. The Arab chroniclers who recorded the invasion of their lands during the crusades typically referred to the polyglot and multiethnic invaders from Europe as the *Franj,* mainly because a majority of their leaders could converse in French. Sephardim, Ashkenazim, and Hasidim were all one and the same to those who referred to them as *gens Iudeorum.*

Yet communalization through common creed had its limits, as the history of Christianity in Britain demonstrates. For Bede the only acceptable Christianity was, unlike that of the Britons, oriented toward the Mediterranean. Even in times of supposed unity ecclesiastical structures could reflect a racial hierarchy. William the Conqueror decreed that "no member of the English race" (*nullum eius gentis*) would be promoted to the high offices of the church.[43] It could even be argued that the assertion of Canterbury's primacy over the whole of the island of Britain was part of William the Conqueror's program of extending his dominance far beyond the borders of England, attempting "to create one unified centralised kingdom in the British Isles on a scale which had never been realised before."[44] Archbishop Lanfranc may have been happy to oblige in this interpenetration of ecclesiastical and secular power, but such assertion of insular hegemony was challenged not just by Scotland, Ireland, and Wales but also by York.

Though fairly rare, voluntary conversions might allow a Christian to become a Muslim?, or a Jew to become Christian. In the thirteenth century, the cleric William le Convers was assaulted by the Jews of Oxford when he attempted to collect from them a poll tax that funded the Domus Conversorum (House of Converts) in London. William's attempt to extract this money in support of further conversions from people who until recently had been his coreligionists was, to say the least, ill advised.[45] Gerald of Wales wrote of a Cistercian who left his order and had himself circumcised so that he could marry a Jewish woman, an act he labeled "phrenetic madness" and "fleeing to the synagogue of Satan."[46] In the 1270s, Robert of Reading, a Hebrew scholar and Dominican friar, fell in love with a Jewish woman and likewise had himself circumcised. He died in prison after King Edward himself was unable to convince him to return to Christianity.[47] In theory, baptism could transform an unbeliever completely, soul *and* body. In the romance *The King of Tars*, a Saracen's dark flesh is whitened through the sacrament's transformative power.[48] Outside of fantasy spaces like romance, however, converts were regarded with a great deal of suspicion by both their former community and their new coreligionists.[49] Baptism did not simply transform a Jew into Christian. Something in his body seemed to resist metamorphosis, leaving him suspended between categories, a hybrid.

A historical episode involving forced conversion and its aftermath illustrates well the permanent alienation from community this unwilled residency in a middle space could bring. When a group of prominent Jews was refused admission to the coronation of Richard I in 1189, a wave of anti-Jewish violence swept London. A prominent Jew from York named Benedict was badly wounded. He accepted baptism rather than face death at the hands of rioters. Although newly christened William, when summoned before the king he announced "I am Benedict, the Jew, from York." In a moment of disgust the archbishop of Canterbury allowed him to return to his former community. When Benedict died of his wounds shortly thereafter, the Jews among whom he had hoped to find rest refused his corpse. Richard of Hovedon, the medieval narrator of the episode, insisted on referring to the post-baptism Benedict as William, even though he had renounced the faith forced upon him. Richard wrote that the archbishop erred in allowing the convert to return to his people: "He ought to have replied, 'We demand Christian judgment on him, since he became a Christian and now denies it.' "[50] Benedict/William is baptized under duress, recants, and, neither a Christian nor a Jew, suspended even in death between the two groups, loses any possibility of belonging. Who knows, therefore, whether Benedict of Norwich and his son Odard/Jurnepin, likewise caught within unsought but intractable hybridity, ever found a secure place to belong. Circumcised Christians and baptized Jews, such figures were in their very bodies caught in a difficult middle.

Although in fact a heterogeneous and mutable category, religious identity is often represented as self-evident, unchanging, and homogeneous. The knowledge that such a fundamental category of identity might be so fragile was anxiety-producing, a point that Gerald of Wales drives home with a narrative of Jewish skepticism and rebuke. During the translation of the body of the virgin saint Frideswide, an event that Gerald himself may have witnessed at Oxford in 1180, many miracles were reported. At this time, a Jew tied cords around his feet and arms, pretending to be paralyzed. He made a great show of crying upon Frideswide for help and "would pretend that he had been miraculously cured and would leap about the streets shouting: 'Behold, what great miracles the holy Frideswide can work!' " (*Jewel of the Church* 1.51). God avenges his new saint's honor by having the Jew tie the cord around his own neck and hang himself. The Jews of Oxford are shamed by the event, but the Christians experience "great joy and rejoicing." What are they so happy about? Partly their glee comes from having witnessed the hand of God in the world, and partly (we might guess) the death itself is a source of relief, for it removes a troubling point of skepticism. The blaspheming Jew performs a specious miracle, insisting that neither the translated saint nor the Christian God possess efficacy. What if *all* the miracles surrounding the burgeoning cult are likewise dubious? The death of the Jew arrives just in time to prevent that line of questioning to proceed, as definitive proof that there is a God in heaven specially inclined toward the Christians of the world. The Jew of Oxford suggests that Christianity can neither grant nor possess the stability it claims. His forced suicide proves that his words have been rendered impotent in advance.

The Politics of Belonging

More abstractly, and perhaps more potently, collective identity and its performance are a matter of strategy. For the most part the medieval denizens of Ireland, Wales, and Scotland would not have considered themselves intimately related, preferring to dwell upon their differences rather than imagine some pan-"Celtic" unity. By the fourteenth century, however, the Bruce dynasty was declaring common ancestry among the Scots, Irish, and Welsh in order to bolster the fight for independence from England, a common enemy making for a common identity.[51] R. R. Davies reduces the whole of human history to a pithy sentence when he writes, "Most peoples are complex amalgams; but beneath the label of a name they become, and come to believe themselves to be, a single people."[52] Thus Bede assimilates various groups that once dwelled in Germany and Scandinavia into three peoples (Angles, Saxons, Jutes) and thence into one (*Angli*), bestowing to the Middle Ages a myth of a primal Englishness. The myth is built upon an act of radical separation, cleanly preserving a border between the island's fifth-century immigrants and Britain's indigenous populations. The *Ecclesiastical History* simplified as it purified. And it powerfully endured.

Dudo of St. Quentin performed a similar service for the Normans, though in a rather different way. Whereas most medieval races imagined, contrary to historical fact, that they had been possessed of an originary homogeneity still carried in their blood, the Normans acknowledged their initial variety.[53] His great-grandfather a Viking (Hrólfr, or Rollo), his grandmother a Breton concubine (Sprota of Brittany), Duke Richard II of Normandy was obviously of mixed blood. Yet when he realized that through its strengthened ties to Denmark and England his principality was losing some of the veneer of Frankishness that his father had labored to impart, he commissioned Dudo to compose a history of the Normans. This narrative depicted the race as an initially polymorphous collection of peoples who had over time settled into an inalterable Christian

Frenchness. That this shift of identity was enduring aimed to reassure the French allies of Richard that the Vikings with whom he was now cooperating did not indicate a dangerous return of the Norman's to their Scandinavian past. "Whatever was 'French,' " Eric Fernie writes of this period, "constituted what for the Normans was modern, including ties of dependence based on land, fortified residences, the language, Christianity, churches, and the Romanesque style in architecture."[54] As profound as this Francophilia became, however, it did not obliterate the Norman's sense of their own separateness from other peoples, as "Normans descended from Normans." This despite their language, law, hybrid customs, and a tendency to use the words *Franci, Francigena*, and *Galli* as synonyms for *Normanni* when describing themselves.[55] Yet by the late 1130s the Norman conquerors of England were rapidly vanishing, "turned into Englishmen."[56] Lanfranc, a Lombard imported from the Norman monastery of St. Stephen's to serve as the first non-English archbishop of Canterbury (1070), could speak of himself as *novus Anglicus,* a "new" or "novice" Englishman, in order to emphasize the transformation of identity that accompanied his transferal of residence.[57]

William of Whitby, né Tostig, knew that names do not merely describe a preexistent state of affairs, but usher new realities into being. "Names are central to the identity of a people; to change a people's name is to change its identity." So writes R. R. Davies of the reality-making power of collective designation.[58] It does not matter whether the name is a self-chosen appellation that unifies a once varied group (*Cymru, Brytaniaid, Prydein*), or a title inflicted upon a people in order to render them more easily contained (*Wealh, Welsh*). Names are transformative. They render those whom they designate distinct. Thus the writer we today call Gerald of Wales always nominated himself with the Latinate appellation Gerald the Cambrian (*Geraldus Cambrensis*). He detested the origin of the word "Welsh," an Old English term for a foreigner, barbarian, or slave. Gerald lamented the infighting that had sundered the people of Wales into competing factions when, to his mind, they should be cognizant of an ultimate unity:

> Cambria [Wales] knows only too well how, in this same neighborhood and in our own times, through a blind lust for conquest and through a rupture of all the ties of common blood and family connection, evil example has spread far and wide throughout the land, and good faith has disappeared, to be replaced by shameful perfidy. (*Journey Through Wales* 1.5)

Consaguinitas, "shared blood," is more than a metaphorical connection among the people of Wales. It is a fundamental and biological essence at the base of community. The tragedy of the Welsh in Gerald's account is their failure to recognize themselves as belonging to a solidarity that in his formulation is ultimately natal.

Names bestow the appearance of long and singular history to what might in fact be a multiplex, fluid group. In the process names also tend to ossify identities, making them not only seem unchanging in the past but actually resistant to further transformation. By the twelfth century the peoples of the British Isles had part acquired an aura of timeless separateness, a uniqueness "provable" by their individuating histories and the assumed distinctiveness of their cultures. Names separated the volatile, intermixed, and resistantly hybrid particles of collective identity into bounded forms, distilling sheer multiplicity into purified wholes. A people's name is thus inseparable from its history, real or imagined. A people's history, in turn, is nearly always entwined in some foundational mythology about shared descent. Nicholas Howe has called such a narrative "an account of that ancestral past which, despite any evidence to the contrary, gives a group its irreducible common identity."[59] The collective blood such histories bestow could, so long as the myth was believed, solidify collective identity and attach it to specific bodies, thereby circumscribing the parameters of community. The next chapter examines how such origin narratives shaped the identities of the peoples of the twelfth-century British Isles, attempting to give permanence and cohesion to groups that were historically recent, mutable, and porous. Yet a people's distinctiveness comes at a high price, especially when a community collects and knows itself by identifying against other groups. This price was to be paid especially by those who found themselves adrift in the chasm of a middle space, belonging completely neither to the powerful group that set the terms for community, nor to those over whom it attempted to dominate.

Geography and Environment

To explain how the differences that set medieval peoples apart could be simultaneously cultural and corporeal, environmental and astrological determinism were frequently invoked. Aristotle had declared in his *Politics* that whereas the extreme coldness of Europe had rendered its people brave but stupid, and the heat of Asia had generated smart cowards, the temperateness of Greece engendered a nearly perfect Hellenic race.[60] To be Greek like Aristotle is to have a body unblemished by extremes of difference. To be a barbarian, on the other hand, is to be somehow more embodied, because the mark of deviation is imprinted upon flesh and soul. Classical traditions of science argued that climate and celestial pull governed the distribution of the humors, the bodily fluids that were thought to hold dominion over disposition and character.[61] When the encyclopedists Isidore of Seville and Bartholomaeus Anglicus wrote that the men of Africa suffered a solar overheating of their blood, darkening their skin and rendering them spiritless, they were stating a medieval commonplace with roots in Galenism. Ibn Sina (Avicenna) agreed: "Those who are far removed from acquiring virtues are slaves by nature like the Turks and negroes and in general people living in an unfavorable climate."[62] In contrast, cold for Bartholomaeus engendered whiteness. The pale skin of northerners was supposed to be the outward sign of their innate valor.[63] Gerald of Wales wrote that the English were frigid in nature because they originated in icy climes, while the Welsh were fiery, having once been desert-dwelling Trojans. Climate is for Gerald a primal determinant of communal character, inalterable after its force suffuses the flesh:

> The Saxons and Germans derive their cold nature from the frozen polar regions which lie adjacent to them. In the same way the English, although they now live elsewhere, still retain their outward fairness of complexion and their inward coldness of disposition from what nature had given them earlier on. The Britons, on the contrary, transplanted from the hot and arid regions of the Trojan plain, keep their dark colouring, which reminds one of the earth itself, their natural warmth of personality and their hot temper. (*Description of Wales* 1.15)

Climate precipitates a bodily adaptation that is carried forward indefinitely through time. Whereas contemporary science speaks of the genetic inheritance of environmentally induced modifications, medieval science believed the mechanism for passing differentiating traits lay in the balance of the four humors that gave all living bodies, human and animal like, their vitality. Although he does not invoke climatological determinism, William of Poitiers has a theory of originary impression in mind when he writes that the English are a people "by nature always ready to take up the sword, being descended from the ancient stock of Saxons" (*Gesta Guillelmi* 2.24). Christian polemicists, fascinated and repulsed by Muslim culture, foregrounded the ability of environment to mold a people's character. The intense heat of the east and the ascendancy of the planet Venus, it was declared, rendered Saracens bellicose and sensual.[64]

In his version of the call for crusade delivered by Urban II at Clermont, William of Malmesbury has the pope describe race as an amalgam of climate and creed. Saracens and Turks originate in an oppressively dry environment and therefore, despite an inborn cleverness, do not possess sufficient blood in their veins (*sed minus habet sanguinis*). "They flee from battle," Urban declares, "because they know that they have no blood to spare" (*History of the English Kings* 4.347). Beyond Europe, Urban continues, stretch frost-locked islands populated by "barbarous peoples living like beasts—who could call them Christians?" These "less rational" peoples suffer from too much of a good thing, "a generous and exuberant supply of blood." Like Aristotle's Greeks, it is the Europeans themselves, especially the Franks, who represent the mean between monstrous extremes. Originating in "the more temperate regions of the world," they possess in Urban's formulation the perfect amount of blood to render them mentally acute and martially irresistible.

Like geographical location and climate, religion and law were thought to imprint themselves in the flesh. Gerald of Wales assumes that conquest can transform a free race into an innately slavish people when he warns the Welsh not to allow themselves to become like the English, "long since reduced to servitude, which by now has almost become a second nature."[65] When Matthew Paris draws a picture of Mohammed with a banner announcing *Poligamus esto* ("I declare polygamy"), it is difficult to say if Venus has inspired the Prophet's law or if his new law will render his people venereal.[66]

Exclusion and Disidentification

The components of collective identity are given to constant change and internal variation. Custom might evince regional, class, gender differences. So could language. The dialects of English and Welsh spoken in the north differed noticeably from southern permutations; English in the wake of the Norman Conquest became what we today call a creole. Religion never did effect the unity it had promised. When William of Malmesbury attempts to convey a crusade-inspired *Christianitas* that transcends national difference, he does so in unselfconsciously nationalistic terms. The First Crusade, he writes, drew eager participants from around the world, even those dwelling *in penitissimis insulis uel in nationibus barbaris* ("on remotest islands and among barbarian nations"). William then describes these "distant" races according to what each must abandon in order to join the cause: "The time had come for the Welshman to give up hunting in his forests, the Scotsman forsook his familiar fleas, the Dane his constant drinking, and the Norwegian left his diet of raw fish" (*History of the English Kings* 4.348). This litany of stereotypes indicates how difficult it could be for medieval writers to think of peoples outside of such assumptions. Christian intellectuals might speak of a Latin race, but behind such collectivizing rhetoric lay the fact that Latinity remained a minority achievement to which the vernacular-speaking masses exhibited a frustrating indifference.

Welding dissonant heterogeneity and hybridity into some harmonious collective is not easy to accomplish. The process typically proceeded through exclusion. It is far easier to point to what one is not than to embrace some essence shared equally among a newly integrating community. Thus King Alfred of Wessex was able to rally a sense of pan-English identity, a new national unity, by emphasizing the vast difference between the *Angelcynn* and the "Viking" Danes who had seized and were living quite comfortably in a large section of the island. Because the Normans were a mongrel concatenation of peoples, to imagine their own unity they routinely dehumanized other peoples, especially when they wanted to seize their land. In the mid-eleventh century, the Bretons and the English were in their turn depicted as barbaric races, patently in need of the Normans' civilizing overlordship.[67] Composite in fact, homogeneous in theory, the English of the twelfth century similarly began to demarcate themselves from those monstrous peoples that limned the margins of their kingdom. The Welsh, Scots, and Irish had once been trading partners, fellow Christians, possible allies. Now they were thought to inhabit a primitive and unruly Celtic Fringe badly in need of the humanizing imprint of anglicization.[68] The author of the *Gesta Stephani*, possibly a bishop of Bath who moved through the highest circles of King Stephen's court, describes the Scots as

> barbarous and filthy [*barbaros et impuros*], neither overcome by excess of cold nor enfeebled by severe hunger, putting their trust in swiftness of foot and light equipment; in their own country they care nothing for the awful moment of the bitterness of death, among foreigners they surpass all for cruelty. (*Gesta Stephani* 1.26)

This debasing description obscures the fact that the Scots were actually an amalgam of peoples (Picts, Danes, Scots, Britons, Angles), and that the "Scottish" army being described in the *Gesta* contained numerous English soldiers in its ranks and Anglo-Norman nobles among its leaders. David, the leader of these "barbarous and filthy" people, was not just the king of Scotland but, through the affection of his brother-in-law Henry I of England, had also been made Earl of Huntingdon, "the apex of English nobility."[69] David was raised and educated in England. He spread Francophile ways in his Scottish court, reformed the native church to make it conform to continental and English Christianity, and assigned bishoprics and lands to Anglo-Norman imports. David's wife was the daughter of Waltheof, the famous Earl of Northumbria. His mother Margaret was sister to Edgar the ætheling. David could therefore trace his descent from England's Æthelred II and the royal house of Wessex. Yet this intimacy to

England also meant that David was uncle to the Empress Matilda, claimant to the very throne Stephen sat upon. For the royalist author of the *Gesta Stephani* this consanguinity meant that the Scottish king's name would never be mentioned in the narrative. His people meanwhile are transformed into a degenerate race. The English—the proper English—would recognize themselves by defeating everything the Scots embody, a disidentification that renders both the English and the Scots pure, self-contained, utterly separate. That this sharp differentiation has little basis in the intractable hybridities of historical reality rendered it neither less powerful nor less ideologically effective.

The monsterization of the Celtic Fringe allowed England to stake a claim to the British Isles in their entirety. British barbarians were not, however, the only peoples who allowed the English their self-differentiation. As Christians living in the midst of ongoing crusades, the English steadfastly defined themselves against the infidel Saracens who held the Holy Land. The crusades may have been fought in a geographically distant locale, but they were never far from contemporary minds.[70] In the years following the Norman Conquest, moreover, a non-Christian group had taken up residence in England itself. By the twelfth century, Jews lived among the English in their largest cities. At once intimate and alien, these domestic foreigners did not practice the kingdom's shared religion and therefore could not participate in the rituals that structured contemporary lives. Considering the implicit challenge they posed to a supposedly self-evident superiority of the realm's unifying creed, it is perhaps not surprising that the Jews were eventually imagined to pose a grave danger to the safety of the community.

Medieval processes of collective self-delineation were frequently attended by violence, whether bluntly physical (expulsion, relocation, colonization, genocide) or more abstractly social (enforced legal disparity, systematic devaluation of culture, regulation of language and custom). Thus the border regions between England and Scotland and Wales were, like much of Ireland, places of battle and blood. The same could be said for the edges of Christendom. Some English knights fought in the Second Crusade, especially in Portugal. Many thousands more joined the third. Among these was the elderly archbishop of Canterbury, destined to perish among soldiers "in a state of desolation of despair," at the siege of Acre in 1190.[71] Closer to home, late in the twelfth century the domestic tranquility of several English cities was disturbed by massacres of Jews, especially in the wake of the coronation of Richard. This violence climaxed in the *shabbat hagadol* of March 15, 1190 (the Great Sabbath of 4950), when many Jews of York took their own lives to escape forced conversion. Those who did not were murdered, despite promises of safety. Even after England became

Judenrein, completely emptied of Jews, following the Expulsion of 1290, Englishness continued to be defined against Jewishness, an especially easy category to manipulate now that the only figures to inhabit it were ghostly remembrances.

The starkest visions of collective identities are seen during times of conquest. The seizure of occupied land becomes unproblematic when indigenes are assumed to be not adequately in possession of civility. The model for this process of representation is to be found in the Hebrew Bible, when the spies sent by Moses to reconnoiter the Promised Land discover that, inconveniently enough, its fecund hills are already populated. The aboriginal Canaanites are imagined to be monsters, a race of giants called the Anakim. Because their lack of humanity is so evidently written upon their bodies, the Anakim can be displaced by the migrating Israelites without worrying about the possibility that they, too, might have a claim on the territory.[72] Medieval Hebrew chronicles sometimes employed a similar technique of hyperbolic disidentification, even when the Jews were the people under attack. Hence this account of the violence of Christians against Jews that erupted during the First Crusade:

> For then rose up initially the arrogant, the barbaric, a fierce and impetuous people, both French and German. They set their hearts to a journey to the Holy City, which had been defiled by a ruffian people, in order to seek there the sepulcher of the crucified bastard and to drive out the Muslims who dwell in the land and to conquer the land.[73]

The passage reinforces the heroism of the Jews who find themselves besieged by crusaders. It represents the Jews as timeless in both their elemental goodness and their subjection to persecution. Other peoples might vary in their geographical origins and religion, but are homogeneous in their unrelenting animus.

Medieval peoples were fond of imagining themselves as a contemporary version of the biblical Israelites. Secure in the knowledge that they, among the manifold nations of the world, had been specially chosen by God, they could then explain even their defeats as signs of divine affection. For Gildas the Saxon subjugation of his people, *praesens Israel*, reveals that like their biblical counterparts the Britons are being punished by a God who loves them dearly.[74] For William of Malmesbury the crushing defeat of the English by the Normans was a similar token of God's parental vigilance, a celestial reprimand for having forgotten their own holiness. The author of the *Gesta Stephani*, troubled that England should experience such turbulence during the reign of King Stephen (*Anglia turbaretur*), transforms his country into a contemporary Israel, its troubles a signal of God's abiding interest (*Gesta Stephani* 1.39). The divine punishment of England cannot abate *usque dum completa essent peccata Amorreorum, et Æthiops mutaret pellem suam*, until "the sins of the Amorites were full and the Ethiopian changed his skin" (1.40, citing Genesis 15:16 and Jeremiah 13:23). Here as elsewhere in the writings of church-trained authors the Hebrew Bible provides the palimpsest for interpreting the travails of the present. The historical Jews vanish to be replaced by a more recently chosen people. Just as God inflicted calamities like the Babylonian captivity upon the Israelites to recall them to their forgotten identity, so likewise the battered Britons or conquered English would rise again, renewed.

Animality and Monstrosity

Divine favor also meant that these latter day Hebrews had license to treat other peoples as if they were Canaanite Anakim, perilous and perhaps not fully human peoples whose lands of milk and honey might be unapologetically colonized.[75] Monsters, savages, and barbarians do not possess territorial rights. Thus the *Gesta Stephani* labels the Welsh "swarming savages" (*barbara Walensium multitudine*) who plunder and burn (100). William of Poitiers, an unabashed Norman apologist, could imagine that the triumph at Hastings was all the more providential in that the English were a bellicose race descended from the Saxons, "the most savage of men."[76] Denial of sufficient civilization often meant denial of sufficient humanity. Take away the customs that order a human life, the ability to express oneself in meaningful language, the rule of law, a belief in the divine and the essence of humanity likewise vanishes. Perhaps that is why supposedly inferior peoples—those whose customs, language, law, and religion are bluntly denied meaning, if not existence—were so frequently imagined as animals.

   Cary Wolfe has coined the useful phrase "discourse of animality" to designate the "constellation of signifiers" that structure "how we address others of whatever sort (not just nonhuman animals)." Though built upon the assumption of an ontological divide between the human and the animal, the discourse of animality has, Wolfe notes, "historically served as a crucial strategy in the oppression of *humans* by other humans."[77] Medieval conflations of denigrated peoples with inferior species followed ample classical precedent, since civilization (willing subjection to law, the state of being a citizen) was typically portrayed as a possession demarcating Romans and Greeks from the feral peoples at the margins of their polities. Claudius Ptolemy described the inhabitants of India, born under the influence of Capricorn and Saturn, as dirty, ugly, and "having the character of wild beasts."[78] Gildas, the British polemicist who combined Roman and biblical modes of historiography in his *De excidio*, labels the Picts wolves, the

Saxons dogs, his own Britons sheep, and heretics like the Arians venomous snakes.[79] Gildas was in good company. Disparaged medieval groups were frequently represented as bestial. Typically such denigration was general and metaphorical. Richard of Hexham condemns the Scots because they do not practice the sexual restraint of the English ("those bestial men who think nothing of committing incest, adultery, and other abominations").[80] Odo of Cambrai, astounded at the fact that Jews cannot be reasoned into an acceptance of Christianity, wonders if they are not humans but senseless beasts.[81]

At other times animalized representations of collective identity were more bluntly physical. The Jews could be transfigured into owls, a bird thought to roost in its excrement, or hyenas, believed to be hermaphroditic corpse-eaters. The Aberdeen Bestiary betrays its author's conflation of Jewishness and animality in an illustration of a hyena with circumcised genitals.[82] Saracens were literally depicted as dog-headed men (cynocephali), or metaphorically dismissed as canine. "The Holy Land," Gerald of Wales asserts, is "profaned by filthy dogs" (*On the Instruction of Princes* 2.30). The same author paints dehumanizing portraits of the Irish in the *History and Topography of Ireland* (1185), a text that often allows little difference between the native inhabitants of the land and the herds of cattle they prize. Gildas mixed leonine, canine, and lupine traits when he called the Saxons "a race hateful both to God and men" and described their invasion of Britain in the fifth century as "a multitude of whelps [which] came forth from the lair of a barbaric lioness" (*De Excidio Bntanniae* 23). Because his sympathies lay with the Britons, the Anglo-Saxon conquest is for Gildas the ruinous advent of a "brood" of "wolfish offspring" and "bastard-born comrades," fiercely devouring the land's bounty with their "doggish mouths." Gildas continued to be read throughout the Middle Ages. Whereas Bede silently dropped the inhumane adjectives for his people, Geoffrey of Monmouth was happy to restore the lupine degradation.

The Normans kept the doggish rhetoric of race in place when they as invaders claimed to be met by canine indigenes. According to Wace, the Normans at the Battle of Hastings heard in the bellicose language of the English only the agitated baying of dogs: "Normant dient qu'Engleis abaient/por la parole qu'il n'entendent."[83] This comparison holds the weight of something more than simple simile, for a story told by Wace in his *Roman de Brut* helped to promulgate the idea that the native English were different in their very bodies, specifically in the caudal appendages they were said to sport. In an episode he added to the *History of the Kings of Britain* as he translated Geoffrey's clerical Latin text into a courtly French (ca. 1155), after Augustine was sent by Pope Gregory to Christianize England he found himself denounced and persecuted. Intent on humiliating the holy man, the heathen English who lived near Dorchester affixed skate tails to his cloak. The holy man prayed to God that these malefactors would be appropriately punished. God immediately responds, bestowing upon Augustine's persecutors a permanent change to their corporeality. These English and their descendants, writes Wace, were transformed into a tailed people:

> [Augustine] begged our Lord that for this great dishonour and dreadful disgrace they should receive a sign and a reminder, and indeed they had one, and will have one forever, for all those who mocked him and hung tails on him got tails and were tailed [*furent cué e cues orent*] and could never lose them thereafter. Everyone from this family has been tailed ever since; they were and are tailed, they had and have tails, tails hanging behind them as a reminder that they mocked God's friend by humiliating him with tails. (*Roman de Brut* 13731–45)

Henry II probably enjoyed Wace's vigorously narrated story about English disobedience and its lastingly embodied consequences, especially as he continued the hard work of engendering a community of consent within his realm. Its appeal to anyone not of English origin was obviously great, too, because it was swiftly generalized into a racializing narrative about English bodily difference. In his translation of Wace's poem, Laȝamon wrote of the shame that the English abroad felt when the insult was hurled at them (*Brut* 2:772). The abusive epithet of *Angli caudati* (tailed English) found its most unforgettable expression in the romance *Richard Coeur de Lion*, which depicted the French taunting their enemies for the dog-like tails they suppose them to bear. The insult endured for centuries. In 1433, Margery Kempe found herself degradingly referred to as a *sterte* (tailed one) while traveling through Germany.[84]

Only the enemies of a people delimit its contours through such animal bodies. Because animals were considered to be reasonless and therefore did not pose troubling questions of agency and autonomy, because God had given primal stewardship of beasts to Adam, because medieval peoples lived so closely with animals and trusted that the proof of human superiority lay in humanity's ability to domesticate, commodify, and profit from the world's fauna, animals were perhaps inevitable receptacles for uneven discourses of race, especially in the wake of conquest. It would be exaggerating only slightly, I think, to say that the representational matrix for collective difference in the twelfth-century British Isles derived from and centered on a discourse of animality rather than a vocabulary for human variation. Animal bodies give to collective identities a definitiveness they would not otherwise possess. They are therefore productive, demarcative, and carceral.

Yet the English clearly are not dogs, the Welsh are something more than grazing beasts, Jews are not simply owl-like plotters, the Irish can be represented as indistinguishable from their cattle but are not ultimately reducible to their own herds. The racialized body is a playground for animal elements, but it is still in the end a human form. Impure and hybrid flesh mingling beast and human, the body of the other was in the end not an animal but a chimera, a monster on whose body unresolved differences in species stood in for inassimilable differences of culture.

The Crisis in Community of the Twelfth Century

This chapter has attempted to gather the various elements from which collective identities were constituted in twelfth-century Britain, and especially in England. I have tried to indicate the long history of medieval thinking about communal bodies, and have as well suggested the futures such conceptualizations experienced on the island. My emphasis throughout has been on how collective identities are established via acts of separation that purify as they sort. These segregations are built upon the denial of compoundedness, impurity, and hybridity. The remainder of this book examines what happens when disavowed middle spaces return to trouble the integrity of the categories built upon their exclusion. The chapters that follow will examine individual authors as they articulated and modified received discourses for the sorting of the world's variety, especially in the long wake of the Norman Conquest.

The process of transformation initiated by the Normans in 1066 was ongoing throughout much of the twelfth century, but was especially evident during its first five decades. In the aftermath of conquest collective identities were riddled with differences, contradictions, complications. When martial violence ceased, subjugation continued via forced acculturation. Through the middle of the century much of England was still being Normanized, especially in its architecture and social and ecclesiastical organization, but also in law, literature, and customs. Because the cultural elites who had once been Normans were calling themselves English within two generations of Hastings, this process could just as easily be called Anglicization. From the southeast the imposition of linguistic, legal, and customary unity proceeded rapidly north and west. As regions like East Anglia and Northumberland became increasingly London-looking, assimilation began to spread elsewhere on the island through the steady agency of what Davies has called an "English diaspora," an immigration that dotted formerly Celtic landscapes with mini Englands. The progress of this secondary conquest via Anglicization was never straightforward, however, and the tempestuous reign of Stephen complicated all these processes, reversing some acculturation and leaving much of Britain wondering about historical continuity and the possibilities for future community.

The next chapter turns to a succession of three writers who, in the wake of history's perturbations, attempted to imagine the English, the Normans, and the Welsh as enduring peoples. Although Bede was able to bequeath to later generations a vigorous myth of the primal unity of the Angles (and, in a way, the Britons), his follower and admirer William of Malmesbury lived after a martial campaign waged by ambitious foreigners had profoundly interrupted that history. William did what he could to mend history's broken chain, though his own narrative is frequently derailed by visually spectacular embodiments of the hybridity he felt surround and even inhabit him. Geoffrey of Monmouth, meanwhile, formulated a counterhistory to hurl against William's careful repair work, a narrative which—if taken seriously—would erode the very ground of English history.

CHAPTER 2

BETWEEN BELONGINGS: HISTORY'S MIDDLES

Despite the tendency of medieval authors to speak of the world's peoples as if they were unchanging and self-consistent, collective identities are messy. Confected from mutable elements like law, custom, language, and environment, they rest upon unstable boundaries and are haunted by their own exclusions. Trace any people far enough back into history and they dissolve into heterogeneity. Moments of imagined community seldom solidify, therefore, without some powerful architecture to circumscribe their volatility, some narrative frame to contain their dispersive vectors. In the absence of a persuasive history to anchor its claims to enduring distinctiveness, a community will have great difficulty gaining substantiality.

To make the fugitive components of a shared identity cohere requires a foundation story, an account of origins that calls into being a shared past. This chapter examines how individuating histories were imagined and to a degree effected by three historiographers writing in medieval Britain: one in a kingdom called Northumbria that did not know it would someday be swallowed into a larger realm called England; one at the heart of this England, now annexed to a transmarinal empire; and one who likewise belonged to this transformed kingdom, but who traced his origins from that stormy edge where England and Wales interpenetrated. Bede, William of Malmesbury, and Geoffrey of Monmouth knew that insular history unfolded in discordant spaces where disparate cultures mingled. Bede lived at a time when the immigrant populations from whom he traced his descent were still absorbing as well as displacing indigenous peoples. For convenience's sake the first group is usually labeled the Anglo-Saxons or English, the second the Britons, Welsh or Celts. Such capacious designations hide what was likely a great deal of internal variation among those whom they collect. Although ecclesiasts outside of Britain often spoke of its fifth- and sixth-century invaders as if they constituted a single people, it is unclear whether anyone but insular elites like Bede believed or even cared that the inhabitants of Bernicia, Kent, Lindsey, Mercia, Essex might really constitute a *gens Anglorum*. Likewise the so-called Celts, "ancient peoples" who, it has been argued, were a romantic invention of the eighteenth century.[1] Since crisp distinction was unlikely to have been the case in the tumultuously hybrid environment of early medieval Britain, the unity and primordial separateness of the English and Britons seems more passionate fantasy than historical fact.

Yet throughout Bede's *Ecclesiastical History* both peoples are represented as discrete in language, custom, character, and history. William of Malmesbury and Geoffrey of Monmouth inherited Bede's sanitized cultural geographies. While neither writer questioned his sorting of collective identities, both were faced with an uncomfortable proximity to the kinds of admixture he had disavowed. William and Geoffrey wrote in the wake of the Norman Conquest. William carried the blood of victor and subjugated in his veins. How could he, a compound creature, write an account of the English past that would seem continuous with that narrated by his revered predecessor, a monk who never had to worry that history's chain, forged to culminate in English ascendancy, might someday suffer disruption? Likewise an heir to the insular past as dreamt by Bede, Geoffrey of Monmouth attempted a counter-narrative of the island. In his version of the past, the English were reduced from history's heroes to rapinous interlopers. The Britons, meanwhile, Geoffrey cleansed of the taint of monstrousness Bede had attached to them as part of his project of differentiating the *gens Anglorum* from the island's aboriginal population. This tinge had grown more pronounced in twelfth-century accounts of the Welsh, especially as England moved fiercely into Wales.

Like Bede, both William and Geoffrey had faith in the solitariness of the island's peoples. Like Bede, neither writer developed a vision of history that could easily accommodate the recklessly alchemical tendencies of the past. They composed narratives in which collective identities appear to be placid in the present and relatively unchanged over monumental spans of time. Yet both their texts are haunted by unquiet middles. Home to a Saracen pope, an acrobat transformed into a donkey, conjoined twins, a tempest of blood that transforms the island into a rotting cadaver, and men who espouse purity of descent while populating the world with mongrel progeny, these regions are roamed by figures of troubling hybridity.

Bede's Austere History

Composing "at the extremity of the known world," the Venerable Bede finished his *Historia ecclesiastica gentis Anglorum* (*Ecclesiastical History of the English People*) around 731.[2] The heart of his narrative spans the fifth through early eighth centuries, a time when the isles were a maelstrom of cultural clash, admixture, and alliance. The Picts and the Britons (disparate and shifting collectives of peoples, some Romanized, some not) formed their greater and smaller collectives, many enduring for years, others coalescing as briefly as the life of a warrior-king. Immigrants from Ireland arrived in what would someday be called Scotland and Wales, establishing the maritime kingdom of Dál Riata. Lively exchange with the continent was a constant. Beginning in the fifth century ethnically various peoples migrated from southern Scandinavia and northern Germany, assimilating or loosely incorporating some indigenous groups, displacing or eradicating others. Over time these plunderers-turned-settlers combined warbands with more sedentary pursuits. Medieval writers referred to this settlement as the *adventus Saxonum*; modern historians label it the Anglo-Saxon migration, the foundation for what becomes England.[3] Recent archeological and historical work has stressed the survival of native polities. Out of patchy amalgamations of Anglo-Saxon and Romano-British elements emerged kingdoms like Hwicce and Mercia.[4] Upstart realms fought relentlessly for hegemony, incorporating conquered rivals to form larger kingdoms, expanding into lands still held by Britons and Picts. These peoples, meanwhile, continued to form their own shifting solidarities, especially in the form of competitive principalities.

By the time Bede set pen to vellum, the inhabitants of Britain had long spoken a variety of languages in an abundance of dialects. No doubt rapidly changing *patois* enabled trade and other less ephemeral forms of exchange. Many islanders would have been multilingual, indeed multiracial. The peoples of Britain were for much of this period more alike than different: possessing cultures and speaking tongues that lacked internal uniformity; prone to forming princely, kingly, and familial factions of variable scope and duration; mixing pastoral and pillage economies with less mobile religious and agrarian pursuits; willing to ally themselves militarily and matrimonially with those outside their linguistic and cultural circles. The British archipelago was, in short, as unsettled as it was compound, a dynamic expanse engendering what contemporary theorists of the postcolonial label creolization, *métissage*, doubleness, *mestizaje*, or hybridity. No surprise, then, that "Anglo-Saxon England" is famous for its syncretism, its ability to embrace diverse and even contradictory traditions simultaneously.

Yet Bede stresses throughout his *Ecclesiastical History* the separateness and the supersession of insular peoples, a point emphasized even in his opening observation that Britain was "formerly known as Albion" (1.1; by whom he never says). He acknowledges hybridity only obliquely.[5] In the narrative arc formed by the *Ecclesiastical History* 2.13–3.3, we witness Edwin of Northumbria forsaking his native ways and converting to Christianity, reorienting his northern kingdom along a Mediterranean axis.[6] The same king unites Britons and Angles in paninsular dominion. Rædwald of the East Angles, we are told, once erected a temple in which one altar served Christ and the other heathen deities. Papal epistles travel the world to ensure that the Northumbrian and Irish races (*gentem Nordanhymbrorum, genti Scottorum*) celebrate a unified Christianity. The pagan English of Mercia enthusiastically join forces with the Christian Britons of Gwynedd to over-throw Edwin. The exiled sons of Æthelfrith, the king from whom Edwin had captured the Bernician throne, dwell with their retinues among the Irish and Picts, awaiting Edwin's death. When these men return to their native kingdom, they immediately revert to their indigenous religion, a worship they had rejected after accepting baptism abroad. Oswald, the newest successor to Northumbria, is witnessed mediating the Irish tongue of the visiting bishop, Aidan of Iona, as he addresses the Angles:

> It was indeed a beautiful sight when the bishop was preaching the gospel, to see the king acting as interpreter of the heavenly word for his ealdormen and thanes, for the bishop was not completely at home in the English tongue [*Anglorum linguam perfecte non nouerat*], while the king had gained a perfect knowledge of Irish [*linguam Scottorum iam plene didicerat*] during the long period of his exile. (*Ecclesiastical History* 3.3)

Bishop Aidan oversees monasteries that conjoin his native country to the Picts and the Angles. He lives on an island, Iona, that straddles the space between Britain and Ireland. His monastic community (if Adomnán of Iona is to be believed) amalgamates the Irish, Picts, English, and Britons. Through Aidan's friendship with Oswald, English Britain is transformed by Irish learning into a composite space (3.3).

Despite these multicultural vectors, however, most interminglings unfold only to be condemned. Rædwald's East Anglia is the location of the famous Sutton Hoo burial, an archeological discovery that—like the corpus of Old English poetry itself—suggests that Rædwald's syncretism is far more indica-tive of the practice of Christianity in England than Bede's absolutist vision of pagan/Christian separation. Because Rædwald stations Christ alongside native gods and privileges neither, because his desire is to combine rather than to sort, the monarch must in Bede's account be deplored. The "Anglo-Saxan" Mercians are allowed their alliance with the Britons only because they are pagans, and therefore as detestable as the confederates they treat as equals. The sons of Æthelfrith deserve their violent deaths because they move back and forth between the categories Christian and heathen, a trou-bling inconstancy rather than an easy fusion (they must be wholly one or the other; they are not permitted the strategic embrace of both). Oswald is allowed his Irish tongue and his subjects their Irish instruction because this source of Christianity does not come from a people, like the Britons, vying against Bede's Angles for possession of the island.

Onto Britain's historical heterogeneity Bede projects a reductive separateness. Bede's narrative is rather like the Hadrianic and Antonine walling projects that he describes early in the text, demarcations that engender unity through exclusion. In his vision the entirety of the island constitutes the natural dominion of a singular *gens Anglorum*, the English people. This group did not quite exist in Bede's day. Yet by imagining the island's past as a story heroically accomplished by this putative collective, by distilling a complicated historical field into the chronicle of a single people, Bede breathes life into the collective identity *English* and aids in the genesis of what is to become Europe's most precocious nation. The *Ecclesiastical History* imagines a past that, despite ample evidence to the contrary, seems monolithic, pure.

In the Beginning

Bede's historical narrative starts, tellingly, not with the arrival of the Britons but centuries later, with Rome's first conquest of the island (1.2). Because the narrative is initiated from a Mediterranean rather than indigenous point of view, other possible histories recede. Like the complex multiculturalism discernable in the Edwin to Oswald arc of books two and three, however, these alternative beginnings can be glimpsed as they quietly trouble Bede's project of separation. In the topographical overview that introduces the *Ecclesiastical History*, Bede offers a precise and seemingly neutral delineation of the islands: the Orkneys; proximate Ireland; the *Oceanus infinitus* or "boundless sea" that encloses these fertile expanses in its watery embrace; massive *Britannia* shared by the Picts, Irish, Britons, and Angles. Describing the contours of the archipelago and its present population means acknowledging that the islands possess a past lengthier than that initiated when Britain was drawn into the orbit of Rome. Yet as geographical survey yields to history, insular time begins with Caesar's arrival, not with the advent of the peoples he warred against, the contemporary *Picti* and *Brettones*.

Four living languages thrive on the island, Bede continues, each straightforwardly representing a single insular people: Irish, Pictish, British, and English (*Ecclesiastical History* 1.1).[7] By demarcating Britain linguistically, Bede is able to delineate four peoples who did not typically conceptualize themselves within such massively collective frameworks. True, writers like Julius Caesar, Tacitus, and Gildas had for their own purposes collected insular inhabitants into vast categories. Even if such communal nomination was available and at times effective when Bede wrote, grandiose designations did not necessarily have much import for the quotidian struggles in which the denizens of Britain engaged. Political realities more frequently eroded than buttressed the efficacy of overarching linguistic and cultural unities. Yet Bede took as a foundational assumption that, in stepping back far enough and surveying all of Britain as if with the eye of God, the island's scattered population would resolve into four groups, naturally and patently distinct. United by language, Bede implies, each was formed by an individuating history and a particularizing origin.[8]

Bede nominally composed an account of the Roman Church in England, a Church still in its infancy. Bede was born a mere seventy-five years after the arrival of the missionary Augustine in Kent, and his own country of Northumbria had been Christian for only five decades.[9] Given this relative precariousness, it could be argued that Bede's ambition was only to provide the English church with a stable history, probably in the hopes of engendering a more secure future. Along the way, however, Bede's *Ecclesiastical History* also furnished the English race (*gens Anglorum*) with a narrative structure that would enable dispersed and heterogeneous peoples to embrace their own community. This harmonizing bent is most evident when Bede describes his favorite "English" kings—beloved, we suspect, because they happen to be Christian kings of Northumbria, and the monk was ethnically a Northumbrian.[10] In a culminating moment of insular harmony, the glorious Edwin reigns peacefully over "the whole realm of Britain" (*omnes Brittaniae fines*, 2.9), both "the English and the British race" (*genti Anglorum simul et Brettonum*, 2.20). One of Edwin's men famously imagines that the world is a fire-lit meadhall, shielding the king and the thanes from the wintry storms that rage outside (2.13). This potent image of community is in a way a figure for Edwin's kingdom itself, capacious and durable, but thoroughly and unthinkingly English in its terms of belonging (the Britons did not dream of meadhalls when they wanted to symbolize harmonious earthly unity; it is not possible to imagine the *gens Brettonum* seated with Edwin by that warming fire). The stability Edwin achieves comes to a cataclysmic end, however, when he and his army are slaughtered in battle. They fall against a twofold enemy: the nefarious heathen Penda, ruler of the rival kingdom of Mercia; and Cædwalla, *rex Brettonum*, "king of the Britons." Bede's title for Cædwalla is a typical exaggeration on his part, for Cadwallon ap Cadfan was king only of Gwynedd, a powerful British kingdom in what would someday become northwest Wales.

Penda is easy to detest, since he remains an idol-worshipping pagan after the Christian destiny of the *gens Anglorum* has been made clear.[11] Cædwalla is another story. Like Edwin, Cædwalla is a Christian king. Welsh literary tradition suggests that Edwin spent time in exile at the court of Gwynedd, probably at the time it was ruled by Cadfan, Cædwalla's father.[12] Yet despite a shared creed and historical alliances that clearly crossed cultural boundaries, Bede distances Cædwalla at every opportunity, introducing him as "a barbarian who was worse than a heathen" (*barbarus erat pagano saeuior*). By insisting that in taking arms against the English Cædwalla committed an act of insurrection (*rebellauit*), Bede not only grants Edwin more power over the Britons than he likely exerted, he renders what may have been military self-protection on Cædwalla's part an unforgivable revolt.[13] After Edwin of Northumbria dies in fierce battle at Hæthfelth, the Britons and their king are described in monstrous terms:

> Cædwalla, although a Christian by name and profession, was nevertheless a barbarian in heart and disposition and spared neither women nor innocent children. With bestial cruelty he put all to death by torture and for a long time raged through all their land, meaning to wipe out the whole English nation from the land of Britain. Nor did he pay any respect to the Christian religion which had sprung up amongst them. Indeed to this very day it is the habit of the Britons to despise the faith and religion of the English and not to co-operate with them in anything more than with the heathen. (2.20)

Barbaric, cruel, bloodthirsty, bestial: these are the very terms that the British polemicist Gildas had used to describe the invading Saxons, now turned against the Britons themselves.[14] These are the same racializing slanders that will be disseminated by the English against the Welsh four hundred years later, with a similar emphasis on distancing two Christian peoples and reducing complicated interrelation to an impermeable binary.[15] Cædwalla attacks with genocidal intention (*erasurum se esse deliberans*), making the object of his fury not mere Northumbrians but *totum genus Anglorum*, "the whole English people." Bede's hyperbolic Latin term for Cædwalla's military objective, *erasurum*, comes from *eradere*, "to abolish, to extirpate." This harsh verb can also mean "to obliterate, to cause to be forgotten," making it clear that the Britons pose a threat to the very memory of the English on the island—a threat, in fact, to the project of Bede's *History* itself. The passage is, moreover, just as reductive in its treatment of the English as it is of the Britons, depicting both peoples as impossibly homogeneous collectives. Imperiled by the blood they share, the *totum genus Anglorum* must now shed the blood of the monster-like Britons to endure. Cædwalla and his savage race are foundationally excluded from this emergent community because they are its catalyst, the endangerment that brings the possibility of a pan-English union into being.

The disaster at Hæthfelth sets the stage for the ascendancy of Oswald, the king who will spectacularly destroy the abominable (*infandus*) leader of the Britons (3.1). The fevered pitch of Bede's Latin in describing Cædwalla deserves notice here. The adjective *infandus* carries the literal meaning "unspeakable" ("*in-*" + *for,* "say, utter") and is employed to indicate those moments when language fails, as when Vergil describes the man-eating Cyclopes of the *Aeneid*.[16] *Barbarus* (barbarian) and *atrocitate ferina* (animal savagery) are little better, but when hitched to a litany of his crimes do a good job of speaking that which in Cædwalla was supposed to be unutterable. Oswald, on the other hand, is a figure of supreme unity a harmonizing force so potent that he evokes a repetition of the same cultural geography that delimited the island at the opening of the *Ecclesiastical History* (3.6). So immune to division is this king that after his royal corpse is dismembered by Mercian enemies, the severed pieces retain their potency. The soil from "that very place where Oswald's blood was spilt" absorbs its curative powers (3.9–10); his bones shimmer with numinous light (3.11); a splinter of the wooden stake on which his severed head was displayed heals the sick (3.13); his hands "have remain uncorrupt until this present time . . . and are venerated with fitting respect by all" (3.6). The body of Oswald can be broken, scattered, made to seem as if it could never again constitute a whole. Yet corporeal fragmentation only serves to disseminate the king's power more widely into his community. Oswald's cadaver is a powerful figure for the *gens Anglorum*, diverse peoples that Bede's *History* consolidates by imagining for them a collective history and a durable corporate future.

"Very Many Peoples"

Every collective identity needs some narrative architecture to shape its contours and harmonize its content. History and myth delimit the bodies from which can be traced descent, barring others (such as *Caedualla infandus* and his monsterized Britons) from this emergent collectivity. Such a foundational narrative will bolster a people's claims to power, distinctiveness, superiority.[17] No less potent for being specious, such unity often comes about by ostracizing peoples perceived as competitors or threats. Origin myths tend to grant each people its singular descent in order not only to explain how present segregations came about, but to uphold such a configuration as the culmination of inevitable historical processes.

Bede bequeathed to the later Middle Ages the idea that the sundry ethnic and political groups that marauded in Britain beginning in the fifth century composed a single entity, the *gens Anglorum*. It is often *not* pointed out, however, that Bede knew well the originary variousness of the peoples who comprised these "Anglo-Saxons." In describing the intended mission of Egbert he writes:

[Egbert] knew that there were very many peoples in Germany from whom the Angles and the Saxons, who now live in Britain, derive their origin; hence even to this day they are by a corruption called *Garmani* by their neighbours the Britons. Now these people are the Frisians, Rugians, Danes, Huns, Old Saxons, and *Boruhtware* [Boructuari]. (5.9)

Bede's list is woefully partial. It contains laughable inaccuracies as well as opaque references. Yet its presence makes clear that Bede was cognizant of the multiplicitous beginnings of his people. Such an acknowledgment is rather surprising on Bede's part, for elsewhere he distills from the ethnic hodgepodge of the island's invaders three impossibly neat groups: Angles, Saxons, and Jutes.[18] Even this tripled origin is not as varied as it seems, since in Bede's account these groups lack distinguishing difference. All are in fact reducible to the umbrella term *Angli*, as is evident in Bede's Latin title for his work. Bede no doubt borrowed such collective language from the Roman Church, an institution that had long promulgated the useful myth that a singular English people actually existed. Thus Pope Gregory's slave market insistence that the blond-haired denizens of England are as angelic as they are apparently unvaried (2.1), and thus the same pope's addressing Æthelberht, king of the Cantuarii—a Jutish people—as "king of the English."[19] Yet no matter from where Bede drew his unitary frame, its effect was undeniable. The numerous and quarrelsome "Anglo-Saxon" kingdoms and their varied populations now had a history within which they could recognize themselves as having always already constituted the English. Hybridity and overlap, meanwhile, simply vanish. Bede makes nothing of the fact that Cædwalla, the detested British king of Gwynedd, shares his name with a beloved ruler of the Gewisse, the West Saxons. This second Cædwalla is a pagan who "harshly" reduces his kingdom to a "state of slavery" (*Ecclesiastical History* 4.15), but his genocidal intentions are practiced against the natives of the Isle of Wight (4.16), and he does become a Christian in Rome a week before his death (5.7). Like Cerdic, mythic founder of Wessex, Cædwalla possesses a name that could be used by Britons or Anglo-Saxons, suggesting that divisions between the two were not necessarily wide. Yet Bede's *History* replaces the fluidity of insular identities with a reductive past in which peoples were and ever remain Britons, Romans, and Angles. Like Oswald's incorruptible body, like his alembic blood that drenches the battlefield to persist into the present, Bede's *Angli* are a people who are ultimately devoid of internal difference, inflexible in their refusal to intermix with other peoples, immune to hybridity and historical change.[20]

Bede died in 735. About sixty-five years later, Wearmouth and Jarrow were abandoned, probably having fallen victim to Viking raids. The stone of the empty monastery crumbled. Yet the structure of belonging that Bede erected for the *gens Anglorum* endured. So did the exclusions upon which this vision was based. Bede set influential but not inalterable terms for future relations between the English and the people who had been the Britons and were more frequently being called the Welsh. Alfred the Great owes his biography to a Welshman named Asser, attached to Alfred's court because of the overtures the English king made to the principalities to his west. Yet Bede's exclusions and monsterizations were reinvigorated when his work was adopted by twelfth-century historiographers, who had their own reasons for wanting to render Welsh Christians as barbaric as possible. What Bede envisioned textually took several centuries to realize fully politically, but England possessed a remarkably corporate identity from at least the tenth century onwards.[21] Bede's formula of "Angles, Saxons, and Jutes" became "Angles and Saxons" (as in Asser's description in the 880s of King Alfred of Wessex as *Angul-Saxonum rex*), thence to *Angli* or English (a reduction already, as we have seen, anticipated by Bede). By the time Edward the Confessor ascended the throne in 1042, the southeast portions of the island had long been in fact as well as in narrative possibility a singular English nation populated by a singular English race, the *Englisc* or *Angelcynn*. Even if its unity proved ultimately precarious, as the multiple claimants to the throne at the Confessor's death made clear, England before Hastings had been the "largest area of integrated power" in the west, a "precocious" and formidable "nation-state."[22] Bede's triumphal vision of English history was no longer a mere vision of the past, but had become the past itself, in all its imperturbability. Any disruption to this intimate entwining of people with polity was destined to be traumatic.

Things Fall Apart

The venerable collectivity that for convenience's sake we now refer to as "Anglo-Saxon England" shattered in 1066. Harold Godwineson was slain in battle at Hastings, William of Normandy crowned king at Westminster. Though both these men were of quite mixed blood, to medieval historians Harold was English, William was Norman, and 1066 was a clash between two distinct peoples—again, despite the fact that their respective armies were far from homogeneous. Known in Latin as *victor* (the Conqueror) to those who revered him, and by the epithet of *nothus* (the Bastard) to those with a more conflicted bent, William deeply transformed the kingdom now his. Most troubling for the suddenly subaltern English, he systematically replaced the secular and ecclesiastical elites who had governed the island with men who differed from the native population in custom, language, descent, allegiance, and history. This purge severely frayed the meshwork that had previously bound country to people. As French-speaking settlers from across the Channel buttressed their new positions of power, peppering the landscape with castles and peopling its towns with an arriviste *haut monde*, England (and later Wales, Scotland, Ireland) was entangled within that web of rapid change, violent clash, pervasive anxiety, and ambivalent desire that we have come to label postcoloniality.

To some extent William and his followers endeavored to play down the historical disjunction that the conquest engendered, especially in the years immediately following Hastings. After all, William had justified his claim to the throne of England by asserting consanguinity with the royal line. In the youth of his reign, the Norman king's impulse was to emphasize continuity, drawing up the majority of his early royal writs in English, retaining priests like Edward the Confessor's trusted Regenbald in his chancery, and so on.[23] Recent interpreters have emphasized that the Norman turn to those strategies that were to produce a bifurcated, recognizably postcolonial society did not happen immediately.[24] The narrative strategy of some twelfth-century historiographers was likewise to underscore a continuousness between pre- and post-conquest England, even if both were ultimately most alike simply in being recipients of a *translatio imperii* that divided insular history into discrete epochs of limited duration.[25]

Yet despite William's claim to the throne through descent, despite even the occasional attempt by Norman nobles to "discover" English ancestors for themselves, the Normans never seriously attempted the promulgation of a shared national mythology, of a harmonizing heritage. Cognizant of their impure origins, the Normans nonetheless cultivated a strong sense of themselves as a people set apart, *Normanni ex Normannis*.[26] In England, this unitary ideology no doubt aided in establishing themselves as the minority government of a population who vastly outnumbered them. It has been estimated that the Normans and their allies numbered perhaps 10,000 after the conquest, constituting less than 1 percent of the country's inhabitants.[27] Yet into the hands of this small group came control of the church, the government, and almost the entirety of the land.

The English meanwhile were quickly transformed from *indigeni* to *gens subacta*, from native dwellers to a subject people. As William's reign progressed and the foundations of his power strengthened, the English were systematically dispossessed of territory, goods, cultural, and linguistic prestige.[28] After the conquest neither language nor a shared sense of the past conjoined England's rulers to those over whom they exerted their authority. As hard as the new divisions in custom and language must have been for the English, the loss of a communal history was the most difficult blow to be borne. Robert Stein describes the lasting historiographic repercussions of this gulf best: "In the writing of history in the twelfth century, the

Norman conquest of the English marks a crisis of cultural identity, of the principles of legitimate sovereignty, and of historical explanation."[29] England's long, culminating chain of history had been severed, and it was difficult to imagine how it might ever be repaired.

The Interrupted Chain of Time

The *Gesta Regum Anglorum* (*History of the English Kings*) was not just William of Malmesbury's magnum opus, the achievement of long years spent in tireless research and hand-cramping composition. The *History* was, quite literally, the product of William's blood.

The first complete account of the English people undertaken since Bede finished the *Ecclesiastical History*, William writes that his intention in composing his monumental text was is "to mend the broken chain of history" (*interruptam temporum seriem sarcire*). This restorative work was required because a historiographic void separated his own day from the terminus of Bede's account.[30] Yet William was himself the result of a more literal *interrupta temporum series*, a rupture in the chain of time. The son of an English mother and Norman father, William would not exist to be writing in the 1120s if the conquest had not derailed the trajectory of English history sixty years prior. In connecting Bede's *Ecclesiastical History* to the present day, William also aimed to accommodate the Norman Conquest into an unbroken historical chain that might conjoin the two peoples who met biologically as well as culturally in him.

By William's day, Bede had become *tout court* the truth of England's distant past.[31] No alternative existed, the annalistic *Anglo-Saxon Chronicle* being too sparse to compete with Bede's rich pageant of kings, popes, abbots, martyrs, and miracles. The first book of William's *History of the English Kings* is therefore mainly derived from the *Ecclesiastical History*, though with a telling difference. Like his bureaucratic counterparts in the burgeoning administrative apparatus of Norman England, William was far more of a systematizer than his Northumbrian predecessor. As he reworked Bede's sprawling data, he neatly divided monarchs into chronologically and geographically precise successions. Despite this Norman reordering, however, William never questioned that the history of the island was *English* history, singular and reductive. The Irish, Britons, Picts, and Scots might provide expedient havens during kingly exiles and convenient enemies for heroic regents to destroy, but William kept the non-English at his narrative periphery. Even within his account of England under the Norman kings, other peoples are introduced only to rebel, to menace border settlements or the Holy Land, and to offer a foil for English superiority. Although William allows that the *gens Anglorum* may once have been similarly uncouth, especially in the days when Hengest and Horsa led the first invasion troops to British shores, he insists that they had long ago progressed into more civilized ways. The other island peoples, however, remain as they have always been, locked in eternal archaism. A devout classicist, William describes them as barbarians.

The Normans and the English were to William very different peoples. The English, he writes, are incorrigible in their love of strong drink (3.245). They possess an inborn credulity (*innata credulitate*, 2.125); speak a rough language (Prologue; 2.165); appreciate neither good architecture nor good manners; cannot restrain their own rashness; overindulge in food and drink to the point of illness; wear too much gold jewelry; and sport gaudy tattoos (3.245). In the wake of the conquest, they also seem a race of permanent losers, irreparably downtrodden: "No Englishman today is an earl, a bishop, or an abbot; new faces everywhere enjoy England's riches and gnaw her vitals, nor is there any hope of ending this miserable state of affairs" (2.227). There are few positive attributes on this list, suggesting that William might simply have performed the same identification as many children of intermarriage, embracing the more powerful component of a mixed heritage. The Normans of his text are, after all, kindly disposed to strangers and foreigners (2.178, 3.254). They build grand structures but live moderately (3.245). Not only "well dressed to a fault," they are also fussy—in a good way—about their food (3.246). Although not always faithful, Normans are reliably ambitious, pious, tolerant of cultural variation, and generous (3.246). His version of William the Conqueror seems to have this natural gulf between peoples in mind when he declares that no man of English descent may be a part of the post-conquest hierarchy of the church (3.254).

William of Malmesbury was, however, no Norman manqué. He describes the Battle of Hastings as "a fatal day for England, the deadly ruin of the sweet homeland in the change of new masters" (3.245). Such elegiac language would seem to betray an indigenous identification. Yet this *dies fatalis* that conjoined the fate of the English to that of the Normans brought into power the very people from whom William of Malmesbury seeks literary patronage. Indeed, the conquest was the precondition of his own conception. How can William, unintentional byproduct of a sweet country's ruin (*excidium*, the very word used by Gildas to describe the devastation of Britain at the hands of the Saxons) narrate the connection between a singular English past and a compound present?

William's uncertainty in the face of this question is evident as he describes the return of Edward the Confessor to claim the English throne. Æthelred II had broken with English tradition and married outside his kingdom, taking as his wife Emma of Normandy. Edward was therefore, like William himself, of mixed blood. After Harthacnut's boozy death he sails from exile in Normandy, bringing numerous friends. When these *nouos homines et aduenas* ("new men and foreigners," 2.197) are granted comfortable positions at the court, native nobles chafe. Chief among these grumblers are Godwine and his sons, men who prospered under the Danish kings and who do not want their power diminished. William attempts a balanced account of Godwine. English reasons for praising him are followed by the Norman charges against his character. The English, he notes, fault Edward for importing foreigners for undeserved promotion. The Normans, he says, insist that they were simply attempting to aid a king misused by his English retinue. William admits that he cannot tell which side interprets this tumultuous moment in history more truthfully. He realizes that the two versions of the events at Edward's court are wholly incompatible:

> It is these differences of opinion which . . . put my narrative at risk, since I cannot decide what precisely is the truth, either from the natural division between the two nations or because the fact is that the English are scornful of any superior and the Normans cannot endure an equal. (2.198)

Both of William's explanations for the deadlock of historical interpretation at which he has arrived have in common the assumption that the Normans and the English are so innately separate that never the two shall meet—a possibility that would not bode well for William himself, in whom the two have in fact quite literally met.

William introduces his frustrated discussion of Edward's court with a warning to the reader that the course of his unfolding history is becoming uncertain (*lectorem premonitum uolo quod hic quasi ancipitem uiam narrationis uideo*, 2.197). That he portrays his narrative as following a road (*uia*) is straightforward enough, but that this road should be *ancipitem* is notable. *Anceps* is a rare Latin adjective that figuratively means "doubtful, ambiguous, hazardous." More literally, however, *anceps* is "two-headed" (*ambi* + *caput*). This bicephalic image suggests that William's hesitation may not be propelled so much by Norman and English difference as by the fact that he has reached a moment of recalcitrant hybridity. Edward the Confessor's court is a place of *métissage*, blending imported and indigenous ways. Its discordant fusion of differences troubles William's narrative because monolithic frames of interpretation cannot separate an admixed history back into its constituent parts: the English version and the Norman version of history are contradictory, and there is no space for the middle that Edward's court inhabits. All William can do is to admit that English and Norman historians interpret the moment incompatibly and move on. Yet the *ancipitem uiam*—"doubled path" "ambiguous course" or "two-headed way"—would be a road he would find himself treading repeatedly in the course of his increasingly troubled narrative.

Cohabitations of Difference

William of Malmesbury arrives at an exegetical impasse not because he could not decide who interpreted history correctly, the Normans or the English, but because their austere perspectives exclude the difficult middle inhabited by William himself, the medial space also occupied by Edward the Confessor and his Danish-Norman-English court. The *History* is pulled in conflicting directions by its author's divergent bonds. William loves the English for their glorious past. He sympathizes with their wretched present, especially because they continue to be barred from positions of authority once enjoyed. He loves the Normans for their cultivated manners, their arts, and their architecture. He is a Benedictine monk, an order that flourished under the reform-minded Normans. William resents both peoples for their numerous vices, and especially (it seems) for their mutual, destructive hatred. The Normans are clearly the elites, and therefore the most beneficial group with which to identify—and William is fully capable of being a Norman apologist. Yet he is writing a history of England, not Normandy; he is resident not in some new Norman foundation but in a monastery founded by Aldhelm (ca. 709), an institution dating from the days of his beloved Bede.[32]

William's typical strategy for advancing beyond impasses of analysis and identification is to provide two irreconcilable views and then move forward without synthesis. He often weights such bifurcated accounts toward the side that eventually prevails (for example, the account of Godwine's death is clearly Norman in its sympathies). Yet the fact that William allows history a constitutive doubleness makes his text very different from the accounts of most contemporary writers, a point that he makes himself. The preface to the third book of the *Deeds* notes in frustration that historians of William the Conqueror have allowed partisan zeal to vitiate their accounts. The Normans praised William to excess, while the English saw only wickedness in his reign.[33] Because he has the blood of both people flowing through his veins (*utriusque gentis sanguinem traho*), William declares, he will blaze a "middle path" (*temperamentum*, literally a "proper mixture"). This intermediate way consists for the most part of setting history's contradictions next to each other, without turning noisy difference into some counterfeit harmony.

"Proper mixture," the alchemy of doubled blood, is in fact the key to understanding the aftermath of the conquest in William's text. His

Normans do not so much interrupt English history as provide another link in history's chain of progress, albeit a transformative one. Unlike Bede, William writes history in an evolutionary mode. The English, he observes, have changed over time.[34] Their elemental barbarism slowly gave way to a more advanced culture, as they learned to live in towns and foster commerce.[35] After the Normans introduce England to sophisticated architecture, customs, laws, and manners, the English remain the English, only better. "In William's view," John Gillingham observes, "it was French culture, not Christianity alone, which made the English civilised."[36] Yet Gillingham overstates the permanence that William grants to the stages peoples achieve as they move from primitivism to cultured modernity.[37] By the eve of the conquest, William thought, the English had regressed to their pre-Christian ways, wallowing in sin and forgetful of their former religious fervor. Perhaps that is why Godwine comes off so badly as he attempts to anglicize his regent Edward. The advent of the Normans restores the English to their Bedean sanctity (3.245). The conquest is a punishing reminder from God of the importance of past achievements rather than a movement to some new mode of being. English accomplishment in refined manners and increased civility seem to be an added bonus of the Normans' arrival rather than the catalyst that moves them out of some enduring barbarity. William is careful, moreover, not to conflate the Normans with the French. The former people are for him as Germanic as England's primal Angles, sent forth like them from an overpopulated motherland in search of a better life (1.5). Like the primordial English, the first Normans are rather uncouth (Rollo, their founder, is possessed of an "innate and uncontrollable barbarity"), becoming progressively more civil as they transform from *Northmanni* to *Normanni*. No matter how different the Normans and English might seem in the eleventh and twelfth century, William implies, they are nonetheless intimately bound.

After narrating the reign of the Conqueror, William tends no longer to dwell upon the Normans and the English as distinct groups. It is possible to see in this tendency to speak of conquerors and conquered as a single national collective evidence that widespread acculturation had been quickly effected and that England remained divided only for a very brief period. Yet William was a monastic writer whose brethren had much at stake in insisting that what had been a wholesale eradication of native political and ecclesiastical leadership had not left in its wake enduring disparities. English monasteries were mainly dedicated to indigenous saints. The stable Englishness of these foundations—both before and after the conquest—therefore needed to be emphasized. William's *History* was, moreover, dedicated to a queen who, with her husband, had viewed the present monarchy as continuous with the pre-Norman past, as a part of English history rather than a disruption or innovation.

Perhaps William's doubled perspective and compound blood are as potently continuist as he claims. Perhaps he could offer some confidence in an unbroken chain of time, one in which compound identity resolves conflict, synthesizes difference, and mends ruptured history. If the path of interpretation that William treads is peacefully dual, then its patron deity may be two-faced Janus, the Roman god of doorways and journeys and good beginnings, often described as *bifrons* or *anceps*. Yet the *via anceps* finds a far less reassuring embodiment later in William 's text, where it returns as a monstrous portent, a conjoined twin who declares the impossibility of placidly combining two identities within a single body.

Middle Paths

Although he acknowledged that peoples might become more civilized or pious over time, William seems to have accepted unquestioningly Bede's vision of collective identities as enduringly separate. When he described his blood as Norman and English, William meant that both identities coexisted within him, not that they had fused into some novel, third category of being. Yet William's historical account is perturbed by spectacular marvels and monsters that embody a hybridity of a very different sort, a tumultuous admixture that offers exactly such intermediacy. Like Gerald of Wales after him, William seems never to have found in his Latin vocabulary terms sufficient to capture precisely what it means to find two collective identities mingled but not assimilated by a single body. He therefore explored hybridity through visual representations that could sidestep the demand to choose one perspective or belonging over another. These richly imagined word-portraits amount to what we would today call fantasy: bodies, identities, and realms that do not respect the accepted rules for how the world should look, move, and work. For twelfth-century writers, however, such moments were an integral part of historiography, a thoroughly self-conscious genre that frequently employed the marvelous and the monstrous as a means of examining cultural problems difficult otherwise to frame.[38] William used the fantastic to ruminate over uneasy or unlooked-for admixture, creating complicated visions that were never simply affirmative.

The most negative figuration of mixed blood in William's text is the ominous birth of conjoined twins at the Norman-Brittany border. This woman or women possessed two heads and four arms, but only one stomach and two legs (2.207). One sister dies, the other endures for three years before she herself expires. This prodigious creature both singular and plural, alive and dead, is interpreted as a figure for England and Normandy, a thriving kingdom conjoined to a moribund duchy. Its ancient nobility all dead (*omni nobilitate antiquorum extincta*), England will be happy again, William observes, only once it regains its freedom (*libertatem*). The trouble with this formulation, however, is that the twins are not simply joined by some inconvenient band of flesh, but inextricably *melded*, two identities in permanent corporeal union. There is no way to separate them, no way to free a Norman or an English being from a body that fuses differences. The conjoined twins at the Norman border figure a monstrous return of William's *via anceps*, the "two-headed way," here in a form that offers not the providential mixing of two nations' blood but a horrific impasse of decidability that eventually becomes lethal.[39]

These unreconciled but amalgamated identities appear in William's narrative shortly after his famous account of the sorceress of Berkeley, an extraordinary woman who has always dwelled outside the limits of an acceptable life (2.204). In both her sexuality and her will to power she is, among twelfth-century Englishwomen, a nonconformist. Yet she realizes that in death she will be reclaimed back into the punitive system that she has so far employed her every wile to escape. Enjoining her children to sew her cadaver within the skin of a deer and to wrap chains around her coffin, she attempts to cheat the devil of her soul. Satan knows his own, however, even when they reside in alien dermis. He removes the witch from her doubled body and flings her upon "a stallion, black, whinnying proudly, with iron barbs set point upwards all down its back." Literally fixed into place and destined for unending torment, the sorceress is last heard screaming for help as she and the demonic retinue vanish. William has been condemned in the past by critics who do not see the point of such marvels. These episodes perhaps seem extraneous when they interrupt a narrative filled with the sober minutiae of kingly reigns and episcopal achievements. Yet, like the imperfectly melded sisters of the Norman border, the sorceress of Berkeley offers a compelling meditation on difficult identities and limited possibilities for belonging. To embrace a selfhood without acceptable historical precedent—to be something novel, compound, plural—is to risk obliteration.

Related themes enliven the long account of the necromancer Gerbert of Aurillac, also known as Pope Silvester II. This figure of intimate otherness functions as a doppelganger for William of Malmesbury himself. William opens the second book of the *Deeds* with a prologue describing his own voracious reading. From childhood he has been obsessed with books and learning, he writes, progressing through the study of logic, medicine, ethics, and history. William tells us that he built a capacious library of foreign historians and native chronicles through exhaustive searching, but never satisfied his ardor for knowledge (2.Prologue). Later in the same book, another expansive search for erudition unfolds, this time with clearly transformative consequences. "John, also called Gerbert" is introduced into the historical narration as the author of a papal letter mandating peace between King Æthelred of England and Duke Richard of Normandy (2.165–66). This peace will be cemented through Æthelred's marriage to Richard's daughter, Emma, setting the stage for Edward the Confessor's ascension as well as that, eventually, of William the Conqueror. Gerbert is, in short, a mediator who ensures that a hybrid Anglo-Norman England will come into being. Gerbert precipitates the series of events that will bring William of Malmesbury into a confused world.

Gerbert's letter is offered in full, followed by an account of his remarkable life—an interpolation so long that it cannot be dismissed as mere digression. The narrative demands, in the words of Monika Otter, "to be accounted for rather than dismissed."[40] Initially a monk, this ambitious scholar leaves the cloister for Spain, where he spends years among the Saracens, the twelfth century's favorite figure for racial and cultural otherness (2.167). Gerbert quickly masters the classical subjects that fascinated the author of the *Deeds* himself, but then turns to the dark arts. He pursues arcane books with a zeal uncannily similar to that animating William's own pursuit of scholarship. Once the former monk has been infected by alien knowledge—once his solidly Christian identity has been opened to unprecedented cultural impurities—he is capable of accomplishing wonders unknown to history. The greatest of these feats is the discovery (though not the attainment) of a realm fashioned of the purest gold, a dangerous and much sought-after kingdom hidden to all previous human eyes (2.169). Yet despite his earthly and intellectual triumphs, despite rising all the way to the papacy, Gerbert's unconventional identity cannot endure. He misinterprets a prophecy about his own place in the world, thinking that the Jerusalem that will herald his death is the distant Holy Land and realizing only too late that it is the name of a church intimate to him. As his death nears he orders that his corpse be chopped into small pieces and scattered. The fragmentation of his body aligns Gerbert with the sorceress of Berkeley and the conjoined twins of Normandy as a mixed creature who, despite a startling innovativeness, cannot possess the secure future he so passionately desires, literally coming apart before its advent.

William's account of John-Gerbert-Silvester (his tripled names well indicating his multiplicitous identity) is uncharacteristically dilatory, containing similar stories of identities brought beyond acceptable limits. A Jewish mage knows the "ineffable name of the Lord" and can snatch the treasures that Christians fail to apprehend (2.170). Two elderly women delight in imprisoning men in the bodies of animals, selling them at the market to embark on new lives, alive in compound forms they never

dreamt would be their own (2.171). The story of these two witches culminates the arc instigated by the Gerbert digression by bringing its themes of
racial and cultural admixture into a bluntly corporeal register. The narrative
emphasizes the confusions engendered by hybridity, as well as the purifying power of speech:

> On the high road that leads to Rome lived two old crones, altogether filthy
> and given to liquor, who shared one cottage and were filled with one spirit
> of witchcraft. If ever a traveller came to lodge with them by himself, they
> used to make him take the shape of horse or hog or some other animal and
> offer him for sale to the dealers in such things, spending on their stomachs
> the coin they thus obtained. One night, as it happened, they gave lodging to
> a youth who earned his living as an acrobat, and made him to take the shape
> of an ass, thinking that donkey whose astonishing capers could hold the
> attentions of passers-by would be a great addition to their assets; for whatever
> movements were dictated by one of the dames the donkey followed. He had
> not, you see, lost a man's intelligence, though he had lost the power of
> speech. (2.171)

The two women find their performing donkey a lucrative addition to their
business, but eventually sell the animal to a rich man. Although the new pet
entertains at drunken feasts, its novelty quickly fades. The crones had
warned the man never to allow the ass to approach water. Now unguarded,
the donkey runs to a pool and rolls in its cleansing embrace. He is restored
immediately to his former shape. Soon thereafter the acrobat is asked if he
happened to have seen an escaped donkey. The artist admits that he was
once that very animal, the case goes all the way to the pope, and eventually the witches are convicted of their crimes.

William's marvels, vivid eruptions of the new, contrast sharply with the
cold functionality of the few wonders Bede describes in his *Ecclesiastical
History*. Bede employed supernatural events to make theological or moral
points, to edify, and to reveal divine favor, well precedented uses of the
marvelous in historical writing.[41] Those wonders William narrates have
seemed to some scholars inconsequential by comparison. Yet the three
marvels just discussed arrive at particularly perilous times for the English in
William's historical narration. Gerbert's story and the tale of the transformative crones are inserted into the section of William's *History of the English
Kings* when Æthelred is rapidly losing control over a kingdom ravaged by
Danish marauders. The sorceress and the conjoined twins appear shortly
after William turns to a consideration of Earl Godwine and his children, a
prelude to the events at Hastings. The arrival of the Normans is imminent,
their cultural transformation of England already started. "Pure" Englishness
is coming to an end, the advent of vexing impurities nears. Two women

in one body, witches who entrap men in animal casings or don such second skins themselves, a necromancer-pope who unites Christian certainties to Saracen possibility: these are powerful icons of hybridity and cultural overlap.

Since all three perish horribly and seem to merit their ends, since the acrobat yearns for escape from his composite form, it could be argued that these are unremittingly negative figurations, warnings against the dangers of not keeping identities pure. Yet the acrobat's intelligence (*intelligentia*) at work in a body that renders him strange combines the human and the animal in ways that at once entrap and delight (he yearns for the contours of an ordinary form while performing feats of invention that neither ass nor man could do alone). The artist in a donkey's skin is an alternative figuration for racial and cultural hybridity, and thus an energetic answer to the moribund twins who had earlier symbolized the forced conjoinment of England to Normandy. Possessed of a vitality that these two sisters lack, this conjunction of identities within a single body offers a powerful if temporary resolution to all the anxieties about hybridity that circulate in William's narration. True, the acrobat in his new skin lacks the power of speech (*amiserat loquelam*), and true, he must submerge himself in the sanitizing power of water to gain the ability to describe his compoundedness, yet William's breathless narration betrays a deep-seated fascination on his part, an enchantment that no restoration to human ordinariness can diminish. Riddled with contradiction, difference, and possibility, these ambivalent figures who cannot find the "middle path" its author so ardently espoused offer an alternative articulations of hybridity, foregrounding its difficulty.

William of Malmesbury was capable of speaking about the past of his beloved homeland with great confidence. As in Bede's vision of history, Englishness is never examined so much as assumed; it dominates, collects, purifies. His strange figures of ambivalence and hesitation provide another version of that past as it limns the compound present, offering branching and ambiguous paths that if acknowledged could disrupt the chain of history once again, ruining William's careful repair work. William does not follow these uncertain roads to their unknown destinations, preferring stable histories and secure futures. He distances his wondrous bodies geographically or through gender. Despite his allowance of contradiction into his narrative, despite his admission that history is difficult to sort, his *History* ultimately sides with continuity and firm foundation over invention and disruptive innovation. The blood of two peoples harmonized into his seemingly pacific body, William composes a history that, although undercut at times by a captivating ambiguity, is in the end an accommodationist text, allowing the Normans and English a past to share and a national community to inherit.[42]

Alternative History

In a world altered by conquest, in the aftermath of broken time, William of Malmesbury's strategy for conducting historiographic repair work was to add the new to the old, aggregation without synthesis. To an English past recorded by Bede (book 1 of the *Deeds*) and still evident in later native sources (book 2), he adjoins a full account of the three Norman kings (books 3–5). The narrative is neither seamless nor unperturbed. Still, it is possible to trace a quietly ascending movement toward harmony in William's text, propelled by an underlying belief that history's uncertainties cannot derail the progress of the English nation. His positing of a continuity, however thorny, between Anglo-Saxon and Norman England effectively united two epochs that threatened to remain disjunct. Upon its publication William's *History of the English Kings* became the authoritative account of English history, subsuming and completing Bede.

William of Malmesbury's text was soon asked to share its prestige with a work penned by another historian of mixed descent, Henry of Huntingdon, archdeacon of Lincoln. That two ambitious English histories should have been composed so closely together by men of compound heritage suggests that an anxiety over history's continuity was felt most acutely by those who carried the meeting of two peoples in their blood. Henry published a first version of his *Historia Anglorum* (*History of the English*) around 1133, and continued to revise the work until 1154. Written in a straightforward Latin that betrays little of William's elegant classicism, Henry's *History* was meant to instruct about their shared past the "less educated multitude" (V.Preface), the literate clergy who staffed a burgeoning governmental and ecclesiastical bureaucracy, ministering to the secular and religious needs of the nation. As his confident use of the first person plural pronoun indicates, Henry's seven book, all-encompassing account of "the origins of our people" (1.4) was securely English in its outlook. Tellingly, Britain vanishes in a single line, the victim of abrupt translation: "this, the most celebrated of islands, formerly called Albion, later Britain, and now England" (1.13). Henry's England is a harmonized place where, as the narrative unwinds, the Normans silently vanish, taking with them the possibility of enduringly separate differences within the kingdom's populace. By the Battle of the Standard in 1138, English and Norman history has been assimilated (4.9). Henry solves the problem of England's interrupted past by discretely merging the two peoples, offering the synthesis that William of Malmesbury could not.

Not all post-conquest historiographers were so eager to embrace narratives of congruity, especially because assimilationist history of this kind diminishes cultural complexity. Henry's blunt declaration that the island was "formerly called Albion, later Britain, and now England" would be galling to anyone who did not approach the past with his Anglophilia. Since Bede's *Ecclesiastical History* was the primal source of English history, and since Bede had not been favorably inclined toward the indigenous inhabitants of Britain, to compose an account of the insular past that did not disparage the Britons would necessitate unseating Bede from his ancient throne. For Britain to stop being swallowed into England, for the country that occupied only the southeast corner of the island to begin to share insular space, a counter-narrative would have to be discovered—or invented.

Geoffrey of Monmouth's *Historia regum Britannie* [*History of the Kings of Britain*] was wildly successful from the moment it first appeared sometime between 1136 and 1138. Proclaimed by its author to be a translation of an ancient book in the British tongue, Geoffrey's text provided an unbroken account of two thousand years of insular history, all through non-English eyes.[43] Although he adopted from the ninth-century *Historia Brittonum* the notion that the Britons were of Trojan descent, Geoffrey composed a fully enfleshed narrative that bore little resemblance to this skeletal amalgam of Welsh and Latin sources.[44] *The History of the Kings of Britain* is an exuberantly hybrid text, masterfully interweaving material derived from Welsh annals and legend, biblical and classical tradition, real and invented history, and from its author's fecund imagination. The sprawling narrative describes how exiled Trojans were given Britain by divine mandate, through a prophecy from the goddess Diana. Like the Israelites arriving in Canaan, this chosen people exterminate the aboriginal giants who inhabit their promised land and render the emptied island a new *patria*. Christening themselves *Britons* and their island *Britain* after their leader Brutus, they establish a nation already ancient by the time Julius Caesar arrives. British glory endures through a succession of spectacular kingships and a series of civil wars, culminating in the sovereignty of Arthur, who extends British dominion over the known world.

Arthur's magnificent reign directly contradicts Bede, who insisted that the arrival of the Angles, Saxons, and Jutes in the mid-fifth century marked the termination of the Britons' insular hegemony. Geoffrey has his heroic king die almost a hundred years *after* the advent of Hengest and Horsa, implying that either Bede got his chronology wrong or that the *Ecclesiastical History* had omitted from its pages some of the most remarkable events to have unfolded on the island.[45] British *imperium* might even be destined to return some day, resurgent and revitalized, at the hands of the latter-day Britons, the Welsh. It was as if someone had hurled a Molotov cocktail against the histories of Bede and William of Malmesbury, challenging their seemingly imperturbable authority through the time-changing power of a prequel.[46]

Geoffrey of Monmouth was an active participant in the celebrated twelfth-century efflorescence of historiography. He clearly admired William of Malmesbury, so much so that Michael A. Faletra aptly calls him William's "most wayward historiographical heir."[47] Henry of Huntingdon esteemed Geoffrey in turn.[48] Yet the *History of the Kings of Britain* was not a narrative that aimed respectfully to supplement or collegially to contribute to the vision of insular history originated by Bede and reinvigorated by William of Malmesbury.[49] Even if shorter in its total number of vellum pages, Geoffrey's millennia-spanning narrative details such a *longue durée* that by comparison the *Ecclesiastical History* and *Deeds of the Kings of the English* dwindle into brevity. Just as important as what Geoffrey includes, moreover, is what he strategically omits: any human presence on the island before the arriving Trojans/Britons, and any indication that the ascendancy of the Saxons is anything but a temporary seizing of British insular dominion.[50] Geoffrey ends the *History of the Kings of Britain* with these invaders in triumph, yet he intimates that the "British people [will] occupy the island again at some time in the future, once the appointed moment should come" (205 12.16).[51]

By passing over Bede's grand procession of monarchs, abbots, missionaries, and saints, Geoffrey's text relegates to silence the very stuff of English history. Absent are iconic figures like the cowherd-poet Cædmon; Gregory, the pope whose slave market browsing leads him to take a special interest in the angelic *Angli*; Coifi, the pagan priest who joyfully smashes the idols he has spent a lifetime attending. Absent too are the brilliant minutiae of kingdoms and successions that so fascinated William of Malmesbury. The ascendancy of Wessex and the unifying glory of Alfred and Edward likewise vanish, too recent to merit notation.[52] When history familiar from English sources does appear, the perspective from which the story unfolds is sharply altered. Sent by the pope to Christianize the English, the missionary Augustine requests help from British bishops. The prelates curtly rebuff him with the declaration that "they had no interest whatsoever in the Saxons' faith or their religion, and they had about as much in common with the Angles as they had with dogs!" (188 11.12).[53] Such episcopal jeers take much of the wind out of Augustine's sails, especially for readers familiar with Bede's adoring account.

The reigns of Edwin and Oswald, the political zenith of Bede's book, fare little better. Earlier in this chapter we saw how Bede described, probably contrary to historical fact, Cædwalla's attack upon Edwin of Northumbria as unmotivated rebellion. According to Geoffrey's detailed account, Edwin had been raised in exile at the court of Cadvan, father of Cadwallo (Bede's Cædwalla). Despite their differences, Edwin and Cadwallo become close friends. The two princes are about to rule the island as dual kings when Brian,

Cadwallo's nephew, reminds his uncle that the Saxons have long intended to "press on with the extermination of our race" (*genus nostrum exterminare insistent*). He argues that his uncle is providing the Saxons the perfect opportunity to complete their genocidal project (191 12.2). When Cadwallo subsequently declines to give Edwin the promised crown, war erupts between the two peoples. Penda of Mercia appears, the notorious pagan and potent ally of Cædwalla in Bede's *Ecclesiastical History*. In Geoffrey's version of the past, however, Peanda finds himself the leader of "a vast horde" (*cum maxima multitudine*) of Saxons, beaten into submission by an utterly dominating king of the Britons (196–97 12.7–8). Geoffrey is happy to repeat Bede's hyperbolic description of Cadwallo as a potent leader bent on eradicating his enemies ("He was determined to scrape the entire English race from the boundaries of Britain" [*omne genus Anglorum ex finibus Britannie abradere uolens*] 198 12.9), but such violence against a people who have invariably attempted the same against the Britons renders Geoffrey's Cadwallo heroic.

As in Bede's version of the island's past, Oswald eventually succeeds Edwin in kingship. Yet whereas Bede's Oswald quickly slaughters "the abominable leader of the Britons" (2.1) and instigates an era of supreme unity on the island, in Geoffrey's account Cadwallo ensures that Oswald is slain at Peanda's hand. He then gloriously presides over the entire isle, the obedient Mercian his subject king. Edwin and Oswald are given an extended presence in the *History of the Kings of Britain* only to erode the authority of Bede's narration. Geoffrey does not admit to conflicting versions of these kings. He writes as if Bede did not exist, even while radically reworking a story poached from him. Confident revisionist rather than self-conflicted accommodationist, Geoffrey is no William of Malmesbury. In the process of rendering the English aliens to the land they have long inhabited, Geoffrey sloughs off onto them the worst of the Normans' own imperialism. These haughty Saxons are also, when compared to the Britons, belated.

The History of the Kings of Britain is as richly detailed as it is (in John Gillingham's words) "shot through and through with ambiguity."[54] Scholars have yet to determine conclusively what Geoffrey of Monmouth's precise objective might have been in composing the text. Gillingham has argued that the *History* attempts to exalt the contemporary Welsh, rendering them suitable allies for the Normans opposed to King Stephen.[55] Indeed, the *History* first appeared not long after the death of Henry I, in the midst of the civil war over his succession. Henry had been especially skilled at subjugating Wales. Seizing upon the uncertainty following the king's demise, many Welsh rose in rebellion, making substantial progress in retaking land. Robert of Gloucester, eager for help in unseating Stephen and placing his half-sister Matilda on the throne, allied himself with these insurgents. Robert's strategy made comrades-at-arms of a people whom his

fellow Normans had been demonizing as part of their program of conquest.[56] Geoffrey's *History*, in Gillingham's view, introduces the magnificent
figure of Arthur to make it clear that this Welsh–Norman confederation is
no mere exigency of war but the joining of two noble peoples allied by
blood. Robert of Gloucester is, therefore, one of the dedicatees of the
History.

But then again, so is Waleran of Meulan, Robert's bitter enemy in the
civil war and an ardent upholder of Stephen's throne. One manuscript is
even dedicated to Stephen himself, making it clear that the work straddles
both sides of the divided kingdom. We may never know what exactly
Geoffrey of Monmouth hoped to accomplish in composing his *History*.[57] No
matter what his intended purpose, however, the Normans obliquely gained
through Geoffrey's text the long insular presence that they so embarrassingly
lacked, since they also considered themselves to be of Trojan blood.[58]
Geoffrey's revisionist historiography employed a dual strategy: explosive
recovery of Britain's full history, and silent passing over of the richness of the
English past. Both these techniques worked to alleviate some of the anxiety
Norman latecomers felt in realizing that their claim to lands that they had
come to consider home rested precariously on recent force rather than
ancient entitlement. Geoffrey's imperial Britons, as J. S. B. Tatlock pointed
out long ago, also granted a historical precedent for Norman ambitions.[59]

By disseminating a new "old" history, Geoffrey asserts discrete pasts and
destinies for the island peoples. If among the ambitions of the narrative is
to glorify the Britons and federate them to the Normans, then the English
will also have to be differentiated and abjected; hence Geoffrey's radical
revision of the *Ecclesiastical History*. Like Bede, moreover, Geoffrey's text
performs the separation of the island's people. His initial description of
Britain is a God's eye view stolen from Bede, similarly stressing the eternal
solitariness of the insular races:

> Britain is inhabited by five races of people, the Norman-French, the Britons,
> the Saxons, the Picts and the Scots. Of these the Britons once occupied the
> land from sea to sea, before the others came. Then the vengeance of God
> overtook them because of their arrogance and they submitted to the Picts
> and the Saxons. (1.3)

The historical narrative that follows builds upon this initial act of separation. Britain's past is a chronicle of the conflicts in which the Britons
engage against giants, against Romans, against Saxons.

Geoffrey's denigration of the English displaces and reverses contemporary rhetoric issuing from England that dehumanized the Welsh. To debase
the *Saxones*, Geoffrey employs abusive epithets lifted from Gildas, a writer

who lived through the invasions and who waxed vitriolic whenever describing those seizing insular lands. Both writers classify the Saxons as barbarians. But Geoffrey goes further, adopting a rhetoric that calls to mind crusading polemic. When the royal House of Constantine retakes Britain from the Saxons, these people are represented as impious pagans, as dog-like as the Saracens whose possession of the Holy Land caused Geoffrey's peers so much concern. Arthur dismisses them as a race "whose very name is an insult to heaven and detested by all men" (146 9.3). His bellicose arch-bishop promises that those who die in battle against such a despicable enemy will ascend directly to heaven (147 9.4), as if they were *crucesignati* storming Jerusalem.

Geoffrey's text assumes with Bede that the island's peoples are patently divisible into neatly bounded communities. Everything is similar but reversed: a subaltern people suddenly becomes the dominant one. No matter what else it accomplishes or attempts, Geoffrey's revisionist history, obsessed with collective descent, connects the proud British past to the present through a continuity the contemporary Welsh carry in their blood.

Impure Blood

Although conquest and colonization have immediate, catastrophic effects, the profoundest of the changes they engender can take decades to register. Marjorie Chibnall has observed that "the most lasting consequences" of the Norman Conquest became evident only "some eighty or a hundred years after 1066."[60] Among these enduring effects was a pervasive, chronic uneasiness over the relationship of England to the polyglot, heterogeneous peoples who composed the population of Britain. Geoffrey of Monmouth completed the *History of the Kings of Britain* about seventy years after Hastings. By stressing epochal history, the indivisibility of the isle, the brevity and perfidiousness of English dominion, the relation of vigorous empire to a nation's civil harmony, and the distinctiveness of Britain's peoples, Geoffrey's narrative offered an implicit defense for the transfer of power in 1066. If his text participates in a process of imagining future community, however, it does so rather perversely: not by connecting the Normans more intimately to the *Angli*, as William of Malmesbury and Henry of Huntingdon do, but by excluding the English from this new vision of insular rule. Even if by the late 1130s the Normans were vanishing as a separate people, "turned into Englishmen," the historical rupture represented by the conquest of the island continued to be evident in lasting disparities between English- and French-speakers.[61] With its viciously reductive depiction of the Saxons as a people unified by their degeneracy, a people "whose very name is an insult to heaven and detested by all men"

(145 9.4), Geoffrey's text went a long way toward naturalizing some of those inequalities, rendering the economic, social, and legal differences that had been promulgated over the preceding decades as differences in the blood.

Blood is a central concern of the *History*. Throughout the millennia that Geoffrey chronicles, blood motivates, catalyzes, unifies, and stains. Arthur's war against the Saxons is not launched to regain stolen land but to take vengeance for the blood of fallen countrymen (*sanguinem conciuium meorum hodie in ipsos uindicare conabor*, 146 9.3). Sanguineous flows are frequent in the *History*, especially in its spirited portrayals of war. A particularly memorable tempest in the narrative is even composed of gore. This deluge of heavy crimson saturates the island, turning what had finally become a placid kingdom into a body violently wounded by history. According to Geoffrey's version of the *King Lear* story, Cordelia and her husband wage a successful campaign against her ungrateful sisters, restoring the repentant father to kingship. When Lear later dies of natural causes, the now widowed Cordelia reigns for five tranquil years (32 2.15). Indignant that a woman should occupy the throne, Goneril and Regan's conniving sons, Marganus and Cunedagius, unseat and imprison her. At first the cousins happily share the kingdom. True to Geoffrey's recurrent theme of divided realms making for tempestuous times, however, an avaricious Marganus provokes his cousin by incinerating his lands. Civil war erupts, ending when Marganus is slain. Cunedagius rules thereafter for thirty-three untroubled years, and at his death the throne quietly passes to his son, Rivallo. The new ruler is described approvingly as a peaceful and prosperous young man who governs the realm well (33 2.16). During Rivallo's sovereignty, however, a rain of blood pours from the sky for three days and "men perished from the flies that swarmed" (*in tempore eius cecidit pluuia tribus diebus sanguinea et muscarum affluentia homines moriebantur*).

Shakespeare's *King Lear* famously erupts in "*Storm and tempest*," a howling embodiment of a kingdom's disintegration. Geoffrey's *pluvia sanguinea* reflects no such disturbance in the social order, since both Rivallo and his father were (or became) peaceful kings with long tenures. Since the deluge cannot incarnate a troubled present, it may recall a traumatic past. Erupting after decades of calm, the hematic storm thunderously brings to Rivallo's reign a reminder of the unsettled history upon which it is built: familial treason against Lear; the rebellion (*insurrexerunt*) of Marganus and Cunedagius against their lawful queen; Cordelia's suicide as she languishes in prison; the ravaging of the land by the warring cousins ("they refused to stop their outrages, they laid waste to numerous provinces"); the division of the island; fatal hostility between power-hungry factions, violence that includes not just the killing of Marganus but the slaughter of innocents caught in the battle for supremacy (*cedem non minimam* is Geoffrey's litotes for the carnage). *Pluvia sanguinea*: soaked in a ruddy flow so overwhelming that it now collects in pools to rot, a land battered by violence rebukes its occupants for the copious blood they have shed.[62] Drenched in pluvial gore, transformed into a pestiferous expanse, Britain becomes a suffering body.

Despite her nephews' indignation at a woman ruling the island, Cordelia was right. "You are worth just as much as you possess," she declares to a father intent on fragmenting the realm, a stern rebuke to his notion that a multiplicity of communities can adequately replace the singular one gathered beneath his crown. Lear's misery lasts just as long as partition endures. Once he has gathered his divided people he can contentedly reascend the throne. Cordelia follows her own advice when she succeeds her father and maintains the integrity of *Britannia* for five happy years, until Marganus and Cunedagius foment revolt. The two cardinal sins in Geoffrey's *History of the Kings of Britain* are civil dissension and division of the realm. After the death of Marganus, Cunedagius becomes *monarchiam totius insule* ("king of the whole island"). His paninsular *regnum* seems to be what allows him his thirty-three years of splendid (*gloriose*) reign. All the good kings in Geoffrey's text—Brutus, Ebraucus, Belinus and Brennius, Aurelius, Arthur—know or quickly learn that violence directed outwards is the path to glory, that the only blood which may be productively shed is the blood of another people. On the other hand, the very possibility of the Britons recognizing themselves as an enduring collectivity, a people set apart, depends upon a knowledge of their shared and sacred blood.

Blood is the most precious of the bodily humors, a sacred substance that suggests suffering and redemption, the most visible marker that the boundaries of the body have been penetrated, and a potent condensation of human life itself. The *History of the Kings of Britain* treats blood with a mixture of reverence and symbolic potential. Most often blood flows as a metonymy for the violence humans commit against each other, as in Geoffrey's description of mortal battle between the Britons and Romans ("the earth was drenched with the blood of the dying," 4.3) or between the Saxons and Britons ("wherever one looked there was blood flowing and the screams of the dying roused to fury those who were still alive," 123 8.5). Sometimes, however, blood circulates to carry with it a collective identity, *consaguinitas*. Most often such blood features in vivid stories meant to separate one group from another. More quietly, however, blood flows throughout Geoffrey's narrative in ways that utterly confound any lasting attempt at keeping collective identities pure. Blood is Geoffrey's difficult middle, a figure for his hybridities.

No matter what else the text might be, the *History of the Kings of Britain* is a foundation myth. As the twelfth-century Welsh who found in its narrative the promise of glory to come would attest, the *History* gives solidity and continuity to a dispersed people. It could legitimate the promulgation of a communal identity based upon shared history. By projecting a Norman mode of kingship and conquest into the past, it also implicitly buttresses the Norman Conquest, and reinforces the distinctiveness of both the Normans and the Britons from the English.[63] Perhaps this desire to keep the insular peoples distinct explains why the text recurrently envalues purity of blood. When a womanless band of Picts arrive from Scythia and ask the Britons for wives, they firmly refuse to intermarry with such an inferior race (4.17). Once the fiercely expansionist leader Maximianus subdues Gaul, he imports a population of Britons for the area. Conanus Meriadocus, left in charge of this "second Britain," strives "to prevent any mixture of blood" between colonists and indigenes. Conanus therefore has seventy-one thousand women imported from the homeland (5.15). The misplaced passion of Brennius for a Danish princess almost causes Britain's ruin (3.2). Part of the great evil of Vortigern, the tyrant who improvidently invites the Saxons into Britain as mercenaries, is his refusal to respect the separation of peoples. He allows "pagans to mingle with the local population" (8.2), degenerating his kingdom to the point at which "no one could tell who was a pagan and who was a Christian, for the pagans were associating with [British] daughters and female relations" (6.13). Vortigern himself marries Renwein, daughter of the Saxon leader Hengest (6.12). Vortimer, Vortigern's pure-blooded son by a previous wife, rises against his father in an attempt to take Britain back for the Britons; he is poisoned by his treacherous stepmother (6.14). Perhaps a certain magical pool described to a wide-eyed Arthur says it all. Naturally fashioned in the shape of a perfect square, the pool harbors four types of fish, and "the fish of any one corner were never found in any of the others" (9.7). Substitute Britons, Picts, Scots, and Saxons for the allegorical fish and Britain suddenly becomes perfectly unmixed, impossibly pure.

Square pools do not exist in nature, nor do fish self-segregate; that is why the pool is a marvel. In Geoffrey's British history, despite the fact that the purity of collective identities is so often declared paramount, peoples nonetheless intermingle. Just like the Norman-English and Norman-Welsh unions of Geoffrey's day, these couplings produce children who carry in their blood a compound heritage. At first glance, it seems that such mixed blood progeny cannot fare well. Assaracus, son of a Trojan mother and Greek father, agrees to help the exiled Brutus because of his anger at having been disinherited by a brother of undiluted blood. Brutus is happy to employ the man so long as he is useful, but the Trojan's subsequent talk of preserving the "purity of noble blood" suggests what he really thinks of his mongrel ally (1.4). Habren, the daughter of King Locrinus by a German concubine, is hurled into a river by his angry wife (2.5). Bassianus, the son of a Roman puppet ruler through a British woman, finds himself raised to the insular throne because his people prefer him over his brother of pure Roman descent (5.2). His reign is quite short, however, because a man named Carausius, humbly born but of untainted British ancestry, rallies the Britons to "massacre the Romans and wipe them out of existence and so free the whole island of that foreign race." The half-blood Bassianus soon lies dead on the battlefield (5.3).

Yet Constantine, the son of a Roman named Constantius and the Briton Helen, becomes not only the king of the whole island but also emperor of Rome, "overlord of the whole world" (5.8). The founding father of the Britons, Brutus himself, takes the Greek princess Ignoge for his wife, mixing his genealogical line with that of an inveterate enemy. It could perhaps be argued that only the race of the father counts in a patriarchal society, overwriting or overcoding the blood of the mother. Such a model seems almost Aristotelian. The mother contributes inert matter to the child, the father gives identity and life. Thus Earl Morcar, an English rebel against the Conqueror, had a sister named Ealdgyth. She bore a daughter to her first husband, Gruffudd ap Llewelyn, upon whom was bestowed the resonantly Welsh name of Nest. Ealdgyth also had a son by her second spouse, King Harold II of England. This Ulf carried an Anglo-Scandinavian appellation that well embodied his royal father's own heritage.[64] In both cases the descent of the father determines the child's name. Perhaps, then, the children of Brutus are just as Trojan, and therefore just as British, as he.

Yet carrying the blood of two peoples in the *History of the Kings of Britain* seldom allows a singular or stable identity to be embraced, or for a dual ancestry to be forgotten. Despite the bias in favor of the separateness of the insular peoples throughout the *History*, in the actual unfolding of historical events Geoffrey demonstrates the impossibility—and sometimes even the sheer destructiveness—of rejecting out of hand hybridity and difficult middles. Attempts to maintain purity of blood invariably fail. Contrary to the British prohibition against taking their women as wives, the Picts do just that, "intermarrying more and more with the Britons" (5.3). These marriages are enabled by Carausius, the pure-blooded Briton who rallied his people to commit genocide against the Romans to keep the island free of foreigners. The intermingling of Saxons with Britons enabled by Vortigern cannot simply be undone, for in the wake of widespread intermarriage pagans and the Christians become indistinguishable (6.13). The desire of Conanus Meriadocus to prevent his soldiers from mixing with the Gauls spectacularly backfires when he imports from Britain suitable wives. Of the 71,000 women shipped across the channel to meet his demand, the lucki-est drown when their ships founder. The remainder is blown so far off course that randy barbarians either slay or enslave them (5.16). Conanus Meriadocus and his men, we must assume, were forced to take their brides from Gaul after all. Even Cadwallo, Geoffrey's reinvented and newly heroic leader of the Britons against the treacherous Saxons, is said to take a sister of Peanda of Mercia as his wife.[65] Their son, Cadwallader, presides over the final loss of British hegemony on the island.

As Peggy McCracken has written in her penetrating analysis of the role of women's blood in medieval literature, descent might be claimed from the father, but the mother's contribution to her offspring's identity can never be completely effaced. Blood, especially when it comes from a woman, tends to be multivalent.[66] A similar observation might be advanced more generally about women's roles in twelfth-century historiography, especially in their relation to collective identity. Although from time to time a powerful female figure will emerge (Hild, Æthelflæd, Cordelia), chronicles of the past are for the most part accounts of the deeds of men. Geoffrey is no exception, imagining a vigorously martial world in which most of the great leaders are male. Women are seldom eligible to have their stories told. There are, of course, vivid exceptions: Gwendolen, Estrildis, Cordelia, Tonuuenna, Genvissa, Judon, Renwein, Ygerna, Guenevere, and Helena.[67] Even women not given a name by the text can sometimes have moving stories narrated about them. Take, for example, the 71,000 women assembled in London to provide wives for the Britons in Gaul. They do not know that they are doomed to perish at sea, be slaughtered by enemies, or become slaves, yet few want to abandon home and family for unknown shores. "They all had their personal wishes in the matter" Geoffrey observes (5.16). When it is acknowledged that the desires of these women are not consonant with maintaining the purity of the Briton blood-line, we realize that the community being built with them is predicated upon a coercive harmonization.

No woman's story in Geoffrey's text resonates more lastingly than that of Ignoge, the Greek princess forced to become bride to Brutus. Geoffrey of Monmouth ordinarily composes his narrative with sangfroid: little human feeling animates its accounts of battles, wonders, political intrigue, and strife. He is not given to moments of aching identification such as William of Malmesbury's wrenching account of the sinking of the White Ship (*Deeds* 5.419). Ignoge has little presence in Geoffrey's text, but as she sets sail with a husband she never chose for a future that is wholly uncertain, we are given a lingering depiction of her last vision of her native land. The episode is at once so evocative and so moving that, as Robert

Hanning observes, it "interrupts the flow" of the narrative, so that "for a moment the issues of national birth and freedom are forgotten; history itself is forgotten."[68] Here is Geoffrey's vivid portrayal of the fading shores of home as glimpsed through bereft Ignoge's eyes:

> The Trojans sailed away . . . Ignoge stood on the high poop and from time to time fell fainting in the arms of Brutus. She wept and sobbed at being forced to leave her relations and her homeland; and as long as the shore lay there before her eyes, she would not turn her gaze away from it. Brutus soothed and caressed her, putting his arms round her and kissing her gently. He did not cease his efforts until, worn out with crying, she fell asleep (1.11)

As Ignoge's home slowly recedes, lost are the possibilities for any life she might have desired for herself, for any history she might have dreamed. Destined to become an appendage of Brutus, the source of his progeny, we next see Ignoge in what appears to be an afterthought, legitimating the birth of three sons (2.1). She is not mentioned again. Her children divide the land and carry on their father's work. It never occurs to them that in their bodies Troy mingles with Greece, that they possess hybrid blood in which two enemies have uneasily been conjoined. The sons of Brutus assume that they are simply Britons, as their father christened his people. They never dwell upon the complexities of history and descent.

Ignoge's gaze opens up the possibility of another story. An alien among strangers, suspended between cultures and no longer able to be of one or the other, Ignoge embodies everything her children so easily forget. Yearning for a home that can never be hers, this princess conveyed to an unfamiliar place suggests the difficulties faced by those who carry an identity full of difference, ambivalence, and conflict. Ignoge inhabits that middle space where conqueror meets conquered, where a war unfolds between loathing and desire. She looks back to a receding homeland and forward to the impossible bind of mixed progeny on an island increasingly dominated by a single people. Ignoge is Greek, her husband Trojan, her children Britons, but her tears prevent such easy separations.

Geoffrey of Monmouth dreamed of a world where at first glance history and descent keep insular peoples solitary. As his textual world unfolds in all its intricacy, however, the peoples that populate Britain mingle and become—despite their own fervent belief to the contrary—impure. Geoffrey's ambivalent entwining of purity with hybridity is rather like William of Malmesbury's. Both writers posited clean separations but undercut them with anxious, medial spaces: one through marvels, the other through blood. The separateness of the island's peoples might be an impossible dream, but that did not stop this dream from being passionately embraced, much to the sorrow of those who carried blood that could never seem untainted. For these impure beings history was filled with upset, and the present never ceased to hurt. The next chapter turns to a writer who was born in the middle of the twelfth century. His life provides a useful case study of the stormy fluidity as well as the constricting solidity of contemporary collective identities. Although an international figure, Gerald of Wales was also the product of the late-twelfth-century Welsh March, a geography at which Anglo-Norman invaders had mingled, culturally as well as biologically, with the peoples they were subjugating. His ample writings reveal some suggestive similarities to the conflicted hybridities we will meet later in this book in East Anglia. Both these spaces inherited divisively heterogeneous pasts, and were attempting to reformulate the terms of communal belonging. William of Norwich, child of a colonized city, English boy with a Norman name, never lived long enough to narrate his own story, never had access to the power and privilege that would allow him to commit his own words to vellum. Gerald of Wales, caught between competing cultures and uncertain what community could ever be his own, wrote endlessly, obsessively, about himself and his turbulent world, about the agony of irresolvable difference in the wake of conquest. He felt coursing in his veins a doubled bloodline, Norman and Welsh. He ached to discover a vocabulary in which to express the ambivalences that had formed him.

Suspended between categories, fully neither one nor the other, Gerald of Wales must often have felt himself a monster.

CHAPTER 3

IN THE BORDERLANDS: THE IDENTITIES
OF GERALD OF WALES

Mixed Blood

"Attempting to rationalise and homogenise Gerald's wildly fluctuating allegiances and sympathies," Julia C. Crick has observed, "would prove a fruitless enterprise."[1] That has not, of course, stopped scholars from trying.
Many critics see a movement in the life of the twelfth-century cleric Gerald
of Wales (Giraldus Cambrensis) from early identifications with the francophone English court to a pro-Welsh stance as he lobbied for an independent archbishopric at St. David's. Later he bitterly rejects both possibilities,
embracing the superiority of the French monarchy and retiring to Lincoln.[2]
In the pages that follow, however, I will emphasize a constant within these
alterations: Gerald's enduring struggle to articulate his hopelessly compound
identity. Celibate ecclesiast, multilingual ethnographer, tireless writer and
reviser of unprecedented texts, grandson of Welsh royalty, cosmopolitan
intellectual, descendant of Norman conquistadors, court chaplain, instru-
ment in the conquest of Ireland, eccentric and irascible multiplier of marvels, Giraldus Cambrensis often did not know exactly who he was.

When pressed, the identity he would most frequently declare would
today be described as "Cambro-Norman" or "Marcher," terms designating a
mixed race inhabitant of the Welsh March. This borderland was a middle
space between England and those northeast regions of Wales designated *Pura
Wallia*. "Pure Wales" consisted of territory never been subjugated by the
Normans, or land that had reverted to native rule following the revolts at the
death of Henry I.[3] The March was engendered when Norman adventurers
saw in the land west of England an opportunity for self-enrichment. Their
advance into the country was rapid, their reordering of indigenous social
and political life far-reaching. A native record of these incursions, the *Brut y
Tywysogyon*, speaks of "the unbearable tyranny, injustice, oppression and

violence of the French," and acknowledges their profound reordering of the world.[4] These invaders employed all their favorite strategies: treaty and selective alliance to take advantage of the animosity between competing indigenous factions; the frenzied building of castles, transforming a landscape that had been traversed by somewhat nomadic groups into permanent settlements clustered around massive fortifications; importation of Flemish and English colonists into conquered areas, fracturing native culture, and instigating a process of forced anglicization; the slaying of livestock, the destruction of buildings, seizure of property and land.[5] At Norman hands, native peoples endured torture, dismemberment, murder, imprisonment, and being sold into slavery.

The Normans also practiced strategic intermarriage to penetrate and master the indigenous population. Employed successfully by their Viking ancestors in France, and deployed again to strengthen the occupation of England, matrimonial infiltration enabled ambitious warriors to secure land and wealth. Their kinsmen in Wales did the same, marrying into powerful princely families to fortify their dominion. In Normandy this process had created a partially assimilated French-speaking elite, and in England intermarriage was transforming *Normanni* into *Angli*. Yet whereas in these geographies the Normans had overpowered and then intermingled with a subject people, in Wales fierce and lasting resistance to conquest engendered enduring bifurcation. Swathes of the lowland areas had been seized and their populations expelled. Boroughs were created from which the Welsh were excluded. Wales became an abidingly segregated geography in a way that England never did.[6]

Unlike their counterparts in Britain's southeast, the Norman settlers who eventually became the Marchers staunchly resisted acculturation, insisting on their separateness from the Welsh. No doubt they felt they had little choice. As John Gillingham and R. R. Davies have demonstrated, eleventh- and twelfth-century England was committed to the systematic depiction of the Irish, Welsh, and Scots as bloodthirsty, uncivilized, even bestial races. Such dehumanizing representation is a hoary tool of colonialism. By representing a native population as monstrous, its dispossession becomes unproblematic. The project of rendering the Welsh less than human, moreover, took on a renewed vitality during the reign of Stephen, when a resurgence of resistance led to spectacular reclamations of territory. The propaganda machine kicked into high gear as an astonished England realized that its dominance was not only being disputed for the first time in generations, but that native defiance was proving embarrassingly effective. Unlike the Franks or the English, who had taken a mere span of years to subjugate, the Welsh would be caught in a violent process of conquest for two long centuries. That the monsterization of the Welsh and the Scots

became increasing hysterical in tone at the very time that they were proving to be formidable challenges to the supposedly self-evident superiority
of England suggests that military and political failure was being answered by
an attempt at representational control.

To make matters worse, this people (the Normans and the English
always thought of the Welsh as constituting a single race, even though
the Welsh did not necessarily think of themselves in such terms) never had
the decency or the sense to stop resisting their inevitable defeat.[7] Geoffrey
of Monmouth aside, the representation of the Welsh by English authors
worsened steadily during the twelfth century. The problem for the
Marchers was that the blood of an increasingly denigrated aboriginal people coursed through their veins. The Welsh future was hardly bright. In the
aftermath of the Glyn Dwr rebellion, intermarriage would be forbidden.
By the fifteenth century, children of mixed descent were considered, like
their Welsh peers, to be ineligible to possess castles or fortifications.[8] In the
wake of the demonization of the Welsh by their English compeers, the
Marchers saw little reason to celebrate their mixed heritage. To be tied in
one's very body to a people who were proving an increasingly useful
national enemy was a matter for alarm, not praise.

Hyphenated Names

Collective identities in the Middle Ages tended to be exclusive, assuming
their own uniformity and historical continuity. Contemporary scholars
faced with medieval hybridities typically rely upon hyphenated terms like
"Anglo-Scandinavian" and "Anglo-Norman." Yet these composite names
have no counterpart in medieval terminology. They designate compound
identities that would not be available to those they now nominate. As
Hugh M. Thomas has emphasized, however handy such shorthand might
be for us, medieval people did not conceptualize group identities in terms
that allowed transitional, hybrid, or hyphenated phases. Individuals of
mixed ancestry tended instead to have multiple identities available to them.
The son of an English mother and a Norman father might consider himself
Norman when hobnobbing at court, English when celebrating the history
of his native country. "Ultimately," writes Thomas, "the results would be
the same: as fewer people chose the Norman option, and more came to see
Englishness as their sole or at least primary identity, there would be an
overall shift to English identity."[9] When a person was powerful enough to
choose strategically his or her identity, such multiplicity was unlikely to
cause much concern, especially as mutual assimilation lessened distinctions,
as "English" began to hide an increasing hybridity by becoming a more
capacious term. The problem of mixed blood vanishes as group affiliation

widens to include two peoples within a single designation. William of
Malmesbury's anxiety over his—and England's—dual heritage finds no
counterpart in English historians like William of Newburgh, writing so late
in the twelfth century that "English" has become the only available self-
designation.

Even if his hybridity posed a far greater problem for him than it did for
his Anglo-Norman compeers, Gerald of Wales would sometimes write as
if his Welsh and Norman blood were two equally embraceable possibilities
within a single placid identity. In his *Description of Wales*, having outlined
a program for the complete subjugation of the country in which he was
born, Gerald turns to how the Welsh can effectively defend themselves:

> I have set out the case for the English with considerable care and in some
> detail. I myself am descended from both peoples [*ex utraque gente originem
> duximus*], and it seems only fair that I should now put forth the opposite
> point of view. I therefore turn to the Welsh in this final chapter of my book.
> (2.10)

Gerald writes as if dual blood can course unconflicted veins, as if advice for
subjection and resistance can without contradiction issue from the same
mouth. Yet Gerald is not William of Malmesbury. He is not a compound
of two potentially exalted origins, at least not as far as the world exterior to
the Welsh March was concerned. From the English point of view, the
Welsh were patently inferior, ineligible to imagine effective opposition to
conquest. Gerald's reconciliation of two collective identities that were in
fact at war is wishful thinking. The frightening questions that his cheerfully
amalgamative viewpoint avoids would continue to arise. What happens
when a person is possessed of a duplex nature, a fusion of identities that
remain incompatible? What happens when no terminology exists to
express a self that happens to be fabricated of grossly unequal parts, when
one's inner nature is being constantly defined within a reductive language
one never chose? What happens when, despite the medieval tendency not
to think in terms of mediating, transitional, or composite identities, one in
fact inhabits just such an impossible body?

In the course of the twelfth century, little room existed for some medial
space, for some identity capable of inhabiting the gap between demarcations as keen as English and Welsh. Yet the Welsh March presented precisely such a difficult middle.[10] The term *march* is related to *mearc*, an Old
English word for boundary. From the viewpoint of a dominant culture, a
march limns the border between domestic stabilities and the perturbing
otherness of a geographic elsewhere. Caught between a domineering kingdom centered in London and a vigorous native resistance issuing especially

from northern Wales, the twelfth-century Welsh March was an unstable geography.[11] Belonging to neither Wales nor England, composite in its culture and mixed in its blood, possessed even of its own law, the March was a place where identities, like political boundaries, had yet to be firmly fixed.

To designate his place of origin Gerald typically employed the Latin transliteration *marchia*. When speaking of the people who, like his family, had made the March their home through martial force and matrimonial alliance, Gerald used the terms *nostri, nostrum genus*, or *nostra gens* ("our men" or "our people"). When referring to the Marchers, Gerald's Latin is frequently translated by contemporary medievalists rather neutrally as "family," "kinsmen," or "stock." These modern English terms do not adequately convey the sense of distinction from other peoples—English, Normans, Welsh, and Irish—that he nearly always implies. Thus Gerald describes the Irish garrison (ca. 1188) as composed of three separate races: *Normanni, Angli*, and *nostri*, "the Normans [from Normandy], the English ["Anglo-Normans"], and our men [Marchers]" (*Expugnatio* 2.37). The Welsh, like the *gens Hibernica* [Irish], likewise form a people set apart, sometimes in Gerald's designation a *gens barbara*, barbaric race.

Collective identities in the Middle Ages tended to be conservative categories. "New" peoples were typically slotted into preexistent taxonomies and did not necessarily force classificatory systems to expand. In implying that the Marchers constitute a *gens* in the sense of "separate people" rather than of "family," Gerald is positing what would have seemed to his contemporaries a radical and shockingly recent origin. The last attempt at a new mythology for a people in Britain was Geoffrey of Monmouth's, a project that buttressed identity categories rather than introduced novel ones. Dudo of St. Quentin's *History of the Normans*, a narrative of how that parvenu race arose from a commingling of peoples in the tenth century, was never invoked by Gerald as a precedent, either because he did not know the text or because he assumed that the "fact" that the Welsh March had engendered a new people was too patent to require defense. Not surprisingly, Gerald had immense difficulty convincing anyone besides the Marchers that they did indeed constitute a distinct people.

Collective identity is, as we have seen, the culmination of energetic processes of remembering, of anchoring an uncertain present in a fantastically stable past. Yet collectivity is just as accurately a process of forgetting. Harold Godwineson can be memorialized as the last English king only after the fact that his mother was Danish is passed over in silence. Edward the Confessor's Norman blood must likewise be ignored for his sacred Englishness to be elegized. William the Conqueror might be the first Norman king, but he also carried an English inheritance, and the *Normannitas* that he supposedly embodied derived from mongrel concatenation rather than singular descent. In twelfth-century Britain, the Norman and Angevin descended aristocracy, securely attached to their politically expedient self-designation as English, did not need any uncomfortable reminders that collective identity is mutable, possibly failing to provide the permanence it promises.

Gerald of Wales was, as a result, never allowed to forget his hybridity. His argument that the Marchers might constitute a *gens* was haunted by forced remembrance of constituent impurity. Gerald complained in his *Symbolum Electorum* that his enemies in England dismissed him as Welsh, while to the Welsh he seemed Norman French: "both peoples regard me as a stranger and one not their own . . . one nation suspects me, the other hates me." Gerald's nemesis Peter de Leia could be "two-handed in his persecution of me . . . for to the French he made me a Welshman and an enemy of the kingdom, but to the Welsh he declared me to be French and their mortal foe in all things."[12] Within this rigid binarism little room existed for Gerald's vision of a concordance of differences or of a novel and compound *gens*. The Marchers not only inhabited a difficult middle; they embodied it.

Avuncular Exhortations

We often glimpse Gerald and his family convincing themselves that they are not simply Welsh or Norman, nor some impure amalgamation of both, but a noble distillation of two peoples into a distinct and glorious third. In a speech that Gerald places in the mouth of his uncle, Robert fitzStephen, leader of the Marcher lords in their conquest of Ireland, Gerald envisions how *nostra gens* might happily combine the best aspects of a dual constitution into a transcendent form:

> In part we come of Trojan blood [*Troiano partim ex sanguine*] by direct line of descent. But we are also partly descended from the men of France [*ex Gallis*], and take our character in part from them. From the former we get our courage, and from the latter our skill in the use of arms. So we are equally brave and versed in arms because of our twofold character and noble ancestry on both sides. (*Expugnatio Hibernica* 1.9)

Citing the myth of Trojan descent revitalized by Geoffrey of Monmouth, Robert argues that the Marchers are of a "twofold" or "doubled" (*duplici*, from the adjective *duplex*) nature, mingling classical bravery with the resplendent martial record of the Normans. That this is an act of ventriloquism is indicated by a repetition of the declaration in Gerald's own voice later in the same work. Within a section entitled "Praise of the Race"

(2.10), Gerald describes his kinsmen as being of a "twinned nature" (*gemina natura*), inheriting raw courage from their Trojan forebears and skill at the use of weapons from the Norman French.[13]

Yet despite their evident pride in commingling, both these formulations of Marcher identity betray a fair amount of defensiveness, if not evasiveness. Gerald consistently describes the Marchers' blood as an inheritance from *Troiani* (Trojans) rather than *Britones* or *Wallenses*, the proper Latin words for the Welsh.[14] The contemporary Welsh, by Gerald's own admission potentially *gens barbara*, vanish from the Marcher bloodline, replaced by more revered ancestors.[15] This silent substitution pushes half of the Marcher ancestry back into the mythy depths of classical history. It refuses to acknowledge the bloody and ongoing struggles in which contemporary Welsh identity actually inhered. A patina of Roman epic thereby enables Gerald to formulate with confidence the alchemy producing *nostra gens*, a courageous new people. And even that designation is equivocal: one can refer to *nostra gens* only if one happens to belong to it. Outside of a ridiculously verbose circumlocution like *gens in Kambrie marchia nutrita* ("the people nurtured in the Welsh March," *Expugnatio* 2.38), Gerald must acknowledge that the vocabulary for nominating the people he wants to distinguish simply does not exist.

As he forcefully articulates a synthetic Marcher identity, Robert fitzStephen betrays no hesitation. A speech later in the *Expugnatio Hibernica* by another of Gerald's uncles, however, suggests just how unsteady a foundation this bravado was built upon. About to engage in battle against the Irish, Maurice fitzGerald admits what Gerald was later to learn personally through his own "two-handed persecution" by Peter de Leia. Collective identity is relational, and therefore inherently precarious:

> We are now constrained in our actions by this circumstance, that just as we are English as far as the Irish are concerned, likewise to the English we are Irish [*ut sicut Hibernicis Angli, sic et Anglis Hibernici simus*], and the inhabitants of this island and the other assail us with an equal degree of hatred. (*Expugnatio Hibernica* 1.23)

Alien on two islands, Maurice gives voice in vivid language to what might be called the postcolonial dilemma, the inability of those hybrid beings who live in the aftermath of conquest to find a secure category of selfhood in which to belong. Intermarriage with the Welsh ensured that the Marchers could never be as English as the former Normans who now ruled England, Normans whose own intermarriages had usefully hastened their assimilation. Conquest likewise ensures that the Irish (*Hibernici*) will never see in the Marchers anything but reviled imperialists, no different from the "true" English (French-speaking or not) who were likewise scrambling for their lands.

A stranger abroad as well as at home, Maurice arrives at a simple solution. He will not think too much about the vexing admixture carried in his blood, and urges his family and followers to do the same: "Let us breach the barriers of hesitation [*mora*] and inertia [*ignavia*], for 'fortune favors the brave'!" (1.23). Maurice's Irish battle cry is suggestive. The entire Marcher expedition to Ireland could be seen as bloody attempt to avoid the complications of carrying a twofold (*duplex*) identity.[16] Robert fitzStephen, Gerald writes, originally sailed to Ireland because he was caught in an impossible bind, precipitated by his dual racial allegiances. Captured by his cousin Rhys ap Gruffydd, prince of South Wales, Robert was released only after he promised to battle the incursions of Henry II. Yet to take up arms against England would be to betray another side of his family. Nest, Robert's Welsh mother, gave birth to at least eleven children fathered by five men; one of these partners was a prince destined to become King Henry I. At the age of fifteen, Nest had born him a son, the powerful Robert of Gloucester, whose patronage Geoffrey of Monmouth had sought.[17] These labyrinthine affiliations meant that the Marcher lord Robert fitzStephen, the last of Nest's children (born ca. 1117), was pulled in his blood toward and away from the English court, toward and away from Welsh politics. A complex web of competing gravitational forces, woven from familial demands not easily separated from racial affiliations, threatened to ensnare Robert fatally. His solution to these intractably conflicted allegiances was to "breach the barriers of hesitation and inertia." Robert quit Britain and took up arms in Ireland. Enlisting his half-brothers David and Maurice fitzGerald, Robert convinced Rhys to allow him to aid the exiled king Diarmait Mac Murda in reclaiming a lost Irish throne (*Expugnatio Hibernica* 1.2). On that island Robert could at least wage war against a people who were definitively not of his blood. By crossing a narrow sea, Robert fitzStephen and the Marcher lords who sailed in his company found a geography in which mixed heritage and incompatible allegiances were, for a while, simply beside the point. Battlefields foster neither *mora* nor *ignavia*.

Though born into a warrior family, Gerald had been trained not as a fighter but as a cleric. Yet ecclesiasts can be instrumental in martial endeavors. As a result of the preaching tour Gerald undertook through Wales with the archbishop of Canterbury, three thousand men pledged their weapons and their lives to the reclamation of the Holy Land (*Journey Through Wales* 2.13). Clerics also had immediate access to a crucial military technology not so easily available to others, writing. Although he could not wield a sword or command a garrison, early in his career Gerald learned to allay his

ambivalence of origin by becoming an enthusiastic chronicler of his family's Irish conquests. Though visible from Welsh shores, Ireland seemed
distant enough for Gerald to imagine that its vast expanses were inhabited
by an unambiguously alien people. Detailing the "subjugation and dispossession of the Irish race, and the taming of the ferociousness of this barbarous nation in our own time"—as he described his project to the
ascendant King Richard—allowed Gerald to forget for a while the similarly
violent history that had bestowed upon him the painful gift of *gemina
natura*.[18] Gerald composed two Irish texts, the *Topographia Hibernica* and the
Expugnatio Hibernica. Both have a tendency to wobble under the sheer variety of materials with which Gerald fills their every crevice, especially
because he energetically revised the works over time, adding ever more
data and anecdotes. Yet both are in the end reductive works that
unabashedly glorify the conquest of a foreign land. Neither demonstrates
much of the conflicted identifications that would characterize his later
writing about Wales.

Irish Fauna

Gerald's earliest work is the *Topographia Hibernica* (*The History and
Topography of Ireland*, ca. 1187), an account of the island's history, people,
and wonders. Gerald sailed across the Irish sea twice before composing this
text: once with his brother, Philip de Barri, to claim lands for the family;
and later in the retinue of Prince John, traveling to Hibernian shores to
assert overlordship. Though Henry II had long been intent on curbing the
power of Gerald's family, the *Topography* is nonetheless dedicated to this
monarch, who had personally led an expedition to Ireland in 1171 to
receive the submission of native kings. The book proved quite popular,
even if its veracity was repeatedly attacked. Like many of Gerald's compositions, the *Topography* has no precise model. Its pages commix chronicle,
anecdote, and marvels with ethnography and natural history. It overflows
with unsystematic detail. Stories multiply so rapidly that the reader often
feels like the portal to an alternate universe has been thrust open and its
contents are spilling out. Yet despite the book's sense of wonder and possibility, few contemporary scholars would disagree with David Rollo's estimation of the work as "a written landscape that is inhabited by a bizarre
menagerie of outlandish monstrosities and vitiated by infections of scorn,
disdain and slander."[19] James Cain observes that the *Topography* couples an
odious "blueprint for colonial occupation" to a "scholarly justification" for
the English conquest of Ireland.[20]

Yet a recurrent topic throughout this weirdly exuberant text is the lives
and habits of animals, making the book read more like Pliny's *Natural

History than Macaulay's "Minute on Indian Education." Included among the fauna are lake fish (1.5–6); hawks, falcons, eagles, cranes, ospreys, king-fishers, swans, storks, "barnacle geese," crows (1.8–1.17); badgers and beavers (1.19–20); assorted reptiles (1.21–22); wolves (2.59); ravens and blackbirds (2.60–61). The *Topography* also discusses beasts of a more fantas-tical kind: unboilable little ducks that enjoy the special protection of Saint Colman (2.62); Saint Brigid's falcon (2.70); fleas banished by Saint Nannan and rats expelled by Saint Yvor (2.64–65); a frog that portends the English invasion of the island (1.25); a fish with three gold teeth that likewise fig-ures imminent conquest (2.43). These creatures serve a multitude of pur-poses in the text, from vaticinal allegories to anthropomorphic fables of virtue and vice.

Sometimes, however, these animals are people.

Take, for example, the case of the Irish werewolves. Three years before Gerald arrives on the island, a priest journeying to Meath stopped for the night beneath a large tree (*Topographia* 2.52). A wolf approached his camp-fire. "Do not be afraid!" the beast announced, a lupine version of the angel's declaration of the birth of Christ to frightened shepherds. The ani-mal explains that the denizens of his village have been cursed by Saint Natalis to take turns inhabiting the bodies of wolves, an exile from human form lasting seven years. The werewolf then begs his interlocutor to accompany him to his ill mate and perform last rites. The priest follows but is dubious about giving communion to what is clearly an animal. When the wolf pulls back his companion's fur, revealing a dying woman, the hesitant priest acquiesces. He later informs his bishop of his actions among the Irish werewolves, and the bishop in turn relates the tale to Gerald.

This strange little episode is, like most of the marvels Gerald so casually relates, dense with the themes that obsessed his restless mind. Caroline Walker Bynum has recently interpreted "Gerald and the Werewolf" (as she calls the encounter) as a typical twelfth-century meditation on the stability of identity in the face of somatic metamorphosis.[21] It is difficult to disagree with such a reading, since Gerald himself indicates that it posed exactly such an invitation to theology as he repeatedly revised the *Topography* years after its composition. Yet when the episode is taken as it rather starkly stands in the text's first version, unadorned and uninterpreted, it is difficult not to see in the bodies of the Irish werewolves the flesh of Irish race.[22] Medieval writers were fond of attaching allegorical meanings to fauna, spawning a tradition of bestiaries that were ultimately more about humans than animals. Gerald leaves us in no doubt what the wolf represents when he writes later in the *Topography* that "wolves in Ireland generally have their young in December, either because of the extreme mildness of the climate, or rather as a symbol of the evils of treachery and plunder which here blossom before their season" (2.59).[23] The Irish inside their wolfskins are not very different from the treacherous, plunder-driven Irish inside their human forms. Their lycanthropy only makes visible in their bodies what they already are, and perhaps that is why we never learn why the villagers should have earned a saint's curse.

As we saw in the first chapter, differences between peoples were often expressed in the Middle Ages through the vocabulary of species difference, especially in the case of subalterns and national enemies. Gerald made ample use of this discourse of animality. The Irish are a people, he writes, who do not build towns, mint coins, or codify laws. Their manner of dress, customs, coiffure, and religious practice declare their feral state. In a culminating description Gerald dismisses the *gens Hibernica* in terms that render them indistinguishable from their counterparts in the wildlife:

> Although they are fully endowed with natural gifts, their external characteristics of beard and dress, and internal cultivation of the mind, are so barbarous that they cannot be said to have any culture . . . This people is a barbarous people, literally barbarous. Judged according to modern ideas, they are uncultivated, not only in the external appearance of their dress, but also in the flowing hair and beards. All their habits are the habits of barbarians. (3.93)[24]

The humane possibilities of the Irish ("fully endowed with natural gifts") vanish beneath a wolfskin of barbarous "beard and dress" and a bestial lack of mental cultivation. Just in case we have not yet got the point that there is something not fully human about the race, he adds, "They are a wild and inhospitable people. They live on beasts only, and live like beasts" (*gens ex bestiis solum et bestialiter vivens*, 3.93).

No surprise, perhaps, that the sexual aberration to which the *gens Hibernica* is most addicted turns out to be bestiality, *quo vitio praecipue gens ista laborat*, "the particular vice of that people (2.54)." Whole towns have, in Gerald's account, been wiped from the face of the island in divine retribution for too passionate a love of animals (2.42). In a rite that Gerald takes great relish in narrating, the people of northern Ulster inaugurate their king by watching him have "bestial intercourse" with a white mare (3.102).[25] The ritual culminates in the consumption of the equine's flesh, a transgression of alimentary taboo which, if not as severe as intercourse with beasts, still represents a mingling of human and animal bodies in a proscribed way.[26] To the knightly class to which Gerald belonged, horses were a revered animal, distinguishing the noble *chevalier* from quotidian foot soldiers and archers. Gerald must have known that in Ireland the cow and not the horse was the culturally sacred beast, since for the Irish cattle were wealth incarnate. Ireland was not a monetary economy like England. Possession of herds marked the difference between power and penury. Cattle were by extension the embodiment of status and honor, the foundation of prestige, the concrete expression of hierarchy.[27] How perverse, then, for Gerald to declare that the preferred sex partner for Irish men was their precious cow.

The intertwining of racial inferiority, bestiality (innate Irish animality *and* sexual vice), and an all too literal desire for cattle culminates in Gerald's narration of the brief life of the Ox Man. Placed precisely at the center of the *Topography*, this strange creature is granted a tragic gravity that not only haunts all that follows in the book but—with its uncharacteristic undercurrent of melancholy, ambivalence, and regret—provokes a rereading of the manifold wonders that precede.[28] In 1174, Gerald writes, the same Maurice fitzGerald we earlier witnessed exhorting the Marchers to ignore their mixed blood and blaze into Hibernian battle took possession of a castle in Wicklow. A strange creature appeared, "an extraordinary man [*homo prodigiosus*]—if indeed it be right to call him a man" (*Topographia* 2.54). Hairless except for some tufts of down, he possesses a roughly human form, although his arms and legs end in hooves. His ox-like eyes are huge, round, brown. His flat face possesses instead of a nose mere slits. No intelligible language issues from the deformed mouth (*verba ei nulla*, "he had no words"), only bovine lowing. This prodigy Gerald christens the *semibos vir*, a poetic designation lifted from Ovid's resonant description of the Minotaur as *semibovemque virum semivirumque bovem*, "a man that was half a bull and a bull that was half a man." The creature becomes a dependent of Maurice's castle, where his daily feedings take on all the air of a circus sideshow. Something of both animal and human but fully neither, the Irish Minotaur attends the court at Wicklow for many years. Maurice's young retainers (*juventute castri*, "youths of the castle") never weary of taunting the local Irish that they had begotten many such beings on the local herds (*quod tales in vaccis genuissent*). Some of these natives secretly murder the Ox Man, a fate that Gerald protests he in no way deserved (2.54). It could be that the Irish were acting out of frustration at a racial jeer repeated too many times, but Gerald does not suggest anger as a motive, only innate *malitia*, "malice," and *invidia*, "envy." Could it be that native ill will and jealousy arose because the Ox Man was so well incorporated into the Wicklow settlement while the Irish found themselves physically excluded and verbally denigrated?

Just before the English conquest, Gerald adds, a "human bull calf" (*vitulum virilem*) was born in the mountains around Glendalough, the result of intercourse between a man and his bovine paramour. This creature pastured among its fellows in the herd for a year, happily nourished by its

mother's milk, and was then "transferred to the society of men." No further detail is given of the Man Bull's story, no intimation that the odd
being had difficulty adapting from his maternal herd to his father's *communitas*. The implication is clear. The Man Bull was incorporated easily into
indigenous life, his cow's blood posing no great impediment to Irish
belonging. Indeed, given the native ardor for their livestock, he may well
have possessed an entire herd of friends.

Tied in their body to cattle, the Irish seem little better than beasts themselves. Like the island as a whole, the people need to be domesticated, *in
formam simul et normam redacta* ("subdued into an ordered and measured
state," *Expugnatio Hibernica* 2.34). Other writers such as William of
Newburgh and William of Malmesbury insisted on the barbarity of the
Irish race, yet none took denigration to the detailed extremes of Gerald.
Nor was Gerald's audience wholly without skepticism, especially concern-
ing his repeated narration of Irish bestiality. The *Expugnatio Hibernica*,
Gerald's second Irish text, begins with a vigorous defense of the episodes in
the *Topographia* I have been examining here. His critics, Gerald admits,
found it unlikely that a wolf would talk with a priest, or that there could
exist *bovina humano corpori extrema* ("a human body which has the extremi-
ties of an ox"). Gerald cites biblical and patristic precedent for loquacious
beasts and incredible wonders, but he makes no apology for equating an
entire people with promiscuous fauna.

The Irish werewolves and the Man Bull of Glendalough are animal
bodies that substitute for racialized bodies. Perhaps, as James Cain has
argued, the *semibos vir*, the "unlikely cowboy from Wicklow," is also a
figure for the Irish, a people so subhuman that they have become animals
even in their blood ("Unnatural History" 37). Yet Gerald's narration of
the tragically short life of the Ox Man does not fit the unremittingly
reductive program of representation displayed elsewhere. Gerald links the
Ox Man's sudden presence at Maurice's Wicklow to the arrival on the
island of William fitzAldelin, the king's deputy, sent to exert royal control
over the Marcher conquest. Persecution of Gerald's family begins immediately, with the coldly calculating William swearing to "end the arrogance" of Maurice and his kin. Gerald launches into a formal and
rhetorically ornate defense of his family, then adds the following almost as
an afterthought:

> About this same time, just a short time previously, there appeared at
> Wicklow a monster [*vir prodigiosus*], the result of a vice prevalent among that
> people, who had been begotten by a man on a cow. His body was that of a
> man, but the extremities of his limbs were those of an ox, as is described in
> the *Topography*. (*Expugantio Hibernica* 2.15)

Gerald then resumes his historical narration, announcing that uncle Maurice died shortly after William began greedily amassing land and wealth. Maurice's death causes "great sorrow among his people." We know that the Ox Man will likewise bring sadness at his passing, but this time specifically for Gerald. In the *Topographia*, Gerald evinces little sympathy for the Man Bull of Glendalough or for the Irish themselves.[29] Yet the *semibos vir* of Maurice's Wicklow is, despite some initial hesitation on Gerald's part, undeniably human. Like the Cretan Minotaur doomed to his winding labyrinth, the Ox Man at his uncle's castle carries in his alien body a discordant mixture of identities, of differences not amenable to easy synthesis.

Given Gerald's fondness for expressing collective differences through a vocabulary of species, it is difficult not to see in the monster of Wicklow a figure for *gemina natura*: twinned nature, dual race. Murderously rejected by the indigenous population, sustained by a court amused by his spectacular oddness but discerning in his voice only meaningless sound, the Ox Man nurtured at the Marcher's colonial outpost belongs nowhere. In the irresolvable differences that the *semibos vir* incarnates, in this monstrous body teetering between categories, Gerald reluctantly beheld a vision of a creature achingly new yet strangely familiar, a vision of his own hopelessly heterogeneous self. For the Irish were not the only *gens ex bestiis solum et bestialiter vivens* ("people living on beasts only, and living like beasts"), at least when the islands were surveyed by English eyes.[30]

Journeys Through Wales

Before turning their eyes to Ireland, Gerald's family had been leaders in the conquest of Wales. Gerald's maternal grandfather and namesake was the celebrated Gerald of Windsor, a knight whose redoubtable offspring are often referred to as the fitzGeralds or Geraldines in his honor. Gerald adored his grandfather, however, not for martial prowess but cleverness. According to his *Itinerarium Kambriae* (*Journey Through Wales*), the Norman adventurers who had first assayed the country were beset by native resistance. In order to better secure the land, Arnulf de Montgomery hastily builds a little fortress of turf and stakes in remote Pembroke. Erecting fortifications in territories about to be annexed was a Norman specialty, enabling a secure base of operations from which to raid. Gerald himself had been born ca. 1146 in one of these battlements, the formidable castle of Manorbier. Compared to most Norman edifices, however, Arnulf's stockade was rather miserable, offering little protection from the people whose land he was claiming. He quickly retreated back to England, leaving Gerald of Windsor in charge. Surrounded by Welsh troops enraged by the death of their prince. Gerald and his garrison knew that they could not endure for long. Provisions dwindled and the Welsh showed no sign of lifting their assault. Gerald ordered the remaining hogs to be cut into pieces and hurled at the enemy. He wrote a letter to Arnulf declaring that they would need neither reinforcements nor supplies for at least four months. The missive was "accidentally" dropped a few miles from the fortress, where the besiegers would be sure to find it. The gullible Welsh broke the siege immediately and dispersed. Whereas Arnulf would eventually fall from royal grace, sly Gerald became constable of Pembroke and married Nest, so beautiful that she was called Helen of Wales (*Journey Through Wales* 1.12). Nest also happened to be the daughter of Rhys ap Tewdwr, prince of Deheubarth. By allying himself with a powerful local family Gerald secured a firm foothold in the land. He also introduced Welsh blood into his family line, a fact that was to haunt his descendants in ways he could hardly have dreamt.

The Welsh attempted much the same violence against their invaders as had been unleashed upon them. They fought subjugation with whatever tools came to hand: swords, sabotage, and—in at least one case—the strategic deployment of stereotypes against those who circulated them. According to Gerald's *Journey Through Wales*, when Henry II was preparing to seize Pencader, the king sent a trustworthy knight from Brittany to reconnoiter the terrain and report on local defenses. This unnamed man was accompanied on his mission by Guaidan, Dean of Cantref Mawr, instructed "to lead the knight . . . by the easiest route and to make his journey as pleasant as possible."[31] Gerald describes the Breton's nightmarish sojourn at Guaidan's hands in words that recall his grandfather's laudable subterfuge:

> [The Welsh priest] made a point of taking him along the most difficult and inaccessible trackways. Whenever they passed through lush woodlands, to the great astonishment of all present, he plucked a handful of grass and ate it, thus giving the impression that in time of need the local inhabitants lived on roots and grasses. (1.10)

When the knight from Brittany finally returns to his monarch, he declares in exasperation that the district is impossible to access or settle, yielding enough nourishment only for *genti bestiali et bestiarum more viventi*, "a bestial race of people, content to live like animals." Henry decides that region is not worth conquering and instead releases the captive prince Rhys ap Gruffydd to hold the land in tenure.

That the Breton knight should find the inhabitants of Pencader to be indistinguishable from grazing beasts is likely to have surprised no one in the royal entourage, since it only confirmed a representation of the Welsh that the English had long been circulating. Isidore of Seville declared that word *Briton* derived from the brutish life of those it designated (*Etymologiae* 9.2.102). Bede's *Ecclesiastical History* bequeathed to English history the "fact" that the Britons were an inferior people. The monsterization of the Welsh, however, took on a special urgency in the twelfth century, especially during the reign of Stephen, a time during which the Welsh became (to use Felipe Fernandez-Armesto's term) "internal primitives."[32] In an attempt to assert representational control at a time when military control was proving difficult, the Welsh were declared a monstrous race, suspended between the categories of rational human and dangerous animal. When viewed from the insular southeast, the "barbarous rudeness" of the Welsh contrasted in every way with the "sweet civility" of the English, a formulation that also suggests the way in which the supposed otherness of the Welsh undergirded English self-definition.[33] Like the Irish and the Scots, the Welsh could, once excluded, regain their humanity only through anglicization, through a process of assimilation in which they would lose the markers of their separateness by admitting the superiority of England and its ways.

The ecclesiast and philosopher John of Salisbury (ca. 1115–1180) denigrated the Welsh as *gens enim rudis et indomita bestiali more uiuens*, "a raw and untamed race, living in the manner of beasts."[34] The *Gesta Stephani*, a royalist account of the perturbations in the realm between 1135 and 1154, succinctly described Wales and its denizens as atavistic and animal-like:

> Now Wales is a country of woodland and pasture, immediately bordering on England, stretching far along the coast on one side of it, abounding in deer and fish, milk and herds; but it breeds men of an animal type [*hominum nutrix bestialium*], naturally swift-footed, accustomed to war [*consuetudine bellantium*], volatile always in breaking their word as in changing their abodes. (1.8)

Whereas in this same text the Norman Conquest of England has the simple effect of subjugating its people (*Anglos subiugarunt*), Wales and its inhabitants require a transformative process of modernization that includes instruction in proper architecture, jurisdiction, agriculture, and civic order:

> When war came and the Normans conquered the English, this land [Wales] they added to their dominion and fortified with numberless castles; they perseveringly civilized it after they had vigorously subdued its inhabitants; to encourage peace they imposed law and statutes on them.[35]

Just as the land needs proper cultivation in order to render its raw resources the equal of the English regions of the isle, so its wild denizens require the

transmutative power of proper law, custom, settlement, and social structure. Civilization is here a process that will lead the Welsh out of their
innate animality, into something closer to the full humanity possessed by
the author and his kindred souls among England's political and ecclesiastical elite.[36]

While giving what he believes is a factual report to King Henry, the
weary Breton knight in Gerald's narrative is in fact mouthing official propaganda about the barbaric state of Wales, even employing what had
become familiar Latin terms (*genti bestiali, bestiarum more*) for the representation of the Welsh. The feral Welsh were to be found in contemporary
vernacular literature as well. Chrétien de Troyes deployed a version in *Li
Contes del Graal* (*The Story of the Grail*). The hero of this widely popular
French romance is simple Perceval, a backwoods Welshman who cannot
tell the difference between an angel descended from heaven and quotidian
knights in armor. One of these knights declares of the gaping rustic: "Sir,
you must be aware that all Welshmen are by nature stupider than beasts in
the field [*plus fol que bestes an pasture*]: this one is just like a beast" (242–45).
Though a scene from romance, the passage could just as easily have been
uttered by one of the knights accompanying Henry II through Pencader.
Through Guaidan's mimicry of indigenous barbarism, the Welsh are
reconfirmed as irrational and wild.

No matter how much Gerald disliked a people, he always made exceptions for those who proved themselves clever. The archbishop of Cashel,
confronted by Gerald's snide assertion that Ireland had produced no martyrs because its people have failed to honor their faith, replies in words that
seem to acknowledge Gerald but, like the dean of Cantref Mawr in Wales,
slyly undercut him:

> Although our people are very barbarous, uncivilized, and savage, neverthe-
> less they have always paid honour and reverence to churchmen . . . But now
> a people has come to the kingdom which knows how, and is accustomed to
> make martyrs. From now on Ireland will have its martyrs. (*Topographia
> Hibernica* 3.107)

The archbishop's shrewd reply amuses Gerald, but its challenge to the truth
of Gerald's words does not seem to have stung him into rethinking the
conquest of the island. Guaidan presents a challenge less easy to dismiss.
The priest from Cantref Mawr is connected to Gerald in a way that no
Irishman could ever be, through a bond of history and blood. Perhaps this
tie explains why Guaidan is allowed to take the Irish archbishop's anticolonial cleverness to an extreme, inhabiting the image of Welsh bestiality to
empty it of meaning. Devouring grass with feral gusto, plodding through

trackless forests with the instinctual zeal of a woodlander, the Welsh priest seems the living embodiment of John of Salisbury's *gens rudis et indomita bestiali more uiuens* ("raw and untamed race, living in the manner of beasts"). Guaidan returns to the colonizers the very message they disseminate, but thereby brings about the release of a captive prince and prevents a more forceful subjugation of his country. For Gerald's readers, the stereotype of the animalistic Welsh suddenly loses its ability to monsterize. King Henry and the Breton knight reveal that they are the Perceval-like naïfs, while the Welsh become the clever manipulators of *idées fixes*. The episode specifically redeems Rhys ap Gruffyd, prisoner of the king "more by a trick than by force of arms" (*Journey Through Wales* 1.10), but at the same time it liberates the Welsh in general from dehumanization.

Subtly deploying stereotypes against their promulgators is not Guaidan's invention, even if he is especially endearing in his subversiveness. The postcolonial theorist Homi Bhabha has called such moments of deflective doubleness "sly civility."[37] When colonizers come across such difficult moment of resistance, self-confidence inevitably falters. Sly civility (or, in Guaidan's case, sly *incivility*) challenges not through blunt defiance but perturbing assent, troubling the self-assured foundation upon which differences of culture are sorted, established, and judged. Through his brilliant mimicry of the bestial Welsh, Guaidan brings about a hesitation in the text during which the conquest of "Wild Wales" becomes a problem rather than a program, capturing an underlying uncertainty that Bhabha argues characterizes all colonialism.

Unlike his first two books, focused on the alienation of Ireland, hesitations and conflicted allegiances are everywhere present in Gerald's Welsh texts. In composing a detailed account of the land to which he does and does not belong, for example, Gerald suggests in a chapter entitled "How the Welsh can be conquered" (*Description of Wales* 2.8) that the country be emptied of its barbarous inhabitants and transformed into a game preserve. He then adds another chapter, "How the Welsh can best fight back and keep up their resistance" (2.10).[38] Tellingly, Gerald concludes the *Description of Wales* by returning to Pencader, the site of Guaidan's quietly seditious mimicry in the *Journey Through Wales*. King Henry asks an elderly Welshman serving in the royal army if he thinks that the native rebels, the soldier's kinsmen, will ever be subdued. The man's reply to the king is stunning. Wales may well be decimated by England, he says, just as it has been injured by others since the Trojan forebears of the Welsh settled the island long ago. Nevertheless, he asserts, "I do not think that on the Day of Direst Judgement any race other than the Welsh, or any other language, will give answer to the Supreme Judge of all for this small corner of the earth" (2.10).[39] Gerald here resolves, at least for a moment, the roiling conflict within his own identity by crossbreeding Christian futurity (the Last Judgment) to secular history (the Welsh as bearers of ancient Trojan blood) and articulating its resultant progeny in a language he himself conspicuously never uses. Though translated into clerical Latin, the final answer to God, which is in fact a "final" answer to Henry's colonialist demand, comes in a pure Welsh that binds past to future, a resistant temporality outside of Norman, Angevin, English fantasies of progress. Sly civility indeed.

Welsh Fauna

Like many modern writers, and unlike most medieval ones, Gerald of Wales could seldom resist inserting himself into his texts. It would be no exaggeration, in fact, to say that Gerald's favorite topic was Gerald. About twenty of his compositions survive, most in multiple versions. Many relate, at some point or another, the rich minutiae of his life: a happy childhood passed at Manorbier, where he built cathedrals out of sand and where his dad affectionately called him *meus episcopus* ("my bishop"); the perils of growing up on a frontier, such as the night when enemy raids outside the family castle caused a tearful Gerald to seek the safety of the church; student days in Paris, full of heady intellectualism; travels through Ireland, Wales, France, and Italy; constant struggles to convince kings, bishops, and popes to read the books he so tirelessly produced; travails at the English court, at his archdeaconry in Brecon, at his semi-retirement in Lincoln.[40]

Next to autobiography, however, the topic to which Gerald turned most repeatedly in his early works was the lives of animals. We have seen already the excursions into wildlife that characterize the *Topography of Ireland*. *The Journey Through Wales*, the text he composed after his Irish works, is replete with loyal and heroic dogs (1.7), weasels that poison milk to exact their revenge on human malefactors (1.12), prophetic songbirds (1.2), self-castrating beavers (2.3), a horde of man-eating toads that relentlessly nibble their victim until only a skeleton remains (2.2). As in his Hibernian writings, Welsh beasts so intrigued Gerald because they provided useful figures for human virtues and vices. As Gerald's fascination with Irish bestiality also demonstrated, the flesh of animals served him well for representing the flesh of race. But this is not all negative. Animals might figure race as imprisoning skin, like the werewolves of Ireland, but they can also be the bodies through which are dreamed identities for which an adequate vocabulary does not yet exist.

Because the Ox Man belonged to two categories but could not be absorbed into either—because he had no possibility of home other than the Marcher castle at Wicklow, a place of welcome as well as murderous violence—the Hibernian minotaur (*semibos vir*) inhabits that difficult middle space between stark categorizations. This sympathetic monster engenders what uncle Maurice decried as *ignavia* and *mora*, impedimental hesitation. In Ireland, Gerald had mainly experienced the confidence of conquerors. In his Welsh writings, however, he became increasingly fascinated with hybrid figures like the *semibos vir*. His texts are populated by bodies that lose their integrity, their purity, and bring into the world new and intransigently hybrid possibilities for identity.

The *Journey Through Wales* is obsessed with corporeal commingling. The narrative ostensibly records a peregrination through Wales that Gerald made in the company of Baldwin, elderly archbishop of Canterbury, to enlist military and monetary support for the Third Crusade. Gerald's Latin title for the work, *itinerarium*, bears millennial associations, invoking journeys to the Holy Land and the Christian right to Palestine. *Itinerarium* imbues the work with religious gravitas.[41] Yet the text is far too chockablock to be reduced to its initial raison d'être. A sprawling composite of travelogue, anecdote, imperialist cartography, crusading propaganda, local chronicle, and national history, the *Journey Through Wales* was initially completed around 1191. Gerald continued to tinker with the burgeoning text thereafter, issuing a much-expanded version around 1197 and a third perhaps in 1214.[42] The *Journey Through Wales* tends to progress via associative logic, wandering the byways of a fertile mind rather than offering a pilgrimage to some secure destination.

In a typical narrative arc, a boy steals pigeons from a church in Llanfaes and his hand adheres to the ecclesiastical stone in punishment, triggering an extended account of sinners who suffered similar fates. A woman of Bury St Edmunds once attempted to pilfer gold by taking coins in her mouth as she kissed a saint's shrine, and her lips adhered to the altar for a whole day. In Howden church, a parson's concubine irreverently sat on the tomb of Saint Osana; her buttocks became fastened to the wood until the parishioners stripped and whipped her. In Winchcombe, a monk was divinely rebuked for having had intercourse the previous night when the prayer book he carried attached itself to his unclean hands. At the same abbey, a woman who blasphemed a saint was punished while reading the psalter, so that "her two eyes were torn from her head and fell plop on the open book, where you can still see the marks of her blood [*vestigia sanguinis*] to this day" (1.2). What thematically connects these episodes widely scattered across geography and time is their fascinated gaze upon the human body as the site for the performance of a public spectacle of truth. The flesh is suddenly possessed by an agency that does not originate from the soul inhabiting it, and through a forced fusion with sacred objects (church walls,

altars, prayer books) becomes a hybrid space where the private and the
social interpenetrate. The mistake these sinners make is to believe in their
individuality, their autonomy. Gerald's narrative brings their errant bodies
back within an ecclesiastical ambit, a rhetorical move in every way consonant with the objectives of his and Baldwin's journey.

The episodes of punished flesh melded to sacred objects culminate in a
second saintly blinding and a pair of impious lips fastened to the magic horn
of St. Patrick. A few words about the numinous power of bells over oath
takers are followed by the observation that when held to the ear, Saint
Patrick's horn makes a sweet noise like an aeolian harp. Next comes what
initially appears to be another "pure" (that is, extraneous) wonder: a wild
sow "suckled by a bitch remarkable for its acute sense of smell" matures
into a hunting-pig that can track game better than most hounds (1.2).
Gerald generalizes the episode into a truth about the perduring imprint
parents make upon the flesh of their offspring.[43] A seemingly unrelated
story follows, added by Gerald during his second revision of the *Itinerarium*
(ca. 1197) apparently because it happened in the same region at about the
same time. A man in Wales, it seems, once quite literally had a cow:

> In the same region and almost at the same time a remarkable event occurred.
> A certain knight, name Gilbert, surname Hagurnell, after a long and
> unremitting anguish, which lasted three years, and the most severe pains as
> of a woman in labour, at length gave birth to a calf, an event which was wit-
> nessed by a great crowd of onlookers.[44] Perhaps it was a portent of some
> unusual calamity yet to come. It was more probably a punishment exacted
> for some unnatural act of vice. (*Journey Through Wales* 1.2)

In isolation, the knight's difficult labor and strange progeny is yet another
wonder offered for the reader's consumption, only slightly more remarkable than Saint Patrick's horn and the pig that thinks it is a dog. When
a similar birth occurs in Ireland, the "man-calf" (*vitulum virilem*) of
Glendalough born *ex coitu viri cum vacca* (through a man's cortus with a
cow), the prodigy seems almost dull, so usual is "unnatural vice" (*nefandi
criminis*) on those shores. Yet this story is not set across the sea in Hibernia
but unfolds at the heart of Norman Wales. It involves not some nameless
Irish native who can stand in for the entirety of his race but a knight
whose nomination declares him an alien to the land to which his passion
attaches him. Unlike the disidentification that motivates the narration of
Irish minglings of human and beast, joinings supposed to demonstrate the
utter animality of that people, this unnatural coupling is fraught with
undecidability. It seems that, looking back on his Welsh work around

1197, Gerald is unable to muster the same unwavering confidence that had propelled much of the *Topography of Ireland*. During this major revision of the *Journey*, Gerald began to landmine his text, introducing ambiguities that undermine the unconflicted prose of his earlier days. Gerald, it seems, has taken the vocabulary of race that he developed for the estrangement of Ireland and transferred its animal obsessions to his own locus of origin.

The story of Gilbert Hagurnell, his taurine paramour, and their unanticipated progeny is an intriguing meditation on *gemina natura*, dual nature or difficult middles. The episode is preceded, after all, by a story that declares that a body carries in its flesh the history and the context into which it is born (a wild sow suckled by a domesticated hound becomes a composite form, physically porcine while functionally canine; the flow of breast milk overcodes the biologically innate with the culturally contingent). The man–bull–calf narrative in turn precedes a second story of interspecies procreation: in the ancient past, a mare belonging to Saint Illtyd mates with a stag and gives birth to creature with a horse's head and deer's haunches. These suggestive marvels are then followed by a sexualized account of the mixed past of Brecknock, the Welsh county in which they occur. Bernard de Neufmarché, *primus Normannorum* in the area, seized the land from its inhabitants and married a Welsh woman named Nest. Norman on its father's colonizing side and partly Welsh through a mother's blood, Brecknock is a hybrid space.

Bernard's wife Nest was in fact the daughter of another Nest, the wife of Osbern fitz Richard, lord of Byton (Shropshire). This Nest was in turn the daughter of the renowned Welsh Prince Gruffydd ap Llywelyn and Ealdgyth, daughter of Aelfgar, Earl of Mercia.[45] Bernard's wife also, as it turns out, possesses a second name, for she is called Agnes by the English. As her bilingual nomination suggests, Nest/Agnes is the focus of a great deal of ambivalence in Gerald's narrative. After her son Mahel mutilates the knight with whom she is having an extramarital affair, she wrongly denounces him to Henry I as the offspring of her disgraced lover. The king happily disinherits Mahel and bestows Bernard's land on Milo FitzWalter, a royal relation. This Milo has five sons, including one named Mahel, but each dies upon succeeding to Brecknock.[46] Milo fitzWalter's inability to found a family that can hold the land through history is underscored by Gerald, who punctuates the episode by finally having King Henry admit to Milo that, even though England occupies Wales for the time being to "commit acts of violence and injustice" against its people, he knows full well that it is the Welsh "who are the rightful heirs" (1.2). Brecknock's destiny, Henry and Gerald together declare, is a Welsh future.

But not a *pure* Welsh future. The sow-hound, the man and the bull who engendered a calf, the deer-horse of Saint Illtyd, Nest/Agnes, failures of inheritance in the Neufmarché and FitzWalter families, and the mixed heritage of Brecknock are bound by a logic of monstrous hybridity, condensed in the history of the land as a history of unresolved Norman/English/Welsh violence. Gerald is not telling a reductive or nostalgic story about the eradication of native purity by a colonialist regime. Indigenous culture has not simply been replaced by imported customs, language, modes of being. The Welsh March is irremediably impure, and Gerald is the living embodiment of its complexity. The *Journey Through Wales* explores how both Wales and England were changed when two bodies formed a third that carries with it something of both parents without fully being either.

Keeping in mind here that the Welsh were consistently depicted by the English as a *gens bestialis*, the offspring engendered upon Gilbert Hagurnell when he mixes his flesh with native animals is perhaps not as strange as it first appears. Hagurnell's bull-calf, produced through long anguish and the combination of differences meant to remain discrete, is Gerald's Welsh analogue to the Irish Minotaur. Both suggest that unanticipated hybridity offers an opening up of contradiction-riddled possibility. The knight pregnant with a calf through his alliance with a bull transforms a male into a maternal form, a human into an interspecies amalgam. The offspring of the mare and stag is simultaneously both and neither of its parents, a body that spectacularly displays its constitutive differences without resolution. When translated into Agnes, Nest forgets her mixed descent, forgets that her son is impure but perfectly legitimate. The price of her forgetting is to be rebuked into meaninglessness by history: her own story ends abruptly when she disowns her son. The English Mahel who replaces the mixed-race Mahel dies when a rock strikes him on the head at Bronllys castle, poetic justice accomplished by the land itself—a land that, as Gerald stresses, has been a tumultuous middle space since the long ago days of Bernard de Neufmarché.

Gerald's sympathy is clearly reserved for the Mahel of impure blood, a man who like Gerald himself was the son of a redoubtable Norman knight and a royal Welsh grandmother named Nest. Gerald's father was William de Barri, his mother Angharad; Angharad's mother Nest was the daughter of Rhys ap Tewdwr, prince of South Wales. Conflicting possibilities roil Gerald's compound blood: "Cambro-Norman" denizen of the Welsh March; Parisian intellectual with secular as well as theological interests; cataloguer of the world's wonders; ethnographer; historian of conquest; child of violence; cousin to Welsh princes; aspiring archbishop of an independent Welsh see; royal servant of the Angevin empire; reform-minded ecclesiastic with variable allegiances to England, Wales, Rome, Jerusalem. It seems that whenever I try to contain Gerald's identity in a sentence, my own syntax bloats, adjectives and nouns proliferate. Gerald was no more successful at finding a succinct way to contain his multipartite, multiparoused self. To take the words that he puts in the mouths of his uncles in Ireland, he was at a minimum *duplex* and *geminus*, "doubled" and "twin-born." Trained in classical Latin, Gerald must have known that his beloved poet Ovid had used the adjective *geminus* to describe the blood of Cecrops, half-Egyptian and half-Greek. He must also have remembered that Ovid used the same adjective to describe the centaur Chiron, half a man and half a horse, an indeterminate monster. Gerald was enthralled by such creatures, strange beings who find that they cannot synthesize the differences that they incorporate. It would not be far wrong to label such figures with racialized English nouns like "hybrids," "mixed bloods," "crossbreeds," but it is perhaps better to employ the word familiar to Gerald for such impure, heterogeneous beings: *mixta*, a Latin substantive derived from the verb *miscere* ("to conjoin, intermarry, copulate, confound, disturb"). *Mixta* technically describe paradoxical hybrids and "coincidences of opposites" like stag-mares, man-cows, and other composite monsters.[47] Yet even Guaidan, the grass-eating Welshman, is something of a *mixta*, combining as he does the image of the feral Welsh with the possibility of a body smarter and more civilized than that possessed by the invaders. *Mixta* as "conjoined things" are sly civility incarnate, bodies dwelling at the interstices and forbidden overlap of categories, confounding monsters.

Gilbert Hagurnell and the baby bull that he bore after three years of labor and an unspecified duration of "unnatural vice" figure the boundary-smashing work of medieval hybridity, of difficult middles. As they proliferate, *mixta* bridge in their flesh disparate cultures, geographies, and temporalities, resisting assimilation into placid or predictable totalities. They truly embody what the postcolonial critic Robert Young has called the "incommensurable, competing histories forced together in unnatural unions by colonialism."[48]

Boundless Middles

William Rufus, second Norman king of England, dreamt of building a naval bridge to Ireland (*Itinerarium* 2.1). This transmarinal architecture, Gerald of Wales claims, was to have been erected near St. David's. As the conduit for an invasion force, William's project tacitly acknowledges that Wales having been royally traversed, Ireland will become the next frontier. William's bridge of ships never materialized. Gerald explains its incompletion through the mouth of Murchard, the prince of Leinster, who declares that since the king of England did not qualify his decree with "If God wills," the people of Ireland need never fear his arrogant undertaking. The rebuke has a doubled sting in that the Irish were held by England to be deficient Christians, barely cognizant of the universal laws of their creed. Had not Pope Alexander III himself agreed when he authorized the English invasion of their island?[49]

William's impossible architecture underscores the medial position of Gerald's Welsh March: an intermediate zone that is neither fully other, like barbarous Ireland, nor exactly familiar, like those civil lands already domesticated into England. Contemporary historians have repeatedly described medieval Wales as a *frontier*, a term connoting an incipient space awaiting development.[50] To label a land a frontier is to assume a colonizer's point of view, for a frontier is an expansion's edge, a region where a self-declared advanced culture imagines it discovers a more primitive realm, ignorant of larger cosmographies. This encounter instigates the process of teaching that new land and its alien people their backwardness, their marginality. When "frontier" is invoked, the center of the world is assumed to be elsewhere. Yet William's bridge to Ireland moves southern Wales behind the line of the frontier without assimilating it to England. The Welsh March thereby becomes a middle space, even to the English king. By placing the proposed naval bridge at St. David's, moreover, Gerald illustrates how a multiplicity of differences circulate through such uncertain regions. Discourses germane to Latin Christianity, Norman-English colonialism, the ambitions of the Marcher lords, and the desires of the native Welsh hybridize at St. David's, for the area is for Gerald not a regional but a cosmopolitan center. Throughout his work Gerald argues that St. David's was the ancient seat of the archbishopric of Wales, a place owing no allegiance to English Canterbury but direct, unmediated obedience to Rome. The English rightly saw in this assertion not just defiance but the dangerous possibility of Welsh ecclesiastical independence brought about through a recentering of their world.

The poet and theorist Gloria Anzaldúa describes the borderland as "a vague and undetermined place created by the emotional residue of an unnatural boundary . . . in a constant state of transition."[51] Such indeterminate geographies foster "shifting and multiple identity and integrity," since they are home to multiple and bastard languages. As a place of *mestizaje*, hybridity, the borderlands are traversed by *los atravesados*, "the squint-eyed, the perverse, the queer, the troublesome, the mongrel, the mulatto, the half-breed . . . those who cross over, pass over, or go through the confines of the 'normal.' "[52] Anzaldúa writes as a self-conflicted product of numerous cultural forces, a lesbian feminist with a difficult relationship to her Chicana (Indian-Mexican-white) origin. The *cultura mestiza* that she articulates is a queer composite of races, religions, histories, sexualities, and species. Just like Wales at St. David's, Wales alongside that imaginary colonial bridge.[53] Anzaldúa figures her "new *mestiza*" as part human, part serpent, a body that spectacularly displays its differences without pretending they can be domesticated into a unified form.[54] The Anzaldúan borderlands are analogous to Gerald's vision of a middle space replete with *mixta*, "composites." Although they lack the investment of heroism that Anzaldúa gives to her joyfully contradictory and ambivalent *raza mestiza* and to her patron monsters (the Shadow Beast, the serpent-goddesses), Gerald's *mixta* similarly embody the intimate otherness produced when cultures have crossbred: "hybrid progeny, a mutable, more malleable species . . . an 'alien' consciousness" (*Borderlands / La Frontera* 77). For Gerald, this newness enters the world invested with desire, anxiety, disgust, passion, trepidation—and, when a figure for a wider process of cultural hybridization, a certain amount of promise.

The March was neither Norman nor Welsh, but an agitated melding of the two. Here hybrid bodies were revealed through hybrid names (Henri ap Cadwgan ap Bleddyn, Meilir fitzHenry, Maredudd son of Robert fitzStephen, Gwenllian Berkerolles, John ap Gwilym Gunter, Angharad de Barri).[55] Linguistically, architecturally, and culturally, the March was a mixed form, a bridge conjoining rather than assimilating differences. Here a king of England might dream of starting an invasion of Ireland, as if the land he stood upon were already safely his. Here also a royal messenger might be forced to eat, seal and all, a letter displeasing to the Marcher baron it addressed.[56] In the words of the foremost scholar of the Welsh March, its expanses formed a geographically, chronologically, and culturally diverse place where history "seems to disintegrate into plurality and defy the analytical categories of the historian."[57]

"Gerald of Wales" could in fact take the place of "the Welsh March" in the preceding paragraph, for his is that middle body through which pass *Pura Wallia, Marchia Wallie, Normannitas,* conflicting allegiances to church and world and *natio,* a bridge to the new frontier of Ireland, a form caught perpetually *in medias res.* Gerald's first name is unambiguously Norman.[58] He could have followed it with a francophone toponym like "de Barri," as his father and grandfather had done, in order to emphasize an origin in a geographic elsewhere (Barri is an island off the Glamorganshire coast). Gerald even had a troublesome nephew who called himself Giraldus de Barri and who succeeded his uncle to his archdeaconry in Brecon. But instead Gerald foregrounded his nativity in Wales by styling himself *Cambrensis.* That he chose this particular designator emphasizes his awareness that he inhabited a medial position where established terms fail. Gerald always describes the indigenous people with whom he shares some blood not as *Wallenses* ("foreigners," the English nomination), not as *Britones* (what the people sometimes called themselves), but as *Kambrenses*, an etymologically impure attempt to designate a compound identity.[59] *Cambria* was a possible Latin designation for Wales, mythologized by Geoffrey of Monmouth as the name of a son of the Trojan refugee Brutus. In styling himself *Giraldus Cambrensis*, Gerald was nominating himself in a language at once familiar and strangely new.

Late in the *Journey Through Wales* Gerald arrives in the Marcher settlement of Chester. Perched at the edge of Wales and England, this town incarnates the fluctuating Welsh borderlands, for its castle is built at a river that moves every year. When the fords of the Dee incline toward England, it will be a good year for conquest. When the fords move toward the Welsh side of this fluvial boundary, Wales will have the upper hand (2.11). Because Chester is a Welsh-English interspace, it is not surprising that Gerald reveals that two historical traumas have been interred but not laid to rest in its walls. The bodies of the Holy Roman Emperor Henry V and King Harold of England are, he asserts, buried within the town's limits. Harold was the last English king, displaced by William the Conqueror— the regent who in fact built Chester's castle during his campaign of 1069–1070, when he waged brutal war against the Welsh. Germany's Henry V had been married to Matilda, daughter and designated heir of Henry I; Matilda was in turn the mother of England's Henry II by Geoffrey of Anjou. The cadavers of these two monarchs are intimately connected to the crises of continuity that so perturbed William of Malmesbury and Geoffrey of Monmouth, the Norman Conquest and the civil war of Stephen's reign. Together they serve as reminders of the island's unsettled history.

It seems natural, then, that the appearance of these dead kings should be followed by stories about the generation in Chester of extraordinary bodies (*Journey Through Wales* 2.11).[60] The first of these *mixta* is a deer-cow, an animal that displays domesticity and untamed wildness in different sections of its flesh. This creature, born in Chester "in our own days," is inserted verbatim into the *Journey Through Wales* from its source, Gerald's *Topographia Hibernica* (2.55), where it forms an analogue to the *semibos vir* and *semivir bos*. Next come monkey-puppies, "ape-like in the front but more like a dog behind." These infant monsters meet the same undeserved fate as Maurice's Ox Man when murdered by a "country bumpkin" who fails to understand that their novelty is a source of wonder, not contempt. A third strange body belongs to a woman, likewise of "our own lifetime," who was born without hands. Her limblessness is (rather too literally) no impediment to her becoming a seamstress, for she adapts her sinewy legs and slender toes to accomplish those tasks a "proper" body assigns only to its hands. Gerald finds her intriguing, it seems, because in her corporeal plasticity she proves a point that he has been making throughout the *Journey Through Wales*: human flesh is malleable, always in the process of becoming something that cannot be anticipated in advance.

Gerald calls these fantastic denizens of Chester *deformes biformis naturae formas*—"deformed and hybrid bodies" in Thorpe's translation, but more literally (and playfully) "deformed forms of biform nature." Horace famously used the adjective *biformis* to describe the poet, a creature who is metaphorically half man and half swan (*Odes* 2.20.3). Perhaps for Gerald *biformis natura* evokes his own identity as lyricist of the world's impurities. Like *gemina natura*, the Latin adjective *biformis* was also employed to designate such compound entities as centaurs, the sea monster Scylla, the Minotaur. The border town of Chester, built at a river that moves its fords as it changes its allegiances, seems intimately connected through its "deformed biform forms" to Gilbert Hagurnell and his bulls in Brecknockshire, to the unfortunate Ox Man of an Ireland that no longer seems so distant. The composite monsters of Chester reveal that contested origins and compound identities cannot be buried along with the bones of Harold and Henry, corpses revivified by the turbulent histories their appearance recalls. That the edge of Wales should be the resting place of such problematic monarchs indicates that just as *gemina natura* engenders no secure future, it erodes the seeming stability of the past.

Disidentifications

Although he may at times have felt great uncertainty about who he was, Gerald of Wales could nonetheless confidently demarcate what he was *not*. His celibate clerical identity, steeped in traditions of misogyny, spurred one of the many abjections he performed. Women and their bodies are triggers for Gerald's worst invective.[61] A soothsayer named Meilye gains his unholy power by having sex with a beautiful temptress, really "a hairy creature, rough and shaggy, and, indeed, repulsive beyond words" (*Journey Through Wales* 1.5). The true form of the creature drives Meilye insane, and he is only partially cured by the ministrations of the saintly men at St. David's. Gerald is almost incapable of representing women outside of terms that make them wearily similar to Meilye's succubus. When the adulteress Nest betrays her son Mahel, for example, she deviates "not one whit from her womanly nature" (*Journey Through Wales* 1.2). In the *Topography*, tales of interspecies hybrids in Ireland give rise to anecdotes about women happily abandoning themselves to coitus with animals. When a goat and a lion copulate with human paramours, both partners in the act are, in Gerald's estimation, beasts worthy of death (*O utramque bestiam turpi morte dignissimam!*). Yet for all his stated revulsion, Gerald cannot resist visualizing such scenes at length. A version of the *Topographia Hibernica* not far removed from Gerald's original (MS National Library of Ireland 700) even illustrates in lurid detail a passionate kiss between each animal and his female lover.[62]

Gerald's monsterization of women perhaps helped him to feel secure in his sexual identity, since celibacy could—even late in the twelfth century— carry with it a tinge of queerness, especially in those parts of Wales where clerical abstinence had not fully penetrated. His denigration of what he held to be inferior and subordinate peoples, on the other hand, no doubt alleviated some of the uncertainty he felt about his hybrid constitution. Even the Normans could earn Gerald's venom, especially as he was repeatedly denied the see of St. David's that he so coveted. By the time he was bringing his manual *On the Instruction of Princes* to a close, he dismissed the conquest of England as the work of "Norman tyrants" who took possession of the island "not by natural descent or legitimately, but, as it were, by a reversed order of things [*per hysteron proteron*]" (27). He tells the story of a Norman bishop "of our own times who was like a monster with many heads" (*Jewel of the Church* 2.36). Gerald is probably referring to his inveterate enemy Hubert Walter, whose "many heads" included justiciar, chancellor, and papal legate. Having inherited through his Norman blood both arrogance and verbosity, says Gerald, Hubert gave sermons that demeaned his English audiences:

> He would attack the very English to whom he was speaking for their inborn hatred of Normans and would say: "In former times the English were outstanding both for armies and for learning, but now, because of wantonness and drunkenness, they excel in neither" . . . He was considered a great man because he was long-winded and boldly loquacious, as are all Normans![63]

Considering that Bishop Hubert was not invested with legatine powers until 1195, this episode not only records Gerald's ability to shift his allegiances as his life progressed, but also indicates a very late instance of Norman antipathy toward the native English (and vice versa, at least in Hubert's accusation).

Not every detested people inhabited the British Isles. The *Topography of Ireland* makes the daring rhetorical move of offering that island as an alternative to the beckoning wealth of the East, as a nearby place of wonder awaiting its own kind of crusade (1.27–32). Stealing some lines from Geoffrey of Monmouth, Gerald even imagines that Ireland had once been conquered by Africans, giving the country a Saracen aura (*Topographia* 3.112–14). By the time Gerald turned to the *Journey Through Wales*, however, figurative crusade had been abandoned for literal. This text after all records the mission that Gerald and Baldwin of Canterbury undertook to recruit soldiers and raise funds for the Third Crusade, the first expedition to the Holy Land to really capture the imagination of the British Isles. The cleric and the archbishop were participating in the creation of a homogeneous Christian community capable of transcending national, regional, and even sectarian differences.[64] At the same time, however, their trip through Wales achieved a variety of local political objectives. Baldwin's progress ensured that the church in Wales was publicly acceding to the power of Canterbury—a fact that Gerald must have found particularly galling, since he was an ardent proponent of an independent Welsh see at St. David's.[65] Once Welsh rulers and nobles were transformed into *crucesignati*, they were forced to champion Henry II's crusade, and therefore more deeply under royal control.[66] The distant struggle over the Levant proved a useful distraction from nationalistic struggles closer to home, and even helped to empty Wales of men who were clearly a cause of domestic troubles (including, in Gerald's words, "robbers, highwaymen and murderers"). At the same time, the religious devotion that the crusades inspired should not be downplayed. About three thousand men were recruited from Wales as a result of Gerald and Baldwin's preaching. The elderly archbishop himself died surrounded by "desolation and despair" at the siege of Acre in 1190 (*Journey Through Wales* 2.14).

Crusading polemic united a fractured West by offering a point of transnational identification, placing a monstrous enemy at the heart of the Holy Land. Such agitprop fostered a Christianity capable of the most unspeakable violence to Muslims, pagans, and Jews. Characterized by dark skin, idolatry, and an innate ardor for war, the Saracen is the most familiar product of this demonizing process. Yet because outside of Iberia Muslims did not live among Western Christians, the Saracen was of limited efficacy for galvanizing religious unity close to home. Not surprisingly, crusading fervor was almost invariably accompanied by brutality against Jews, religious and racial outsiders who did in fact cohabit with the Christians in England, Germany, and France. Gerald composed and revised his numerous works in the aftermath of this violence. He never refers to these events. True, Gerald had spent his childhood in an area of Britain lacking permanent Jewish settlements, but as soon as he stepped foot in cities like London, Lincoln, and Paris he witnessed thriving Jewish communities. The massacre at Clifford's Tower in York, the conflagration of Jewish domiciles in Lynn and Norwich, the murder of Jews at the coronation of Richard all took place while Gerald was in England. These bloody episodes seem not to have disturbed him much, for they are wholly absent from his otherwise capacious works. Yet it would not be true to say that there are no Jews in Gerald's writings. The *Journey Through Wales* contains an anecdote in which the philosopher Peter Abelard is challenged by a Jew to explain why lightning so often sets fire to churches, damaging crosses and other sacred objects. Peter offers a reply that makes it clear what both he and Gerald think of Jews: "No one ever saw lightning hit a public lavatory, or even heard of such a thing: by the same token it never falls on any of your Jewish synagogues" (1.12).[67] Gerald's *History and Topography of Ireland* relates how a marvelous goose is spontaneously generated from barnacles (1.12). Gerald seizes the opportunity to address a hypothetical Jew: "Pause, unhappy Jew! Pause—even if it be late . . . Blush, wretch, blush!" Barnacle geese, he argues, are all the proof required that Jesus could be born of a woman without the assistance of a man, and Jews are of "obstinate will" because they will not believe. The apostrophe from Ireland to the unnamed stubborn Jew takes on a special resonance when it is recalled that Josce of Gloucester, a Jew, financed Richard Strongbow's expedition to Ireland in 1170.[68]

Gerald's *Gemma ecclesiastica* (*Gem of the Church*), a book of spiritual instruction focused on canon and moral law, features two vivid episodes of punished Jews not found elsewhere. Both these narratives reveal a fascination with the flow of Christian blood. In a story that he claims to have taken from St. Basil but which does not in fact seem to have a source there, a Jew rents lodgings in Antioch to a Christian. When he eventually returns to his house and hosts a feast, one of his guests notices that a crucifix has been painted upon the wall by the former tenant. The Jews beat their host soundly for allowing the image to remain, then drag him to a judge and demand that he be put to death. The dinner guests remaining at the house poke a lance at the image, "just as they had done to Christ" (1.30). The painting yields to the weapon as if it were flesh. Real blood and water gush from the wound. The Jews dab these liquids upon themselves and are healed of various ailments. Having seen the Passion of Christ enacted in the dining room, having become unwitting participants in this history made real, the Jews decide that they will not make the same mistake as their forefathers: they convert to Christianity en masse. A similar episode follows in which a Jew in Rome hurls a rock at a portrait of Christ. "Blood immediately poured out in such an abundant flow," Gerald writes, that it covered the church floor (1.31). Although some Jews who hear about the incident convert, the stone thrower himself dies instantly, "struck with a terrible agony."

Jews, the Christian body in peril, an unstinting efflux of blood—these episodes from Gerald's late work bring together the components for solving a problem Gerald himself was never able to surmount: how, in the face of vexing hybridities and in the wake of historical trauma, to imagine that divided and heterogeneous peoples constitute a union. Gerald even hints at the resolution itself, not in the Jews who convert to Christianity and vanish, but in the blasphemous Jew who hurls a rock at the church and injures the body of Christ. In imagining a malevolent figure who unleashes a flow of sacred blood and pays for the violence with his own life lay a possible future for the formation of community.

CHAPTER 4

CITY OF CATASTROPHES

Postcolonial England

A poignant scene in *Beowulf* depicts the last survivor of a forgotten race constructing a burial mound or *beorh* (2241). Within its earthen walls he inters the leavings of his people: swords, goblets, gold jewelry, the detritus of a vanished nation. Ages later a dragon arrives to claim for himself this memorial that no longer retains memory, guarding for dozy centuries its lifeless wealth. When some wretch plunders the hoard and awakens its guardian, Beowulf is forced to battle the monster in its adopted home. The poem concludes with the dead king interred with the same treasure inside another barrow, *Biowulfes biorh* (2807), while the enemies of his people gather to obliterate his realm.

The *beorh* constructed by forgotten hands was a familiar sight in the *Beowulf*-poet's day. Some of these mounds were contemporary, such as the Sutton Hoo burials of East Anglia. Others were the remnants of Roman chambered tombs or the funereal structures of Britons. Most of Britain's barrows, however, are the work of prehistoric peoples who enclosed their bones and precious objects but were unable to bequeath to the future more than the barest indication that they had once walked the land. As writers like Bede, William of Malmesbury, and Gerald of Wales knew, the long history of the British Isles consists of repeated migration, invasion, resettlement, fading, commingling. Flows of languages, religion, cultures, and genes washed an archipelago where disparate peoples coexisted, conflicted, and changed. Many of their histories linger now only in tantalizing material fragments. Others achieved consolidations still well known: Roman *Britannia*, Dal Ríata, changing constellations of petty Welsh and Anglo-Saxon kingdoms, the Mercian hegemony, King Alfred's omnivorous Wessex, the Danelaw, Athelstan's united England. Each of these collectives was eventually displaced or transformed by the advent of some new power with its own vision of community and dominion.

Because they unfolded over long spans, few of the major shifts in insular power are attached to specific dates. Even when precise years are known, none exude the same gravitas as 1066, a date every student of insular history can recite, "the year of the Conquest," of the Battle of Hastings and of William's Christmas coronation in Westminster, a year so profoundly transformative that (according to William of Poitiers, Henry of Huntingdon, and the Bayeux Tapestry) Halley's comet streaked across the firmament to announce the profundity of the coming changes.[1] The year retains such demarcative force in part because, compared to previous conquests or invasions, the Norman campaign was meticulously documented. Why 1066 should have immediately attracted a vast historiography is not difficult to explain: growing literacy, the widespread existence of fairly efficient apparatuses for the dissemination of texts, a burgeoning interest in secular history. The arrival of the Normans was also inherently more narratable than, say, the Anglo-Saxon migration, an "event" of protracted duration accomplished through waves of peoples not acting under a single leader or even as a collective. With a charismatic leader, swift denouement, and sheer geographic spread, the Conquest was readymade epic. Yet that so much historiography arose in the wake of 1066 is probably due less to the fact that the Conquest *could* be efficiently narrated so much as that the subjugation of England effected such profound change that its story *needed* to be told, over and over again, to make sense of an altered world.

The arrival of those peoples who became the Irish, the Britons, the Picts, and the English unfolded slowly, fostering gradual displacement and absorption of indigenous populations rather than wholesale subjugation. Most insular polities were as a result predicated on continuity between rulers and governed. The swift Norman Conquest, on the other hand, engendered a bifurcated society, the effects of which could clearly be discerned for at least a century thereafter. Whereas the earlier Danish capture of the monarchy had not excluded the kingdom's native residents from positions of power, William purged secular and ecclesiastical institutions of their indigenous elite. He made it amply evident that the English had become something they were not under the Danes: a subaltern population, inferior to the internationally minded aristocracy who now connected the British Islands with far-flung holdings in France, the Mediterranean, the Holy Land.

The achievement of the Conquest is especially impressive considering that England had been powerfully united from at least the tenth century onwards. Although the English, Danish, and Norman co-claimants to the throne at Edward the Confessor's death make clear that no country's future is as stable as its people might desire, England on the eve of Hastings had enjoyed a lengthy reign as western Europe's earliest, largest, and most politically integrated nation. This vision of collectivity was built upon a cohesive notion of the *gens Anglorum*. By forcibly annexing England to a structure of power that had originated in Normandy and continued to look across the channel for its self-identity, the events of 1066 precipitated a national trauma. Conquest triggered a prolonged struggle to discover how a suddenly polyglot and multiethnic population might imagine itself a community, might again create a sense of shared identity in the face of the linguistic, historical, political, cultural, and economic difference.

Haltingly and with much experimentation, a process of reconsolidation proceeded on at least two levels, the national and the local. The vastness of national space has been well analyzed by medievalists, who have been especially interested in detailing how historiographers transformed the Conquest into narratives emphasizing the continuities straddling both sides of 1066. The progress of subjugation in the closeness of regional space, its relation to smaller solidarities like provincial or parochial *communitas*, has long been the domain of archeologists and specialist historians but has received comparatively little attention from literary scholars. The reason such an imbalance should exist is not difficult to find. Most of the texts that survive from the period are breathtakingly grand in their sweep, taking as their subject matter events that unfolded across immense temporal spans. William of Malmesbury, for example, begins his *History of the English Kings* in 449, as the Angles and Saxons arrive on British shores under Hengest and Horsa (1.1). He concludes the work almost seven centuries later, during the reign of the current monarch, Henry I (5.449). Even when they composed for nearby patrons, writers like Orderic Vitalis, Henry of Huntingdon, and Geoffrey Gaimar narrated the long story of the nation and had comparatively little to say of the localities they inhabited. Geoffrey of Monmouth's *History of the Kings of Britain*, meanwhile, did erase some of the blunt imperialism of 1066. Through its rapid and widespread dissemination, the text helped to contain the contemporary crisis of community, at first for the ruling elites, and then (as it was translated into French and English) for successive layers of the social strata. Geoffrey's book and its vernacular adaptations disseminated new national mythologies, profoundly reconfiguring within a few decades the shared perception of the insular past. Yet the book had a major drawback. Its subject matter was not England but Britain, and more specifically the parts of Britain that constituted Wales. Although he had bestowed a splendid origin myth on London, "New Troy" and glorious seat of kings, Geoffrey was profoundly uninterested in the other English towns and cities, granting these locales no place in his history other than as Saxon settlements for British heroes like Arthur to besiege. *The History of the Kings of Britain* ultimately had little to say, therefore, to the quotidian and provincial power struggles through which the Norman Conquest relentlessly advanced in the decades after Hastings. Until King Arthur could be converted into an English rather than a British regent (a fate that would, inevitably, befall him), Geoffrey's text yielded little material for building a community in which Norman and English difference might be transcended. By tying the Normans to the Britons at the expense of the people he called the Saxons, Geoffrey promulgated a vision of the past that left disjunction intact.

Not all twelfth-century Latin writing is as ambitious as what flowed from the pen of William of Malmesbury and Geoffrey of Monmouth, nor is every contemporary text so obsessed with nations and *longues durées*. A twelfth-century work exists so circumscribed in its ambit and so meticulous in its recounting of local minutiae that, compared to the panoramic vistas of Bede, William and Geoffrey, it seems at times positively claustrophobic. The monk Thomas of Monmouth composed his *Life and Miracles of St William of Norwich* for and about the city in which he lived.[2] An indigent tanner's apprentice, William was transformed a decade after his death into a new patron for a Norwich riven by conquest. An English child christened with a Norman name, William offered in his sacred body a suturing point at which those differences that had formerly divided the city's citizens could be forgotten, mitigating some of the lingering social and cultural trauma endured in the wake of Norman subjugation. The achievement of a civic harmony in the text rests upon a new vision of affinity, a vision demanding new monsters. For the first time in written history we encounter in Norwich a figure destined to become familiar throughout medieval Christendom, the Jew whose murderous hands provoke an unceasing flow of blood.

The final two chapters of this book examine the *Life and Miracles of St William of Norwich* in its relation to local visions of collective identity and community. The current chapter is mainly historical, describing the transformations that Norman colonization induced in Norwich. This prosperous and populous mercantile town was transformed against its will into what I have been describing throughout this book as a compound and postcolonial difficult middle. Some attention will be paid to texts like Thomas's hagiography, but many of the stories told here derive from the stones of massive new buildings and from the radical reconfiguration of an established urban landscape. I will be most interested in hypothesizing how the transformation of physical space leads to changes in the lived experience of that space, and how the architectural wounding of a city affects the subjectivities of those who inhabit its altered geographies. The concluding chapter will then analyze the *Life and Miracles of St William of Norwich* in greater detail, arguing that its bloody imagining of a Norwich united behind a native saint can best be understood as a purifying remedy for a city made hybrid through catastrophe.

English Norwich

In speaking of the Norman subjugation of England, excellent precedent exists for seeing writing as inextricable from conquest. The *Anglo-Saxon Chronicle* insists that William the Conqueror was so enamored of documentation that he would not allow a single grazing beast to go unrecorded:

> 1085. The king . . . sent his men over all England into every shire and had them find out how many hundred hides there were in the shire, or what land and cattle the king himself had in the country, or what dues he ought to have in twelve months from the shire. Also he had a record made of how much land his archbishops had, and his bishops and his abbots and his earls—and though I relate it at too great length—what or how much everybody had who was occupying land in England, in land or cattle, and how much money it was worth. So very narrowly did he have it investigated, that there was no single hide nor virgate of land, nor indeed (it is a shame to relate but it seemed no shame for him to do) one ox nor one cow nor one pig which was there left out.[3]

William's project, according to the *Dialogue of the Exchequer*, was christened by the native English *Domesdai*, "judgment day," because in its penetrative gaze "it seemed to them like the Last Judgment described in Revelation."[4] The Domesday Book is described by the *Anglo-Saxon Chronicle* as a colonial device, transforming into the permanence of text a Norman hold on the land that extends to every mill, farm, and beast. The conquest may have begun in blood at Hastings, but the English author of this entry makes it clear that it long continued through more abstract, penetrative, and wounding modes. No text, of course, no matter how piercing, can in fact provide the kind of all-encompassing account that the chronicler describes and to which, perhaps, Domesday actually aspired. In attempting to capture the sheer diversity of England within a single register, the Domesday project reveals a sangfroid and hubris that deeply troubled the English chronicler. By 1085 the Norman king and his francophone compatriots were transfiguring England in ways that could not have been anticipated two decades previous.

Yet the argument has sometimes been advanced that the Norman Conquest was not much of a conquest after all. Its proponents stress the already apparent Normanization of the land, especially under Edward the Confessor, and invoke the abundant continuities traversing both sides of 1066.[5] Such narratives of unbroken history have a familiar ring to them, for Norman apologists were advancing exactly the same hypothesis in the twelfth century. Still, it would be difficult to convince a medieval resident of a city like York, Lincoln, or Norwich of the smoothness of this transition.

These important English communities saw large, often densely populated swathes of urban topography demolished to make way for immense architectural introductions. Modest English buildings were displaced by some of the largest structures in Christendom, lofty monuments in stone to a reconfigured nation. The Norman willingness to raze established areas of cities, erecting settlements of their own directly on top of the ruins of their English predecessors, prompts Eric Fernie to observe that

> there could hardly be a more direct statement, as physical and literal as it is symbolic, of the imposition of one culture upon another. It has been argued in recent years that the Norman Conquest had little impact on the history of eleventh-century England and the fact of its occurrence would not be apparent on the evidence of the material record alone. The remains of cities such as Norwich suggest that this conclusion is wrong.[6]

The subjection of England found bluntly material expression in the spectacular reconfiguring of countryside, cities, and towns. In York, for example, the construction of a castle bisected the city's commercial district, disrupting a network of streets dating back to Roman days. When the new occupiers of the city damned the River Foss, two mills were submerged. With them were lost not just places where an essential labor was carried out but centers of commerce and community. The erection of the archbishop's precinct and a second castle destroyed almost a thousand tenements. *Francigenae* displaced English residents from 145 manses by 1086.[7] In Lincoln at least 166 English tenements were laid waste as a Norman castle rose. Building projects in Cambridge obliterated 27 houses, while Huntingdon lost 20, Gloucester 16, and Stamford 5.[8] The castle in Norwich apparently claimed 98 houses and at least 2 churches, while the cathedral and other new edifices took many more.[9] Like Lincoln, Nottingham, Shrewsbury, and York, the city of Norwich was subject to a complete Norman restructuration, the devastation of its pre-conquest contours and content. English Norwich was obliterated to make way for a new Norman city. Because few written records germane to the city survive from the period, a possible way to uncover some of the effects of Norman subjugation on the city's community might be to map its architecture and physical space both before and after the alteration in national governance.[10] Scholars have long taken it for granted that medieval communities reveal themselves (no matter how partially or in what idealized form) in the texts they produce; the same must certainly be true of the edifices that they construct and inhabit, and in the changing topographies that these architectures form.

By the time William, Duke of Normandy, and Harold Godwinson, former Earl of East Anglia and briefly king of England, fought on their distant battlefield at Hastings, Norwich had long been a wealthy and heavily populated urban center. Along with London, Winchester, and York, it was among the most significant cities of the realm, and possessed neither peer nor rival in the region. Well situated for overland and transmarinal trade, it straddled the River Wensum at an ideal spot: the waters were low enough to be forded, narrow enough to be bridged, and deep enough to be navigated by ships sailing into the estuary at the North Sea. Wide pastures and fertile soil could sustain varied agriculture; flourishing livestock and the availability of the river would encourage leatherworking and tanning; nearby woodlands such as Thorpe provided ample timber; the area was rich in iron for metalworking and clay for pottery; easy access to the ocean meant that the quays would eventually see much traffic in fish, especially herring. It is possible that several of the roads that converged on the medieval city were laid during the Roman period, but evidence for the earliest history of the area is scanty. A buried Neolithic henge survives at Arminghall, about a mile away, while the abandoned Roman market-city of *Venta Icenorum* is about three miles distant.[11] Immigrants from northern Europe eventually displaced or assimilated indigenous Romano-Britons. These newly arriving raiders and warriors were also, as they had been in their native lands, dedicated farmers. After an initial contraction in population and economic recession, Norfolk steadily regained both people and affluence. Archeological evidence suggests that the area which was to become Norwich possessed a Saxon population since the sixth century, and perhaps even from the fifth. These settlements were likely modest and fairly separate. James Campbell suggests 850–925 as the likeliest time span for Norwich's congealing out of a sweep of rural hamlets to form a united borough with regional, national, and international importance.[12]

Of the several Saxon villages that were to become the future city, two bestowed their names upon later urban quarters: Coslany (north of the river) and Conesford (the southeast section of the city). "Norwich" may have been the designation for a third area, perhaps even a part of Conesford, that eventually gathered the others beneath its name as the settlements grew together. *Norwic* is formed of the English words *north* and *wic* ("fort," "settlement" or—as Ælfric glossed it—"*litelport*").[13] Churches dedicated to saints like Etheldreda (East Anglian queen and nun of the seventh century) and Ethelbert (East Anglian king killed in 794) may have originated fairly early, perhaps as centers of village life. The area's growing importance is indicated by the fact that the Danes executed the martyr-king Edmund nearby in 869. Scandinavian raids of East Anglia had begun four years previous, and Danish rule endured from about 870 to Edward the Elder's reconquest in 917. Although some pagan elements were probably reintroduced at this time, the first Danish king (Guthrum, ca. 870–890) did convert to Christianity, easing the accommodation between new rulers and subjects. Significant Scandinavian settlement is likely to have occurred in the Norwich communities, especially given that nearby Thetford was, according to the *Anglo-Saxon Chronicle*, a base for Viking raiders. Several streets of medieval Norwich were called *gates* (for example, Pottergate, Fishergate), a Danish nomenclature suggesting that not all residents in the eighth and ninth centuries spoke *Englisc* as their first language. Thorpe ("new settlement"), the area east of the city, is a Danish word, as is half of the compound designation Cow*holme* ("water meadow"), a section of Norwich eventually surrounded by the Norman cathedral close.[14] The quarter of the city called Conesford probably records how the English word "king's ford" sounded when spoken by a Danish mouth, while another quarter, Westwick (west of Conesford), may have originated as a colony of Danes.[15] Campbell has reasonably postulated that the Danish conquest united what had been separate English villages into a single, thriving settlement by stimulating international trade and triggering rapid growth.

After East Anglia was absorbed under Edward into the burgeoning holdings of the house of Wessex, it was thereafter ruled by the king's *ealdorman*, later to become the Earl of East Anglia. The city of Norwich enters written history as the word NORVIC stamped upon coins manufactured during the reign of the great unifier Athelstan (924–939). A mint may have been established north of Conesford, perhaps in a fortified area being called the "north settlement," or *Northwic*. Royal mints were always located in walled areas (*burhs*) with their own marketplaces. It could well be that through their circulation these coins bestowed the name of Norwich upon the merger of the separate villages (Coslany, Conesford, Westwick) that had burgeoned into East Anglia's chief city. Any settlement large enough to boast a royal mint possessed not just wealth but cultural cachet. It may even have been a royal residence.[16] Perhaps for these reasons Swein Forkbeard, king of Denmark, decided to pillage Norwich early in the eleventh century. The *Anglo-Saxon Chronicle* narrates the destruction in the city with grave terseness:

> **1004** Her com Swegen mid his flotan to Norðwic. 7 þa burh ealle gehergade 7 forbærndon.
>
> [In this year Swein came with his fleet to Norwich and completely ravaged and burnt the borough.][17]

The entry goes on to describe how the English warrior Ulfcetel and his companions attacked the marauding Danes at Thetford, a bloody battle in which "the flower of the East Anglian people was killed." It is possible that the *Knútsdrapa*, a praise poem composed for Cnut, son to Swein and future king of England, records his participation in his father's campaign. *Knútsdrapa* contains the lines "Gracious giver of mighty gifts, you made corslets red in Norwich."[18] Considering the *Anglo-Saxon Chronicle* describes Norwich as "completely ravaged and burnt" ("ealle gehergade 7 forbærndon"), the destruction must have been substantial.

In attacking the city, Swein may have been seeking vengeance. His sister Gunnhild had been murdered a year earlier during the St. Brice's Day Massacre, racial violence ordered against the Danish population of England by a paranoid King Æthelræd. Nor was Swein's the last Danish campaign in the area. Cnut, soon to ascend to the throne, was involved in a second battle at Norwich at some time close to the end of Æthelræd's reign. England shortly thereafter found itself conjoined in empire to Denmark, a geographic reorientation strengthened when in 1028 Cnut received his third crown, Norway. Because of its proximity to the North Sea, the body of water that this newly transmarinal polity spanned, Norwich was well positioned to benefit from a circulation in goods and people. Domesday Book records numerous Scandinavian names in the area. Although the total immigrant population from Denmark and Norway was probably fairly low, these transplants constituted an elite minority, and contemporary English absorbed many words from their Scandinavian tongues. Late Saxon Norwich became, like the densely inhabited geography that surrounded the city, an Anglo-Scandinavian milieu.

Despite the destruction inflicted upon the city in 1004 and despite whatever damage occurred when Cnut campaigned there later, Norwich quickly rebounded. The years leading up to 1066 saw rapid development, especially in the area surrounding what was called Tombland. *Tom* is the Danish word for vacant, so "Tombland" was a space kept intentionally empty, probably so that it could house the city's market and serve as a place for civic meetings such as courts. Tombland was likely to have been the community's economic, social, and juridical heart. The orderly nature of the settlement surrounding the locale suggests urban planning, perhaps at the hands of the powerful English magnates who owned land in Norwich: the king, the bishop, and Earl of East Anglia, the abbots of Ely and Bury.[19]

Most contemporary accounts of medieval England tend to take London as the kingdom's natural center. Yet a London-centric approach can obscure the vitality of other regions of the kingdom, especially in the years when the royal household tended to be peripatetic and London was simply one large city among several. The importance of Norfolk in general and Norwich in particular can be glimpsed at the eve of the conquest in small details, like the fact that the last English bishop to hold the see of East Anglia was Æthelmaer, a man with family intimately connected to the royal court. Most likely a native of Norwich, Æthelmaer had succeeded to a bishopric recently vacated by his legendary brother Stigand. Among England's most powerful magnates before the conquest, Stigand was simultaneously the bishop of Winchester, the archbishop of Canterbury, and an unparalleled force in the governing of Edward the Confessor's realm. Though the seat of the East Anglian bishops remained outside the city until the 1090s, the fact that Æthelmaer, Stigand, and their kin possessed extensive land and several churches in Norwich suggests their intimate ties to the area and makes clear why William the Conqueror secured the city so quickly. In April of 1070, during the so-called Norman purge of the episcopate, Æthelmaer was—along with Stigand—deposed.[20] As was William's practice in the wake of the English revolt of the previous year, Æthelmaer was replaced by a man devoid of local connections, a Norman named Herfast. Not long thereafter, a royal castle began to rise in the see's most important city. The fortification would have served as a constant threat to any lingering sympathies toward Stigand's family, or toward those favorably inclined to another powerful pre-conquest family with deep local connections, the Godwinesons.

Eleventh-century Norfolk was the most densely populated shire in England. Its chief city of Norwich was among the kingdom's most expansive, populous, and prosperous. A nexus of industry and the location of thriving regional and international trade markets, Norwich was East Anglia's primary port. By the time of the conquest, its considerable wealth lay in watermills; diverse agriculture; catches of herring (a staple of the medieval diet, prized for its meat as well as its salt content); flint and lime from nearby quarries; wood for building and fuel, derived especially from the dense forest at Thorpe; international trade; and the manufacture of consumer goods, especially pottery jars and lamps. Though not self-governing, the city was administered separately from the remainder of Norfolk. Taxes and rents were paid to a royal official, who owed £20 a year to the king and half that again to the Earl of East Anglia. We are fortunate in that Norwich is included in the detail-rich volume called Little Domesday, rather than the more condensed and elliptical Great Domesday. According to this record, by 1065 the city's burgesses lived in three jurisdictions. The majority (1,238) were responsible directly to King Edward and Earl Gyrth Godwinson; Gyrth's brother, Harold Godwinson, former Earl of East Anglia and briefly to become England's King, held some land here with 32 burgesses; and Stigand, last English archbishop of Canterbury and the former bishop of East Anglia, had the allegiance of 50 burgesses. The number of tax-paying burgesses indicates the city's great affluence.[21]

The vigor of the smaller communities that constituted the city of Norwich can be glimpsed in the city's expansive system of parish churches.[22]

Anglo-Saxon East Anglia had experienced a rapid proliferation of churches, modest and ambitious alike. Domesday records more than 300 chapels and churches in Norfolk. An astounding 50 of these were in Norwich itself, and at least 25 are known to be pre-conquest. Some of these structures were quite small. The communities centered around them could consequently be fragile. Since they were considered private property and therefore divisible and inheritable, churches could be modified, torn down, or sold. As Colin Platt has shown, some endured for only a single generation.[23] Yet many of Norwich's known pre-conquest churches (including St. Sepulchre, St. Edward, St. Clement, St. Andrew, St. Gregory, St. Swithun, and St. Martin at Oak) were likely of great age before being recorded in Domesday. By 1086, some churches probably dated back two hundred years, and a few may have been founded in the eighth or ninth century.[24] St. Clement Colgate, for example, was named for the patron of sailors, a popular figure in Scandinavia and Anglo-Scandinavian towns.[25] The activity of raiders from across the sea probably engendered the proliferation of parish churches, mainly by eliminating centralized sources of ecclesiastical oversight. Because the monasteries had been sacked and the episcopal see lay vacant for decades, local landowners could erect revenue-generating churches without interference. Ownership of a church was open to anyone who could afford to acquire the land and build the structure, or to purchase a preexisting edifice. Parish churches in Norwich, therefore, would have been in the possession of laymen, secular priests, monks, or some combination of these as joint owners.

Churches could be profitable investments, or they might remain tiny and impoverished. St. Michael's Tombland, demolished to make way for the Norman cathedral, was a pre-conquest church of great prosperity, while the nameless wooden church destroyed to build the northeast bailey of the Norman castle clearly ministered to an indigent congregation.[26] Neighborhood and district centers, churches functioned as meeting places, spaces for commercial transactions, and architectures inside which Christians could perform those rituals that bound them together in camaraderie and faith. Ælfric once complained about men drinking and chatting idly in churches, prompting James Campbell to observe that they "fulfilled some of the same functions as public houses and [were] needed as much for general social purposes as for worship."[27] A great deal of intimacy would have existed between the priest and his parishioners, not only because of the modest size of most structures but also because English priests were typically married, bound to their communities not just by pastoral duty but through familial ties.[28] This sense of unity would have been especially palpable in a church owned by the priest himself, particularly if it had been passed from father to son as an inheritable building and office.

A priest hired by a church's owner lived a more precarious existence, and may not have had the same opportunity to become an important civic figure as his more firmly established counterparts did.

By the time Thomas of Monmouth wrote the *The Life and Miracles of St William of Norwich* in the mid-twelfth century, the Norman cathedral that had been erected in the city served as mother church (*mater ecclesia*) to the manifold parishes. The imposition of the cathedral's authority must have organized through subordination what had been a vast patchwork of nearly autonomous religious communities. Thomas describes a feast day managed by the cathedral that transported parishioners out of their local allegiances to the public acknowledgment of the superlative status of the new church: "That day was the Absolution day, on which the penitents of the whole diocese were accustomed to assemble in crowds in the Mother Church at Norwich, and the streets of the whole city were crowded with an unusual multitude of people walking about" (1.7). Once the cathedral was erected, parish priests were superintended through its archdeacons and synods. Thomas offhandedly describes a diocesan synod held in the cathedral in 1144, suggesting that such gatherings were a regular event. Yet the bishop's seat was not moved to Norwich until the days of East Anglia's third Norman bishop, Herbert de Losinga. The English bishops had resided in bucolic Elmham, and Æthelmær's Norman successor Herfast (1070– 1084) moved to Thetford around 1072.[29] Prior to the cathedral's establishment in Norwich, no local ecclesiastical body directly or effectively oversaw the city's abundance of churches and priests, leading to independence and variation. These same circumstances probably encouraged the parish churches to circumscription in their mission, fostering neighborhood solidarities rather than encouraging the growth of a larger urban community or promulgating a feeling of belonging to a national or international Christianity.

When William of Normandy crossed the Channel and won his new throne, Norwich had a population of between five and twelve thousand. Like most of East Anglia, the city was possessed of a fairly homogeneous populace, mainly of Anglo-Scandinavian descent. Archeological evidence such as pottery shards connect Norwich to Rhineland trade routes by the ninth century, and to France by the eleventh. Domesday states that Norwich furnished the king with a bear, a detail that hints at an enduring Scandinavian connection.[30] It is also possible that even into the eleventh century the port of Norwich saw traffic in humans as slaves were shipped abroad.[31] One of the city's pre-conquest churches was dedicated to the Flemish saints Vaast and Amand, indicating that a group might have settled in the city from Flanders.[32] Yet by the time of Edward the Confessor, the citizens of Norwich were likely to have felt themselves, like the people of England more generally, united by a sense of shared language and history.

On a quotidian level this sense of community was likely to be unconscious, vague, and implicit. Community did not need to be fought over because, at the eve of the conquest, ethnic difference did not offer some source of long simmering tension or enduring resentment; no historical event, legal system, or division in cultural cachet had fragmented the city into inimical or highly differentiated groups. Whatever civil unrest it may initially have engendered, Danish settlement does not seem to have created lasting collective divisions, probably because mutual assimilation quickly occurred. A lack of enduring disparities based upon origin or history may also have much to do with the economic benefits brought about by stronger connection of the city to Scandinavian and German trade routes. This increase in the city's prosperity was apparently not only substantial but mutual, benefiting the indigenous English and immigrants from across the sea.[33]

Violence between ethnic groups was not unknown. Yet the xenophobia manifested acutely in the St. Brice's Day massacre or more chronically in the demonized deployment of the term "Dane" by the *Anglo-Saxon Chronicle* and other texts was balanced by quiet accommodation of immigrants into existing communities. While it is true that Cnut initiated his English reign with bloodshed (for example, the Christmas murders of 1017, which effected the demise of several important members of the indigenous political elite), the Danes quickly realized that assimilation and parity would achieve a secure tenure more quickly. A few years later both peoples were living comfortably under Cnut's rule without any lingering damage to the established social structure or even, it seems, to the perceived continuity of the nation.

Amalgamative and synthetic, the reign of King Cnut was in the end a widening rather than a transfer of power. With its thorough, enduring, and bifurcated reassignment of status, wealth, privilege, and power, the Norman Conquest was to be a completely different story.

Postcolonial Norwich

That the body of King Harold lay lost among the carnage at Hastings suggests the sheer human toll of the clash, the bloodiest moment of the Norman Conquest. Though crowned a mere eighty-eight days after landing in England, the new king would face further violent encounters. His subjugation of the English was, by both medieval and modern criteria, brutal.[34] The English nobles who rebelled in 1068–1070 so threatened William's grip on the throne that he devastated Yorkshire as part of a counter-campaign, engendering widespread misery.[35] In 1075, Ralph Guader, the Breton-English Earl of Norfolk, allied himself with Waltheof of Huntingdon, the only remaining English earl, and Roger of Hereford, a disgruntled Norman magnate. The conspiracy was plotted at a wedding feast held in Norwich, a genesis so captivating in its day that it became a popular rhyme. The *Anglo-Saxon Chronicle* cheerfully records the lines: þær wæs þat bryd ealo / þat wæs manegra manna bealo ("There was that bride-ale / That was many men's bale").[36] King William's forces crushed the rebels and their Danish support troops and laid siege to Ralph's wife in Norwich castle. It may be that Ralph found the citizens of Norwich supportive of his struggle against William, perhaps because Ralph's father had been a Breton highly favored by Edward the Confessor. It may also be significant that Ralph's predecessors as earl of East Anglia were Harold Godwinson and his brother, suggesting the possibility that the city might not have been overly sympathetic to the new Norman regime. The uprising led by the three earls ended with Waltheof beheaded, Roger perpetually imprisoned, and Ralph permanently relocated to Brittany. In the wake of the rebellion, Norwich found its castle equipped with a substantially larger garrison, and many Norwich citizens are recorded in the Domesday survey of 1086 as ruined or having fled the city.

Once William had quashed military insurgences, the conquest proceeded with a violence no longer corporeal so much as cultural. A francophone elite was installed in ancient English seats of power. The replacement of the native ruling class with Norman, French, and Breton imports was made vastly easier by the fact that so many indigenous nobles had perished in the battles of Stamford Bridge and Hastings; English survivors of the latter were, moreover, ineligible to retain their lands. Arriviste and land-hungry secular elites were joined by their ecclesiastical brethren, abbots and bishops who sailed across the channel to take control of existing church structures and bring new ones into being. William's men quickly entrenched themselves in the kingdom through the erection of finely tuned bureaucracies and massive fortifications. Norman knights erected a profusion of castles atop large-scale earthworks. Norman clerics rebuilt the major English abbeys and cathedrals, creating towering stone monuments to proclaim the shift in national power. Secular settlers of more moderate means often took English properties and domiciles, adapting them to their own tastes; sometimes they carved out completely new boroughs within the English cities, constructing markets and homes for their own use.

Even in the monasteries, tension between the Normans and the English was endemic. As at Glastonbury in 1083, discord between native brethren and their freshly arrived superiors could result in bloodshed, even murder. Abbot Turstin, annoyed that his monks were refusing to follow the chanting practice he imported from Fécamp, sent his knights after the disobedient brothers. Archers shot at those who sought the safety of the church's altar. The E version of the *Anglo-Saxon Chronicle* vividly recounts the scene, allowing the slaughter of the English monks to stand in for the brutalized English nation:

> A grievous thing happened that day. The Frenchmen broke into the choir and threw missiles towards where the monks were, and some of the retainers went up to the upper story and shot arrows down toward the sanctuary, so that many arrows stuck in the cross that stood above the altar; and the wretched monks were lying round about the altar, and some crept under it, and cried to God zealously, asking for his mercy when they could get no mercy from men. What can we say, except that they shot fiercely, and the others broke the doors down there, and went in and killed some of the monks and wounded many there in the church, so that the blood came from the altar on to the steps, and from the steps on to the floor.[37]

The transfer of a monastery's abbacy becomes in this horrific narration Hastings in little. English blood flows across what had been shared and sacred space, rendering it an invaded geography. The world, the chronicle makes clear, will never be the same.

The Glastonbury "massacre" (despite the hyperbolic tone of the chronicle, only three monks were killed) occurred almost twenty years after the conquest began. The transformations engendered by the Normans were apparent long before. Robert Bartlett succinctly describes England a decade after Hastings as a conquered nation where "a small armed group speaking a language incomprehensible to the majority of the population controlled virtually all the landed wealth."[38] These ascendant Normans not only spoke an alien tongue, they at times seemed set apart in their very bodies, short hair and clean-shaven faces contrasting sharply with the long tresses and moustaches of the natives. William of Poitiers describes the Normans curiously gazing upon the longhaired English brought back to Normandy by William in 1067, finding them to yield nothing "to the beauty of girls."[39] A more negative depiction of English coiffure is found in the *Carmen de Hastingae Proelio*, which declares that the combed and oiled hair of the English renders them "effeminate young men."[40] Ann Williams argues that such anecdotes, entertaining as they might be, reveal

> little about the interaction between newcomers and natives in post-Conquest England, nor do they touch the deeper changes and compromises that both groups were forced to make. The imposition of a foreign aristocracy involved more than manners, more even than a change of personnel. It produced a different way of reckoning status.[41]

In the abstract, of course, contemporary references to English versus Norman hairstyles or customs may not amount to much. Yet the sheer number of such comments suggests that corporeal differences obsessed contemporary writers because they made a radical, deep-reaching change in power instantly and empirically visible. It was not so easy to talk about the Norman erosion of the prestige attached to English earlship and thegnage, or about the remaking of tenurial rules. The arrival of baronage and the vanishing of sokeland also did not make for riveting narrative; likewise the realization that power was now far more intimately tied to landholding, and that landholding was inextricable from service to the king—even if such Norman changes amounted to a fundamental transformation of social relations. On the other hand, it was viscerally satisfying to be able to take the realization that the world had been profoundly altered and *embody* it, dwelling upon differences in grooming, customs, and language—that is, in race—as a way of comprehending the exclusions and inclusions upon which access to status had been newly built.

Assimilation born of intermarriage and cultural osmosis would lessen these differences over time. Yet distinctions between the regnant French and the subaltern English became entrenched, receding only slowly. Thus Aelred of Rievaulx could write ca.1163 of those who still deeply (*maxime*) lamented the disappearance of the English aristocracy (*Anglorum nobilitatem*), bewailing the fact that their descendants were not the realm's current king, earls, bishops, or abbots.[42] Daniel Donoghue has analyzed the lingering resentment that men like the English poet Laȝamon and his "dispossessed contemporaries" must have felt a century after the advent of the Normans as they contemplated their people's dwindled authority and prestige.[43] "Then came the Normans with their evil power," wrote Laȝamon of the conquest, late in the twelfth century, "They harmed this nation" (*Brut* 3547–48).

The city of Norwich was no exception. No doubt its economic vitality and strategic promise were what drew the Normans so quickly. By the early twelfth century, Norwich had been so completely transformed that it bore little resemblance to its former self. In 1066, the city was a conglomerate of three districts (Conesford, Coslany, and Westwick) that together formed a unified borough. Its residents spoke a single language, the Norfolk dialect of English, possessed of a lexicon that revealed that the Danes who had settled in the area had been absorbed but not wholly forgotten.[44] As a result of the conquest, this unity shattered. Conesford was cut off from Coslany and Westwick when a "foreign zone" was implanted in the city's midst.[45] With its ponderous stone buildings and demarcative walls, this new area rendered Norwich suddenly quadripartite. The Normans fragmented the urban topography, isolating the most important English district in order to disempower all three indigenous quarters. In so doing they quickly exerted a military, financial, ecclesiastical, and symbolic dominance over all of Norwich. James Campbell, the foremost historian of the medieval city, has observed that the Normans changed more urban topography in five decades than their successors were able to alter in five centuries.[46] This forced metamorphosis was accomplished through the agency of what (in homage to the philosophers Gilles Deleuze and Félix Guattari) might be called three *machines* or *assemblages*, gatherings of human and nonhuman elements into open but nonetheless ruthlessly efficient structures of alliance.[47] These machines were geographical and architectural as well as social. They consisted of a castle, a cathedral, and a new French borough.

The first step in the Norman colonization of the city, the castle-assemblage brought together massive earthworks, towering walls, disciplinary officers, and networks of authority and privilege. Though carved from Norwich itself, its gaze did not for the most part look inward toward the city but swept across Norfolk and Suffolk, its eye turned always toward London. A local outpost of the king's wide-reaching power, this machine was connected mainly to other royal assemblages, the monarch's court, Norman castles elsewhere, and the emergent mythologies of the nation. Meanwhile a cathedral-assemblage brought together a relocated East Anglian see, a bishop and his palace and his extensive episcopal holdings, a priory, a new foundation of Benedictine monks, and a sprawling jurisdiction exempt, like the castle fee, from any dues or taxes the city might impose. The cathedral-machine was beholden in part to the king. Domesday records that William the Conqueror had given land in Norwich for the cathedral to be built upon; Herbert de Losinga, founder of the city's cathedral, purchased his bishopric from William's son, prompting William of Malmesbury to quote a contemporary poem about Herbert that ended "O the injustice of it! Bishop and abbot are made by money!" (*History of the English Kings* 4.338). Yet the cathedral could be a place of monarchal defiance, as when Herbert later sought absolution for his simony from a pope that the throne had yet to recognize.[48] The cathedral was, moreover, often in direct competition with the royal imperatives animating the castle, especially regarding jurisdictional reach.[49]

Norwich's cathedral-machine was connected to ecclesiastical assemblages in Canterbury, Normandy, and Rome. Like them, it promulgated with variable degrees of conviction a transnational and supposedly universal code for the governing of the body that could be at odds with the values of the castle-assemblage and of the local parish church system. The latter might be described in turn as a "parochial-assemblage," bringing together mainly indigenous priests attached to a galaxy of small churches. Compared to the English parish and chapel-based priests, their counterparts in the cathedral and the Norman parish churches were substantially wealthier and more likely to be celibate. The monks who staffed the cathedral, for example, lived among (in the words of William of Malmesbury) "imposing, uplifting buildings" and "beautiful ornaments," the aesthetic trappings of Norman affluence.[50] The cathedral priory, moreover, possessed an educational apparatus that was quickly capable of producing new leaders for East Anglia. Trained there was William Turbe, bishop of Norwich from 1146–1174 and partisan of Saint William's burgeoning cult. Herbert de Losinga's surviving letters make it amply clear that he took an enthusiastic personal interest in the education of the monastery's youth.[51]

Finally, overlapping and to an extent competing with castle and cathedral (and contending as well with Norwich's native secular assemblages) was a new civic-machine, a Norman borough whose mainly French-speaking citizens possessed their own provincial and national aspirations, their own legal rights, their own economic, political, and corporeal desires. Eventually christened Mancroft, this borough recentered Norwich, shifting the city's economic and social gravity through the introduction of a new marketplace. Composed of heterogeneous elements, the castle, cathedral, and civic assemblages were riven by their own inner conflicts.[52] Herbert de Losinga had the king's support as the building of the cathedral progressed, but he did not find that same enthusiasm expressed by the monks who were its staff.[53] A similar internal rift will be seen in the battle over the sanctification of the boy William, when the bishop of Norwich and the monk Thomas will be opposed by the monastery's prior, Elias. Yet internal conflicts did not hinder these three machines from profoundly reordering social and private life in the city of Norwich, perhaps not least because they were so intimately connected, often in surprisingly complicated ways. To give but one example taken from the *Life of St. William*: Simon de Novers, a local noble accused of ordering the death of the moneylender Eleazar, turns out to be the mesne tenant of Bishop Turbe, giving the cathedral's head another reason to insist upon the wickedness of the city's Jews and the sacredness of the dead child.

Each of the three Norman assemblages found concrete expression in massive architectural structures. One reason for the military success of the Normans was their perfection of the art of quickly constructing wood and stone castles upon land they wished to claim, rendering it difficult to force them to leave once they had set up housekeeping.[54] The Bayeux tapestry depicts the Conqueror's army, having just disembarked at Pevensey, frantically erecting *ceastra*. Already crowned king of England and desirous of inhabiting London, William was forced to bide his time in Barking while (in the words of William of Poitiers) "fortifications were being completed in the city as a defense against the inconstancy of the numerous and hostile inhabitants." The structure that would be known as the White Tower was William's lasting mark on London's cityscape. It was quickly joined by at least two other Norman castles.[55] Orderic Vitalis described castles as the surest way for William to secure control of not only individual cities but his entire kingdom:

> The fortifications called castles by the Normans were scarcely known in the English provinces, and so the English—in spite of their courage and love of fighting—could put up only a weak resistance to their enemies . . . William appointed strong men from his Norman forces as guardians of the castles, and distributed rich fiefs that induced men to endure toil and danger to defend them.[56]

Perhaps these edifices made such a vivid impression because English nobles had traditionally relied upon walled settlements and fortified manor-houses as defensive works. Such structures must have seemed pathetically meager in the lengthening shadow of a rising motte and bailey castle, a construction that typically consisted of an expansive, flat-topped mound of earth (motte); a large, fenced-in courtyard (bailey); a series of defensive ditches; and, crowning the summit of the earthwork, a tower that could serve as lookout, lodging, and last line of defense. They required only a small force to be manned effectively, and were extremely useful for exerting control over a subject population who outnumbered their new masters. The Normans could erect a simple version of such a structure in a little more than a week. Over time the defenses would be shored up and timber fortification might be replaced by stone.

Although the Normans did not invent the castle, they perfected its speedy strategic deployment. The relation between castle-building and the Norman colonization of the land deeply impressed the English, as the *Anglo-Saxon Chronicle* entries for 1067 make clear. Once William returned to Normandy, we are told, his men Bishop Odo of Bayeux and Earl William fitz Osbern "built castles far and wide throughout the country, and distressed the wretched folk."[57] The obituary for King William in the Peterborough Chronicle begins with the declarative *Castelas he let wyrcean* ["He had castles built"], prompting Seth Lerer to observe the following:

> From these first words, the poem signals a new architectural, political and linguistic order in the land. Castles were foreign to the Anglo-Saxons, who did not build monumentally in dressed stone but in timber or flint. The word itself, a loan from Norman French, makes clear the immediate impress of Norman life on English soil, as if the very vocabulary of institutional rule had changed with the Conqueror's coming.[58]

The Normans erected hundreds of castles across the island. As they rose in their multitudes, these fortifications served not only as strategically useful havens for occupation garrisons, but also as exorbitant visual reminders of the change in kingly and aristocratic authority. Castles enabled new structures of governance and regulation to be imposed.[59] A Norman strategy for military as well as symbolic domination, castles ensured not only that England belonged to the Normans and their allies, but that their subject population possessed an enduring declaration of this fact.

At some time during the decade after Hastings, a typical motte and bailey castle was erected in Norwich, the first step in the architectural transfiguration of the city. The fortress appears to have been built adjacent to what had been since the middle Saxon period an especially densely populated area.[60] Constructed initially of wood, the castle included palisades, two baileys, and a keep, and it was perched upon a partly natural, partly man-made mound more than sixty feet high. The structure was expansive enough to obliterate its immediate urban surroundings, and enters the textual record through Lanfranc, William's replacement for the deposed Stigand. The archbishop of Canterbury composed a letter reporting to his absent king on the rebellion of Ralph Guader. Installed under the Normans as Earl of East Anglia, Ralph failed rather miserably at his attempted insurgence. As a result, the castle at Norwich ceased to function as a baronial fortress (if that is what it was) and became thenceforth a royal possession. Thus when King Henry held his Christmas court in Norwich in 1121, the castle would have served as a suitably sumptuous residence for his itinerant household.[61] When not inhabited by the king, however, the castle was the home and center of operations for the sheriff of Norfolk and Suffolk. This powerful agent of royal authority was destined to be in frequent conflict with the citizens of the city, since his political allegiances were not civic but national. Though the office of sheriff could be inherited, its possessors proved just as changeable in their loyalties as the earls.[62]

Archbishop Lanfranc's letter on Ralph Guader's rebellion mentions in passing that the *castrum Noruuich* could by 1075 harbor three hundred *loricati* (heavily armed mounted knights) as well as "a large force of slingers and siege engineers."[63] At twenty-three acres, more than 10 percent of the size of Norwich itself, the castle was immense. The mound its munitions sat upon was the largest in England.[64] Around 1100, the castle's central tower was already being remade in stone, a sign both of its strategic importance and of the city's enduring prosperity.[65] Much of this stone originated in Normandy. Although it is hypothetically possible that the Normans built the castle with their own manpower, given the sheer size of the structure it is likely that residents of the city and its environs participated in its erection.

Whether they were forced, bribed, or agreed willingly to assist in the massive project is unknown.

A royal jurisdiction set apart from the rest of Norwich until 1345, the castle Fee, as the area of the fortification came to be called, provided royal administrators such as sheriffs and tariff collectors a secure area in which to conduct the king's business and to store the wealth and livestock they had confiscated. The separateness of the Fee may have been emphasized by a circumscriptive series of posts bearing the king's arms, a visual boundary to separate the castle's jurisdiction from city.[66] The castle's mound, ditches, walls, and edifices not only dominated the urban landscape but obstructed the approach to Norwich from the older settlements. The castle was surely in part a defensive structure, but its strategic position in Norwich makes it clear that the building's primary function was to dominate visually and symbolically an essential East Anglian city associated with the Godwinesons, the English family who had been bitter enemies not only of William the Conqueror but of all things Norman.

Just to the north and east of this edifice soon rose the impressive Romanesque cathedral that looms over Norwich to this day. This immense Norman building implanted at the city's heart further transfigured Norwich, immuring a large area and towering watchfully over the rest. Conesford was now effectively cut off from the rest of the town, with direct access possible only through the constricted opening between the edge of the castle fee and the beginning of the cathedral precincts, an architectural circumstance that shifted mercantile activity to the more easily reached market in the French borough. Well-defined and self-contained worlds, both castle and cathedral were built with formidable barricades and other defenses to control who could pass into their limits. This exclusionary function is seen most clearly in the castle, with its palisades and ramparts, but can also be glimpsed in the cathedral. Precinctual walls separated the church, monks and monastery from the city, while at the episcopal palace a defensive structure, East Anglia's first stone keep, securely ensconced the bishop. The proliferation of steep walls and ever-ascending towers began to overshadow the suddenly modest buildings that had been the English settlement. Norman structures, royal and ecclesiastical, forced a city long accustomed to spreading along a horizontal plane of sight to begin to reconceptualize urban space as sharply vertical.

Even the materials from which these edifices were fabricated would have seemed an alien presence: white slabs of limestone that shimmered in the sunlight, their ethereal coloration counterweighted by the sheer mass of each component block. The Normans on both the continent and in England were enamored of substantial stone constructions that hearkened back to the architecture of imperial Rome. Before the erection of the cathedral and its close (and, later, the stone replacement of parts of the castle, such as its central keep), there had never been a construction project in Norwich undertaken on such massive scale or utilizing such stone. The arrival of the raw materials for the Norwich projects must have been breathtaking. Some of the limestone derived from Barnack in Northamptonshire, a favorite Norman quarry, and some was imported from Caen. After departing its native Normandy and crossing the sea, this latter stone would have been shipped up the River Wensum and then through a specially cut canal to the cathedral site, where masons and other laborers went about their noisy work.

The cathedral church of the Holy and Undivided Trinity and its walled precinct were the crowning achievement of Herbert de Losinga, the ambitious Norman who held the see from 1091 to 1119. Although the precise origin of *Losinga* is not known for certain, William of Malmesbury wrote that Herbert obtained his surname "because of his skill in flattery" (*lusingare* is Italian for "to flatter"), an indication that this ambitious man was especially good at getting his way through his verbal dexterity.[67] Herbert's letters, many of which survive, reveal a writer enamored of the expressiveness of Latin, a mind that has mastered wide-ranging classical and biblical materials, and a cleric who took his pastoral charge seriously. Previously the prior of Fécamp in Normandy, Herbert gained lasting notoriety by purchasing from William Rufus the bishopric of East Anglia for himself and an abbacy for his father. Herbert moved the episcopal seat from Thetford to Norwich, a relocation William of Malmesbury describes as attractive because Norwich was "famous for its trade and large population" (*Deeds of the Bishops* 74) and "a busy (*insignem mercimoniis*) and populous town" (*History of the English Kings* 4.338). With its castle and thriving French borough, Norwich offered access to wealth, prestige, and urbanity. With its proximity to river and sea, it also enabled the importation of stone to initiate the grand building projects Herbert so loved.

Although Herbert's career reveals a penchant for self-dramatization and occasional opportunism, William of Malmesbury preferred to see in the bishop's life a model for turning from initial sin to redemptive works. His teary-eyed Herbert declares at his arrival in Norwich, "I confess my coming here has been bad, but with God's grace helping me my going hence shall be good" (*Deeds of the Bishops* 74). William spoke reverently of the beauty of the buildings that Herbert erected. A Benedictine monk himself, William of course singled out the monastic edifices: "Finally, how can I weave into my work fitting praise for Herbert's action, as a bishop without much money, in making the monastery so magnificent that nothing was missing, neither imposing, uplifting buildings, nor beautiful ornaments, nor God-fearing monks who showed concern and charity towards all" (*Deeds of the Bishops* 74). Herbert imported not only the stone and the monks to fabricate his cathedral, moreover, but transplanted the cathedral's liturgical customs from his home monastery in Normandy as well. Anyone of native blood entering the cathedral would be well aware that its walls enclosed a cultural space very different from what was to be experienced in English monasteries or parish churches.[68]

Monastic cathedrals in which a bishop took the place of the abbot were an English custom retained and amplified by the Normans.[69] Some of the monks attached to the cathedral in Norwich were drawn from the local population, English and Norman descended alike. Among the local monks were Richard, the son of Bishop William de Beaufeu by his wife Agnes; and later Robert, the brother of Saint William and an important figure in the legal proceedings over his death.[70] Yet despite the odd Briton and the more numerous English in their monasteries, the Benedictines were an order especially well populated by Normans. Eric Fernie has argued that the importance of the order to the advancement of the conquest cannot be underestimated: "Monasteries were an integral part of the system of government, important as schools for servants of Church and State, with the king appointing abbots and priors, treating their estates as his own and using them as the chief means of reforming the English Church."[71] William the Conqueror's dying words were, according to Orderic Vitalis, an acknowledgment that the Benedictine monasteries that had proliferated during his reign were the fortresses through which the Normans had been made strong.[72] The bishops, abbots, and priors who ruled over these Benedictines were, inevitably, Normans. That the inhabitants of the priory enjoyed a wealth and prestige that the impoverished parish churches did not is indicated by the size of their grounds and the extent of their holdings. Monastic lands were so expansive that they engulfed the city's limits. According to James Campbell, Herbert de Losinga

> built not only a great cathedral but also a very considerable ecclesiastical empire and turned the hitherto poor see of East Anglia into a power in the land. The consequences of his success for Norwich were lasting. Besides establishing a powerful monastery with franchisal jurisdiction within the city, he acquired the greater part of the rural environment of Norwich for the church.[73]

No wonder, then, that Neil Batcock has labeled Herbert's policy of stamping his authority across county and diocese "episcopal imperialism."[74] Another version of this imperialism can be glimpsed unfolding inside the walls of Herbert's cloister. A series of letters written by the bishop to various youths of the Norwich monastery survives, letters in which Herbert reveals his concern to discipline the young men bodily (warning them against spending money given by their parents on games, and "useless articles of self-indulgence") and intellectually (enjoining them to toil in their acquisition of Latin, admonishing against the reading of Ovid and Virgil). As a good monk and an enthusiastic teacher, Herbert's ambition was to mold these youthful subjectivities in such a way that their primary attachment would be to cathedral and cloister, not to family and city.[75]

Herbert was forced to purchase a considerable portion of Norwich in order to fulfill his dream of erecting an elegant and immense cathedral. Twenty-four houses were held already by 1086, but they constituted "a fraction of those to be swallowed up within the Cathedral Close after 1096."[76] Nor was it simply houses that vanished as this architecture burgeoned. The cathedral's ecclesiastical and monastic structures required the destruction of native churches and civic space. Through Norman expansion the English city lost its original meeting place and market, thought to have been located at the open space referred to as Tombland. The death knell had probably been sounded for this vital area when the entrance to the castle fee was located facing the new French borough, allowing Norman traffic to bypass the English commercial and civic area in favor of the amenities of Mancroft. The reconfiguring of Tombland through the encroachment of the cathedral would have hastened the process of dissolving a center of indigenous community. At least two parish churches, St. Michael Tombland and Holy Trinity, were also demolished. Standing adjacent to the original market, St. Michael Tombland was the wealthiest church of the pre-conquest city. The cathedral's imported stone sits atop the ruined pieces of the English church to this day. A beautiful crucifixion scene carved from walrus ivory was discovered when underground lavatories were dug at the site in 1878. The piece is now held by the Victoria and Albert Museum, and only hints at the glory that St. Michael may have possessed.

The Benedictine priory that spread into Tombland was large enough to house at its full occupancy no less than sixty monks. It may have been founded with something more than the needs of the cathedral in mind. R. B. Dobson sees the Benedictines who established themselves in England after 1066 as part of the process of colonizing and holding the land, at least in the north: "Norman kings and magnates were well aware that the foundation of new monasteries was a useful method of consolidating power in regions under territorial dispute or of doubtful allegiance."[77] These words may have proven equally true of Norwich, a city that may at one time have housed the palace of the pre-conquest earls of East Anglia. A structure that would have served as an urban residence for a pre-coronation Harold Godwinson (among other members of his family), the palace was supposed to have been located at Tombland, and was perhaps destroyed to build the cathedral.[78] That the city's sympathies leaned toward the Godwinsons is suggested by the fact that in 1065 the ill-fated King Harold owned a soke in Norwich with 32 burgesses, while another 1,238 Norwich burgesses lived on land that Harold owned jointly with Gyrth Godwineson, his brother and successor as Earl of East Anglia.[79] If the earls of East Anglia did maintain a palace near Tombland, it may have been Gyrth's residence that was destroyed.[80] Erecting a grandiose cathedral and carving away a section of the city's economic heart through the walls of the priory's close made it clear that the city's Norman future was to be very different from its English past.

Construction of the cathedral began in 1096, two years after Herbert de Losinga moved the episcopal seat from Thetford to Norwich. The church, its monastery, and the bishop's palace were completed less than fifty years later, during the reign of Eborard (1121–1145). Enough of the cathedral had been finished by 1101 to consecrate the building and place its roofed section into use. Herbert provides an energetic portrait of the massive labor required and the sheer scope of the project in a letter complaining about the slow pace of its progress. He reproves the lack of enthusiasm from his own monks while acknowledging the help of the king's men:

> But alas! The work drags on; and in providing materials you show no enthusiasm. Behold, the servants of the king and my own are really earnest in the works allotted to them, gather stones, carry them to the spot, when gathered, and fill with them the fields and ways, the houses and courts; and you meanwhile are asleep with folded hands, numbed, as it were, and frost-bitten by a winter of negligence, shuffling and failing in your duty through a paltry lack of ease.[81]

As the "fields and ways, the houses and courts" were transformed into stone edifices, the cathedral was joined by an episcopal palace to its north and priory to its south. What the native inhabitants of the city thought of this transformation is unrecorded, but can be guessed at: ambivalent at best, aggrieved and resentful in many cases, grudgingly appreciative in others.[82] It may not have helped that work on the cathedral's Caen stone was apparently being overseen by royal masons ("servants of the king" in Herbert's letter) rather than locals, ensuring that the cathedral shimmered as a "cosmopolitan rather than provincial" monument.[83] Although it is not possible to know with certainty what the Norwich natives felt about their changed cityscape, when taking into account the difficult (and sometimes deadly) relations between cathedral and town later in history, it does seem unlikely that early relations were anything less than vexed.

The new cathedral functioned as the mother church for the Norwich parishes. As a Norman institution, however, it was more internationally focused than any of its parochial communities could ever be. There is nothing local in the cathedral's conceptualization, authorization, or design, and little of Norwich itself present in its walls. The edifice rose at the expense of native buildings and disrupted an established way of life; the space it occupied had been torn from the city and immured against it; though spoken in comfortable Latin, the actual liturgy celebrated inside was unfamiliar to the English denizens of the town; even the architectural style of the cathedral and its precincts was foreign to the island, as William of Malmesbury pointed out more generally of the massive Norman edifices erected after the conquest, looming in alien majesty above the English landscape.[84] The new church's national and international orientation, as well as its disregard for its local context, is also exhibited in its sheer immensity. Norwich was a big city by contemporary standards, but it did not have a population that required a building as large as St. Peter's in Rome.[85]

Herbert located his episcopal palace and a chapel alongside the cathedral, and built the monastery of St. Leonard's and two hospitals as well.[86] Though none of these buildings matched the ambition or scale of his cathedral project, each in turn transformed another swathe of unassuming timber and masonry into a stone monument to the conquest's permanence. The construction of the cathedral has been described as "wounding" and "devastating" to the city, especially because it was sited in a densely populated urban area and appears to have destroyed the existing configuration of streets.[87] With the castle, the cathedral carved about 50 acres from English Norwich, a city that extended about 200 acres to begin with.[88] Thus Eric Fernie describes the two structures as together "obliterating the centre of the old town."[89] The addition of a French borough brings the Norman occupation of the Anglo-Saxon city up to almost half its total area.[90] Roads, churches, and houses vanished, replaced by prohibiting walls, structures built in nonnative styles and of nonindigenous materials, the habitations and workplaces of foreigners. The Normans, it seemed, were colonizing not just the city's flat expanses but the very sky:

> The cathedral must have been a staggering sight in the context of contemporary buildings in Norfolk and Suffolk. In the mid 1090s the architectural landscape consisted mainly of wooden structures, whether houses or churches of high and low status, defences . . . and some small masonry churches.[91]

No doubt the castle and cathedral, looming in monumental splendor above the suddenly tiny wood and masonry structures of the city, functioned like the jar imagined by Wallace Stevens which when placed on a hill in Tennessee "took dominion everywhere," reorienting the world by forcibly introducing in its midst an overwhelming visual ordering principle.[92]

The difficulties between the rebellious Earl Ralph Guader and the king illustrate well another tension affecting all these assemblages: the relationship between aristocracy and monarch. The Anglo-Normans and their allies inherited from their forebears across the channel a sense of political community that stressed the interdependence of subject and king, with "individuals [within this community] replaceable and manipulable, as was their chairman-king."[93] Ralph will revolt and be displaced, while future regents will struggle to maintain their leadership in the face of powerful peers. The new borough of Norwich will be profoundly influenced by the fortunes of both—as well as by the ambitions of the cathedral, and so forth—since it is straightforwardly controlled by none. It perhaps did not help that Ralph was not a Norman in a Norman-dominated regime; he was part Breton, and many of his followers were from Brittany.[94] That Ralph's men were allowed to depart the siege of Norwich castle "with limbs" (as Archbishop Lanfranc put it in his letter) was taken as a great mercy. After all, the rebel Bretons of Winchester were, in the same year, blinded and maimed.[95]

Ralph was the first post-conquest Earl of East Anglia. By agreeing to share his land with King William, he was able to create from his holdings near the castle the French borough. This settlement was probably introduced in tandem with the castle, since they appear to be contemporaneous. The creation of an entirely new borough populated by Normans and their allies was unprecedented. Only Nottingham saw a similar borough implanted among its English population. By 1096, this Norman settlement supported a thriving market, destined to put out of business its suddenly inconvenient native counterpart at Tombland. The arrival of nonindigenous flora in this reconfigured city suggests vividly the changes in its orientation, connections, and appetites. Seeds found in the medieval debris of the city are the first instances of marigolds and hops in England, while the shell of a walnut is the first known reimportation of the food on the island since the departure of the Roman legions.[96] After Ralph's rebellion in 1075 the new borough, like everything the earl owned, was seized by the crown and remained royal property thereafter. Protected by the fortress and in the elongating shadow of the cathedral, the *novus burgus* (new borough) was quickly settled by French-speaking immigrants (Domesday Book calls them *Franci de Norwic*) whose ambition it was to take advantage of the city's booming economy.[97] This community was eventually called Mancroft, a word that hints that it had been formed in part from the English city's common grazing area. St. Peter Mancroft, a Norman church likely founded by

Earl Ralph himself, was destined to eclipse in importance all other parish churches in the city. In 1086, there were 125 inhabitants in the borough, of which at least 41 were French burgesses. In the space of ten years it added at least 90 new French burgesses and possibly many more, illustrating its steady growth. If these burgesses were similar to those who settled Battle, they would likely be mostly craftsmen and administrators.[98]

Norman redevelopment was often ruinous for the native population of the towns in which it occurred. In Ipswich, the English citizens were reduced to *pauperes burgenses* (impoverished burgesses). The French borough in Norwich flourished at the expense of the ravaged English city. Things were so desperate that, according to Domesday, the number of English burgesses fell from 1,320 in 1066 to 665 twenty years later. Even as the English population dwindled, taxes increased sharply, placing a growing burden on those who remained. Most of the "disappearing" English burgesses had probably lost their status due to financial ruin. Thirty-two of them are known to have fled, and Domesday notes that "those fleeing and the others remaining have been utterly ruined [*vastati*]." Almost 300 Norwich houses are described as destroyed or empty in 1086—and, as Alan Carter has noted, Domesday generally "minimizes the significance of the devastation in the English borough."[99] The reasons listed for the devastation of Norwich's citizenry are manifold: Earl Ralph Guader's forfeiture following his rebellion; damaging fires; and the activities of Waleran, an official of the king who held the city in fee, paying the royal dues for Norwich and then farming the tax (that is, collecting what money he could from the city's population to make up what he had paid the crown and to clear a profit for himself). Through these and other catastrophes much English land in the city passed into alien hands. It is important to keep in mind that Domesday was composed after the construction of the castle and the new borough but before work on the cathedral had begun. As bad as things were for the English of Norwich twenty years after the conquest, they would grow worse.

The Norman parvenus were clearly not welcomed with open arms by the inhabitants of the older sections of the city, for they had to be provided with their own sheriff, an officer of the king charged with protecting their bodies and their interests. That royal officers were necessary to inhibit what could become deadly antagonism is also made clear by William the Conqueror's declaration of the *murdrum* fine, the sum of money that was levied against the English inhabitants of any district in which a Norman was found dead by unknown hands.[100] At its worst this ethnic hatred could manifest itself in group violence, such as the disturbance that erupted in London at Michaelmas in 1130. Thirteen men of English and Norman descent were fined *pro assaltu navium et domorum Londoniae*, an incident that

Stenton describes as "a riot on a considerable scale."[101] Cecily Clark points out that some indication that French and English "did not always live in the closest harmony" is also provided by the fact that Domesday records thirty-six Frenchmen initially sharing the new borough in Norwich with six Englishmen, but by 1086 the English had been replaced by five Frenchmen.[102] Although the civic-assemblage of this *novus burgus* was destined to merge with native (Anglo-Scandinavian) structures of urban sociality to create a secular, amalgamated Norwich, the townspeople would long exist in an uneasy relationship with both the castle and the cathedral. Indeed, tensions between citizens and ecclesiasts were destined to explode later in the town's history, culminating in a deadly attack against the fortified cathedral and its priory in 1272.[103]

In short, post-Conquest Norwich found its cultural, economic, political, and linguistic cohesiveness torn as an alien presence was forcibly implanted at its heart. The city was irreparably split between the heterogeneous and competitive Norman machines (castle, cathedral, borough)—united most by their shared language of French—and an older collection of native assemblages (urban and agrarian settlements, parish church structures, even a priestly sex/gender system that varied rather remarkably from the one that obtained in the Norman section of town). A dominated majority, the English-speaking and Anglo-Scandinavian descended population of Norwich now struggled to compete economically, juridically, and symbolically with these uninvited entities in its midst.

Things Fall Apart

Medieval as well as Contemporary history has proven that Norwich is a resilient City. No cataclysm has ever so set it back that it could not recover. An economist would no doubt speak of the city's vitality, of its enduring health. Yet unlike a fire, bombing, or riot, the Norman Conquest broke upon the city in waves, some small and subtly erosive, others with full tidal force. The castle was in place by 1075 when Earl Ralph rebelled, because the king's forces lay siege to it at that time. Thus we know that a decade after Hastings at least a hundred houses had been lost and the city now had huge earthwork and a series of timber fortifications peering watchfully over its expanses. The new French borough was implanted at about this time. It grew rapidly and immediately challenged the vitality of the English districts. Thirty years after the conquest, perhaps at the same time as the wooden castle was being replaced with a stone edifice, the cathedral and its close began to rise. Houses were demolished, native churches fell, walls and monastic buildings appeared, transforming what had been open space and modest habitations into soaring, monumental stone. Norwich harbored the kind of heterogeneity in tempestuous admixture that Gerald of Wales embodied in figures like the Ox Man of Wicklow, a body irresolvably at war with itself.

The next chapter examines a heinous murder that occurred just outside the city in 1144, at a time when the Norman building projects that had so transformed Norwich were at last coming to their end. Norwich was assuming the contours it would retain for centuries thereafter. At this critical period in the mid-twelfth century, at a time when what had been a deeply divided population was finally growing into an urban community, it became necessary for Norwich to imagine itself as not just unhealthy but as imminently imperiled. In the mid-twelfth century, a city that had been fragmented after the conquest was starting to feel the possibility of imagining itself a harmonious and integrated entity again. A turbulently hybrid expanse was on the verge of embracing a newly purified communal identity. This emergent vision of unity, however, demanded both a new monster and a ceaseless flow of blood.

CHAPTER 5

THE FLOW OF BLOOD IN NORWICH

Local Mythologies

A few decades after Geoffrey of Monmouth completed his *History of the Kings of Britain*, another cleric who likewise christened himself *Monemutensis* produced a text similarly obsessed with collective identity, blood, history, community, and monsters. Thomas of Monmouth composed the *Vita et passio sancti Willelmi martyris Norwicensis* (known in English as the *Life and Miracles of St William of Norwich*) while attached to the Benedictine priory supporting Norwich cathedral. Whereas Geoffrey dedicated his *History* to powerful nobles of international renown, Thomas addresses the *vita* to William Turbe, the bishop of Norwich who had previously been a member of the cathedral's monastery.[1] Whereas Geoffrey's epochal narrative was preoccupied with nations and empires, Thomas aimed his saint's life at a local community. The text has been the subject of much penetrating scholarship over the years, most of it attempting to determine whether Thomas was the inventor of the blood libel, the myth that Jews murder Christians for ritualistic purposes.[2] Thomas was recording a mythology blossoming around a Norwich boy supposedly sacrificed at Jewish hands, a mythology so potent that it could be deployed a few years after William's death in northern France and the Rhineland (places intimately connected to Norwich through trade routes) in support of violence against Jews. Anti-Jewish sentiment was certainly an international phenomenon in the Middle Ages. Yet these stories told about the murdered William were also disseminated to achieve more circumscribed ambitions.

Having explored the penetrating effects of conquest on Norwich, I would now like to excavate from Thomas's *Life of St William* some of the tenacious traces of postcoloniality visible in the city around the time of the boy's mid-century death. I will suggest that the martyr becomes for

Thomas integral to the imagining of a purified collective identity for Norwich's discordant and heterogeneous populations. Thomas's text records, in polemical form, popular beliefs circulating within the city to which both monk and murdered boy belonged.[3] In promulgating a narrative centered upon innate Jewish desire to shed Christian blood, Thomas attempted to give authoritative form to a story that could bring into unity a Norwich long splintered by history. Though other contemporary sources allude to the martyrdom of William, only Thomas recounted the boy's death in any detail. His is also the only text to imagine secret Jewish rites occurring in the city and to describe the sanguinary flows supposed to have accompanied them.[4] In recording a lurid story that a group of Jews living in Norwich had crucified a young boy, a story that transformed his fellow French-speaking inhabitants of the town into an innately homicidal race, Thomas, like Bede, was purifying a dominant collective identity and disavowing the medial spaces where differences had already merged into intricate hybridities. In Norwich English and francophone worlds met in roiling confluence. It was a space that, it seemed, could be made placid simply by abjecting a people undeniably alien, even monstrous. The exclusion of the Jews would allow at last the emergence of a harmonious civic community in which historical antagonisms among the anglophone and francophone Christians of Norwich could be forgotten, the difficult middle that was post-conquest Norwich at last abandoned for a more certain future.

Or so Thomas of Monmouth dreamed.

The Body of Murdered William

Thomas of Monmouth's narration begins with the body of a child, a boy whose bruised and punctured flesh proclaimed the tortures to which he had been subjected. Such was the discovery made on March 24, 1144, when the holy woman Legarda and a forester named Henry de Sprowston made their separate way through Thorpe Wood, a dense swathe of trees and brush just outside the city. According to Thomas, both travelers came across a youth, dead for several days, dumped beneath the trees, "dressed in his jacket and shoes, his head shaved, and punctured with countless stabs" (*Life of St William* 1.10). Legarda and her companions watched as ravens attempted to devour the corpse, but the body proved invulnerable to beak and claw. Convinced that she had witnessed a miracle, Legarda returned home "rejoicing" (*gratulabunda*). She seems never to have mentioned her discovery to anyone else.[5] Henry de Sprowston later passed the same spot in his own travels. He immediately noted numerous wounds, and discovered that someone had placed in the boy's mouth a wooden "device of torture" (*ligneum tormentum*, in reality a teasel, a device for raising nap on cloth). Anxious to be home for Easter, Henry likewise left the cadaver where it lay. The body caused "strange excitement" throughout the city (1.12). Members of the community wandered into the trees to gaze upon the signs of abuse. On Easter Monday, Henry returned and buried the corpse beneath the tree on which it had at one point been hanging. Those present at the interment agreed that they could smell divine flowers, the odor of sanctity. The deceased was eventually identified as a twelve-year old named William, an apprentice leatherworker (*pelliparia*) who had vanished some days earlier.

William had disappeared during Holy Week at the hands of a mysterious stranger. Claiming to be a cook attached to the household of the archdeacon of Norwich, this man of unknown identity appeared at his mother's door and offered William a job. Even though she did not believe this imposter who begged to "make away" with her child (1.4), William's mother allowed him to take the boy after a payment of silver—just as, Thomas is quick to point out, Jesus was betrayed through monetary exchange. According to a young girl sent by William's aunt to spy on this louche cook, the boy was brought to the house of a prominent Jewish moneylender. A few days later, his maltreated body was discovered in the woods. In modern times we would not hesitate to blame the murder upon a pedophile or serial killer. Norwich in the twelfth century had no such prefabricated answer to the mystery of why the boy should have died so horribly. Perhaps not surprisingly, the monster deployed to make sense of this senseless act was the Jew.

Surveying the flourishing of the belief that Jews desecrated the Eucharistic, Miri Rubin writes that whereas the host represents Christian community, the Jews "carried difference in their bodies, in their rejection of Christian truths, in their palpable mundane otherness."[6] In mid-twelfth-century England, much of the mythology of ethical, bodily, and cultural deviance that would be so well established by the close of the Middle Ages had yet to be attached to the Jews.[7] Not yet notorious poisoners of wells nor spreaders of the plague, Jews had also still to be accused of forcibly circumcising or cannibalizing Christians. It had not yet been "discovered" that the key ingredient for matzo was innocent blood. The bodies of Jews need not be represented with hooked noses, large ears, horns, or a tail.[8] The decrees of the third and fourth Lateran Councils that Jews wear distinguishing clothes were still decades away. No claim had yet been advanced that Jewish men bled once a month like women, sanguinary proof of their difference from Christian somatic normalcy. Although the accusation that Jews murdered children as part of their religious rituals had been made in the past, the last time such a story circulated was seven centuries ago, in a text unknown in twelfth-century Britain.[9]

On the other hand, as John McCulloh has pointed out, when the Jews arrived in Norwich, probably in the early 1130s, negative expectations were already in circulation.[10] Herbert de Losinga once concluded a Christmas sermon with a story in which a Jewish father, enraged that his son has received communion, hurls the boy into an oven. The tale is meant to convey the triumphant power of the Virgin, who keeps the child safe from harm until Christians rescue him. Yet the narrative demonizes the Jewish father, who would rather incinerate his son than lose him to conversion. His punishment, along with that of coreligionists refusing baptism, is to be hurled into the fire himself. Herbert describes these deaths as "a most just vengeance on the heads of the Jews."[11] Another of the bishop's sermons, this time for Palm Sunday, speaks of Jewish malignity, perfidy, and deicide. The homily mentions Christ's rebuke of Jewish moneychangers in the Temple, and emphasizes Jewish responsibility for the crucifixion.[12]

Yet in the end we do not have any documentary evidence that the Jewish newcomers to Norwich were greeted with animus. When in the *vita* a Jew of the city is summoned to the nearby woods to meet the men of Simon de Novers, he rides a horse and carries a sword but brings no retinue, a sign of the safety he assumed when traveling among Christians. Perhaps the absence of widespread anti-Jewish feeling explains why when William's uncle, Godwin Sturt, proclaims at a diocesan synod that the Jews must have been responsible for his nephew's death, the accusation fails to arouse much outrage. While some citizens are sympathetic to Godwin, none are impassioned enough to commit those crimes that within a few decades will inevitably follow such allegations: the forced conversion or murder of Jews, the ransacking and destruction of their homes. Promoted mainly by Godwin and attracting only weak support from the city's bishop, William's incipient cult seems destined to become an early version of the sanctity abortively attached to John of Hampton, a participant in the plunder of Stamford's Jewish domiciles in 1190. According to William of Newburgh, John was murdered by a greedy accomplice and his body was abandoned. When signs and dreams convinced the local people that the corpse was sacred, the local clergy attempted to profit from its veneration. Bishop Hugh of Lincoln squelched the burgeoning movement, and the enthusiasm for the unlikely "martyr" quickly ebbed.[13] More innocent but no less unlikely a candidate for sanctification, William of Norwich was similarly buried and—despite the efforts of some supporters—the memory of his murder receded from public consciousness.

Thomas of Monmouth arrived on the scene around 1150, a monk attached to the cathedral priory. For unknown reasons he took an immediate interest in the dead boy and became an ardent lobbyist for his sanctity. His eventual reward was to be appointed the new saint's sacrist, responsible for the maintenance and continued honor of William's tomb. Several years after the events he describes, Thomas composed a narrative of William's suffering, death, and posthumous miracles, supposedly based upon eyewitness accounts.[14] Thomas appeared in Norwich at a particularly opportune time for the revival of Godwin's accusation. Servants of Simon de Novers had murdered a man named in the Latin text "Deus-adiuuet," probably an imprecise translation of the Hebrew name Eleazar, the richest Jew in the city and a moneylender to whom Simon was deeply indebted. William Turbe, the cathedral's third bishop and the man from whom Simon held his land, announced that no enquiry should proceed into the murder until the Jews were first brought to justice for William's death.[15] The city found itself sundered along ecclesiastical, regnal, and civic lines as the case was passionately argued and eventually brought before the king. Stephen left the affair unresolved by postponing judgment sine die (2.14). Thomas seems to have been living in Norwich within perhaps a year of these events and would therefore have found himself a new resident in an uneasy milieu.

The aftermath of William's murder mainly unfolds during the episcopacy of William Turbe, a Norman from the cathedral priory who—much against the wishes of Sheriff John de Chesney, the local agent of the throne—was elected by his fellow monks rather than nominated by the king. The first two bishops to reign from Norwich cathedral, Herbert de Losinga and the former royal chaplain Eborard (or Everard, as the name is sometimes written), were recipients of the seat through monarchical fiat. Bishop William was, unlike the men who preceded and followed him in office, neither a well-connected aristocrat nor a cosmopolitan royal administrator. Turbe had probably entered the monastery as child oblate. He seems to have been a protégé of Herbert himself. His ascension through the monastery's offices was a sign of his brethren's regard. Turbe had proven himself a vociferous critic of royal prerogative by opposing the will of Sheriff John and the justices over the prosecution of the Jews for William's murder. That Stephen had refused to dismiss the accusation and left the case without closure meant that the bishop and his obedient cathedral, united in a way they had not previously been, now had a unique opportunity.

"In the Tempest that was Stephen's Reign"

The first book of William of Newburgh's *History of English Affairs*, composed at the end of the twelfth century, envisions "real and recent blood" flowing at two traumatic historical moments: beneath the soil of Hastings, as a lasting reminder of the violence of the conquest, and in Ramsey Abbey, where it figures the turbulence brought by civil war during

Stephen's reign.[16] This blood runs down the walls of the formerly sacred space as if just shed, linking the turmoil of Stephen's tenure back to the conquest. The death of William of Norwich and the attempt to render him a saint unfolded during what was for England a tumultuous time, an era during which some of the progress that had been made in harmonizing the kingdom came undone. The author of the *Gesta Stephani*, loyal as he was to the crown, realized that during Stephen's reign long-buried traumas were being, quite literally, exhumed. When the rebel Geoffrey Talbot attacks the royal troops at Hereford, he drives the priests from the cathedral church and renders the ecclesiastical structure "a haunt of war and blood." In order to construct a defensive rampart for his forces, Talbot disinters a graveyard:

> The townsmen were uttering cries of lamentation . . . the earth of their kins-folk's graveyard was being heaped up to form a defensive rampart and they could see, cruel sight, the bodies of parents and relations, some half-rotten, some quite lately buried, pitilessly dragged from the depths. (1.53)

Like the bloody walls of Ramsey Abbey, the incident at Hereford is a reminder that even when the past seems laid to rest, fresh upheaval can revivify its pain. As a war for the throne erupted between Stephen and the Empress Matilda, England was forcefully reminded of the strife that had earlier divided its history and was having lingering effects now.

The line that Thomas of Monmouth employs to set the scene of the *vita* says it all: *Ea tempestate qua Regis Stephani florebat regnum, immo iusticia languente degenerabat*, "In the time [*tempestate*] when the reign of King Stephen was flourishing, or rather, in the decline of justice, was languishing" (2.10). *Tempestas* is a Latin noun that can innocuously designate "time" but also carries the meaning of "tempest" as well as "calamity." It is clear that Thomas means to play on all these possibilities to describe the unsettled nature of the kingdom.[17] Stephen was the nephew of Henry I and had taken the throne on his uncle's death. Despite Stephen's anointment by the archbishop of Canterbury, Henry's daughter Matilda was not willing to cede him the crown. Her disembarkation in England in 1139 precipitated nine years of unrest which, even if not as pandemic as medieval accounts indicate, were nonetheless deeply wounding to national solidarity. Questions of origin, history, and community that had faced the realm in the wake of the conquest resurfaced. Yet despite a resurgence of a bifurcated vocabulary for collective difference, seven decades of intermarriage and acculturation had permanently changed the realm. Normans and English had fused, precipitating hybridities that could not be decomposed. As we have seen repeatedly in this book, hybridity is not some third term that synthesizes two warring elements and renders them placid. Hybridity tends to remain a tumultuous, conflicted state, easily roiled by changes in social context. The turmoil Matilda and Stephen engendered induced not a return to binarism but a diffusely pervasive anxiety over the future shape of national community. In the words of John Gillingham, during Stephen's reign England's slow transformation into a united, "culturally homogenous island" was "halted, in some senses reversed, and in others profoundly transformed."[18] No province of England was immune to a perturbation that was as much psychological and social as visceral.

The city of Norwich was the site of a major siege. According to Henry of Huntingdon, the royal castle was occupied by Hugh Bigod, a future earl of Norfolk destined to be in frequent revolt against Stephen. When the king arrived to retake the fortification, Hugh released his prize with great reluctance: "So already the madness of the Normans," Henry wrote, "was beginning to spread, in faithlessness and treachery."[19] A version of the *Anglo-Saxon Chronicle*, composed at the monastery in nearby Peterborough, contains an extended visualization of the civil war's toll in human suffering and lives. In an entry dated 1137 but composed perhaps two decades later, the author condenses events that unfolded over a span of several years. This narrative compression attempts to convey, in retrospect, the unraveling of the kingdom's cohesion. Rebels against the monarch's authority

> oppressed the wretched people of the country severely with their castle-building. When the castles were built, they filled them with devils and wicked men. Then, both by day and night they took those people that they thought had any goods—men and women—and put them in prison and tortured them with indescribable torture to extort gold and silver—for no martyrs were ever tortured as they were. They were hung by their thumbs or by the head, and corselets were hung on their feet. Knotted ropes were put round their heads and twisted till they penetrated to the brains. They put them in prisons where there were adders and snakes and toads, and killed them like that. Some they put in a "torture-chamber" [*crucethus*] . . . I have neither the ability nor the power to tell the horrors nor all the torments they inflicted upon wretched people in this country; and that lasted nineteen years while Stephen was king, and it was always going from bad to worse.[20]

For ne uuœren nœure nan martyrs swa pined alse hi wœron. "for no martyrs were ever tortrued as they were." The narration continues for many more lines in a similar vein, an ever-dilating chronicle of rapine, sacrilege, murder, torture, anarchy. Violence against the bodies of the people is paralleled by violence against the land itself.[21] Populous villages empty; cultivated ground reverts to waste. Time seems to be spinning backwards as signs of humanity recede from the landscape, and humaneness vanishes from the country's powerful. The entry culminates in the following:

> The Jews of Norwich bought a Christian child before Easter and tortured him with all the torture that our Lord was tortured with; and on Good Friday hanged him upon a cross on account of our Lord, and then buried him. They expected it would be concealed, but our Lord made it plain that he was a holy martyr, and the monks took him and buried him with cere-mony in the monastery, and through our Lord he has worked wonderful and varied miracles, and he is called St. William.

William died in 1144, not 1137. The author of this portion of the chroni-cle places the murder here, it seems, because he perceives a link between those who were tortured "as no martyrs were ever tortured" and this boy tormented by Jews (the same Old English verb, *pined*, is used to describe the pains endured by the tortured English, the martyrs, and William). The knotted cord twisted about suffering heads, suspension upon beams, and perhaps the crucifixion reference implicit in the strange torture called the *crucet-hus* all seem to refer to William's death.[22] Though Thomas describes William as a victim of the Jews, for the Peterborough chronicler he is by association a victim of civil war. He becomes a figure for a nation that even though torn apart endures. *Sanct Willelm* serves as the perfect body with which to close the narrative of Stephen's reign because, once "buried with ceremony in the monastery," he offers the possibility of at last transcending a recurring dividedness.

In the preceding chapter I cited the opening line from an obituary poem provided by the same chronicler for William I, *Castelas he let wyrcean*. These structures function as powerful symbols of the sea change in island politics brought about by the Normans. As war tears the kingdom apart, castles rise to oppress the *earme men* in the entry for 1087, then the *uurecce men* in 1137. The latter entry brings us inside one of these structures, where we witness innocents crushed by rocks, strung on chains, miserably imprisoned. Through this architectural twinning, the *Peterborough Chronicle* makes clear that England has been returned to the worst days of the conquest, when the kingdom was so deeply divided that it seemed it would never again cohere. One of the few miracles to receive extended treatment by Thomas unfolds in the same horrifying space envisioned in such gruesome detail by the *Peterborough Chronicle*, a castle dungeon. Having earlier brought his readers inside a Jew's house where rather similar tortures are being blasphemously performed, Thomas later conveys them to a dank prison where a group of captives find themselves in a scene uncannily like that imagined in the chronicle:

There was, then, a woman of Brandney named Wimarc, who in the time of Stephen, when the days were evil, was given as a hostage at Gainsborough for her husband who had been taken by pirates. In his stead she was committed to prison with three other women and one man, and there she remained for long. These people, after long enduring miserably cold, hunger, stench, and attacks of toads, began to plan in concert the death of their gaoler. (6.13)

Toads in both the *Peterborough Chronicle* and the *vita* embody quite literally the poison of civil war. *Bufones* (Latin) or *pades* (English) were thought to be as lethal as adders. The prisoners in the *Life of St William* squeeze the venom from some of these amphibians to mix with the gaoler's drink. Suspecting treachery, he forces them to imbibe their concoction, and all but Wimarc perish. Her flesh swells grotesquely, to the point where her skin nearly tears. Once released from prison, for seven years Wimarc is possessed of the body not of a human being but of "some portentous new monster." A pilgrimage to William's shrine brings instant relief. She vomits the toad's venom over the pavement in front of the shrine ("there was enough of it to fill a vessel of the largest size") and is restored to her slender figure. The poisons of the past having been disgorged, Wimarc can cease to be a monster and settle back into the moderate contours of a regenerated body, all through the mediation of William.

Contemporary events may also be what provoke Thomas to connect Candlemas so strongly to the cult of William. The boy was born, we are told, on this day commemorating the purification of Mary (*Vita* 1.2). Perhaps not coincidentally, the celebration of Candlemas was infamously connected to Stephen's troubles. On that feast in 1141, against much advice to the contrary, the king decided to initiate hostilities at Lincoln, a disastrous campaign culminating in his capture and imprisonment. Henry of Huntingdon, Orderic Vitalis, and the *Gesta Stephani* record that when the bishop had given Stephen a burning candle to carry into mass that morning, the stick shattered and the flame was snuffed out—a portent, it was thought, of impending catastrophe.[23] For anyone who knew this widely disseminated story, the association of William with the Feast of the Purification and the burning of candles must have been a reminder of these bad days, now laid to rest at the martyr's peaceful tomb.

William's corpse was discovered in the spring of 1144, five years into the civil war. Norfolk tended to be securely royalist, with its sheriff John de Chesney supporting Stephen. Yet the bishop sided with Matilda, and Earl Hugh Bigod pledged himself to one side and then another, avoiding secure alliance.[24] Duress was compounded by devastating famines in 1150 and 1151. Thousands died of hunger and disease throughout England.[25] Stephen's reign was filled with crises: the contested crown, bloody Welsh resurgence, Scottish invasions into England, famine, plague, the rekindling of old worries about the inclusiveness of the English nation. These tempestuous times, difficult as they were to endure, seem to have assisted in the mid-century emergence of a new national unity.[26] William's cult begins to burgeon once Henry of Anjou, son of the Empress Matilda, has been accepted as successor to a suddenly heirless Stephen. Perhaps it is no coincidence that Thomas appears to have composed the first six books of his *Vita* shortly after Stephen's death, a period when the future of the realm looked increasingly more settled. The time was right for sorting out the new rules of exactly who is to belong to this emergent community, national and local.

Outsiders

The *Life of Saint William of Norwich* affords an extraordinary glimpse into the microdynamics through which these new possibilities for community proceeded. Though Thomas rhetorically embraces a national audience, speaking of an all-encompassing *Anglia* and an undifferentiated *Angli nostri* (I.Prologue), the narrative is an intended catalyst for struggles over *communitas* specific to *Norwicensem prouintiam* ("the parts about Norwich," 1.1). The *vita* is an activist text, envisioning a fractured and disharmonious urban collective as united in order to bring that harmonization about. The local and comparatively modest ambitions of the cult of St. William make it different in kind from the veneration of most other English saints, particularly East Anglian ones. James Campbell has demonstrated that the cults of the pre-conquest English saints were politically useful for their ability to bind nation to king, functioning as "nodes and links in a network which connected royal power to local piety over most of England."[27] William's cult demonstrates that revered bodies could become "nodal points" for communalizations profoundly uninterested in monarchs, epochal histories, and the stories nations tell to call themselves into being. My use of the adjective "local" to examine the relation between William and his fellow citizens of Norwich, moreover, should not obscure the fact that seemingly circumscribed communities are not necessarily any less internationally minded than, for example, nation-states.[28] The impression of Norwich that develops from the *vita* is at once provincial (minimal rhetoric connects the city to the kingdom) and global (the text demonstrates repeatedly that Norwich maintained important ties to the continent through trade and through its own citizenry, including the Jews).

A refreshingly recalcitrant boy in life, a rascal, the murdered William was transformed by Thomas and other supporters into the purest of saints, the first of many child martyrs imagined lost to Jewish torture. Thomas admits William's improbable sanctity from the start. When glimpsed in heaven he appears with "raiment . . . whiter than snow, and his face brighter than the sun, and upon his head there shown a golden crown, studded everywhere with precious stones" (2.4). This transfiguration into blinding purity and stunning opulence comes as quite a shock to many of those who actually knew William in life. Chief among the doubters of the boy's miracles, Thomas writes, are those residents of Norwich who remember him as *puerulum pauperculum pannosum* ("a poor, ragged little lad"). Perhaps as a result of familial poverty, William was training for a profession generally scorned because of the sheer nastiness of its materials: "this poor neglected little fellow [was] picking up a precarious livelihood at his tanner's business" (2.8). William possessed an adolescent's attraction to outsiders. His uncle, Godwin Sturt, and Wulward, the man with whom William lives, warn him not to associate with the Jews. Being a twelve-year-old boy, he promptly does just that, and the Jews return the affection by giving him extra business. Transforming this amicable relationship into homicide does not, Thomas knows, have textual precedent. Nor have the elaborate tortures to which the Jews supposedly submit William been previously enacted on anyone but Christ. Thomas must therefore constantly acknowledge his subject matter's evident unlikeliness. "If some things introduced in this book should seem to any improbable," Thomas writes defensively, "let him therefore not account me guilty of falsehood" (1.Prologue). The *vita* is therefore an extended argument, an account that envisions a community of believers partly in order to bring that community into being.

The proof of William's sanctity rest upon dreams, miracles, supernatural endorsements, and eyewitness narratives. No less an authority than Bishop Herbert de Losinga appears to Thomas to provide a founder's benediction for the boy's burgeoning cult, as if the cathedral had been built in anticipation of this newly arrived saint.[29] A Christian maid is located who formerly worked for the Jews. She announces that she peered through a crack in a door and watched as they gagged their young victim, pierced him with thorns, bound him with rope and nails to a cross-like structure, punctured his side all the way to the heart.[30] In a culminating moment that entangles the Norwich murder in an international conspiracy against Christians, a converted Jew from Cambridge named Theobald is introduced. He confides to Thomas that a Jewish tribunal in Narbonne yearly decides which of their far-flung communities will shed Christian blood.[31] In 1144, the

charge falls upon the Jews of Norwich, who obediently enact a ritual supposed to hasten their dispersed people's reunion:

> Theobald, who was once a Jew, and afterwards a monk . . . verily told us
> that in the ancient writings of his fathers it was written that the Jews, with-
> out shedding of human blood, could never obtain their freedom, nor could
> they ever return to their fatherland. Hence it was laid down by them in
> ancient times that every year they must sacrifice a Christian in some part of
> the world to the Most High God in scorn and contempt of Christ . . . as it
> was because of Christ's death that they had been sent from their own coun-
> try, and were in exile as slaves in a foreign land. Wherefore the chief
> men and Rabbis of the Jews who dwell in Spain assemble together at
> Narbonne . . . and they cast lots for all the countries which the Jews inhabit;
> and whatever country the lots fall upon, its metropolis has to carry out the
> same method with the other towns and cities . . . Now in that year in which
> we know that William, God's glorious martyr, was slain, it happened that the
> lot fell upon the Norwich Jews, and all the synagogues in England signified,
> by letter or by message, their consent. (2.11)

This worldwide conspiracy removes the Jews from local community by
placing their controlling cabal in a distant Elsewhere, transnationalizing in
order to exclude.

As Stephen Kruger has documented, Jews who became Christians were
imagined as ambivalent figures: "uncertainty [remained] about whether
religious conversion truly transformed bodies, cleansing them of their
impurities, repairing their imperfections . . . The convert remains somehow different, still of another people, *gens*, race than the Christian society
to which he is assimilated."[32] Anxieties about the fragility of Christian self-
identity might also be projected upon converted Jews. If a Jew were trans-
mutable into a Christian, might Christians be susceptible to becoming
something else, something that would sow further division in a world desperate for a vision of unified *Christianitas*? To find the Theobald, *ab hoste
conuerso* ("a converted enemy," as if *iudeus* and *hostis* were synonyms),
assisting in the promulgation of William's cult makes a certain amount of
sense, too, given England's experience that the line demarcating one *gens*
or *hostis* from another might, to the advantage of one group, be rendered
over time traversable, allowing *Franci* a transmutation into *Angli*.
Theobald's narrative of the Narbonne tribunal is meant to have the opposite effect for the Jews, rendering them permanent outsiders whose presence poses a bodily threat to Norwich's Christians. Theobald's hybridity is
supposed to promulgate a strict separation between two groups who in fact
commingle in him.

Blood

As the gory demand of the rabbinic cabal suggests, Thomas is fascinated throughout his text with sanguineous efflux. His Jews are characterized by desires that Thomas labels *innatus*, "inborn," and chief among these seems to be a hunger for Christian blood. They are described as *christianicidae iudei* and *sanguinis innocentis effusores*, "Christian-slaying Jews" and "shedders of innocent blood" (1. prologue; 1.16). William is meanwhile "crowned with the blood of glorious martyrdom" (*gloriosi sanguine martyrii laureatus*, 1.5). His birth is presaged by a dream in which his mother takes into her womb a fish with fins "red and as it were dabbled with blood" (*piscis . . . pinnas utrimque rubicundas et tanquam sanguine aspersas habebat*, 1.1). In 1144, Passover and Easter overlapped, so that while the Christians were contemplating the suffering, death, and redemptive blood of their messiah, the Jews are commemorating a sanguinary sign that once saved their firstborn from death. Returning from the synagogue on Wednesday, March 22, the Jews of Norwich slay William as if the murder were part of their observation of Pesach (1.5).[33] While William is eating a meal, they approach him from behind, hold him immobile, and insert into his mouth a wooden gag, the teasel that will one day be removed from his cadaver. A rope braided with knots is secured around his head, a makeshift crown of thorns. They shave his hair and perform a version of the scourging of Christ, stabbing repeatedly "with countless thorn-points" so that "blood came horribly from the wounds" (*inlictisque uulneribus miserabiliter cruentant*). To the physical tortures are added jeers and mockery. The spectacle culminates in a savage crucifixion:

> And thus, while these enemies of the Christian name were rioting in the spirit of malignity around the boy, some of those present adjudged him to be fixed to a cross in mockery of the Lord's passion, as though they would say, "Even as we condemned the Christ to a shameful death, so let us also condemn the Christian, so that, uniting the Lord and his servant in a like punishment, we may retort upon themselves the pain of that reproach which they impute to us."

The boy is bound to some cruciform beams, an architecture that (Thomas assures us) still bore the marks of its employ many years later when he entered the house to examine the sanctified timber. William's right hand and foot are tied to the beams, while his left limbs are transfixed by nails.[34]

In having the Jews reenact the passion of Christ as the Christians of Norwich are commemorating the same ancient drama in their churches and cathedral, Thomas imagines that, although more than a millennium separates the death of Christ from the martyrdom of William, both Christians and Jews remain locked in an unchanging enmity. The idea that the Jews as a people bear a blood guilt for the death of Christ has a long history that begins, intentionally or not, in the gospels. A Jewish crowd absolves Pontius Pilate of his role in the crucifixion of Jesus by declaring "His blood be upon us and on our children" (Matthew 27:25). Thomas will repeat this very line in the *vita* to condemn all Jews as culpable of deicide (2.15), broadening its scope to include those who, like Sheriff John de Chesney, sympathize with Jews. In Thomas's narrative, the Jews progress from slayers of Christ to slayers of Christians. Their reasoning is especially perverse—"so that we may retort upon themselves the pain of that reproach which they impute to us"—as if the crucifixion of William were payback against the Christians for the pain that Jews endure at the Christian taunt that they are primal crucifiers. The unfolding of the passion drama in Norwich effectively transforms Christian community into the fragile and endangered band of the faithful that they were in their earliest days, a nostalgic reimagining of the present that allows the history behind the formation of Herbert's cathedral, the priory in which Thomas writes, and all the other ecclesiastical power so evident in the city to simply vanish. As potential victims of a savage torture that unfolds not only in the vellum pages of the Bible but in the very bodies of contemporaries, the Christians of Norwich become as united as they are imperiled.

The Jews finally end the boy's life by inflicting a *uulnus acerbum* on William's left side, a wound reaching to his heart. As they puncture his crucified flesh, blood emanates in streams, "running down from all parts of his body" (*et quoniam per totum corpus plurimi sanguinis defluebant riui*, 1.5). Hot water must be brought to close his wounds and stop the spreading red stain from traveling through the house. As if the scene were not horrible enough in its first iteration, Thomas returns to it again in his second book. Here the crucifixion is vividly renarrated through the eyes of the maid spying on the Jews through a chink in the door. The episode culminates as the torturers frantically pour water upon the boy's injuries, unable to staunch the sanguinary flow (2.9).

A binding substance that, at least symbolically, cannot thereafter be washed away, this Christian blood henceforth stains their Jewish hands, *manus cruentae* (1.5, 2.12). A double-edged adjective, *cruentus* means both "spotted with blood, ensanguined" and "delighting in blood, bloodthirsty": Thomas's dual signification for the Jews themselves. The special power of William's blood to stain red whatever person or object to which it adheres is emphasized in the excessive rhetoric describing the creation of his saint's stole, "dyed [red] with the rosy blood of martyrdom" (*roseo martyrii sanguine rubricauit*, 2.2). This reddening power continues in his miracles, the first of which is the production of a red rose on his grave during winter (2.3) and the rubification of a pale man named Lewin, about to die of an unknown sickness (2.4). Later miracles include the cure of a swineherd's wife who, like the biblical woman who touched the cloak of Jesus, is "freed from a bloody flux" (*a sanguinis profluuio liberata*, 4.4), and the restoration of a sacrist experiencing a bloody genital flow (3.13). The sanguinary efflux associated with the saint finds its most vivid postmortem depiction, however, when thirty-two days after his death William's body is exhumed from its resting place at the city's margins to rebury within the boundaries of the cathedral precinct, in the monk's own cemetery. The nostrils of the corpse pour forth *recens sanguis*: "while they were washing his face, fresh blood suddenly issued from his nostrils . . . the blood kept flowing drop by drop" (1.18). Accompanying the streaming blood is for a second time fragrant evidence of the boy's sanctity ("so strange a fragrance of exceeding sweetness greeted their nostrils"). This *recens sanguis* also allows the creation of multiple sanguinary relics, red-stained cloths to disseminate William's blood further into the community.

Community in Norwich

To understand what is at stake in the emanation of all this Christian blood, we need only recall the devastating reconfiguration of Norwich in the wake the Norman Conquest, and the abiding divisions that marked the city. In the years immediately following the conquest, the rift between French settlers and English indigenes in many towns was acute. Domesday records the bitter lament of the English burgesses at Shrewsbury, economically devastated by the fact that their French counterparts were exempt from paying the Danegeld. The "new castle boroughs" (as James Tait called them) were eventually assimilated "to the model of their English neighbors," and yet the process was slow, leaving scars and lasting inequalities.[35] Gillingham has argued that within seventy years of 1066 the gulf between the Norman French and the native English ceased to be a source of what "national or ethnic tension."[36] It could be objected that this imagined unity was perhaps true of cultural elites, but that blunt differences of class and status divided this deeply hierarchical society and that regional, civic, urban, or parochial identities might in many instances mark the outer boundary of a shared and quotidian sense of community, leaving little room for or interest in big designators like the nation. Thomas of Monmouth's text portrays a Norwich in which the possibility of imagining a community of the realm, a homogeneous *patria*, is of little practical import. The pulls of nationalism seem barely to penetrate an intense localism.[37]

Even if those who had once been *Normanni* or *Franci* and Anglo-Scandinavian *Englisc* can now be gathered beneath the descriptor *Angli*, the residents of the city and its environs continue to find themselves segregated socially, economically, and to a degree linguistically by the tenacious effects of the conquest "accomplished" in the previous century. In the course of narrating the life of the saint and the struggles to foster a cult, Thomas alludes repeatedly to disparities entrenched within the city's populations. The English of indigenous descent are comparatively poor and low in social status. They do not live in the Norman-created urban center; they do not have the same access to structures of ecclesiastical and civic power, especially cathedral and castle, and in general they do not appear to speak either the prestige language of the wealthiest members of the city or (except perhaps for the priests) the official language of ecclesiastical and governmental administration.

William is a local boy, the son of two English (judging from their names, non-Norman-descended) parents. His kin seem to have lived in or near Norwich for some time. The family of his mother, Elviva, is clearly part of the fabric of provincial and parochial community, especially in their recurring role as parish priests. Elviva's father, Wlward, is described as *presbitero famoso quidem illius temporis uiro* ("a priest, a man very famous in his time," 1.1). His special skill is the interpretation of dreams, a talent he puts to good use when his daughter beholds a ruddy fish portending William's birth. Wlward's *plurimam exponendarum uisionum* ("great experience in the expounding of visions"), it can be assumed, is also a service he provides his parishioners. Elviva's sister, meanwhile, is married to Godwin Sturt, a priest who seems to have been a well-established local leader and a voice for the community. It is Uncle Godwin, after all, who makes the formal accusation against the Jews at an ecclesiastical synod, and it is Uncle Godwin who is later seen administering the parochial version of William's cult. Given the familial state of Godwin and Wlward, and if other incidental details provided by the *vita* are to be taken seriously, twelfth-century Norwich was a city racially divided not just in its architecture and its spatial segregations but even in its clergy and their sexuality. William's grandfather, uncle, and a maternal relation (named Edwin of Taverham) were secular priests who—like many provincial English lower clergy at this time—were married and had children.[38] As C. N. L. Brooke has observed, the enforcement of clerical celibacy among the English clergy was at this time creating "a devastating social revolution . . . with many victims," destined to produce "broken homes and personal tragedies."[39] The imposition of a differently configured sexuality would likely also have engendered hostility between married secular priests and the monastic communities who demanded their abstinence be emulated.

Wlward, Godwin Sturt, and Sturt's son Alexander the deacon were attached to the local parish system, composed predominantly of English-speaking communities centered around small churches. The chasm that could divide parish priests from their francophone superiors in the cathedral is well illustrated in an incident from the *vita* of Wulfric of Haselbury. This famous hermit miraculously grants a mute man the power to converse in both English and French. Wulfric's servant, a priest bearing the resonantly English name of Brictric, complains bitterly at the gift: " 'I've served you for years, all for nothing. You've never enabled me to speak French, and when I come before the bishop and the archdeacon I have to stand dumb as any mute."[40] Wulfric died in 1154, at a time when the upper echelons of the church, abbots and bishops, were primarily of French descent, while the lower clergy of East Anglia remained provincial and anglophone.[41] Wulfric's *vita* was composed around 1185, suggesting just how long this division in language, origin, and access to power endured.

As components of the diocese, the parishes owed their ultimate obedience to the Norman-built cathedral, called by Thomas *matrem ecclesiam Norwicensem*, "the Mother Church of Norwich" (1.6). The cathedral's founder, Herbert de Losinga, had carefully emphasized English-Norman continuity when he took the ancient stone of the English episcopal throne at Elmham and installed it in the new Norwich building behind the high altar. In the north transept, just above the doorway leading to the episcopal palace, was placed a large statue of a bishop, likely St. Felix, the missionary who converted the East Angles to Christianity in the country's youth.[42] Yet despite these attempts at symbolically interweaving English past and Norman present through architecture, a combination of history, culture, descent, and sexuality sundered the parishes from the cathedral to which they now owed allegiance. Æthelmær, last English bishop of East Anglia, had a wife. He presided over his see from Elmham, a community of secular priests. They were not monks, and English priests frequently were, like Æthelmær, married. The founder of the cathedral at Norwich was something altogether different. By blood as well as culturally, Herbert de Losinga was Norman. Possessed of a monastic background, he had previously risen to the office of prior at the Norman monastery of Fécamp, the foundation where he passed his youth.

Herbert was appointed bishop at a time of accelerating clerical reform. Celibacy for parish priests was being repeatedly mandated, not only because chastity had long been thought an inherent good but because priests without children could not expect to pass their benefices to inheritors, thus increasing the real estate and property available to the church. By ensuring that the upper echelons of the ecclesiastical hierarchy were overseeing the staffing of more diocesan offices, the parochial system was becoming more thoroughly subordinated to the local episcopacy. Herbert reigned over his vast see from a cathedral seat maintained by a community of Benedictines, a community modeled on Herbert's beloved Fécamp. The cathedral assemblage, staffed by monks and enamored of monastic ideals, was a world away from that inhabited by the secular priests who maintained the local parish system, priests who might have devotional reasons to eschew wealth, worldly involvement, and sexual activity but who had not taken vows promising any of these things.

Thus we see in the course of the narrative one parish priest who has established himself as a reliable interpreter of dreams (Wlward), and another who raises livestock and trades in modest miracles worked from his nephew's relics (Godwin Sturt). Differences in sexuality between cathedral and parish were, however, likely to be the most visible of these racialized ecclesiastical divisions. When, thirty-two years after Æthelmær had been forced from his bishopric, the Council of Westminster attempted to eliminate clerical marriage (1102), Herbert de Losinga had to complain from a practical standpoint that should the married clergy be dismissed, the parish churches of Norwich would have no one left to serve them.[43] Considering the frequent mention in the *Life of St William* of priests and their children, and considering that this text was written at least half a century after the promulgation of the Westminster reforms, Herbert was not exaggerating.

Given that Monmouth was an important Norman settlement on the Welsh border where many Bretons also lived, Thomas *Monemutensis* was probably of Norman, Welsh, Breton or mixed extraction. Like Henry of Huntingdon, William of Malmesbury, and Geoffrey of Monmouth, Thomas was presumably French-speaking. He consistently notes that whenever Saint William restores speech to supplicants with unambiguously English names, the language that bursts forth from their mended mouth is their mother tongue of English, an observation that would be unnecessary if Thomas and the recipients of William's power always shared the same language.[44] Thomas was likely to have been born into social advantage, since, historically, the Benedictines in England drew members and sponsorship from the Norman baronage, resulting in a francophone orientation.[45] Thus among Thomas's fellow monks named in the *vita* are Peter Peverell and Richard de Ferrariis, members of distinguished Norman families.[46]

As Andrew Galloway has noted, the Benedictines were integral to the emergence of post-conquest historiography because they "possessed the fullest resources for archival and literary collection, manuscript reproduction, and the gathering of news from the constant stream of guests that their substantial and often well-positioned abbeys drew."[47] Although three or four decades separated their writing, Thomas of Monmouth and William of Malmesbury were brothers in the same order. They both benefited from the renewed prestige that the Normans bestowed upon the Benedictines, as well as access to an educational apparatus capable of forming learned writers and disseminating their work. Medievalists seldom see Thomas of Monmouth as participating in the twelfth-century flourishing of Latin writing, a blossoming that also includes the Benedictine monks Orderic Vitalis, Eadmer of Canterbury, and John of Worcester. Yet Thomas differed from these writers not so much in the desires that motivated his composition but in the rather circumscribed ambitions of his text.

Post-conquest England witnessed a boom in monasticism, perhaps a tenfold increase from 1066 to 1200.[48] Stephen's reign saw acceleration of this trend: twice as many monasteries existed in 1154 than twenty years previous.[49] With their communal but cloistered style of living, their vow of obedience, and their espousal of chastity, these clergy posed numerous challenges to native systems of inherited benefices and parish-based churches. This proliferating commitment to celibacy no doubt furthered on a quotidian level the gender crisis precipitated by the Gregorian reform. Priests and monks who define themselves through their continence will necessarily have a different relation to women than priests who are married.[50] Norwich was in short a city possessed of a heterogeneous, segregated, and far from harmonious population, even in its clergy. Mutual assimilation was no doubt producing an increasingly synthetic urban culture, but in the years following William's death, the city was still composed of a privileged minority of former aliens living alongside a majority population who could not fail to notice that differences in status and prestige may have lessened over the years but continued everywhere to be visible. Norwich was a hybrid space, a geography that melded differences but left them disjunct.

The Jews of Norwich

A third community precariously inhabited this uncertain city, a group both alien and alienated. Within the powerful Norman minority was a more tenuous francophone community: the Ashkenazic Jews who had begun to make permanent settlements in England in the days of Conqueror. Having followed the international trade routes that linked Norwich to their communities in Normandy and the lower Rhineland, these Jewish immigrants had been resident in the city for no more than a decade when the events narrated by Thomas occurred.[51] Although the Norwich Jews lived among the Christians rather than in a separate Jewry, according to V. D. Lipman's extensive research their habitations were for the most part located in

what Domesday had called the city's *novus burgus*, the French borough of
Mancroft, founded in the shadow of the castle:

> To the south and south-east of the market place lived most, though not
> all, the Jews of medieval Norwich. They lived between the castle and
> market . . . Thus they were in the midst of the most populous part of the
> city; and near to the centres of royal and civic authority . . . It is noticeable
> that these groups of houses are all near the new market place in the new
> "French" settlement and that they are also within easy reach of the castle,
> which was the headquarters of the representative of royal authority specially
> charged with the oversight and protection of the Jews, and which also served
> as a refuge for them in times of disturbance.[52]

The Jewish community was at once marginal and central: small in number,
nonparticipants in the rituals that bound Christians to each other, but as
moneylenders the lifeblood of Norwich's commercial prosperity.[53] They
were geographical and economic intimates with the *Franci de Norwic*, a people with whom they shared a language and in many cases an origin, since
most English Jews prior to 1154 arrived from Normandy.

Although they must have known some English and a modicum of Latin
to conduct effective business, French was the vernacular of the Jews, a
domestic and conversational tongue spoken among themselves and with
Christians of the upper classes. Because it was the language they employed
at home, English Jews tended to bear francophone appellations, often
translations of their Hebrew names. Contemporary Jewish literacy consisted of facility in Hebrew, sometimes in Latin, and invariably in French.[54]
Norwich's cathedral, castle, and new borough might be inhabited by people of Norman heritage who conducted many of their interactions *en
français*, but these residents of the city likely thought of themselves as
English. Anglicization did not penetrate England's Jewish communities as
it did the households of former Normans. The Jews remained a French-
speaking people who continued to cultivate ties with their relations on the
continent, especially Rouen. At a time when the kingdom of England was
literally becoming more insular (Normandy was temporarily lost during
Stephen's reign), the Jews maintained strong connections to the continent,
making them an international group resident within a dwindled national
community.[55]

Even to francophone Christians, the Jews seemed a people set apart.
Whereas for most citizens of Norwich the centers of community were the
local church and the city's cathedral, the Jews attended their synagogue and
did not live according to the ritual calendar that gave the Christian year its
structure. The long solemnity of Lent and Easter, the festivity of Christmas,

the multiplicity of holy days that called the city to communal prayer, celebration, or repentance meant nothing to a people who still awaited their
messiah and who could not believe in the sacred magic of the saints. Few
as they were, the Jews formed a national community more than a local
one—evidenced, for example, by the fact that they sent their dead to
London to be buried in a Jewish cemetery.[56] They enjoyed royal protec-
tions not available to local citizens; they continued to speak French in an
environment that was becoming increasingly dominated by English; even
their households were different, Jewish women more fully participating in
domestic governance and public business than Christian women did.[57] The
Jews seemed ultimately to be *alieni* of a different order, disturbingly uninterested in or incapable of the assimilation that their neighbors in the new
borough were undergoing.

Linguistic, religious, and cultural otherness rendered the Jews easy tar-
gets for animus and anxiety that endured in the wake of the city's profound
social, structural, architectural transformation. As the first Jewish settlers
arrived in Norwich, the wooden fortifications of the Norman castle had
just been replaced with a stone keep. The cathedral church, monastic
buildings, and bishop's palace were likewise nearing completion or had just
been finished.[58] Jurnet, Norwich's wealthiest moneylender, had a stone
house built for his family in the 1170s and employed the same masons who
had previously toiled on some of the cathedral buildings. Emily Rose spec-
ulates that this house was meant to replace the wooden domicile in which
William had supposedly been crucified, allowing Jurnet to raze the now
notorious building.[59] In the decade following William's death, this house
was perhaps on its way to becoming an unofficial pilgrimage site where
observers hoped to spot the boy's blood on the timbers, just as Thomas of
Monmouth had done. Jewish homes in the new borough's marketplace
provided a constant visual reminder of the shift in the city's economic and
social gravity. This transferal of power would have accelerated after the
Jews arrived in the 1130s, catalyzing further mercantile and monetary
activity. Norwich's Jewish population appeared, in other words, just in
time to embody every Norman transformation wrought upon the fabric of
English Norwich. Perhaps that is why when the supposed messenger
arrives to offer the boy William a position in the archdeacon's kitchen, his
mother cannot tell whether the man who leads away her son is a Christian
or a Jew (1.4). In her English eyes and to her English ears, all the francophone residents of the new borough—whether attached to the cathedral
or practicing an alien faith—are foreigners. As much as their difference in
creed, it must have been the Jews' lingering Frenchness that triggered historical resentments having much to do with the lingering memory of the
effects of the conquest.[60]

The first public declaration that the murder of William had been accomplished by Jews, it should be noted, is made by townspeople of ethnic English descent, specifically by his mother Elviva (upon learning of the death of her son, she races through the streets of Norwich, screaming out their guilt, 1.15) and his uncle Godwin (who formally accuses the Jews of the crime during a diocesan synod about two weeks after Easter, 1.16). Godwin's wife Liviva sends her daughter to follow the "cook" and William to Eleazer's house (1.5); William's brother Robert was entrusted with "the business of carrying out the accusation against the Jews" (2.10). As Godwin's words of denunciation in front of Bishop Eborard make clear, the crime reverses the terms envisioned by William's long ago institution of the *murdrum* fine. This murder, Godwin declares, is an outrage committed against *communem omnium christianorum*, "the whole of the Christian community" (1.16), against the solidarity that William Turbe will later call *nos christiani*, "we Christians" (2.14). Bishop William is arguing before King Stephen for Jewish guilt, and like Godwin at the synod he imagines that the *murdrum* offense has been inflicted by a minority upon a majority, an urban collective imagined as both coherent and imperiled, or coherent *because* imperiled.

Such unifying rhetoric has in the world of Thomas's narration its intended effect. Eborard immediately summons the Jews to an accounting. The Jews in turn reply through the sheriff that in the absence of the king they need "make no answer to the such inventions of the Christians," indicating why both Norman-and English-descended residents of the city might have reason to dislike them. Unlike other citizens of Norwich, the Jews were not subject to local authorities, not even the bishop. "We are thy Jews" (2.14), Thomas imagines them declaring to King Stephen as they remind the rest of Norwich that, since they are royal property, they are a community set apart from civic and ecclesiastical jurisdiction.[61] When the Jews refuse the ordeal demanded by Godwin Sturt and Bishop Eborard, they take refuge in the Norman castle and confidently await the arrival of a royal edict ensuring their immunity. The galling separateness of the Jews from local community is referenced repeatedly, and is intimately related to Thomas's representation of them as a people living a precariousness existence in Norwich, a city to which they do not and cannot belong. When the guilty Jews gather to debate how best to dispose of William's body, one of their leaders points out that they cannot fling the corpse into a cesspool or bury it in a basement because they do not own houses and may, at any moment, "be forced for some reason to leave these premises and go elsewhere" (1.6). They are made to wonder aloud if *genus nostrum ab Anglie partibus funditus extermininabitur* ("our race will be utterly driven out from all parts of England")—or, even more ominously, *rapiemur ad mortem, dabimur*

in exterminium, "we shall be delivered to our deaths, we will be exterminated" (1.6). Thomas's point is clear: if Norwich is a unified community
forged of former *Franci et Angli*, it is one in which the Jews in their leased
houses lack the possibility of a future.

Perhaps an associate of Geoffrey of Monmouth, at any rate as obsessed
by collective difference and differentiation as the author of the *History of the
Kings of Britain*, Thomas of Monmouth maps in his text not just the tensions but the possible alliances among Norwich's diverse population, especially as they fight over sacralizing the body of dead William. Godwin's oral
accusation is amplified, validated, and textualized by Thomas, creating
a moment of civic unity in which the divisions that fragment the city
are suddenly overcome. Norwich becomes simply *communitas omnium
christianorum*, the community of all Christians (Godwin's formulation as
ventriloquized by Thomas, 1.16). Like the aboriginal monsters through
which Geoffrey of Monmouth solved the problem of "To whom belongs
Britain?" the Jews temporarily alleviate a crisis in community by displacing
anxieties about its irresolvability. The Jews, as non-Christian others who
are clearly *not* English, allow through their monsterization the emergence
of a new civic totality. Through the Jew who was at once blood-stained
and blood-loving (*cruentus*), former Anglo-Normans and Anglo-Saxons
catalyze a tentative harmony, communalized by their not being Jewish. As
these two populations lose their distinctiveness, moreover, the Jews
become all the more immutably set in their denigrated identity, *uersutis-
sima iudeorum gens et auarissima*, "that most crafty and avaricious race, the
Jews" (2.14).

Medieval imaginings of collective identity frequently include a fascination with blood, especially that of excluded groups who, once identified
and alienated, allow the coming into being of purified, dominating identities like *Christian* and *English*.[62] Difference tends to be possessed most visi-
bly by the ostracized. Thomas and the other sanctifiers of William's blood
discover in a horrific murder the chance to transcend differences that have
hindered the forming of local concordance. Dead William, English boy
with a Norman name, slain by Jewish malice, is transformed by the *vita* into
blood that flows and washes away epistemological uncertainties, into blood
that cleanses not just the trauma of finding a child brutally murdered, but
also the trauma of a conquest initiating a postcolonial era with repercussions that continued to be palpable for a century.

That the forced reconfiguration of Norwich continued to haunt the
imagination of its citizens is seen best in an uncanny vision granted to
Liviva, the wife of Godwin Sturt. A few days before her nephew is found
dead, she dreams that she is standing in the market created by the town's
Norman resettlers and inhabited by even newer francophone immigrants.

In a Latin narration that achieves the claustrophobia of a nightmare through its jarring repetitions, Liviva describes how Jews pour from their nearby houses and dismember her:

> As I was standing in the High Street of the Market Place, suddenly the Jews came upon me running up from all sides, and they surrounded me as I fled and they seized me. And as they held me they broke my right leg with a club and they tore it away from the rest of my body, and running off with all speed it seemed that they were carrying it away with them. (1.14)

Locating the dream's unfolding in the Norman marketplace and centering its action upon the ripping apart of a Christian body by the Jews who live and conduct their business there ensure that the vision becomes something more than a private fantasy shared in confidence between husband and wife. The fact that Thomas renders the dream a rhetorically complex addition to his own argument (his Latin is really at its best here, suffocating and oneiric) invests the dream with an important, community-directed meaning. Liviva's body, torn asunder by rapacious hands in the heart of the Norwich's new borough, horrifically figures the rifts and fragmentations (ethnic, civic, economic) left in the wake of conquest and revivified during the turbulence of Stephen's reign. The Jews at the heart of this symbolic geography, avidly wrenching a limb from a Christian's body, eager to kidnap and sacrifice an innocent member of Norwich's *corpus Christianum*, conveniently enflesh all those differences that, once expelled, might allow the violent history behind the formation of that difficult middle to be forgotten, all its dismembering divisions to be transcended.

Community of Blood

The martyred boy's sacred blood (which, as Liviva makes clear, is the *shared* blood of the Christians of Norwich) brings about a necessary suture, conjoining temporarily the French-descended and indigenous English, bringing together the clerics and the laity, monks and priests, the celibate and the married, the privileged and the impoverished, the women and the men. First the clergy and people (*cleri plebisque*) who carry William's cadaver from the woods for interment in the cathedral monastery's cemetery are met by "so vast a concourse of the common people . . . that you would have thought very few had stayed behind in the city" (1.18). Then as the body is laid to rest in its new grave,

> the cemetery was filled by thousands of men who entered by the gate on the other side, and the area was hardly large enough for those who kept coming

in. On the one side were the clergy and monks who were celebrating the exequies with songs of praise, on the other were the laity who were taking their part with exceeding joy. But though they who were present differed in grade and in sex, they were all of one mind in wishing to see the sight. (1.19)

A fragrant and effulgent climax to the first book of the *vita*, this interment provides a satisfying moment of transcendence in which nightmares of bodily loss, unavenged corpses, murdered young men who do not rest easy, and histories of violence yet to be forgotten are finally laid to rest. Thomas's narration transforms a hagiographical commonplace (the *adventus* of saint's relics for burial) into a culminating moment of civic unity.[63]

As William's body is lowered into the sacred ground, buried with him in Thomas's utopian rendering are the disparities sundering the city. The only important differences now find their embodiment in the Jews and in those Christians who announce a Jew-like nature by sympathizing with them. The punishment of a Jewish refusal by a Christian to participate in the civic solidarity of William's cult finds its most memorable—and bloodiest—expression in the death of Sheriff John de Chesney, the representative of the king who repeatedly gave the Jews shelter in the castle whenever the citizens of Norwich united in their desire to massacre them. Immediately upon first protecting the Jews, John suffers an "internal hemorrhage" (*per posteriora eius sanguis guttatim profluere inchoauit*, 2.15).[64] For two years his blood flows incessantly, but John continues in his obstinacy until, "exhausted by the incessant flow of this blood, his strength and his blood alike failing him," he dies miserably. Thomas notes tartly: "And so clearly was the vengeance of God shown in this case that he might in very truth say with the Jews, 'Let the innocent blood be upon us and upon our children' " (2.15).

Sheriff John is the only truly national figure to play a significant role in the *vita*. His surname *de Caineto* means "from Caen," the site in Normandy that was the source for the stone of the cathedral and castle keep. John's father Robert had preceded him as sheriff, while Robert's father Walter had been in the service of William Malet, renowned companion of the Conqueror.[65] Sheriff John, frequently recorded as being in attendance upon King Stephen, carried prestigious blood, and was a living reminder of the change that had come to England in the previous century. Yet this representative of royal interests, an embodiment of what Thomas calls *regi regiisue ministris* (perhaps best translated as "king and castle," where the latter is the castle-assemblage and its attendant officials, 1.16), simply gets in the way of the local unity-making mechanisms engendered by the veneration of St. William, a veneration efficacious for the surmounting of Norwich's post-conquest dividedness The vast majority of the visitors to William's shrine recorded by Thomas were, after all, city residents. Ronald Finucane emphasizes the local aspect of William's miracles:

> Most of William's miracles were reported by local folk. More than half (57%) of his recorded pilgrims (94% located) lived less than ten miles from the shrine, and two thirds of these came from the city of Norwich itself. After ten miles or so there was a sharp decline in pilgrims' villages. This decline continued until, at a distance of about fifty miles, very few individuals felt sufficient thaumaturgic radiation from the child's bones to experience a cure or to undergo a pilgrimage to seek one.[66]

In a final symbolic gesture, Thomas emphasizes that the sheriff who had abstained from local community by protecting the Jews died as he was desperately trying to reach Norwich from London. In the Latin of the *vita* this city is given the same grandiose name attached to it by Geoffrey of Monmouth, *Trinovantum*. Sheriff John's spectacularly painful death as he races homeward from New Troy suggests that the community solidifying in Norwich around William's cult has no room for extravagantly national mythologies that would account for the founding of London, that would provide a pedigree for and unity to the *patria*.

Whereas Sheriff John's anguish and the murder of Eleazar figure blood intolerable to Norwich's commonality, the gush of William's Christian blood—viscous blood, binding blood—erases those distinctions that divided the city. These are not simple Norman versus Saxon differences, with the *Ivanhoe* connotations such a hoary binary conjures. True, William has parents with unambiguously English names, Elviva (that is, Ælfgifu) and Wenstan.[67] His priestly uncle bears what is possibly the most resonantly Anglo-Scandinavian of all possible names for the time: Godwin was, after all, the appellation of the infamous Earl of Wessex who rose to power during the reign of Cnut, who energetically anglicized the Norman-leaning court of Edward the Confessor, and who fathered Harold, William of Normandy's coclaimant for the throne.[68] Godwin's anti-Norman sentiment was legendary, a fact surely not lost on Godwin Sturt's own parents when they christened their child. Given that Norwich had until 1066 been a city in which the Godwinsons held land and possibly an urban residence, and given that the Norman construction of castle, borough, and cathedral may have been aimed at securing what had been their stronghold, it is not surprising that Godwin Sturt enters Thomas's narrative as an illustrious local figure with a personality as large as his historically loaded name.

Immediately after the conquest a name like William, Robert, or Walter would invariably indicate Norman ethnicity. These prestige monikers

were, however, quickly adopted by the English. By the time Herbert de
Losinga was bishop of Norwich, two troublesome brothers were residents
of his priory. One bore the named Godwin and the other William, a
cacophony of French and English eponyms within a single family that indicates the linguistic hybridity that quickly proliferated.[69] Robert, the
brother of Saint William, was christened with the second most popular of
French names, while the boy martyr himself carries a name so thoroughly
Norman that its popularity was something of a joke. "William" was originally a Frankish name, bestowed upon the eldest son of a famous Viking
(Hrólfr, AKA Rollo, founder of the Norman dynasty) in order to give a
veneer of culture to his progeny. The Normans adopted the appellation
with gusto. Robert Bartlett provides a wonderful example of what this
multiplication of Williams could bring about: a Christmas court in
Normandy in 1171 attended by, among other guests, 110 knights named
William. These Williams segregated themselves in a private room and
refused to allow anyone not bearing their name to dine with them.[70] As in
Normandy so in England: William was quickly established as the single
most popular name in the Middle Ages, adopted as ardently by the lower
classes as it was by the aristocracy.

Nor was Norman influence on England limited to the period after the
conquest. Edward the Confessor, the second to last "English" king, was (as
the previous chapter pointed out) a hybrid regent who created an admixed
court. Even Thomas's chosen geographic designator, *Monemutensis*, places
his own origin in the ethnically plural Welsh March, a borderland that
Michelle Warren aptly describes as a "multiple zone" of "interactive and
often improvised identifications."[71] Mid-twelfth-century Norwich was,
like England itself, irreversibly hybrid. But hybridity is not assimilation,
synthesis, or harmony. As Homi Bhabha has pointed out, when hybridity
marks a conjoining of cultural differences, the meeting tends to be irremediably conflictual.[72] Obscured by the harmonizing bent of Thomas's text
and deflected by the Normanizing of names like Robert and William are
some of the incongruities and intractable differences that the *vita* must
silently acknowledge. A power struggle plays out among the cathedral,
with its entwined local, regional, national, and transnational vectors;
local citizens like Godwin Sturt, who think, work, and move within a
parochial ambit; Norman aristocrats and the citizens of the new borough,
with their multiple loyalties; the king's representatives like Sheriff John,
faced with their own monarch's fluctuating ability to influence regional
dynamics of power.

Divisions in Norwich that may be labeled ethnic, moreover, are just as
accurately divisions of class, prestige, and power. Yet a suggestive passage
composed by Richard fitzNigel (ca.1130–1198) is frequently cited to back

the assertion that the Normans and English achieved something close to parity by the middle of the twelfth century. When in his *Dialogus de Scaccario* he considers the *murdrum* fine instituted by William to discourage the "conquered English" (*Anglicis subactis*) from ambushing and secretly killing the "mistrusted and hated Normans" (*suspectam et exosam Normannorum gentem*)—evidently a common crime in the wake of the conquest—Richard ponders whether the death of a contemporary Englishman "like that of a Norman" should result in the same fine. Richard asserts that the Normans and English have so intermarried as to be indistinguishable. Yet the synthetic description contains an important qualifier:

> Nowadays, when English and Normans live close together and marry and give in marriage to each other, the nations are so mixed that it can scarcely be decided (I mean in the case of freemen) who is of English birth and who of Norman; except, of course, the villeins, who cannot alter their condition without the leave of their masters. For that reason whoever is found slain nowadays, the murder-fine is exacted, except in cases where there is definite proof of the servile condition of the victim.[73]

Some of the realm may have become *permixte*, mainly through Norman men taking English wives and concubines, but servile class is for Richard an immediate marker of unalloyed Englishness.[74] Social class and collective identity continue to be inextricable, with pure Englishness and enduring servility synonymous.

The example of Norwich, further, demonstrates that it is not just the lowest classes (villeins) who are relatively poor and unambiguously English. Whether they are farmers, parish clerics, or an apprentice skinner aspiring to the upward mobility of a cook's assistant, the indigence of William's family is continually underscored in Thomas's text. After an initial description of William's family as moderately well-off dwellers in the rustic fringe of the city, their poverty is mentioned repeatedly. This reduction in circumstance perhaps resulted from the death of William's father, since he is never mentioned in the text after his son's birth. William's status as *pauperculus* (later *pauper et neglectus*) suggests why his mother apprenticed him to the master leatherworker Wulward, at whose Norwich residence William lodges. The family's penury also helps to explain why his mother would have so quickly accepted payment from a mysterious stranger to take him away to more rewarding employment in the archdeacon's household. That William's family dwells at the bucolic margins of Norwich (*rus*) and is moved to the city (*urbs*) to become an apprentice likewise indicates an attempt to trade rural poverty for a more lucrative urban life.

Before his disappearance William was learning the craft of the *pelliparia*, leatherworker. As Maryanne Kowaleski points out, leather was the plastic of its day, the malleable substance from which were manufactured the quotidian items of medieval life.[75] Skinners, tanners, and other leatherworkers were professions integral to the local economy, the bridge between countryside and the city. But they were also "notorious offenders in matters of public hygiene," mainly because the materials they required generated noxious odors and wastes.[76] Working with hides, skins, and the chemicals used to prepare them was perceived as a typically English craft, at least by Gerald of Wales, probably because of its lack of prestige.[77] The offensive smells and water pollution engendered by the leather trade ensured that it was practiced at the margins of cities, a geographical fact that nicely spatializes Gerald's social commentary.

In seizing the opportunity to leave behind his dirty life as a *pelliparia*, William was hoping to abandon an impoverished English world for a milieu created by the Normans. The position of archdeacon was a Norman innovation to the English ecclesiastical system, introduced by bishops who found themselves overwhelmed by administrative responsibilities. The *oculi episcopi*, archdeacons assisted in the efficient oversight of their sees, and were especially active in the discipline of diocesan priests.[78] An archdeacon was therefore a person of considerable local power. Their households were notoriously opulent and offered access, as Thomas makes clear, to *multa commoda* ("many advantages," 1.4). Given that archdeacons were also the policemen of clerical celibacy, William and his mother were also potentially rejecting the English world of married priests to which they were so closely related.[79] Inclusion in the archdeacon's household would give William the chance to move from the literal and figurative margins of town to its center, to belong to the community that supported the majestic cathedral of stone. Here too would be his chance to mingle with the dwellers of Mancroft, the prosperous borough of Norwich that enjoyed a standard of living higher than that of the city's other quarters. Even when their habitation was a priory in which they were bound by a vow of poverty, the residents of the cathedral close lived surrounded by a splendor that must have been impressive to an English boy raised at the outskirts of the city, a boy whose extensive familial experience of the church had been of modest parish structures staffed by the members of the social class to which he belonged, the English free peasantry.

In the mid-twelfth century, most abbots and bishops were of French ancestry, while the priests at the lower end of the ecclesiastical hierarchy were English.[80] The monasteries would have held a mixed population of French- and English-descended monks, typically led by a French abbot. William probably saw in the promises of the supposed cook his chance to enter a world offering far greater access to prestige and prosperity, a world very different from what he was experiencing at his leatherworking and from what he glimpsed in the life of his priestly uncle. To become a cook's apprentice and a member of the archdeacon's household was to have the doors of possibility thrown open. It was at the same time the chance to blunt the supposed roughness of an English upbringing with a patina of refinement.

Little did William know that this assimilation into the world of the cathedral was in fact going to take place, but not until it was recognized that his cadaver could provide the majestic establishment with a lucrative relic.[81] The "insolent" Jews, confident of royal protection through Sheriff John, declare to the Christians: "You ought to be very much obliged to us, for we have made a saint and martyr for you . . . Aye! We have done for you what you could not do yourselves" (2.11). The Jews make clear the commercial implications of venerating William. Should the city unite in the worship of the martyr, Norwich cathedral will have the relics that will allow it to compete with nearby but independent Benedictine foundation at Bury St. Edmunds, enriched by its possession of the body of King Edmund, martyred by the Danes in 870.[82] The successive translations of the dead English boy into places of increasing prestige within the Norman ecclesiastical precinct was a perhaps more successful version of Bishop Herbert's erecting a statue of the revered Felix, missionary to the East Angles, within his new episcopal church.[83] Arriving not long after the cathedral had been completed, the relics of Saint William might—like those English saints initially held in contempt by Norman ecclesiasts but eventually adopted as a useful means for engendering community—bridge native English and imported French worlds and might mend at last the broken chain of Norwich's history.

Francophile ways might at times equate with prestige for the Christian dwellers in the castle, cathedral, and the French quarter of Mancroft. The same could not be said for the Jews. In the community imagined by Thomas's text, the sanctification of William allows the assimilation of Norwich's diverse population into a single *Christianitas* at the expense of this second francophone population, the one group living in Britain who (in Marjorie Chibnall's words) were different in kind because they were, "in the conditions of the day, unassimilable."[84] After he is crucified, dies, and is reburied, Saint William guarantees that the only citizens of the city who carry racialized blood are "the enemies of the Christian name," the *sanguinis innocentis effusores* ("shedders of innocent blood," 1.16).[85] Homicidal monsters, spinners of transnational conspiracies unfathomable in their brutality (conspiracies that ensure that the actions of Jews of Norwich cannot be seen by Thomas's audience as some local deviance, but instead render all Jews everywhere both culpable and intimately connected as uni-fied group)[86]—the Jews with their *manus cruentae* (hands that are stained with blood, hands that are thirsty for blood) embody the trauma of 1066 and convey it elsewhere, allowing Norman and English alike the possibil-ity of a placid affinity. Their communalized blood endangered by this intimate enemy, these latter groups suddenly find their common and tran-scendent denominator as Christians of Norwich. Just as their messiah suf-fered long ago at the hands of deicidal Jews and redeemed a fragmented world, so in the *vita* Christians witness one of their own submit to the ago-nies of the biblical Passion and emerge transformed. The martyr William is a diminutive counterpart to the risen Christ, an eternal witness to the fact that the sundered Babel that had been Norwich has been redeemed into wholeness, restored to community.

In my description of what allows the Norwich envisioned in the *vita* to realize a new solidarity in the face of its own heterogeneity there are dis-cernible echoes of recent scholarly analysis of the crusades, which likewise gathered an array of conflictual differences under the banner of a unifying Christianity at the expense of a demonized Other known as the Saracen. These transnational endeavors, moreover, saw the massacre of Jews in Europe before the *crucesignati* voyaged east. The most famous incidents happened during the First Crusade, when Jews living in the Rhineland were killed or chose martyrdom to avoid forced conversion. England would not see similar violence until late in the twelfth century. In 1190 in Norwich, Jewish houses were burned, their contents looted, their occu-pants murdered by crusaders intent on following King Richard to the Holy Land.[87] Perhaps the similarity between violence attending both the inter-national crusades and the provincial sanctification of William is not surpris-ing, given that in 1147 East Anglians were accompanying Hervey de Glanvil on crusade to Lisbon, where he is recorded as delivering a speech urging unity between *Normanni* and *Angli*.[88] Jewish blood must in Thomas's text be spilled in order to purge the community of alien content and allow a homogeneous collectivity to solidify:

> Since then it is certain . . . that the most blessed boy and martyr William was slain by the Jews, we believe that it was brought about by the righteous judgement of God that these same men, being guilty of so horrible a crime, suffered so prompt a retribution for such deliberate wickedness, and that the rod of heaven in a brief space of time exterminated them all. (2.13)

Thus Eleazar, supposed ringleader of the murderous Jews, dies in a bloody ambush, while those who sympathize with the Jews or otherwise act Jewish by refusing participation in William's veneration suffer severe retribution, often by the sanctified *puerulus vilis* himself, now transmuted into a spirit of vengeance. The monk Richard, for example, refuses to make an offering of candles demanded by the saint in a nocturnal vision. William backhands the man across his forehead, an excruciating wound that quickly proves fatal (2.5). Prior Elias, hesitant to endorse William's cult, does not allow Thomas to adorn the boy's tomb with a carpet and candles. Like Richard, he perishes. Walter, servant of the dean of Norwich, made it his habit to ridicule the burgeoning cult of the martyr. William appears to him in a dream, cudgeling every part of his body, "finally letting him go when he was bruised in every limb" (7.13). "It is dangerous to neglect the young St William," Benedicta Ward observes crisply, "or to be remiss in paying him honour."[89] Jews die; Christians who do not answer saintly William's call to community die; and it would seem that the new kind of belonging being promulgated in the city has its terrifying underside, for its unity arises from an unstinting flow of blood.

Yet even if the vision of community espoused by Thomas seems as suffocating as it is relentless, we should at least take note that, as Thomas himself is forced repeatedly to admit, not every citizen of the town was easily convinced that William was entitled to the *cultus* spreading under his name. The moment of harmony with which Thomas closes the first book of the *vita* does not endure long. The glorious translations of William from the monastic cemetery into the cathedral church, where he is placed beside the high altar and next to Herbert de Losinga's tomb (5.2), and thence—because of the "unwontedly large crowds"—to his own chapel (6.1), indicate the burgeoning popularity of the saint between 1150 and 1154. The movements of the relics are public performances of unity, enacted by the whole convent of monks and "plurima populorum . . . caterua" (a phrase that could be translated blandly as "a very large throng of people" or more classically as "the majority of the community," since *populus* indicated for the Romans a nation, a collective populace). Yet these translations of the martyr's body are preceded by a dissension-provoking relocation of the corpse to the chapter house (3.1). The second book of the *vita* opens with an extended defense of the boy's martyrdom against the "saucy insolence and insolent sauciness" of those who not only deprecate the cult but turn its divine mysteries to ridicule (2.1). Dissension within the monastery over the veneration of William also appears from time to time, with Thomas in book 4 still unable to forgive Prior Elias for having ordered him to remove the unauthorized carpet (4.1). Enthusiasm for the cult wanes and waxes irregularly as Thomas's narrative unfolds. Just as his new cathedral tomb has begun to radiate healing powers (5.6), moreover, St. William is observed punishing Godwin Sturt for demanding that a poor woman surrender a hen before he will allow her to partake of some healing water he possesses. This potent fluid is created with the wooden teasel that Godwin took from the mouth of William's cadaver long ago. Clearly the priest is making quite a profit by selling the sanctified water to the local community. His demand for payment incurs the wrath of his sanctified nephew, so that very night

> every one of his fowls died; and of the whole number, which was large, not one remained; so that for the one which he unjustly demanded he deservedly suffered the loss of many. In the morning on hearing of his mishap, the priest was at once repentant . . . In fear he vowed that he would never thenceforth seek gains of this kind by conferring spiritual benefits. (5.5)

The veneration of William, it seems, has made Godwin rich in livestock. The parish priest's entrepreneurship and the demand for modest miracles among the local population yield an intriguing glimpse at the popular, parochial version of William's veneration and hint at a competition between at least two versions of the cult. The episode also betrays Thomas's effort to establish the primacy of the cult centered at the cathedral over that being managed by William's family. A miracle narrated shortly after Godwin's punishment features William appearing to a lady near Lynn and pulling a gold ring from her finger as she sleeps. Because the valuables are to be donated to the shrine at Norwich, the episode illustrates this time not the exploitation of William for financial gain but properly Christian devotion to the martyr (5.7).[90] An episode that similarly demarcates the "official" cult centered at the cathedral from that associated with William's family occurs a few chapters thereafter, when William extorts a cross from his mother before allowing her to die in peace. The narrative stresses that William remains alive in his tomb, now translated into the cathedral itself ("I have lain for many days on my left side," he declares in a vision, "because I would have the Cross of the Lord [in the cathedral] always before my eyes"), and this uncanny afterlife is located securely beneath the watchful eye of Thomas (5.21). The *vita* records Thomas's attempt to envision, foster, and promulgate a harmonious community, but it also reveals that this unity of which he at times seems so confident was not as monolithic as he desired.

Aftermath

Though the Jewish population of England was to be expelled wholesale in 1290, a community of Jews not only endured in Norwich for a century and a half after William's death, but it fostered under wealthy patrons, like the Jurnet family, a thriving center for rabbinic scholarship. Norwich even produced an extraordinary poet, Meir ben Elijah, who could declare in the acrostic of a poem on Exodus "I am Meir, son of Rabbi Elijah from the city of Norwich, which is in the land of the Isle, called Angleterre."[91] As Ivan Marcus (among many others) has observed, the Jews experienced a flourishing of their culture similar to what for the Christians has been labeled the "Twelfth-Century Renaissance"—only for the Jews, this explosion of creativity "was a response to an oppressive challenge" rather than the alchemy of a moment of international community.[92] The murder of the child William in Norwich in 1144 was brutal, but in a way it arrived too early: England was not yet as reflexively anti-Semitic as it proves itself to be a few decades hence. Some scholars have detected in Thomas's narrative an edge of desperation in the "marketing" of the boy as a saint: "Well into the 1160s and 1170s, some thirty years after William's 'murder,' Thomas and the monks at Norwich were collecting miracle stories and trying new ways (such as the dedication in 1168 of the 'Chapel of St William in the Wood') to invigorate the cult and make it lucrative."[93] The events surrounding William's death did not inspire the contagious awe and national fascination to be awakened by the boy martyr Hugh of Lincoln in 1255. Few in number and never in fact capable of posing much of an actual threat to local communities, let alone to national *communitas*, the Jews were perhaps of greatest ideological use once they had been expelled from the island and transformed, in the wake of 1290, into specters or virtual bodies.[94] Beginning in the twelfth century, as we have seen, England began to imagine that it was ringed by vast geographies populated with people irremediably different in culture, ethics, and perhaps even blood. At the same time as Norwich was transforming its resident Jews into monsters, writers like William of Malmesbury were transforming the Welsh, Scots, and Irish into bloodthirsty barbarians whose passion was to murder, maim, and enslave English Christians. Jews may have temporarily provided those others over whose excluded bodies a local or even national collectivity might condense, but the creation of a primitive and ripe for conquest Celtic Fringe was to offer a more enduring invitation to the imagining of a community of the realm, allowing a postcolonial England to transform itself into an insular empire.

The call for vengeance heard from the mouths of Godwin Sturt and Thomas of Monmouth, the demand for blood proclaimed from parish church, cathedral, and city street alike goes unheeded. So far as we know, no Jew was killed as a direct result of William's murder. Yet it is worthwhile considering whether Jewish blood need flow in order to save the *vita* from being dismissed as the record of a failed attempt to monsterize the Jews. Would the document feel more weighty if a pogrom or a Jewish choice of martyrdom lay in its immediate history? The events, accusations, and animus recorded by Thomas are, by any measure, chilling. Though it would take four more decades for the people of Norwich to start to bring death to the Jews of their city and conflagration to their dwellings, as they did in 1190, it is difficult to believe that this later hostility could be wholly unconnected to the conspiracies, fantasies, and enthusiasm for murder documented in the *vita*. The stories that circulated about William were clearly precedent-setting, for other cases of supposed ritual murder of children by Jews followed: Harold of Gloucester (1168), Robert of Bury St. Edmunds (1181), Hugh of Lincoln (1255). The last incident saw nineteen Jews hanged for their supposed part in the sacrifice, and royal endorsement was given to the boy martyr's burgeoning cult. By the close of the twelfth century anti-Jewish violence was erupting across East Anglia, having been kindled by a riot against some Jews at the coronation of King Richard. By the close of the thirteenth, England would be the first country in Europe that had declared itself *Judenrein*.

Even if violence took some years to arrive, the *vita* remains the first text in English history to imagine that Jews pose a grave and bodily danger to Christians, and it is the first to record a desire to massacre a Jewish community in revenge. *The Life of Saint Thomas of Norwich* is punctuated by demands for Jewish blood: "And so the earnestness of their devout fervor was urging all to destroy the Jews, and they would there and then have laid hands upon them" (1.12); "Everybody began to cry out with one voice that all the Jews ought to be utterly destroyed as constant enemies of the Christian name and Christian religion" (1.15); "Because it was not safe for them to remain outside, the Sheriff protected them within the defenses of the Castle" (1.16). Thomas repeatedly labels the Jews *iudei christianicide* ("Christianicidal Jews," as in the rubric to 2.13) and makes it clear that the only safe Norwich is one cleansed of its religious, cultural, and racial aliens. Thomas composed a narrative obsessed with the flow of blood; blood that in its movement purified a collective identity and conveyed difference elsewhere. It is not likely an exaggeration to say that this text and the cult it promulgated were to trigger many more such flows.

EPILOGUE: *IN MEDIAS RES*

The Norwich described by Thomas of Monmouth was a hybrid space, a difficult middle. In some ways the city would have been easier for its own residents to comprehend when the difference between peoples had been as lucid as the language that spilled from a particular set of lips. By the time Thomas arrived, the powerful lived and worked in architectures that, having only recently been completed, must still have seemed alien to residents with long memories. In these same buildings, however, were held convocations like diocesan synods that gathered together anglophone and francophone populations, the affluent and the impoverished, married priests and celibate monks, peoples with long and with brief Norwich histories. French-speakers were no doubt slowly adopting English; native families were christening their children with French names. Economic and social disparities still sundered the city's populations. Friction caused by competition and hauteur is amply evident in Thomas's *vita*. Yet the former Normans and the native English had clearly interpenetrated in Norwich, creating a civic milieu that, even if turbulent, was also on the brink of forming an enlarged community. The Jews, transformed by Thomas and his supporters into monsters, could transport away the troubling power of lingering difference, and allow a hybrid space to believe in its unifying purity.

The Jews as represented by the *Life of Saint William* are rather similar to the Britons in Bede's *Ecclesiastical History*: an inimical race whose evident similarities must be denied in order to purge a collective identity of troubling heterogeneity—in order, really, to render that identity substantial, possible. The first chapter of this book examined how medieval authors passionately detailed the customs, laws, histories, and other cultural and corporeal phenomena that were supposed to separate peoples into natural groups. Because these various markers were mutable, their power to differentiate never long endured. The perennial human tendency to engender a shared sense of community through definition *against* other peoples, moreover, meant that those who found themselves *between* belongings faced great difficulty in attempting to articulate their identity. Thus William of

Malmesbury, Norman and English blood uneasily admixed in his historian's body, dreamed hybridity through marvelous figures like witches,
conjoined twins, a Saracen-stained pope, men transformed into animals.
Geoffrey of Monmouth composed what must be medieval Britain's most
deeply ambiguous text, a revisionist history that confidently offered a novel
vision of past, then quietly and thoroughly eroded it. Gerald of Wales spent
his life seeking a vocabulary sufficient for expressing his multifarious identity. Like William of Malmesbury, he found a strikingly visual lexicon for
this hybridity in the unnatural mixing of human and animal, in strange
bodies marked in the flesh by their divergent histories and headed toward
futures for which no precedent existed. William of Norwich was in a way
just such a hybrid body himself, suspended between worlds. Installed in the
cathedral as a saint, he was supposed to bring about a unity that had long
escaped the city, but Norwich's postcolonial legacy was not so easily
interred.

This book has attempted to move between the world as keenly divided
by authors like Bede and Thomas and the lived experience of writers who
dwelled in the intermediacies such division foments. William of
Malmesbury's historical narration arrives at an almost insurmountable
obstacle at the Norman Conquest because, despite William's protestations
to the contrary, a synthetic point of view was not truly possible at the time
he wrote. Geoffrey of Monmouth seems serenely untroubled by this same
state of affairs, bequeathing a text that multiplied difficulties rather than
attempted to resolve them. Early in his life Gerald of Wales wrote with
confidence, believing that his compound identity could bridge a riven
world. When rivals at the English court used his hybridity to bar him from
privilege, however, Gerald turned with increasing bitterness against the
milieu that he had sought to master. His last days were spent in a kind of
self-imposed exile in Lincoln, revising his youthful texts, multiplying their
marvels and perversions. What all of these authors shared was their
Christian Latinity, granting them access to an international community of
educated and powerful men. Like Bede in the eighth century, William,
Geoffrey, and Gerald never seemed to worry that their words, even when
troubled or beleaguered, might not be heard or endure.

I would like to end this book by briefly mentioning a voice that likewise
survives from medieval Britain, but that possessed no such reason to be
confident of future comprehension. Meir ben Elijah of Norwich was the
thirteenth-century author of about twenty-one Hebrew poems. Writing in
those difficult days when the persecution of the English Jews was moving
toward its crescendo of expulsion, Meir wondered if God might have forgotten his chosen people. His poem "Oyevi bim'eirah tiqqov" ["Put a
curse on my enemy"] is filled with despair, a dilating catalogue of hardship

and distress.[1] Meir wrote in the wake of martyrdoms and violent persecutions. Many of his fellow Jews had been lost to conversion, while others had embraced a passionate but fruitless messianism. Every declaration of the dimming of the world, however, is met in Meir's poem by the possibility of daybreak to come: "When I hoped for good, evil arrived, yet I will wait for the light" (5). Indeed, the biblical refrain of the work is the line "You are mighty and full of light, You turn darkness into light." Its seventeen repetitions in the fifty-one line composition have an incantatory quality, washing around the poem's long litany of suffering with a countercurrent of breaking futurity.

"Oyevi bim'eirah tiqqov" is temporally rather odd. Its recitation is clearly meant to follow the *havdalah*, the ceremonial end of the Sabbath, a transition that is typically seen as a movement from light to the gathering darkness that ends the sacred day—exactly opposite to the movement of this poem in which light pierces gathering gloom. Meir was the poet of a community at the edge of oblivion. He penned lines that have lost their faith in the present, that express confusion about why God should allow his people to be so assailed ("The words of the seer are garbled, for the foe has mocked your children," 7; "Have you forgotten to be gracious, my God?" 19). The poem is also, somehow, a record of impossible hope. Its words belong to an author lost to history. They are composed in a language shortly to be exterminated in Britain. Yet "Oyevi bim'eirah tiqqov" arrives eight hundred years later to declare what it is like to be stuck in a difficult and darkening middle, longing for a radiant end. I let Meier ben Elijah come last in this book because it seems to me that he knew as well as any medieval writer the suffering that humans inflict upon each other in the name of creating community. His is the voice of someone who was almost made to vanish, but who somehow after all this time possesses a voice that still resounds.

NOTES

Introduction: *In medias res*

1. *Colonial Desire* 18.
2. Review of Marjorie Chibnall, *The Normans* 466.
3. " 'Gens Normannorum'—Myth or Reality?" 114.
4. Simon James argues that the Celts, for example, are a modern construct (*The Atlantic Celts*); though not quite as modern, collectives like the Britons and the Welsh are also more imagined than real (Christopher A. Snyder, *The Britons* 2–5 and R. R. Davies, *Conquest, Coexistence and Change* 13–14). The Scots were fifth- and sixth-century immigrants from Ireland who intermingled with the Picts, Britons, Angles, and Norse. That the so-called Anglo-Saxons were a mongrel confederation of peoples has been widely enough accepted to have become a critical commonplace. Patrick Geary sums up much recent writing on their hybrid past in *The Myth of Nations* 115, 141–42. As Peter S Wells has made clear, moreover, processes of collective transformation tend to be mutual, rapid, and ongoing at times of contact: Rome was as changed by its barbarians as the barbarians were changed by Rome (*The Barbarians Speak*).
5. It should be noted at this point that in this book I refer to both the English and the Britons/Welsh as indigenous peoples, when of course the varied ancestors of both arrived from elsewhere. Britain had no autochthonous population; its long history is one of ceaseless migration, colonization, intermingling. I will use words like *indigenous* and *native* with the caveat that these are simply convenient terms for collectives who imagine they have lived on the island for a long time, even if they never claimed to be an aboriginal population.
6. Review of *Medieval Europeans*. See also Curta's inspirational work on the evolution of collective ethnic identities in *The Making of the Slavs*.
7. Medievalists have been inspired by postcolonial modes of analysis for many years now, and the postcolonial Middle Ages is certainly a communal project. In addition to the essays in *Postcolonial Middle Ages*, see especially the work of Catherine Brown, Geraldine Heng, Bruce Holsinger, Patricia Ingham, Lisa Lampert, Clare A. Lees and Gillian R. Overing, and Michelle Warren.
8. David Wallace has recently made this point clear in *Premodern Places*, a book likewise populated by intermixed spaces. For an acute discussion of borders

and hybridity, see the breathtaking analysis of Calais in 22–90. I have, as always, found Wallace's work to be intellectually bracing, though I approach my middles rather differently. I concentrate on proximate spaces within Britain and Ireland that were instrumental in shaping—and purifying, and subverting—the Englishness whose vagrant later history Wallace traces. Other medievalists whose work on hybridity has been of great value to me in this project include Glenn Burger, Patricia Ingham (whose emphasis on the productive and potentially affirmative possibilities of hybridity throughout her work closely matches my own), Clare A. Lees, and Michelle Warren (see bibliography).

9. "Introduction: Hybridity" 184.
10. *Location of Culture* 219, 207. Bhabha's notion of hybridity as a playful "third space" has frequently been attacked, mainly by critics who insist that he does not sufficiently acknowledge the suffering that occurs among those forced to inhabit such cultural interstices (see, for example, Marjorie Perloff, "Cultural Liminality, Aesthetic Closure?"). What such critiques tend to have in common, besides a holier than thou attitude, is a failure to acknowledge that Bhabha does indeed describe these spaces as difficult, but chooses to emphasize what is subversive and positive about them. Bhabha's emphasis on hybridity as conflictual contingency resonates well with Glenn Burger's deployment of métissage in his essay "Cicilian Armenian Métissage," a work that likewise stresses the productive power of hybridity (see especially 78).
11. Anzaldúa's writings aided immensely in the emergence of the field called border theory. For recent work that attempts to extend this project beyond the Mexico-US borderlands, see the collection of essays by Scott Michaelsen and David E. Johnson. I have also found useful the work of Néstor García Canclini in *Hybrid Cultures* and José Esteban Muñoz's *Disidentifications*.
12. "'Turn It Again'" 2. Lisa Lampert similarly speaks of "attempting to de-center Christianity from a normative position" in *Gender and Jewish Difference from Paul to Shakespeare* 1.

1 Acts of Separation: Shaping Communal Bodies

1. For an excellent examination of critical race theory and identity as performance, see Gayle Wald, *Crossing the Line*. Elizabeth Robertson brings many of the same insights to her discussion of race in "The 'Elvyssh' Power of Constance"; see also the work by Carolyn Dinshaw, Thomas Hahn, Geraldine Heng, Sharon Kinoshita, Steven Kruger, and Lisa Lampert in the bibliography.
2. See my entry for "Race" in the first supplement to the *Dictionary of the Middle Ages* for a fuller version of this argument. Patricia Ingham makes a related point throughout *Sovereign Fantasies,* a book that admirably captures the tension between "fantasies of unification" (13) and those doomed by them to exclusion and fragmentation.

3. Though the performativity of identity is associated with the gender theorist Judith Butler and critical race studies, it is important to note that both Bartlett and Davies are keenly aware in their work of the *processual* nature of collective identity formation. Bartlett writes insightfully of Europe's need to "Europeanize" itself in *The Making of Europe*, while Davies traces the anglicization of Britain in *The First English Empire*.

4. The events are imperfectly known from the historical record, but are reconstructed by V. D. Lipman in *The Jews of Medieval Norwich* 59–64. I base my discussion on the documentary evidence he assembles.

5. That Benedict was a convert was first proposed by Rye and is amplified by Lipman, who stresses that the entire Jewish population should not be assumed to be acting in concert here, since it is clear that not all the Norwich Jews knew the details of the event (for example, some of the Jews paid for a coroner to examine the child, believing that the circumcision charge would be disproved, 62). On other attempts by Jewish communities to "rescue" children from parents lost to conversion see Robert C. Stacey, "The Conversion of Jews" 270. From the medieval Jewish point of view conversion to Christianity was not really possible: "Their view of the renegade was that of Rashi: 'although he has sinned, he remains a Jew' " (Paul Hyams, "The Jewish Minority in Mediaeval England" 276).

6. Although William's army consisted mainly of Normans, it also included a multiethnic array of allies. Citing R. L. Graeme Ritchie, Marjorie Chibnall writes that the "Norman Conquest" is really just shorthand for " 'Duke William's Breton, Lotharingian, Flemish, Picard, Artesian, Cenomanian, Angevin, general-French and Norman Conquest' " (" 'Racial' Minorities in the Anglo-Norman Realm" 50). On the reduction of these multiple peoples into one legal designation, Franci, see George Garnett, " 'Franci et Angli' " 114.

7. This process of Norman assimilation coupled to Celtic differentiation is explored in much of John Gillingham's opus, collected in *The English in the Twelfth Century*. Gillingham asserts that the shift from Norman to English identity had been accomplished by the 1140s, but Hugh M. Thomas has recently argued in convincing detail that assimilation was "extremely complex and progressed in a lurching and uneven manner" until the end of the twelfth century (*The English and the Normans* 57).

8. On the Welsh as a community of blood see R. R. Davies, *Conquest, Coexistence, and Change* 16; on the utility of disidentification to medieval constructions of race see Steven F. Kruger, "Medieval Christian (Dis)identifications: Muslims and Jews in Guibert of Nogent." Such disidentifications can hold an enduring power of definition over those placed into the negative category. Cf. James Muldoon, *Identity on the Medieval Irish Frontier* x.

9. Examined by Bartlett in both *The Making of Europe* (197) and "Concepts of Race and Ethnicity" (47). Cf. the fuller list offered by Davies for the medieval definition of a people in "The Peoples of Britain and Ireland 1100–1400: I. Identities" 11.

10. Ann Williams gathers much of the material on Norman versus English hair and dress, pointing out some contradiction in the evidence, in *English and the Norman Conquest* 188–90. Such differences, it goes without saying, were susceptible to strategic exaggeration or downplaying depending upon their reporter.

11. *Chronica majora* 2.418. Robert Bartlett examines Paris's statement in "Hair in the Middle Ages" 45.

12. Monika Otter explicates the complexity this text betrays in its relation to the Norman Conquest in "1066: The Moment of Transition" 571–72, 578.

13. Eadmer reported that the men of William Rufus's court would "grow their hair long like girls . . . with locks well-combed, glancing about them and winking in an ungodly fashion." Ann Williams treats this passage from the *Historia Novorum in Anglia* in *The English and the Norman Conquest* 190.

14. Joe Hillaby, "The Ritual-Child-Murder Accusation" 80. A description of the medieval circumcision festival survives in the *Mahzor Vitry* of Simha ben Samuel of Vitry-le-François, Champagne.

15. See John Boswell's translation of the spurious "Letter of Alexius Comnenus" in *Christianity, Social Tolerance, and Homosexuality* 279–80, 367–69. See also Steven F. Kruger, "Racial/Religious and Sexual Queerness in the Middle Ages" 34.

16. Rhonda Knight explores this paradoxical assertion in "Procreative Sodomy in Gerald of Wales."

17. James Cain contextualizes the passage from the *Topographia Hibernica* in "Unnatural History" 35.

18. Jewish menstruation or anal bleeding was a popular myth throughout the later Middle Ages. Its most famous early populizer was Thomas de Cantimpré in the *Miraculorum et exemplorum memorabilium sui temporis libri duo*. Albert the Great linked Jewish nature and diet to their propensity for bloody hemorrhoids, *Quaestiones de animalibus* 9.7. The topic is well explored in Irven M. Resnick, "Medieval Roots of the Myth of Jewish Male Menses" and Willis Johnson, "The Myth of Jewish Male Menses."

19. For a full discussion of the pseudo-biographies of "Mahomet," see Norman Daniel, *Islam and the West* 79–108.

20. Geraldine Heng has demonstrated how the consumption of pig meat can differentiate races in unforgettably visual ways in *Empire of Magic* 63–113.

21. Gerald of Wales narrates the scene in the *Expugnatio Hibernica* 1.33. Davies describes it as an episode of Anglicization in *The First English Empire* 170 and as "a gastronomic, and thereby cultural, *coup de théâtre*" in *Domination and Conquest* 49. John Gillingham sees it as part of a program of acculturation that saw the importation of 569 pounds of almonds along with the weapons of war that Henry brought to Ireland (*The English in the Twelfth Century* 104). A somewhat similar feast is recorded by William of Malmesbury, when William of Normandy catches Harold's spies poking around his camp on the eve of the battle of Hastings and feeds them "a substantial dinner" (*Gesta Regum Anglorum* 3.239).

22. The best treatment of the medieval fascination with national character is Paul Meyvaert, "Voicing National Antipathy."

23. See the *History of the English Kings* 2.165 for Danish stereotypes (and Williams' refusal to translate the *barbariem linguae* of the counties the Danes attack) and 2.121 for William's comment on Guthrum's unaltered character.

24. Letter LV in *The Life, Letters, and Sermons of Hebert de Losinga* 1.100–1. The translators provide their own racist support for the timeless shortcomings of the "Keltic race" in their footnote.

25. Cf. R. R. Davies: "A people's character and customs were grounded, like its law, in the distant past; like the law, they were almost immemorial and thereby congenital" ("The Peoples of Britain and Ireland 1100–1400: III. Laws and Customs" 13).

26. See Bartlett, "Hair in the Middle Ages" 59.

27. *Statutes, Ordinances and Acts of the Parliament of Ireland* 430–69. Kathleen Biddick discusses the Statutes of Kilkenny as colonial violence in *The Shock of Medievalism* 54. See also R. R. Davies, "Race Relations in Post-Conquest Wales" 36.

28. Robert Bartlett discusses changing Anglo-Scandinavian names in *England Under the Norman and Angevin Kings* 539–40.

29. Davies, "Race Relations in Post-Conquest Wales" 34.

30. *The Making of Europe* 254.

31. *Travels of John Mandeville* 166.

32. Brynley F. Roberts, "Writing in Wales" 183.

33. N. J. Higham, *An English Empire* 219.

34. See Paul Freedman, *Images of the Medieval Peasant*.

35. Marjorie Chibnall, *The Debate on the Norman Conquest* 19.

36. The lines are from Gerald's *Invectiones* (ca. 1200). Robert Bartlett observes that even as the distinction between Norman and English was failing in England itself, the "conditions of settlement in Wales" could magnify the divide, *Gerald of Wales* 14. Gerald provides a similar if less vivid condemnation of English servility in *On the Instruction of Princes* 3.30. See also Gillingham, " 'Slaves of the Normans'?"

37. "regnum vestrum purgatum est spurcicia Britonum," *The Letters of Lanfranc*, no. 35, 124. *Spurcitia* can refer to filth in general as well as more specifically to bodily products like vomit and dung.

38. Marjorie Chibnall, " 'Racial' Minorities in Anglo-Norman Realm" 51.

39. *The Chronicle of Matthew of Paris* 142–43; Anthony Bale, "Fictions of Judaism" 136; Colin Richmond, "Englishness and Medieval Anglo-Jewry" 217.

40. "Imagining Communities" 11. I have examined the myth at greater length in *Of Giants* 45–60.

41. This intermixture makes medieval race uncannily similar to what Etienne Balibar calls "neo-racism," a racism based on religious difference. See "Is There a 'Neo-Racism'?"

42. A brief overview of the Hasidei Ashkenaz can be found in Leonard B. Glick, *Abraham's Heirs: Jews and Christians in Medieval Europe* 180–83.

43. The decree is reported by William of Malmesbury in the *Gesta regum Anglorum* 3.254.

44. Richter, "Canterbury's Primacy in Wales" 177.

45. V. D. Lipman writes of the episode from 1289–1290 in "Anatomy of Medieval Anglo-Jewry" 64. On the Domus Conversorum and the conversion of English Jews more generally, see Stacey, "The Conversion of Jews."

46. Joseph Jacobs treats the episode in *The Jews of Angevin England* 283–84.

47. See D. B. Dobson, "A Minority Within a Minority" 47 and Hyams, "The Jewish Minority in Mediaeval England" 275.

48. See Heng's sophisticated treatment of the romance in *Empire of Magic* 229–30.

49. On the enduring suspicion that greeted converts, both by their former and new communities, see Jeremy Cohen, "The Mentality of the Jewish Apostate"; Hyams, "The Jewish Minority in Mediaeval England" 276–77; William Chester Jordan, "Why 'Race'?" 166; Stephen F. Kruger, "Conversion and Medieval Categories"; Carolyn Dinshaw, "Pale Faces" 26.

50. Translation from Jacobs, *The Jews of Angevin England* 105–6. Jacobs also provides accounts of the London massacre from William of Newburgh, Robert of Gloucester, and Ephraim of Bonn.

51. "In such cases as these, those making the appeals calculated that there was some strength and meaning in calling up common descent and language and that a feeling of ethnic and linguistic solidarity might shape and direct political action" (Robert Bartlett, "Concepts of Race and Ethnicity" 51).

52. "The Peoples of Britain and Ireland II. Names, Boundaries and Regnal Solidarities" 3. Later in the same address, Davies writes that names like "the English" are "treacherous," because they create the impression that the group designated by that name is unified, timeless, and immutable when in fact just the opposite is likely to be true historically (9). On the assumption that all peoples will possess an individuating history, see Walter Goffart, *The Narrators of Barbarian History* 4.

53. On the extraordinary nature of this acknowledgment see Cassandra Potts, "'*Atque unum ex diversis gentibus populum effecit*'" 142.

54. *The Architecture of Norman England* 11.

55. The Normans broke their long alliance with the Capetians in 1052. A movement toward assimilation had long been stalled and in some ways reversed by enduring rivalry. David Crouch treats the permutations of Norman identity well in *The Normans* 32–75, where he argues that by about 1050 the Normans gave up their desire to seem French, confident in their own distinctiveness.

56. The phrase "turned into Englishmen" is the succinct formulation of R. H. C. Davis, *Normans and their Myth* 122. Chibnall discusses the process and surveys recent scholarship on the subject in *The Debate on the Norman Conquest* 128–29.

57. Williams, *The English and the Norman Conquest* 5 and 136 n43.

58. "The Peoples of Britain and Ireland 1100–1400: II. Names, Boundaries and Regnal Solidarities" 2.

59. *Migration and MythMaking in Anglo-Saxon England* 5. Cf. Susan Reynolds on myths of Scandinavian or north-German origin: "Yet the stories of Scandinavian origin, like all the others that I am considering, seem to *assume* that 'peoples' were not only enduring political and cultural communities but were biologically homogeneous too. This seems to have been an important attraction of the origin-stories during the middle ages, as well as in later centuries when 'Germanist' ideas began to grow." Reynolds argues that this assumption must be wrong, although it endures in our tendency to refer to barbarians as living in self-contained tribes and to distinguish them from the Romans they lived among ("Medieval *Origines Gentium*" 379).

60. Aristotle, *Politics* 7.7 (1327b 23); Bartlett "Concepts of Race and Ethnicity" 46.

61. Mary Floyd-Wilson labels the phenomenon "geohumoralism" and provides a useful survey of classical sources for the concept in *English Ethnicity and Race in Early Modern Drama* 23–47. See also Gail Kern Paster, *The Body Embarrassed and Humoring the Body*.

62. The passage is quoted in a discussion of non-Christian racism in the Middle Ages by Jordan in "Why 'Race'?'" 167. Maimonides, following Miskawayh, made a similar statement; see David M. Goldenberg, "The Development of the Idea of Race" 566.

63. Suzanne Conklin Akbari, "From Due East to True North."

64. I survey the scholarship on these points in *Medieval Identity Machines* 199–202.

65. *De iure et statu Meneuensis Ecclesiae* 4, trans. H. E. Butler in *The Autobiography of Gerald of Wales* 247.

66. The illustration is found in a manuscript of Paris's *Chronica Majora*, Cambridge Corpus Christi College 26.

67. David Crouch makes this point at some length in *The Normans* 102.

68. See especially Gillingham, *English in the Twelfth Century* and Davies, *First English Empire*.

69. The description is David Crouch's, *The Normans* 198.

70. This is Christopher Tyerman's point throughout *England and the Crusades*.

71. Gerald of Wales narrates the death of Archbishop Baldwin the *Journey Through Wales* 2.14.

72. I examine this biblical episode in its relation to Geoffrey of Monmouth's *History of the Kings of Britain* in *Of Giants* 34–35.

73. Quoted and translated in Robert Chazan, *European Jewry and the First Crusade* 152.

74. The biblical typology that Gildas employs and its origins have been searchingly explored by Hanning, *Vision of History in Early Britain* 55–58.

75. The biblical Gog and Magog also offered another monstrous category for the subsuming of the unknown and putatively inferior. See Scott D. Westrem, "Against Gog and Magog."

76. The description of the English appears just after Harold's death and reads, "Gens equidem illa natura semper in ferrum prompta fuit, descendens ab

antiqua Saxonum origine ferocissimorum hominum" (*Histoire de Guillaume le Conquérant 202*). Robert Stein discusses the passage in "The Trouble with Harold" 183.

77. "Introduction," in *Zoontologies* xx. See also Wolfe's monograph *Animal Rites*.

78. *Tetrabiblos* 2.2, quoted by Meyvaert, "Voicing National Antipathy" 745.

79. Hanning (*Vision of History in Early Britain* 54–55) and A. C. Sutherland ("The Imagery of Gildas's *De Excidio Brittanniae*" 159–62) explore Gildas's use of animals. Gildas's stress upon the Saxons as race that is *ferocissimus* ("extreme ferocity") and his penchant for turning them into "brutal carnivores" is explored by Higham, *The English Conquest* 37.

80. *Chronicles of the Reigns* 3.156–7, cited by John Gillingham, *The English in the Twelfth Century* 11.

81. Abelard makes a similar observation. Anna Sapir Abulafia treats these and other partisans in the debates between Christians and Jews who thought of Jews in animalistic terms in "Bodies in the Jewish-Christian Debate."

82. For these examples and for an excellent overview of Jews as "blind beasts" see Bale, "Fictions of Judaism" 141–42. Bale writes perceptively of the bestiary tradition that it "offers us clear evidence that Jews' bodies (as well as the Jewish religion) were thought of as degraded and corrupt entities, foreshadowing later antisemitic material and a 'racial' conception of Judaism" (141).

83. *Le Roman de Rou de Wace,* ll.8067–69. This passage prompts Susan Crane to argue that "The distinction between 'French-speaking' and 'not French-speaking' was sharper than any single ethnic opposition [in post-Conquest England], and language continued to be the most salient difference between conquerors and conquered" ("Anglo-Norman Cultures in England, 1066–1460" 36). Yet Searle asks if we should really imagine that Harold Godwinson and Earl Waltheof had to rely on interpreters to speak to William: "The Normans obviously spoke French—and used it in England to distinguish themselves from those who land they had taken. Distinguishing themselves from their prey was part of what made Normans. But we surely underestimate the multilingual nature of the restless world of the eleventh century if we imagine that they could not get along in what one might call a 'trade-route' (or invading-route) *patois*" (*Predatory Kinship* 243). Most important, then, is how language is imagined to call into being an inviolable separateness, despite the fact that linguistic hybridities and bilingualism are more likely the norm (on which see Susan Crane, *Insular Romance* especially 2–7).

84. On English tails see Arthur Langfors, "'L'Anglais qui couve' dans l'imagination populaire au Moyen Age" and. Thomas, *The English and the Normans* 303. Malcolm Jones produces a picture of Edward I as a tailed Englishman in *Secret Middle Ages* 67. In her discussion of *Richard Coeur de Lion*, Heng describes the tailed English as a racialized body, but is confused about the source of the legend (*Empire of Magic* 91–98). Like Bradford Broughton (*Legends of King Richard* 94) Heng places the first recordation of the myth in

William of Malmesbury's *Gesta pontificum anglorum*. In fact, while this text contains an episode of aggressive fish tail hanging at the hands of irate villagers and Augustine's subsequent pique, the narrative culminates in repentance and baptism, not a vindictive curse (1.84). William borrowed the story from the "greater" (*major*) life of St. Augustine, composed by a Flemish monk named Goscelin whose special passion was composing lives of English saints. Wace may have taken the description of the malevolent affixing of fish-tails from William's *Gesta*, but the curse and its consequences come from an unknown source, oral tradition, or Wace's fertile imagination.

2 Between Belongings: History's Middles

1. Simon James, *The Atlantic Celts: Ancient People or Modern Invention*?
2. "Nearly at the extremity of the known world" is James Campbell's description of Bede's native Northumbria (*Essays in Anglo-Saxon History* 29), and well captures its position vis à vis Rome—though not necessarily Bede's own experience of place. Nowadays we are used to situating Bede with reference to London, unthinkingly describing him as a resident of the north of England (a nonexistent entity in Bede's day). London was not a possible point of reference for Bede; Northumbria is clearly for him its own center.
3. The best consideration of how the *adventus Saxonum* is rendered into— indeed, invented by—later historical narrative remains Nicholas Howe, *Migration and Mythmaking in Anglo-Saxon England*.
4. A good, recent survey of this mixed historical origin in its relation to the textual promulgation of a seemingly all-encompassing Anglo-Saxon culture is Alfred K. Siewers, "Landscapes of Conversion," especially 8–12. Also of note is the revisionary work of N. J. Higham, especially *The Kingdom of Northumbria, AD 350–1100*; *The English Conquest*; *An English Empire;* and *The Convert Kings*. Walter Goffart has trenchantly reconceptualized Bede as a writer actively engaged with shaping the social reality of his time, an antidote to previous scholarship that saw him as an unworldly voice: *The Narrators of Barbarian History* 235–328. I will not be concerned with Bede's motivations so much as the effect his text had of establishing a purified vision of insular history.
5. Kathleen Biddick offers an "articulation" of Bede that surfaces his hybridity rather differently than I do in *Shock of Medievalism* 96–101.
6. The source of Edwin's Christianity is crucial: not the Britons, living near and perhaps among his own people, but missionaries tied to the church in Rome. By denying the possibility of an indigenous connection for the Christianity adopted by the *gens Anglorum*, Bede instigates his process of clearly separating the two peoples. For a reading that stresses the overlap and interchange between the two groupsduring this period, depicting a world very different from Bede's purified spaces, see Patrick Sims-Williams, *Religion and Literature in Western England*, especially 25–33, 77–84. Sims-Williams argues forcefully for the role Britons living with the Anglo-Saxons

played in their conversion, at least among the Hwicce and Magonsætan. Goffart observes that the Roman and Irish vectors in Bede's narrative of Christianization are meant to exclude the Britons in *Narrators of Barbarian History* 250.

7. Bede also includes ecclesiastical Latin on his list. Latin offered the possibility of a unifying tongue, even if Bede had his doubts over whether the Britons could be Christian in the same way as the converted English.

8. In fact the topographical first chapter of the first book of the *History* gives a brief origin for the Britons (who arrive from Armorica), the Picts (originally a band of men from Scythia), and the Irish. A cursory arc of chapters gives the Romans their presence on the island (1.2–13), intermingling them with the Christian Britons. The remainder of the work is then devoted to the English.

9. George Hardin Brown emphasizes the fragility of Christianity in Anglo-Saxon Britain in *Bede the Venerable* 9.

10. Specifically, Bede was a native Bernician (Northumbria was made up of the former kingdoms of Bernicia and Deira). Higham goes so far as to call him a "Bernician jingoist" (*An English Empire* 65). Goffart similarly observes that "Bede's *History*, in spite of its title and grandiose incorporation of the English microcosm into the macrocosm of providential time, is predominantly concerned with Northumbria . . . Bede's interest in other kingdoms and in Canterbury is genuine, but subordinate to his narrower homeland" (*Narrators of Barbarian History* 240; see also 251–52). Bede gives a brief account of his own life in the *Ecclesiastical History* 5.24.

11. Though of course that is exactly what Edwin was, until he converted six years previous to this battle. That Penda has such power in Mercia also suggests how much wishful thinking Bede is displaying in writing that Edwin "held under his sway the whole realm of Britain" (2.9).

12. Higham gathers the sources in *The Convert Kings* 149 and 195 n51, as well as *An English Empire* 137. See also the notes in the Colgrave and Mynors edition of the *Ecclesiastical History* 162 and 202–3. Bede is vague on Edwin's wanderings during his exile (2.12).

13. Cf. 2.9, where Edwin is glimpsed spreading his control across the island by force.

14. Higham makes this point in *An English Empire* 133–35; for an analysis of the animal attributes deployed by Gildas see Higham's *The English Conquest* 53–56. Goffart describes Bede's manipulation of Gildas to indict the Britons and pave the way for the arrival of his own people: *Narrators of Barbarian History* 302–3.

15. Thus according to Joaquín Martínez Pizarro: "What modern historical scholarship has had to correct in Bede's account of the Anglo-Saxon *Landnahme* is precisely this sense of alienation and lack of contact and mutual assimilation between Britons and English, together with the idea that the spread of the latter pushed the former into Wales and the areas of the North" ("Ethnic and National History" 66).

16. Higham argues that *infandus* has its suggestive counterpart in the description of the Saxons by Gildas as *nefandus*, and therefore constitutes part of Bede's reworking of Gildas's terms (*An English Empire* 134).

17. On this point see Susan Reynolds, "Medieval *Origines Gentium*" 381.

18. On the complicated ethnicities behind Bede's three categories, see the provocative essay by John Moreland, "Ethnicity, Power and the English."

19. See the letter that Bede reproduces in 1.32. On the papal tendency to make vast unities out of disparate peoples (*Gallia, Germania, Italia, Anglia*), see G. G. Coulton, "Nationalism in the Middle Ages" 29.

20. Cf. Walter Pohl: "In Bede's ethnic model, there is no room for what we might call ethnogenetic processes—people can come and go, or even be destroyed, but they do not mix or change. Thus, after almost 400 years of Roman rule, the Romans can simply leave or be killed, and leave the Britons they have once conquered to themselves. Bede also disregards—or rather denies—he possibility that many Britons might have become Angles or Saxons . . . Such a view could in the long run lead to contradictions between the actual situation and a text as influential as Bede's *Ecclesiastical History*. But it could also contribute towards stabilizing ethnic identities as a basis for political legitimacy" ("Ethnic Names and Identities in the British Isles" 25)

21. See the wide-ranging work of James Campbell, especially "Was it Infancy in England?" "The Late Anglo-Saxon State: A Maximum View," and "The United Kingdom of England." See also R. R. Davies, *The First English Empire* 50–55 and 196–200, and "The Peoples of Britain and Ireland, 1100–1400: II Names, Boundaries and Regnal Solidarities" 10–12; Sarah Foot, "The Making of *Angelcynn*: English Identity Before the Norman Conquest"; and Patrick Wormald, "*Engla Land*: The Making of an Allegiance."

22. The quotations are from Campbell, "The United Kingdom of England" 31.

23. Simon Keynes, "Regenbald the Chancellor (sic)," especially 217, 220. Though, as David Crouch observes, symbolic gestures often cloaked the harsher reality: "William's rhetoric was all about continuity and inheritance; his actions spoke of high-handed superiority and dispossession" (*The Normans* 103).

24. Ann Williams argues that the true turning points for the conquest were marked by the resistance offered to William by the citizens of Exeter in 1068 and the revolt of 1069–1070 (*The English and the Norman Conquest* 44). The conquest, in other words, is best seen as a changing, multiregister national reconfiguration of long duration and lingering effect.

25. Michael A. Faletra rather too flatly advances this argument for William of Malmesbury and Geoffrey of Monmouth in "Narrating the Matter of Britain," concluding that "the historians active in the eleventh and twelfth century . . . together created a series of texts that celebrate Norman achievements and provide a discursive foundation for the Norman conquest of Britain" (60). Robert M. Stein usefully explores the rhetorical complexity

of William of Malmesbury's text by mapping it across his divided personal allegiances and emplacing the *Historia* within the contradictory, post-conquest desire "to make history English" ("Making History English" 104, 98). See also Andrew Galloway's account of the mutability of William's allegiances in "Writing History in England" 264–66. John Gillingham advances a similar argument for Henry of Huntingdon's changing affiliations in *The English in the Twelfth-Century* 128–30.

26. The phrase is taken from a charter composed for Richard de Montgomery, a follower of William the Conqueror, as he speaks his identity. See Eleanor Searle, *Predatory Kinship* 242. On Norman heterogeneity and *Normannitas* as a performative rather than pregiven identity, see 244. Norman unity has sometimes been overplayed, as Pauline Stafford points out in *Unification and Conquest* 105–6.

27. Eric Fernie, *Architecture of Norman England* 20.

28. A century later, Richard fitzNigel described the implicit philosophy as well as the mechanics of this dispossession in the *Course of the Exchequer*, where he writes that William was surprisingly merciful to "the conquered, and probably disloyal, English" when he allowed them to hold lands through service or contract but not through inheritance. See 53–54, from which the terms *indigeni* and *gens subacta* used above are also taken.

29. "Making History English" 97. Stein is following R. W. Southern's observation about "historical activity" being a "therapeutic" mode in the wake of social upheaval. Southern labels the period from 1090 to 1130 as a time when "a crisis in national affairs . . . seemed to alienate men from their past": "The Sense of the Past" 244, 246.

30. William claims that the project was motivated by affection for his homeland and the urging of Queen Matilda, wife to Henry I. His complex ties of patronage and the ways in which contemporary constructions of William as a disinterested "modern" historian efface the ambitions of his text are well examined by Laurie B. Finke and Martin B. Shichtman in *King Arthur and the Myth of History* 21–34. My own reading of William is deeply sympathetic to Finke and Shichtman's, for these are two of the few scholars who take notice of how the "dialogically agitated environment in which William wrote, an environment of uneven, unsettled, and conflicted cultural, political, ideological, linguistic, and economic agendas" (31) penetrated William's historiographic and artistic project.

31. On Bede's "hovering, magisterial presence" see Nancy Partner, *Serious Entertainments* 5.

32. Rodney Thomson relates the history of the monastery to William's background in *William of Malmesbury* 98–99. Southern lingers over William's masterful reconstruction of Aldhelm's life in the *Gesta Pontificum* in "The Sense of the Past" 255.

33. The bluntness of such a complaint needs to be taken with a grain of salt. The E text of the *Anglo-Saxon Chronicle*, for example, contains as an entry for the year of the Conqueror's death (1087) an account of William's life composed by someone who clearly attended the royal court. The lengthy

obituary commingles criticism with ample praise. Of William of Malmesbury's treatment of the Conqueror and other participants in the events surrounding the conquest Hugh M. Thomas concludes reasonably that around 1125 there were clearly "vociferous disputes between the English and the Normans about the characters and actions of key figures . . . clearly the conquest was still a topic for heated debate over half a century after it occurred" (*The English and the Normans* 241).

34. "Long since had it [that is, the *patria*] grown used to the character of the English—though that changed greatly with the passage of time" (3.245). These are the lines that immediately follow William's observation that Hastings was a *dies fatalis* for England. Cf. William's initial description of the Angles, Saxons, and Jutes (1.4).

35. William contrasts this evolutionary achievement of the English with the Irish, who never progress from squalid rusticity (5.409).

36. See *The English in the Twelfth Century* 29. Cf. p. 6 "In William's eyes the more 'Frenchified' England and the English became, the better." The downside of this emphasis on Franconorman manners and cultivation is that the Welsh are rendered barbarians (18, 27–28).

37. Gillingham's emphasis on William's Francophilia also downplays his classicism. As Monika Otter points out in her examination of William's rendering of a life of St. Wulfstan from English into Latin, this *translatio* enables William to stress both the rupture caused by the Norman Conquest and the continuities that traverse it ("1066: The Moment of Transition" 578–79).

38. Finke and Shichtman say it best: "Medieval history, in both its 'serious' and 'fabulous' forms, invested its world with the power to reveal truths through symbols that were not strictly literal but poetic, or more accurately, that confounded the literal and the metaphoric" (*King Arthur and the Myth of History* 40). See also Monika Otter, *Inventiones*.

39. Stein notes William's juxtaposition of the conjoined twins with a discussion of the incorruptibility of the English saints: "The uncorrupted body of the saint . . . stands over against this form of monstrous integration" ("Making History English" 102). See also his analysis of the twins in "Signs and Things" 108.

40. *Inventiones* 98. Otter argues that Gerbert's wonders are an enactment of the "historian in his lab," animating the lifeless facts of history (101). While I do not disagree with this interpretation, I also argue that other kinds of experimental "lab work" are being conducted through the figure of Gerbert.

41. On the differences between Bede and William in their use of the wondrous see Thomson, *William of Malmesbury* 23–24.

42. He accomplishes this mission, of course, by writing in neither French nor English but in ecclesiastical Latin, a third component to his compound identity. See Stein's sophisticated treatment in "Making History English," especially 104.

43. In his dedication Geoffrey writes that book was given to him by Walter, Archdeacon of Oxford. No such book has ever been discovered. Most scholars now believe that Geoffrey did not have a precise source, but

combined Welsh materials in innovative ways. Multiple versions of Geoffrey's text survive. I have consulted the composite edition by Faral (possessed of many drawbacks, but probably the closest to Geoffrey's original) and the two versions edited by Wright: the "Vulgate" or "standard" version (represented by the Bern MS, which probably circulated in Normandy), and the "First Variant." None of these versions represent some final, authorially sanctioned text. Both Faral and Wright employ the same chapter numbering, and the first reference in my quotations will be according to this numeration, with a note where the two texts differ in ways important to my argument. Lewis Thorpe did not adopt Faral's numbering system but used that employed by Commelin; my second set of numbers therefore gives the chapter and section of Thorpe's translation.

44. Scholars have repeatedly observed that myths of Trojan origin tend to be most actively promulgated as part of a program of imperialism or in an effort to promulgate a sense of shared ethnicity. See Reynolds, "Medieval *Origines Gentium* and the Community of the Realm" 375, 378, and Richard Waswo, "Our Ancestors, The Trojans" 273. Nicholas Birns allows that the Trojan myth was a "secular paradigm which strengthened current political authority," but stresses the uncontrollable "subsidiary reverberations" central to its enduring vitality: "The Trojan Myth: Postmodern Reverberations" 49–50.

45. On Geoffrey's renarration of insular chronology, see R. William Leckie, *The Passage of Dominion*.

46. In her sensitive reading of Geoffrey's project, Kellie Robertson compares his *History of the Kings of Britain* to a minor literature as described by Gilles Deleuze and Félix Guattari: "Geoffrey's claim that he is translating from Trojan-derived Welsh challenges not only the authority of Anglo-Saxon that is privileged in its relation to Latin, but also the Anglo-Latin historiographical tradition in which the Welsh were seen as morally corrupt and their subjugation by the Saxons read as the appropriate corollary to *translatio imperii*" ("Geoffrey of Monmouth and the Translation of Insular Historiography" 46). Cf. R. R. Davies, who writes that Geoffrey "torpedoed" the "smug Anglocentricity" of William of Malmesbury and Henry of Huntingdon "by making Britain, not England, the subject of his work and providing Britain with a glorious pre-English and non-English past" (*The Matter of Britain* 10). For this reason Davies calls the *Historia* a "counter-history." Similarly, Patricia Clare Ingham christens the *Historia* "an influential fantasy productive for an oppositional history of British identity" (*Sovereign Fantasies* 24).

47. "Narrating the Matter of Britain" 61. See also R. W. Hanning, *The Vision of History* 135–36.

48. Geoffrey certainly had his detractors, such as Gerald of Wales and William of Newburgh, but this criticism should not obscure the cross-cultural enthusiasm that Geoffrey's work generated, leading to widespread admiration.

49. The most eloquent examiner of Geoffrey's sheer competitiveness with William of Malmesbury is Valerie Flint, "Parody and its Purpose." J. C. Crick

appropriately calls Geoffrey's work an "un-Bedan un-english account of early insular history" that could disturb the secure anglocentrism of other historiographers ("The British Past and the Welsh Future" 62).

50. Whereas Bede had conflated his ethnically complicated forebears into the three affiliated kinship groups of Angles, Saxons, and Jutes, Geoffrey reduces these peoples to the singular *Saxones*. As E. A. Freeman pointed out long ago, it was only those hostile to the English who called them "Saxons" (*The History of the Norman Conquest of England* 5 825).

51. The Welsh seized upon this confident prophecy of the end of English hegemony, causing the reviser of the Bern MS version of the *History* to add "The Welsh, once they degenerated from the noble state enjoyed by the Britons, never afterwards regained the overlordship of the island. On the contrary, they went on quarrelling with the Saxons and among themselves and remained in a perpetual state of either civil or external warfare" (207; trans. Thorpe p.284n).

52. Geoffrey does mention Alfred as the translator of laws taken from the Britons, a backhanded way of acknowledging Alfred's fame that robs him of any real achievement (39, 47; 3.5, 3.13). Breaking the narration off in the early days of the Saxon occupation allows Geoffrey to leave English history as fairly empty, however.

53. The line is pilfered from Bede, where it is meant to indicate the failings of the British Christians; its meaning becomes very different in Geoffrey's text.

54. Gillingham's discussion of Geoffrey is especially rich; see "The Context and Purposes of Geoffrey of Monmouth's *History of the Kings of Britain*" in *The English in the Twelfth Century* 19–39, quotation at 19. Davies describes Geoffrey as "a deliberate trader in multiple ambiguities" (*The Matter of Britain* 6), and lucidly outlines the challenges that his work posed to the contemporary political order, especially in its "evasive ambiguities" (*The First English Empire* 39–41). See also Ingham, *Sovereign Fantasies,* especially 21–24, 43–49 (which describes Geoffrey's valorization of *ambiguitas,* or hybridity); Otter, *Inventiones* 70–71, 77–80; and Michelle Warren's thorough account of the complexities of the text in *History on the Edge* 25–82.

55. See especially *The English in the Twelfth Century* 19–39. Gillingham argues that Geoffrey was a Welshman determined to give civilization to a people being represented as "barbarians, as brutish peoples without a history" (31). Although they do not seem to have known each other's work, Richard Waswo makes similar though less historically specific observations about Geoffrey's recuperative project in "Inventing Cultural Identity in the Middle Ages" 284.

56. Thus the *Gesta Stephani*, a text written by an author whose sympathies clearly did not lay with either Robert or the Welsh, described the alliance as conjoining rebels against Stephen to "a dreadful and unendurable mass of Welsh, all in agreement, all in complete harmony, together to overthrow the king" (1.54).

57. Long critical traditions connect Geoffrey with parody or the glorification of the Welsh or Bretons. In a sophisticated reading of Geoffrey of Monmouth's

allegiances, Faletra argues that, like William of Malmesbury, Geoffrey's linear historical mode likewise justifies a *translatio imperii* (Britons-Saxons-Normans) but does so "agonistically" (69). At the same time, however, the Troy myth as narrated by Geoffrey and others was full of contradiction (Birns, "The Trojan Myth: Postmodern Reverberations") ambivalence (Warren, *History on the Edge*, 25–30), ambiguity (Ingham, *Sovereign Fantasies* 15, 43), and self-deconstruction (Lee Patterson, *Negotiating the Past* 201–2). Perhaps Waswo puts it best when he writes that Geoffrey's story could "be appealing and useful to almost any faction in the Anglo-French feudal domains . . . the local or racial loyalties of one writer or another do not much matter; the story's appeal is the force of the legend itself, and anyone can use it—anyone, that is, who finds a foundation by invading culture-bringers to be the essence of civilization" ("Inventing Cultural Identity in the Middle Ages" 285–86).

58. Thus Gerald of Wales could write that "the Normans (but not the English), although different in speech, were Trojans *sicut et nostrates*" (Reynolds, "Medieval *Origines Gentium*" 385).

59. *The Legendary History of Britain* 426. On Geoffrey's utility to the Normans see also Patricia Ingham, *Sovereign Fantasies* 9–10; Finke and Shichtman, *King Arthur and the Myth of History* 38–39, 45, 51–52; Warren, *History on the Edge* 25–59.

60. *The Debate on the Norman Conquest* 130.

61. The phrase "turned into Englishmen" is from R. H. C. Davis's succinct formulation, "the paradox of the Normans is that though it was in England that they reached their acme and fulfilled themselves as Normans, yet in the long run the conquest of England turned them into Englishmen." *Normans and their Myth* 122. Chibnall discusses the process and surveys recent scholarship on the subject in *The Debate on the Norman Conquest* 128–29.

62. Cf. Otter, *Inventiones* 69–70, where the spectacular death of Lear's father Bladud (dashed to pieces after an unsuccessful attempt at aviation) anticipates his son's "fragmentation of the realm."

63. Brutus in Geoffrey's account is a conquistador in the Norman tradition. His cultivation of fields, energetic program of architectural development, founding of cities, and vigorous promulgation of law codes were Norman strategies for securing new territory. The struggles over succession, the civil wars, and endless aristocratic power plays that animate the *History* are more characteristic of the English empire from 1066–1036 than of anything that unfolded in the kingdoms of Wales, or in Britain's pre-English past.

64. Williams traces the fates of Ealdgyth, Nest, and Ulf in *The English and the Norman Conquest* 51–52.

65. In fact this nameless woman is only half Saxon, since her mother is said to be "a woman born from a noble family of the Gewissei [Vortigern's tribe]" (12.14).

66. *The Curse of Eve, the Wound of the Hero* ix.

67. On women in Geoffrey's history see Finke and Shichtman, *King Arthur and the Myth of History* 55–61. Gransden sees in these women support

for Matilda's claim to the English throne (*Historical Writing in England* 207–8). The difficult hybridities that women could figure are well illustrated by Emma of Normandy. She was the wife of two kings, one English and one Danish, and thereby the mother of two (Harthacnut [by Cnut] and Edward the Confessor [by Æthelred]). Her Norman name was changed to Ælfgifu when she married Æthelred. While living in Flanders after the death of Cnut, she even commissioned a pro-Danish contemporary history of England that positioned her as the legitimator of future succession to the throne, the *Encomium Emmae Reginae*.

68. *Vision of History in Early Britain* 162.

3   In the Borderlands: The Identities of Gerald of Wales

1. "The British Past and the Welsh Future" 62.
2. See especially John Gillingham's schematic outline in *The English in the Twelfth Century* 154–56; Michael Richter, "Giraldus Cambrenisis" 3.1; and, to a lesser extent, Robert Bartlett's biography *Gerald of Wales*.
3. *Pura Wallia* marks the lost dream of the Cambro-Normans to conquer all of Wales (a loss fully approved of by Henry II, who viewed the power of the Marchers with growing suspicion, especially after their successes in Ireland). Once Henry reached an accord with the Welsh princelings (1171–1172), native Welsh kingdoms such as Deheubarth regained some of their former vigor and the March became more suspended in the middle than forward-pushing frontier. On the ambiguities of the geographical designation "Wales" as a whole and the fluctuations of its border before 1300, see R. R. Davies, *Conquest, Coexistence and Change* 4–13.
4. See the Brut entry for 1098 and R. R. Davies' comments in *The First English Empire* 5.
5. In addition to the writings of Gerald of Wales, my generalizations about medieval Wales are based on the following sources: Bartlett, *Gerald of Wales*; A. D. Carr, *Medieval Wales*; R. R. Davies, *Lordship and Society in the March of Wales; Conquest, Coexistence and Change; Domination and Conquest*; and *The Age of Conquest;* Wendy Davies, *Wales in the Early Middle Ages*; Ralph A. Griffiths, *Conquerors and Conquered in Medieval Wales*; John Edward Lloyd, *A History of Wales From the Earliest Times to the Edwardian Conquest*; Lynn H. Nelson, *The Normans in South Wales*; David Walker, *Medieval Wales*.
6. See Davies, *Lordship and Society in the March of Wales* 304–28, 341–47; *Age of Conquest* 97–100, 371–73, 421; and *Domination and Conquest* 88–89.
7. The native Welsh, that is, began to recognize themselves as a solidarity only after they saw themselves from within the collective terms thrust upon them by their antagonists. See especially Davies, *Conquest, Coexistence, and Change* 4–13. As Michael Richter has observed, "gradually [the Welsh] came to know each other as fellow-countrymen by being fellow sufferers" ("National Identity in Medieval Wales" 38).

8. Patricia Clare Ingham traces this worsening of conditions and gathers relevant bibliography in *Sovereign Fantasies* 68–69.

9. *The English and the Normans* 71.

10. Thus Davies: "To outsiders Wales was a land of exclusive racial groups: French (Norman), English, and Welsh. To the men of the March such a confident simplification was a distortion . . . The ingredients of the making of a 'middle nation'—a group caught between, and sitting astride, the normal categorizations of race—were being assembled in parts of Norman Wales" (*Conquest, Coexistence and Change* 103).

11. Early in his career R. R. Davies argued that the "March of Wales" is a rather misleading designation, given the area's mutability: "There was not so much *a* March as marches," in competition and flux ("Kings, Lords and Liberties" 45).

12. The two passages are quoted and Gerald's dual heritage given a thoughtful reading in Bartlett, *Gerald of Wales* 17–20. Cf. the complaint of the burgesses of Llanfaes that "in Wales they were regarded as Englishmen and in England as Welshman": R. R. Davies, "Race Relations in Post-Conquest Wales" 44. Gerald also relates that he was marked as *English* while studying in Paris. At the birth of Philip, future king of the French, a woman singles Gerald and his companions out for some invective against their king (*On the Instruction of Princes* 3.25).

13. Gerald then acknowledges the suspicion under which the Marchers were held by the English court, hinting at its reason: "what a noble stock, a stock which unaided would have been equal to the conquest of any kingdom."

14. The same diffidence is seen in Gerald's use of the Latinate *Cambrensis* to describe himself. *Kambria* was (according to Geoffrey of Monmouth) the original word for Wales (*Historia Regum Britannie* 23), but was an unusual contemporary term for the geography.

15. It might seem that Gerald also refers to his Norman heritage rather obliquely through the same formula, since he calls that race *Galli* rather than *Normanni*. Yet by Gerald's day *Normanni* typically referred to Normans fresh from Normandy; *Galli* was sometimes used even in the early days of Norman England to designate the Normans, though *Franci* was more typical. When Gerald composes his *Descriptio Kambriae*, a work written at a time in his life when he was more sympathetic to the Welsh, he voices his dual heritage as derived (*duximus*) from both people (*utraque gente*), the English (*Anglis*) and the Welsh (*Kambros*); "English" is of course what the Normans in England had long been calling themselves, while "Cambrians" is Gerald's term (2.10).

16. I do not mean to reduce what was in fact a multifarious and prolonged conquest into so simple a catalyst as identity panic, only to suggest the pivotal role that such alarm played. It is useful to bear in mind that the Marcher lords lost vast amounts of their Welsh territories to native princes during the turbulence of Stephen's reign. When Henry II ascended the throne in 1154, it became evident to the Marchers that their power was going to be curtailed. No surprise, then, that another frontier would be sought. For an

excellent overview of the conflict between the Marchers and the crown, as well as the identity crisis it provoked, see Rhonda Knight, "Werewolves, Monsters, and Miracles" 58–61.

17. A captive to her cousin Owain ap Cadwgan, the prince of Powys, Nest later bore two sons, Llewellyn and Einion. The latter eventually became steward to his half-brother Robert of Gloucester, demonstrating just how intricate were the ties that intermingled the Welsh and English families connected to Nest. Nest's life and her complicated family are lucidly explicated by Gwenn Meredith in "Henry I's Concubines" 16–19.

18. The line from the *Expugnatio Hibernica* quoted at the beginning of this sentence is taken from Gerald's opening address to Count Richard, about to be crowned King Richard, but its negative characterization of the Irish is endemic to the *Expugnatio* as well as to the *Topographia*.

19. "Sex and the Irish Nation" 169.

20. "Unnatural History" 33. Cain also well captures the text's spirit of experiment and play, even if he does not dwell upon it.

21. See *Metamorphosis and Identity* 15–18, 77–111.

22. Knight posits a similar interpretation, seeing in the corporeal changeability that inheres in the lycanthropy a voicing of the Marcher fears of losing their own identities and becoming Irish ("Werewolves, Monsters, and Miracles" 73).

23. Likewise in the *Journey Through Wales*, Gerald writes that the tongue of a wolf can cause death by infecting open wounds with its poisonous saliva (1.7).

24. Gerald's Latin punningly interweaves Irish beards (*barbis*) with their barbarity (*barbarissimi*), creating a rhetorical frenzy that O'Meara's translation does not adequately capture: "Gens igitur haec gens barbara, et vere barbara. Quia non tantum barbaro vestium ritu, verum etiam comis et barbis luxuriantibus, iuxta modernas novitates, incultissima; et omnes eorum mores barbarissimi sunt."

25. The king is said only to "advance bestially" on the mare (*bestialiter accedens*), but as David Rollo points out the same Latin phrase is used to describe the copulation of a goat and woman in 2.56 ("Gerald of Wales' *Topographia Hibernica*" 182). Cain observes that the episode ensures that the reader knows that bestiality "fully penetrates all ranks of [Irish] society: from royalty to clergy to the common people in general" ("Unnatural History" 39).

26. The Christianization of England included persuading its peoples to desist in consuming horsemeat, except under extenuating circumstances. See Robert Bartlett, *England Under the Norman and Angevin Kings* 667.

27. Davies, *The First English Empire* 125.

28. The special prominence accorded the episode has been well argued by Cain, "Unnatural History" 36.

29. This is not to deny that Gerald does betray occasional complexity in his depiction of the Marchers' interactions with the Irish—they had, after all, come to the island at the invitation of an Irish king. The *Expugnatio* in general reveals a more nuanced view of the conquest, complaining (for example) that the new men brought to Ireland by the Angevins alienated former

Irish allies of the Marchers by treating them with contempt, pulling on their beards and taking their lands (*Expugnatio* 2.35).

30. A point dramatically brought home when Gerald accidentally writes *Kambrie* for *Hibernie* in describing the submission of the kings of Ireland to Henry; see the rubric to *Expugnatio* 1.30.

31. Cantref Mawr is weighted with so much history for Gerald that his pen "quivers" (*noster explicare stilus abhorruit*). Nearby are Roman ruins, reminders of an ancient colonization. The place itself had been a "safe haven" for the Welsh, since its forests are impenetrable, but here the king's troops exacted "terrible vengeance" on the indigenous population—including mass decapitations—fter a battle in 1136 (on these events see *Gesta Stephani* 1.8–11). This colonialist trauma experienced in Gerald's body as he inscribes the location's history is clearly meant to be kept in mind as the Guaidan episode unfolds.

32. Ingham suggests this deployment of Fernandez-Armesto's description in relation to the Welsh in *Sovereign Fantasies*, a book that admirably analyzes the postcolonial complexities I am treating here (see especially 11, 22–23, 39–40). See also Laurie Finke and Martin Shichtman on "anachronistic humans," *King Arthur and the Myth of History* 33–34.

33. The quotations are from Edmund Spenser and form the title of Davies' rich chapter on the barbarization of the non-English in *The First English Empire* 113–41.

34. Letter 87, *Letters of John of Salisbury* I 135. For John Welsh bestiality is also manifested in religious deficiency, for even though nominally Christian the race "despises the Word of Life" (*aspernatur uerbum uitae*).

35. *Gesta Stephani* 1.8. Chapters 8–11 of the first book of the *Gesta* are dedicated to the Welsh rebellion of 1136 and contain an extended narration of Welsh bestiality.

36. R. H. C. Davis has convincingly argued that the author of the narrative was likely Robert of Lewes, Bishop of Bath (1136–1166). See the introduction to the *Gesta Stephani* xxxiv.

37. See the essay "Sly Civility" in *The Location of Culture* 93–101, as well as two related pieces on postcolonial mimicry in the same book: "Of Mimicry and Man" (85–92) and "Signs Taken for Wonders" (102–22).

38. In fact the lines about "ejecting the entire population that lives there now, so that Wales can be colonized anew" because the "present inhabitants are virtually ungovernable" were cut from the text by Gerald as he revised the *Descriptio* ca.1214. Such an excision fits well with Bartlett's argument that Gerald in the course of his life increasingly identified more with his Welsh ancestry, especially as he argued the case for St. David's as an archepiscopal seat (*Gerald of Wales* 53–57). Monika Otter agrees, arguing that in the absence of English preferment he "rediscovers his Welshness" later in life (*Inventiones* 146).

39. J. C. Crick argues that this speech is Gerald's rebuke of the Welsh dream of recovering rule of the entire island, a discrediting of those ambitions fostered by Geoffrey of Monmouth. In the old man's statement that only a

small corner (*angulus*) will retain its Welsh identity is an "innovatory" attempt to circumscribe the Welsh desire to recover a lost hegemony, urging them to be satisfied with endurance under reduced circumstances ("British Past and the Welsh Future" 74). It seems to me, however, that by the time Gerald writes this section of the *Description* his self-identification has become conflicted enough that such a straightforward embrace of an imperialist point of view is unlikely.

40. A good overview of Gerald's moments of self-revelation can be found in Yoko Wada, "Gerald on Gerald."

41. Stephen G. Nichols, "Fission and Fusion" 32.

42. Thorpe gives a thorough account of the dating of each version in his introduction, 36–39.

43. Both man and beast, he says, are "greatly influenced by the dam whose milk they suck." Gerald is fascinated by such stories of corporeal imprinting. In a later chapter, for example, he gives the famous example of a queen who "had a painting of a Negro in her bedroom" and, because she looked at it too much, gave birth to a black baby. Marie-Hélène Huet has studied this visual phenomenon and called it "maternal impression" (*Monstrous Imagination*), but for Gerald it is more accurately described as *parental* impression: to prove his point that both parents imprint the unborn child, he gives the example of a man who, during intercourse, thought about someone plagued by a nervous tic, and engendered a son afflicted by the same bodily contortion (*Journey through Wales* 2.7).

44. Although Thorpe's translation does not make this point clear, the gender of *vitulus* can only be masculine ("bull-calf").

45. These complicated interrelations are well mapped on the table compiled by A. J. Roderick in "Marriage and Politics in Wales" 5.

46. More accurately, four of the five sons die upon succeeding to their inheritance; William perished before he could possess the land.

47. The gloss "coincidence of opposites" for *mixta* is from Caroline Walker Bynum, *Metamorphosis and Identity* 43.

48. The quotation is Young's gloss on Deleuze and Guattari's desiring machines read through a postcolonial lens in *Colonial Desire* 174.

49. See *Expugnatio Hibernica* 2.5.

50. The "frontier thesis" advanced by Frederick Jackson Turner in 1893, though much critiqued, continues to occupy the contemporary historiographic imaginary ("The Significance of the Frontier in American History," *The Frontier in American History* 1–38). For an overview of the influence of Turner on medieval studies, see the collection of essays edited by Robert Bartlett and Angus MacKay, *Medieval Frontier Societies*, especially Robert I. Burns, "The Significance of the Frontier in the Middle Ages." A recent critique of the frontier that anticipates my argument here is Amy Kaplan, " 'Left Alone with America.' "

51. *Borderlands / La Frontera* 3. For sensitive readings of Anzaldúa's work, see Carlos G. Vélez-Ibáñez, *Border Visions* 216–21, and Robert McRuer, *Queer Renaissance* 116–54.

52. Quotations from "Preface" (unpaginated), 3, 5.

53. Indeed, "bridge" (*puente*) as that which connects geographies and temporalities is one of Anzaldúa's poetic glosses for "mestiza," as in "Yo soy un puente tendido/del mundo gabacho al del mojado,/lo pasado me estirá pa' 'trás/y lo presente pa' 'delante" (3).

54. Cf. McRuer: "Some overly celebratory understandings of queerness . . . tend to efface the ways in which identities and histories are structured in domination . . . For Anzaldúa, 'the border' and 'queerness' stand as figures for the failure of easy separation. Rather than establishing two discrete identities, each attempt at separation actually produces (mestiza/queer) identities that do not wholly fit in either location" (*Queer Renaissance* 117).

55. On mixed names in the March see Davies, *Conquest, Coexistence and Change* 102 and "Race Relations in Post-Conquest Wales" 52.

56. The story of how in 1250 Walter Clifford forced a messenger to swallow the king's letter is told in Davies, *Lordship and Society in the March of Wales* 1.

57. Davies, *Lordship and Society in the March of Wales* 8. Davies elsewhere observes that the use of the term "March" for south Wales was an acknowledgment that "there was a fairly extensive area between native-controlled Wales on the one hand and the kingdom of England on the other which was intermediate in its status, laws, and governance and had its own recognizable habits and institutions" ("Frontier Arrangements in Fragmented Societies: Ireland and Wales" 81). True to the purpose of the collection of essays for which he writes, Davies here insists on calling Wales a "frontier," even while emphasizing its mediality.

58. Gerald acknowledges this fact in his *De Invectionibus* (1.2) when he writes that Archbishop Hubert Walter, wishing to condemn Gerald as too Welsh to hold a position of ecclesiastical power in Wales, could not link Gerald there through his name (*Sed nomen istud plus Gallicum quam Wallicum redolere videtur*, "But this name of mine seems to smack rather of France than of Wales"). Hubert contents himself with labeling Gerald *natione Wallensis*, "a Welshman by nation." See the *Autobiography* 171–72.

59. Bartlett writes, "In his preference for *Kambrenses* over both *Wallenses* and *Britones*, rejecting both what the English called the Welsh and what the Welsh called themselves, Gerald was attempting to create a new vocabulary for his own particularly ambiguous ethnic and national position" (*Gerald of Wales*, 185).

60. Robert Stein likewise links the monarchs' cadavers and the monstrous hybrids in "The Trouble with Harold" 196–97.

61. Robert Bartlett gives the illuminating example of a misogynistic rant that Gerald superfluously introduced while reworking a saintly *vita* in "Rewriting Saints' Lives" 602.

62. For a smart reading of the inseparability of text and illustration in this manuscript see Knight, "Werewolves, Monsters, and Miracles."

63. This episode appears in Gerald's *Jewel of the Church* (2.36) in a long section on clerical Latin blunders.

64. As Steven F. Kruger has emphasized, "Christianity encountered difference not only as it expanded into previously pagan lands, nor only at its 'frontiers' or in its Jewish ghettoes; 'heretical' differences always threatened to erupt within the heart of European Christendom" (review of James Muldoon, *Varieties of Religious Conversion in the Middle Ages* 146). These internal differences are especially salient in considering Gerald of Wales, who colonized the "irregular" Welsh church in order to bring it into conformity with England and Rome.

65. To make matters worse, not only was Gerald forced to undertake the trip with the archbishop of Canterbury, they were joined by Bishop Peter at St. David's in celebrating a mass that performed the obeisance of the Welsh seat to Baldwin. This religious ritual as public theater was surely scripted by the Angevin rulers of England, who saw that the submission of the Welsh church to Canterbury and the submission of the Welsh to the English throne were inextricably linked.

66. For an excellent discussion of the complicated context of Gerald's preaching tour through Wales, see Christopher Tyerman, *England and the Crusades* 156.

67. A source for the story has not been found in Abelard's work; it seems unique to Gerald.

68. See Joseph Jacobs, *Jews of Angevin England* 51.

4 City of Catastrophes

1. Henry of Huntingdon, *Historia Anglorum*, VI.30; William of Poitiers, *Gesta Guillelmi* II.27. Yet, as R. R. Davies crisply points out, even if 1066 is "the one date which every schoolboy knows," in actuality it all depends "where the boy goes to school." Welsh and Irish annalists, for example, barely mention Hastings, and saw the Norman events of 1093 as far more important (*First English Empire* 4).

2. The *vita* survives in a single manuscript copy: Cambridge, University Library, Additional MS 3037. It dates from the late twelfth century and does not appear to have made it out of East Anglia. This manuscript is clearly not the original, which seems to have resided at Norwich cathedral (Barbara Dodwell, "The Muniments and the Library" 336).

3. *EHR* 2 168.

4. M. T. Clanchy examines the English mythology that quickly surrounded Domesday in *From Memory to Written Record* 18–21 (quotation at 18). On Domesday as a misguided Norman attempt to arrest time and transform description into possession, see 20.

5. The trajectory for the "evolution versus revolution" argument was set in the nineteenth century by E. A. Freeman and J. H. Round, liberal English partisan and conservative Norman apologist respectively. For a review of the copious relevant scholarship, see C. Warren Hollister, *Monarchy, Magnates and Institutions in the Anglo-Norman World* 1–6; R. Allen Brown, *The Normans and the Norman Conquest* 1–5; and Marjorie Chibnall, *The Debate*

on the Norman Conquest. Chibnall also discusses the analytical impasses that the evolution/revolution binary entails in her introduction to *Anglo-Norman England* 1–5.

6. *An Architectural History of Norwich Cathedral* 7. The works he cites that argue the relative unimportance of the conquest to the material record are H. G. Richardson and G. O. Sayles, *The Governance of Medieval England from the Conquest to the Magna Carta* and T. Rowley, *The Heritage of Norman England.* Fernie treats the subject again in *The Architecture of Norman England,* concluding that "whatever the case may be in other areas of life, the architectural evidence indicates that for large sections of the population the effects of the Conquest were dramatic, far-reaching, and visible" (19).

7. Robin Fleming gathers copious evidence for the systematic seizure and destruction of urban property and architectures to make room for Norman edifices in *Kings and Lords in Conquest England* 194–204; my description of the changes in York are based on 195–96.

8. H. R. Loyn, *The Norman Conquest* 178.

9. Susan Reynolds, *An Introduction to the History of Medieval Towns* 43. Brian Ayers writes of the recently discovered remains of a timber church, demolished to erect the castle, in *Book of Norwich* 33, 37–38; see 43 for the second ruined church. As Eric Fernie has pointed out, it is unclear if every one of the 98 houses were destroyed when the castle was constructed, since the phrase used in the Domesday Book (*in occupatione castelli*) may describe their legal status rather than imply their razing (*An Architectural History of Norwich Cathedral* 5). Yet most scholars assume that, given the sheer size of the Norman edifice and its defensive mound, the English houses must have been eradicated.

10. My discussion of pre-and post-conquest Norwich owes most to Stephen Alsford, "History of Medieval Norwich"; Ayers, *Book of Norwich*; James Campbell, "Norwich" and "The East Anglian Sees before the Conquest"; Alan Carter, "The Anglo-Saxon Origins of Norwich"; Eric Fernie, *An Architectural History of Norwich Cathedral* 5–17; Barbara Green and Rachel M. R. Young, *Norwich: The Growth of a City*; and V. D. Lipman, *The Jews of Medieval Norwich* 3–33. I have also gained important background from Brian Ayers, "The Cathedral Site Before 1096"; Barbara Dodwell, "Herbert de Losinga and the Foundation"; and Norman Tanner, "The Cathedral and the City."

11. Arminghall is the only great henge monument in the area and consists of a large round earthwork, ditches, and, at one time, a horseshoe of eight wooden posts. Williamson surveys the literature on Neolithic Norfolk in *The Origins of Norfolk* 20–23; see also David Dymond, *The Norfolk Landscape* 37–48, who labels Arminghall the Norwich cathedral of its day (42). As many as 1200 barrows have been identified in Norfolk, many long since destroyed (Williamson, *The Origins of Norfolk* 22); a few of these are near Arminghall and related perhaps to its religious function (Green and Young, *Norwich* 7). Although Norwich certainly was not a Roman city, its site may nonetheless have had some settlement during Roman times.

12. "Norwich" 5. Campbell follows a theory of nucleated development for the city, but some archeologists have more recently posited an "extended ribbon development" that spread along the river's edge as a single settlement with various areas. See Ayers, *Book of Norwich* 24.

13. See Carter, "The Anglo-Saxon Origins of Norwich" 176.

14. On these examples and the Anglo-Scandinavian borough more generally, see Ayers, *Book of Norwich* 25.

15. In the twelfth century, Conesford was spelled *Cunegesford*, betraying "a Danish modification of an earlier Saxon name" (Green and Young, *Norwich* 8). That is, the Danish word *kunung* may have taken the place of the English word *cyning*, both of which mean *king* (so that Conesford = king's ford).

16. This residence or center might have been in Norwich proper or in Thorpe; see Campbell, who points out that thorp means "small or secondary settlement" in Old Norse, Old Danish, and Old English—where it can also mean villa or estate (2).

17. Old English from *Two Saxon Chronicles*, ed. Plummer135; translation from *EHD* 239.

18. See *EHD* 1 336.

19. Ayers makes this suggestion in *Book of Norwich* 33. Planned areas of town are not evident again until after the conquest, especially with the formation of the French borough from what may have been a common grazing area and the mid-twelfth century implantation of a series of stone of tenements north of the cathedral, in space formerly occupied by English timber structures.

20. The phrase "Norman purge" is from Campbell, "The East Anglian Sees before the Conquest" 18. Cf. Ann Williams, *The English and the Norman Conquest* 45–46.

21. On the relative wealth of Norwich in 1065 and the tripartite jurisdictionary division of its burgesses, see Green and Young, *Norwich* 9–10.

22. See the excellent introduction tracing the evolution of the English parochial system by John Blair in *Ministers and Parish Churches* 1–19.

23. *The English Medieval Town* 149.

24. Stephen Alsford provides a useful sketch-map of the Anglo-Saxon churches of Norwich and compiles evidence for their dates at his "History of Medieval Norwich" site; see also the map of pre-conquest churches by Jayne Bown included in Ayers, *Book of Norwich* 26.

25. This expansive parish was eventually carved into many smaller ones; see Ayers, *Book of Norwich* 25–27.

26. The nameless church was in existence for perhaps seventy-five years before the castle mandated its destruction. Its population was wholly Anglo-Scandinavian. About 130 skeletons from the church's graveyard have been studied to determine something of the pre-conquest population of the city, and indicate that at least in this poor parish the people were malnourished, prone to diseases like rickets, and lived lives "full of hard, physical labour" (Ayers, *Book of Norwich* 37–38).

27. "Norwich" 22.

28. I will have more to saw on the marital status of English priests in the following chapter.

29. On the pre-conquest location of the bishop's seat, see Campbell, "East Anglian Sees before the Conquest." Dodwell argues that Herfast saw Thetford as a temporary move, aiming for Bury St. Edmunds as the permanent seat: "Herbert de Losinga and the Foundation" 37.

30. Unfortunately no documentary evidence survives to detail what was sold in the late Saxon Norwich markets. Green and Young list likely merchandise as pottery from the Midlands; millstones, swords, wine and wine vessels from the Rhineland; furs and ivory from Scandinavia and Russia; wool from Flanders (*Norwich* 10).

31. William of Malmesbury notes that Earl Godwine's first wife, the sister of King Cnut, shipped English girls to Denmark (*History of the English Kings* 2.200), but it is impossible to know how much truth the story holds.

32. On the international connections of the city see especially Campbell, "Norwich" 6 and Lipman, *The Jews of Medieval Norwich* 13.

33. For an overview of the Scandinavian settlement on English towns, especially as a stimulus to growth, see Reynolds, *An Introduction to the History of English Medieval Towns* 37–42.

34. The violence of the conquest is often underplayed by contemporary scholars, but the evidence gathered by Hugh M. Thomas in *The English and the Normans* 59–62 is a salient reminder of its ferocity.

35. William of Malmesbury gives a moving portrait of the destruction's lingering aftermath, *History of the English Kings* 3.248.

36. The entry is quoted from the D version of the chronicle, *EHD* 162. John of Worcester placed the bridal feast at Exning rather than Norwich.

37. Anglo-Saxon Chronicle entry for 1083, *EHD* 168–69.

38. *England Under the Norman and Angevin Kings, 1075–1225* 1.

39. The passage describes how Franks and Normans at Fécamp admire the English youths, *Gesta Guillelmi* 2.44.

40. Williams gathers much of the material on Norman versus English hair and dress, pointing out some contradiction in the evidence, in *The English and the Norman Conquest* 188–90; the quotation from the Carmen is taken from 189. Such differences, it goes without saying, were susceptible to strategic exaggeration or downplaying depending upon their reporter.

41. *The English and the Norman Conquest* 190.

42. *Vita Edwardi Regis et Confessoris*, ed. J.-P. Migne, *Patrologia Latina* 195, col. 774.

43. "Laȝamon's Ambivalence" 561.

44. Cf. Jocelin of Brakelond, writing at nearby Bury St. Edmunds a century after the conquest, who said that he "could read books written in English most elegantly and he used to preach to the people in English, but in the Norfolk dialect, for that was where he was born and brought up." *Chronicle of the Abbey of Bury St Edmunds* 37; Williams, *English and the Norman Conquest* 130.

45. Green and Young's term for the French borough, *Norwich* 11.

46. "Norwich" 8.

47. On these *machines* or *agencements*, see *Anti-Oedipus* and *A Thousand Plateaus*, as well as my *Medieval Identity Machines*.

48. James W. Alexander examines the difficult relations among William Rufus, Herbert, and Urban in "Herbert of Norwich" 127–31.

49. This jurisdictionary battle is seen most vividly in Thomas of Monmouth's text as Bishop Eborard attempts to force the Jews to submit to an ecclesiastically administered ordeal. The sheriff then protects the Jews in the castle until the king sends an edict prohibiting the bishop from judging them (1.16). Marjorie Chibnall underscores the power of the church to make the king in times of vexed monarchal succession: "Since the prelates controlled substantial landed wealth and could raise a force of some 700 knights, church support was more than merely moral" (*Anglo-Norman England* 57). Jacques Beauroy labels this coming into power "la conquête cléricale de l"Angleterre" in his article of that name.

50. William of Malmesbury, *The Deeds of the Bishops of England* 74.

51. On William Turbe's tenure as bishop of Norwich, see Christopher Harper-Bill, "Bishop William Turbe and the Diocese of Norwich." Turbe is probably the "Willelm" so frequently—and affectionately—addressed in Herbert de Losinga's letters (*Life, Letters, and Sermons of Herbert de Losinga* 281).

52. Loyn memorably describes the "heterogeneity of jurisdiction" spawned by such proliferations of authorities and interests as producing in places like London, York, and Norwich "an elaborate honeycomb" of competition and alliance (*Norman Conquest* 183).

53. Letter XIV, *The Life and Letters of Herbert de Losinga* 131–33.

54. William of Jumièges writes of the strategic superlativeness of these fortifications in seizing and holding land: *Gesta Normannorum Ducum* 2.92. See also the essays by R. Allen Brown gathered in *Castles, Conquest and Charters*; Richard Eales, "Royal Power and Castles in Norman England"; Stephen Morillo, *Warfare under the Anglo-Norman Kings*, 85–88 and 94–97; and N. J. G. Pounds, *The Medieval Castle in England and Wales*, especially 3–53.

55. *Gesta Guillelmi* 2.34. Frank Stenton provides a good, rapid overview of the Norman reconfiguration of the city, stressing the centrality of their building program to their occupation in "Norman London."

56. *The Ecclesiastical History of Orderic Vitalis* 2.194–5, 218–19. The passage is treated by Chibnall in two concise discussions of Norman motte and bailey castles in England, *The Normans* 44–45 and "Orderic Vitalis on Castles" in *Piety, Power and History in Medieval England and Normandy* XVI.

57. F. M. Stenton discusses the passage in *Anglo-Saxon England* 597.

58. "Old English and its Afterlife" 16. The Peterborough passage is a bit misleading in that the first Norman castles were of timber, not stone, but its point is well taken. There is some evidence for a few pre-conquest castles in England (see especially Eric Fernie, "Saxons, Normans, and their Buildings" 7–8 and *The Architecture of Norman England* 52–53), but the widespread erection of these fortifications was a predominantly Norman strategy.

59. Paul Dalton captures this last function well when he writes that "the construction of Norman castles and the establishment of Norman estate management and administrative authority often went hand in hand." See *Conquest, Anarchy and Lordship* 31.

60. That the castle was built by "a major middle Saxon nucleus" (possibly called *Needham*, later *Cowholm*) is argued by Carter, "The Anglo-Saxon Origins of Norwich" 198–99.

61. The king's Christmas court is recorded in the E version of the *Anglo-Saxon Chronicle* in the entry for 1122, *EHD* 197.

62. Thus Roger Bigod rebelled against William Rufus (who was, fortunately for Bigod, merciful to the insurgents), but remained faithful during an attempt in 1101 to replace King Henry I with his luckless older brother, Robert of Normandy.

63. *The Letters of Lanfranc* 126–27. Earl Ralph's rebellion is also narrated by Henry of Huntingdon in the *Historia Anglorum* 6.34.

64. For the most recent archeological data on the castle see Ayers, *Norwich*. The figures above are derived from 56–57, which detail the excavations of 1999.

65. Eric Fernie provides a date of ca.1100 for the great tower's construction because of the similar mason marks on the keep and the cathedral's east arm: *The Architecture of Norman England* 72.

66. On this possibility see Ayers, *Book of Norwich* 45.

67. See *The Deeds of the Bishops of England* 74. John of Worcester makes the same claim. Both are probably indulging in purely speculative etymology; Losinga appears to be Herbert's actual cognomen, since he shared it with his father.

68. Thus Eric Fernie calls the importation of the Fécamp customs (themselves derived from that center of monastic reform, Cluny) as part of "the Norman cultural invasion of England" ("The Building" 52).

69. David Knowles, *The Monastic Order in England* 619–31. Canterbury, Winchester, and Worcester were also monastic cathedrals.

70. William de Beaufeu succeeded Herfast as Bishop of Thetford in 1085, a position he held for about five years. William's son Richard became the cathedral's archdeacon in 1107. See *The Life, Letters, and Sermons of Herbert de Losinga* 114–15.

71. *The Architecture of Norman England* 32.

72. *Ecclesiastical History* 4.92–3; Fernie treats the passage in *The Architecture of Norman England* 33.

73. "Norwich" 8.

74. "The Parish Church in Norfolk in the 11th and 12th Centuries" 188.

75. See especially letters XX and XXVIII in *The Life, Letters, and Sermons of Herbert de Losinga*.

76. Carter, "The Anglo-Saxon Origins of Norwich" 187.

77. "A Minority Ascendant: The Benedictine Conquest of the North of England, 1066–1100" 19.

78. There is a late (thirteenth century) reference to the existence of an earl's palace (*palatium*). Campbell writes that, whether or not this particular

reference is true, "late Saxon earls of East Anglia probably had a substantial establishment somewhere in Norwich" ("Norwich" 6). If it existed at Tombland as has often been supposed, the destruction of this building would have been among the most spectacular acts of the Normans reconfiguring the area.

79. These numbers are taken from the Domesday comparison of 1086 to 1065. See Alsford, "Effects of the Conquest" in "History of Medieval Norwich" and Green and Young, *Norwich* 9.

80. Alternately, if the palace survived the transition to the Normans, it may have been knocked down to punish the rebellious Ralph Gauder.

81. Letter XIV, *The Life and Letters of Herbert de Losinga*, 132–33.

82. In the absence of evidence it is easy either to underplay or to overplay the imagined resentfulness of the inhabitants. The "ruthless destruction of property and the establishment of a privileged community of foreign monks in their midst," reason Green and Young, "were hateful to the English inhabitants" (*Norwich* 12). After surveying the position of the cathedral via-à-vis the English city, Norman Tunner writes similarly (though more mildly): "It is not difficult to see the potential for possible grievances in these arrangements" ("The Cathedral and the City" 256).

83. Deirdre Wollaston's phrase in "Herbert de Losinga" 33.

84. On this point see R. Allen Brown, "William of Malmesbury as an Architectural Historian," in *Castles, Conquests, Charters* 12.

85. At 433 feet, only three contemporary churches were larger than Norwich cathedral: Bury St. Edmunds Abbey, Cluny Abbey, and Winchester cathedral. See Stephen Heywood, "The Romanesque Building" 111.

86. Wollaston comments that "few Anglo-Norman patrons rival Herbert in the number, size and variety of the buildings he created." See "Herbert de Losinga" 34. Ayers points out that the palace was at one time connected to the cathedral at the north nave. It was built over an English cemetery, probably that of Holy Trinity or Christ Church (*Book of Norwich* 56; see 57 for the archeological remains of St. Leonard's and the hospitals).

87. The adjective "devastating" is from Brian S. Ayers, "The Cathedral Site before 1096" 59. Tanner, "The Cathedral and the City," describes the removal of land from city control as "wounding for Norwich, which was already a large and prosperous town. The transfer to the priory's jurisdiction of Tombland (or Tomland, Danish for an open space), which appears to have been the centre of the late Anglo-Saxon borough, a market and a meeting-place, may have been particularly painful" (258).

88. Carter, "The Anglo-Saxon Origins of Norwich" 202.

89. *An Architectural History of Norwich Cathedral* 6.

90. Fernie, *The Architecture of Norman England* 72.

91. Eric Fernie, "The Building: An Introduction," 51.

92. "Anecdote of the Jar," in *The Collected Poems of Wallace Stevens* 76.

93. Eleanor Searle, *Predatory Kinship* 246.

94. Williams provides a good account of Ralph's rebellion in *The English and the Norman Conquest* 59–63, stressing Ralph's complicated ethnicity and the

possible racial tensions centered around the struggle. Ralph's father was a Breton who became a staller in the court of Edward the Confessor; see Marjorie Chibnall, " 'Racial' Minorities" 50–51.

95. Ayers, *Book of Norwich* 43. William was not so forgiving. When he returned to England at Christmas he had the Bretons of Norwich blinded, shamed, and banished.

96. Ayers gathers this and other biological evidence in *Book of Norwich* 52–3.

97. Domesday is also the source for labeling the area formed by Earl Ralph the *novus burgus*: "Franci de Norwici. In novo Burgo XXXVI burgenses" (Domesday, Norfolk 2.118a).

98. See Cecily Clarke, "Battle c.1110: An Anthroponymist Looks at an Anglo-Norman New Town."

99. "The Anglo-Saxon Origins of Norwich" 194.

100. George Garnett, " 'Franci et Angli' " 116–21; F. C. Hamil, "Presentment of Englishry and the Murder Fine"; H. E. Yntema, "The *lex murdrorum*: An Episode in the History of English Criminal Law."

101. "Norman London" 35. Stenton's work suggests an important difference between London, which retained numerous civic liberties after the conquest and had a long history of its "conception of its place in the world" (35) and Norwich, a more recent settlement lacking London's tradition of corporate urban identity. Norwich was not granted a charter, royal privileges, and a degree of self-determination until 1194.

102. "Women's Names in Post-Conquest England: Observations and Speculations" 241. She adds that "At Southampton some demarcation between the two groups is implied by a 'French street' running parallel to the main 'English street' "

103. This episode saw the looting and burning of the monastery. Notably, participants in the attack included women and secular priests, an indication of the heterogeneity of the civic-machine. See Tanner, "The Cathedral and the City" 259–62, 268.

5   The Flow of Blood in Norwich

1. Thomas's Prologue contains a dedication to Turbe, and 2.2 asserts that he writes at the charge of bishop and convent.

2. See Gavin I. Langmuir's seminal article "Thomas of Monmouth," as well as his later generalization of some of the claims advanced there in *Toward a Definition of Antisemitism* (especially 100–33) and *History, Religion, and Antisemitism* (esp. 275–305). John M. McCulloh has argued against locating the origin of the accusation in Thomas, presenting evidence that the blood libel was circulating in the community and being carried from Norwich to the continent before Thomas wrote ("Jewish Ritual Murder").

3. "Thomas makes the case that belief in the crucifixion [of William] was widespread [in Norwich]. In his description of a visit to the murder scene, he states he knew on the basis of common report (*ut fama traditur*) the

structure of the beam and posts that the Jews supposedly employed in place of a cross" (McCulloh, "Jewish Ritual Murder" 732–33). Thomas, that is, cannot have been a lone or eccentric voice.

4. The best critical overview of the scanty medieval sources for the William legend is McCulloh, "Jewish Ritual Murder" 712–16. I am in substantial agreement with McCulloh's suggestion, based upon the pioneering work of Israel J. Yuval, that the ritual murder myth arose in the aftermath of the Ashkenazic Jews' choice of death over forced conversion during the crusader-inflicted persecutions of 1096 ("Jewish Ritual Murder" 699–700, 738–39). This spectacular choice to take one's life *al kiddush ha-Shem* (in the sanctification of God's name) and the flow of blood that resulted from these actions (invariably these martyrdoms were accomplished by the knife, often with parent's taking their children's lives before their own) resulted in a fascination with Jews and sanguinary ritual. For a good overview of the *al kiddush ha-Shem*, a contextualization of its medieval Hebrew inscription, and a warning about the dangers of overplaying its existence as an unmediated historical event, see Robert Chazan, *God, Humanity, and History* and Jeremy Cohen, "A 1096 Complex? Constructing the First Crusade in Jewish Historical Memory, Medieval and Modern." On the memorialization of this violence by Jewish communities, see Susan Einbinder, *Beautiful Death*.

5. On Thomas's deliberate patterning of Legarda's discovery on the Easter story, hoping that some of the numinous aura of the paschal celebration would adhere to this *inventio*. see Monika Otter's thoughtful explication, *Inventiones* 39. Otter writes cogently of the relation of saints' bodies to the sustenance of community at 34.

6. *Gentile Tales* 1. The pernicious narrative emerged toward the end of the thirteenth century.

7. The extent to which the twelfth century witnessed a major deterioration of Christian-Jewish relations is being debated, but critics like Robert Chazan see the "sanguinary assaults" of 1096 and their repercussions as of primary importance in transforming the terms of that relationship. See Chazan, *European Jewry and the First Crusade; Medieval Stereotypes and Modern Antisemitism*, especially 67; and "From the First Crusade to the Second."

8. The most famous medieval English caricature of Jews is possessed by the Public Record Office in London (Exchequer of Receipt, Jews' Roll, no. 87). Dating from 1233, the racialized cartoon depicts Isaac of Norwich, Mosse Mokke, and a Jewish woman named Avegaye. For an explication of the scene see Frank Felsenstein, *Anti-Semitic Stereotypes* 27–29.

9. This is the infamous story of the Jews of Imestar, Syria, who supposedly tied a boy to a cross as part of a Purim celebration. See Joe Hillaby, "The Ritual-Child-Murder Accusation" 69 and Langmuir, "Thomas of Monmouth" 822–26.

10. "Jewish Ritual Murder" 738.

11. The Jewish father is also noted for his madness and cruelty (*patremque parvuli in amentiam et crudelitatem exasperavit*): *The Life, Letters, and Sermons of Bishop Herbert de Losinga* vol. 2, 30–33.

12. *The Life, Letters, and Sermons of Bishop Herbert de Losinga* vol. 2, 114–120. Rubin examines Herbert's version of "the tale of the Jewish Boy" in *Gentile Tales* 10.

13. The inglorious story of John's veneration is narrated by William of Newburgh in his *Historia rerum Anglicarum* and discussed by Nancy F. Partner in *Serious Entertainments* 73–74.

14. Although Langmuir argues that the *vita* was composed in stages, with the first book completed in 1149 or early 1150 ("Thomas of Monmouth" 838–40), McCulloh sees the first six books as a single compositional unit and dates them to no earlier than 1155, just after Stephen's death ("Jewish Ritual Murder" 706–9). Emily Rose has recently argued that these books culminate the flourishing of the cult between 1150 and 1155 ("The Cult of St. William of Norwich" 105). The last two books were added and the *Life* revised in the 1170s.

15. Rose places the origin of the ritual murder charge in these legal proceedings, arguing that it was introduced by Bishop William as a "clever legal tactic" that would prevent the prosecution of Simon de Novers on technical grounds ("The Cult of St. William of Norwich"). Though the truth of this assertion is impossible to ascertain, Rose does argue reasonably that Simon was a member of a conquest-era knightly family who had fallen upon hard times, taking out loans from Eleazar to finance participation in the Second Crusade.

16. For the blood beneath Hastings see 1.1.8 and for Ramsey Abbey 1.11.1. William takes the latter episode from his favorite source, Henry of Huntingdon's *Historia Anglorum*. The bleeding walls seem to have been a wonder well known throughout England, and Henry claimed to have seen the flow of blood himself (*et ipse ego oculis meis inspexi*, 8.22).

17. On Stephen's reign and the turmoil that endured through many of his years, see R. H. C. Davis, *King Stephen* and the collection of essays edited by Edmund King, *The Anarchy in King Stephen's Reign*. As David Crouch has recently made clear, the chaos of Stephen's reign has frequently been overplayed, as has the peace that supposedly pre-existed it (*The Reign of King Stephen*, especially 1–7). Yet as canny a ruler as Stephen may have been, his reign saw England's first prolonged civil war, a series of conflicts spread over a long duration. After the conquest most military violence had been occurring at the country's margins, as England expanded into Wales, Scotland and Ireland; in the conflict between Matilda and Stephen armed engagement returned to England's interior.

18. John Gillingham, *The English in the Twelfth Century* 97. Gillingham's argument has been implicitly expanded by two scholars who disagree with his thesis that references to "the Normans" at this time indicate only a court faction rather than an enduring racial divide: see Judith A. Green, *The Aristocracy of Norman England* 435 and Hugh M. Thomas, *The English and the Normans* 64–65.

19. *Historia Anglorum* 4.4. In 1166 Earl Hugh would be excommunicated by William Turbe.

20. Peterborough Chronicle (Anglo-Saxon chronicle version E), trans. Dorothy Whitelock, entry for 1137. Rose examines this passage, the general impact of the civil war, and resonances with the torture of William in "The Cult of St. William of Norwich" 72–74. Cf. the descriptions of torture in the narrative for 1138, *Gesta Stephani* 1.29.

21. This is Martin B. Shichtman and Laurie A. Finke's observation about the "litany of horrors" in the *Peterborough Chronicle, King Arthur and the Myth of History* 35–38.

22. Clarke renders the word *crucethur* and relates it to Latin *cruciator, Peterborough Chronicle* 107. The word used for William of Norwich's cross is the English noun *rode*.

23. David Crouch gathers the contemporary readings of Stephen's Candlemas disaster in *The Reign of King Stephen* 141.

24. On the allegiances of the sheriff and bishop see Rose, "The Cult of St. William of Norwich" 74. Rose also points out the Bishop Herbert's library was destroyed during the civil war, indirect evidence of unrest within the city limits.

25. Crouch assesses the devastation of the peasantry and the nobility in *The Normans* 274–75, where he sees the famines as integral to the rethinking of royal strategy for the future of the realm.

26. John Gillingham, *The English in the Twelfth Century*, calls it "a new sense of national identity after the traumas of the Norman conquest" (99). He argues that in the writings of William of Malmesbury and Henry of Huntingdon dating from the 1120s one finds a "lingering remembrance" of the English as a "subject" and "downtrodden" population, "oppressed by French (or Norman) lords." Yet in their later writings this feeling of oppression vanishes (99).

27. "The United Kingdom of England" 39.

28. Thus although the great strength of work like Elizabeth Salter's "An Obsession with the Continent" is to place the literature of England into a wide, non-insular context, the problem with assuming that all writing participates in internationalism only at the national level is that it does not allow local-minded texts like Thomas's *vita* to be at once regional, international, and uninterested in collectivities as large as the nation. See Salter's *English and International* 1–100.

29. A gray-haired Bishop Herbert, *Norwicensis ecclesie fundator*, appears in two visions: one granted to a virgin of Dunwich who had been plagued by an incubus (2.7), the other to Thomas himself (3.1).

30. Another eyewitness account is that of Ælward Ded, who on his deathbed relates that he had encountered two Jews bearing a corpse into Thorpe Wood. He had been forced by the sheriff (a royal authority who, we are told, had been bribed by the Jews) to keep the story silent (1.7).

31. As a city with a thriving Jewish population headed by a *Nasi* (prince)—a city, that is, in which the Jews exerted real political power and participated in civic community—Narbonne must have been an especially attractive place for Thomas/Theobald to disparage. On Narbonne and the Jews as a political force, see Kenneth R. Stow, *Alienated Minority* 43–45.

32. "Conversion and Medieval Sexual, Religious, and Racial Categories" 167, 172. Jonathan M. Elukin writes, "From late antiquity on, many Jewish converts never completely escaped the perceived stigma of their Jewishness" ("Jews and Conversion in the Twelfth Century" 63). On the conversion of English Jews, especially by compulsion, see Stow, *Alienated Minority* 288–90.

33. The aura of chronological precision that Thomas creates through his detailed narrative may, however, be misleading. McCulloh has shown that a competing tradition placed William's death on Good Friday (March 24), and Thomas himself once implies that this is indeed when the boy died, suggesting that "information about William's death independent of Thomas's hagiography circulated at least within a limited geographical area" ("Jewish Ritual Murder" 717).

34. Thomas writes that the Jews use this combination of techniques in case evidence of their handiwork should come to light: "Now the deed was done in this way, lest, if eventually the body were found, it should be discovered from the presence of nail-marks in both hands and feet, that the murderers were Jews and not Christians" (1.5, corrected translation at 295).

35. *The Medieval English Borough: Studies in its Origins and Constitutional History* 105.

36. *The English in the Twelfth Century* 4. A limitation of such a sweeping pronouncement is that it tends to conflate group and individual identities, rather than allowing for a complex and fluid relationship between collective designators and self-assertion. On the intricacies of mapping social identities in early England, see William O. Frazer's introduction to *Social Identity in Early Medieval Britain* 1–22.

37. The useful expression "intense localism" is coined by William Chester Jordan in " 'Europe' in the Middle Ages" 73 to capture the tendencies toward self-sufficiency and parochialism that existed in tension with cosmopolitanism during the period 1050–1350.

38. Edwin of Taverham married William's mother's first cousin; his daughter Hathewis is healed by the saint (7.15). Another married priest in the text, Walter of Tivetshall, is not related to William (4.11). Emily Rose also identifies Aelward Ded as a married priest ("The Cult of St. William of Norwich" 140). On married clergy as a persistently English phenomenon, see C. N. L. Brooke, "Gregorian Reform in Action," *Medieval Church and Society* 69–99, especially 78. For an indication of how widespread clerical marriage was before the Conquest, see the references collected under "celibacy" in the index to Frank Barlow, *The English Church 1000–1066*. The son of a cleric and himself a married archdeacon with several children, Henry of Huntingdon perhaps overstates the novelty of Anselm's first reform council (1102), which "forbade wives to the priests of England, something formerly not prohibited"; see Partner, *Serious Entertainments* 12–14 and 39–47. Not all Norman and Norman-appointed clergy were unmarried. Roger Bishop of Salisbury had a wife; Wulfstan's successor in Worcester, Samson, fathered future bishops of York and Bayeux; Herfast, first Norman bishop of East Anglia, bequeathed his cathedral church of

St. Mary in Thetford to his sons, who held it in 1086; Eborard, who resigned as bishop of Norwich in 1145, may also have had children. On married Norman bishops see especially the list compiled by C. N. L. Brooke, "Married Men among the English Higher Clergy, 1066–1200." Yet by the middle of the twelfth century a swift and drastic decline in clerical marriage had occurred among the upper clergy. The circumstances in the Norwich described by Thomas are straightforward: celibate clergy in positions of power tended to be Norman-French and affiliated with the cathedral, while the married clergy were secular priests of native English descent and administered the multiplex parish churches.

39. *Medieval Church and Society* 70.
40. John of Forde, *Wulfric of Haselbury* 29; trans. Pauline Matarusso, 54.
41. Frank Barlow, *The English Church, 1066–1154* 311.
42. James Campbell collects the archeological references and provides a useful illustration in "East Anglian Sees before the Conquest" 9–10. Brian Ayers describes the throne and effigy in *Book of Norwich* 56. See also Eric Fernie, *Architecture of Norman England* 146.
43. The collected documents for the Council of Westminster (ca. September 29, 1102) are contained in *Councils and Synods, with other documents relating to the English Church*, ed. D. Whitelock, M. Brett, and C. N. L. Brooke,. 668–88. Archbishop Anselm's letter to Herbert that contains the reference to married parish clergy may be found on 683–84. Repeated attempts were made to enforce clerical celibacy, but most were eventually abandoned because so energetically resisted. See H. R. Loyn, *The Norman Conquest* 159–60 and M. Brett, *The English Church under Henry I* 77–79, 219–20. For the effects of newly enforced celibacy upon an archdeacon of mixed Norman-English descent, see Partner's sensitive treatment of Henry of Huntingdon, *Serious Entertainments* 11–48.
44. See the restoration of the son of Colobern and Ansfrida to the boy's *loquela materna* in 3.16, where Thomas converses with the family about the miracle. See also the restoration of her *materna lingua* to a dumb girl in 5.16 and of *Anglica lingua* to a speechless child in 5.17. A man named Godric has a son by the niece of Robert of Wales; the mother may have been French-speaking (and was at least most likely Norman-descended) because when the deformed boy is restored to health he calls out in *lingua patria* (6.12) to his father.
45. Ann Williams, *The English and the Norman Conquest* 133.
46. Introduction to *The Life and Miracles of St William of Norwich* xxiii. Richard succeeded Elias as prior. With enthusiastic supporters of William's sanctity now heading both the monastery and the cathedral, the corpse was moved with much pomp from the monk's cemetery to inside the cathedral itself, next to the tomb of Herbert de Losinga. Peter likewise supported the cult ardently. Thomas describes him as a former knight who "had long served King Henry and had been numbered among his attendants in the Privy Chamber" (3.6).
47. "Writing History in England" 260.

48. Brooke, "Gregorian Reform in Action" 79. That these increases further hardened some class disparities by attracting more wellborn men to the newly prestigious upper clergy is suggested at 80.

49. Crouch, *The Reign of King Stephen* 312.

50. This point is made well by Jo Ann McNamara, "The Herrenfrage: The Restructuring of the Gender System, 1050–1150."

51. Jews settled in London during William the Conqueror's reign but probably did not arrive in Norwich until the 1130s. The newness of the Ashkenazic Jewry in northern Europe is essential to Robert Chazan's work on the contemporary development of "innovative anti-Jewish stereotypes" in *Medieval Stereotypes and Modern Antisemitism*, quotation at 2. Paul Hyams offers an excellent overview of the Jews of England in which he stresses their two hundred year status as an immigrant community, "The Jewish Minority in Mediaeval England, 1066–1290."

52. *The Jews of Medieval Norwich* 3, 17.

53. V. D. Lipman has estimated the size of the Jewish community of Norwich at 100–200, perhaps 2 percent of the city's total population ("Anatomy of Medieval Anglo-Jewry" 65, 67). "Financiers" might be the more accurate word for those engaged in monetary occupations, since lending and credit activities engaged in by the English Jews included "pawn broking, mortgaging, granting of fee debts, annuities, and the sale of debts" (Robin R. Mundill, "Christian and Jewish Lending Patterns" 42). Although such activities were vital to the existence of Jewish communities, and indeed money lending became central to the Christian representation of Jewishness from the twelfth century onwards, Norwich's Jewish population was large enough that credit could not have been the only occupation in which Jews engaged. Richardson and Lipman document evidence that English Jews were also doctors, teachers, vintners, cheese and fishmongers, servants and assistants to wealthier Jews, traders, and pawnbrokers: *English Jewry under Angevin Kings* 25–27 and *Jews of Medieval Norwich* 79–81.

54. Robert C. Stacey writes of the origins of the English Jews and their Frenchness in "Jews and Christians in Twelfth-Century England" 341. See also Cecil Roth, *A History of the Jews in England* 93–95.

55. Paul Hyams stresses the enduring connection of the English Jews with Normandy and beyond in "The Jewish Minority in Mediaeval England" 271–72.

56. Thus when Eleazar is murdered, his body must be sent to London (2.13)—the only permitted location for a Jewish cemetery until 1177. Norwich had a Jewish cemetery of its own by 1202, since it was vandalized in that year (Lipman, *Jews of Medieval Norwich* 124–25).

57. R. B. Dobson stresses the "joint marital enterprise" of the contemporary Jews in "A Minority Within a Minority" 28.

58. No exact date for the completion of the cathedral is known, other than that construction concluded during Eborard's reign (ended 1145). Fernie argues that the monastic buildings and episcopal palace were likewise completed by this date in *Architecture of Norman England* 144.

59. See Emily Rose, "The Cult of St. William of Norwich" 41–43. Rose also hypothesizes that Jurnet was the son of the Eleazer slain by Simon de Novers's men.

60. Stacey makes this point obliquely: "The Jews' status as fellow Francophones tended to unite them, at least in the eyes of the conquered English, with the French-speaking military aristocracy created by the Conquest. Jews in the Anglo-Norman period were thus not so isolated a linguistic minority as they would later become. By the mid-twelfth century, however, English was emerging as the first language of virtually all children raised in England, irrespective of family origins or class." ("Jews and Christians in Twelfth-Century England" 343).

61. The declaration *Nos iudei tui sumus*, with its second person singular implication of intimacy and subject status, is taken from Thomas's performative imagining of the Jews pleading with Stephen to condemn Simon de Novers for the murder of Eleazar.

62. While he does not speak specifically of blood and identity, John Gillingham—as noted in the first chapter—argues that the promulgation of Celtic otherness functioned as an effective precipitator of twelfth-century possibilities for English-Norman unity (*The English in the Twelfth Century* 3–18 and 41–58). Whereas the position of the Welsh, Scots, and Irish at martial frontiers was, in Gillingham's argument, essential to their ideological utility, the Jews might be seen as an internal version of cultural alterity deployed to bring about community within the *patria*. See Anne McClintock's discussion of "internal colonization" in "The Angel of Progress" 88 and Sylvia Tomasch's excellent discussion "Postcolonial Chaucer and the Virtual Jew" 250–51. Thomas points out the mixed descent of the perpetrators of violence against Jews in the York massacre of 1190, making a similar argument for the unifying power of hatred toward Jews (*The English and the Normans* 309).

63. On the creative deployment of hagiographic conventions in twelfth-century saints' lives more generally, see David Townsend, "Anglo-Latin Hagiography and the Norman Transition." Thomas writes within a contemporary efflorescence of hagiographic narratives, but as Townsend underscores, the supposedly "static tradition" that lay behind these lives is in fact subverted by the "adhortive agenda" each contains for its readers (387–88, 390).

64. On this bloody fate as appropriately Jew-like, see Willis Johnson, "The Myth of Jewish Male Menses" 280, 285–86.

65. See Jessopp's introduction to the *Vita*, xxxiii. John's brother William succeeded him as sheriff, and is known to have become heavily indebted to the Norwich Jews (xxxiv).

66. *Miracles and Pilgrims* 161. See also John R. Shinners, "The Veneration of Saints at Norwich Cathedral" 134.

67. On Alveva as the Latin transliteration of OE Ælfgifu see Cecily Clarke, "Women's Names in Post-Conquest England" 227.

68. Godwin was, as well, the name of one of King Harold's sons. For a balanced reading of Earl Godwine's considerable achievements in securing both land

and popularity, see Robin Fleming, *Kings and Lords in Conquest England* 53–103, and Frank Barlow, *The Godwins*. There is one other Godwin in Thomas's text, Godwin Creme, freed from his irons by William's intercession (6.18).

69. Herbert addresses a letter about their father to the brothers Godwin and William (XXVII in *The Life, Letters and Sermons of Herbert de Losinga*, 287).

70. Bartlett writes vividly of the English adoption of Norman names in the wake of the conquest, *England Under the Norman and Angevin Kings* 538–41; story of the Williams at 540. For an examination of the complexities of reading ethnicity from post-conquest names, see Clarke, "Women's Names in Post-Conquest England." Clark remarks that English women's names were replaced much more slowly by continental ones, probably due to a "paucity of . . . feminine name-models" (251)—an indication that the Norman immigration into England was mainly a movement of men.

71. *History on the Edge* 25. As the chapter on Gerald of Wales emphasized, the Welsh March was inhabited by Normans, Bretons, English, Flemish, and (of course) Welsh, cultures locked in a long negotiation over separatism, assimilation, and alliance. Joe Hillaby points out that William's miracles and vengefulness are fully in the mode of contemporary of Welsh hagiography, comparing him to David and Cadog ("The Ritual-Child-Murder Accusation" 71).

72. *Location of Culture* 113. Medievalists have used various synonyms for Bhabha's hybridity in their own analyses. Daniel Donoghue, for example, has argued for a wide "cultural ambivalence in twelfth- and thirteenth-century England," glossing ambivalence as "a tension pulling in two directions" that preserves opposition rather than neutralizes its force ("Laʒamon's Ambivalence" 537, 558). In her important work on Geoffrey of Monmouth, Patricia Ingham has developed a postcolonial-inflected notion of *ambiguitas*, which she defines as "inclined to both sides; hybrid" and "wavering, hesitating, uncertain, doubtful, obscure" (*Sovereign Fantasies* 43).

73. *Dialogus de Scaccario* 53–54. Richard himself seems to have been a product of a Norman-English union. See Charles Johnson's introduction to his edition of the *Dialogus de Scaccario* xiv, where it is observed that Nigel may well not have been a priest when Richard was conceived. Richard's uncle was Roger, bishop of Salisbury—likewise the father of children with a woman who was likely English, Matilda of Ramsbury (Marjorie Chibnall, *Anglo-Norman England* 209). His mixed family history no doubt accounts for Richard's somewhat utopian vision of an England united in its hybrid, indistinguishable Norman-English blood.

74. It is also worth bearing in mind that, as. Thomas notes, Richard's statement about the intermixed state of the English and French "is an expression not of unity but of uncertainty about elite identity" (*The English and the Normans* 75).

75. "The Hide and Leather Trade" 57.

76. Colin Platt groups tanners with butchers and fishmongers as "unsocial crafts" in *The English Medieval Town* 47.

77. *Invectiones*, ed. W. S. Davies, *Y Cymmrodor* xxx (1920); 93; cited by Robert Bartlett, *Gerald of Wales* 14.

78. According to Christopher Harper-Bill, because of its immense size Norwich had at least two archdeacons by 1107 and four by 1145 ("Introduction" xxvi). On the office of archdeacon more generally see Partner, *Serious Entertainments* 13–14 and 44–45.

79. Though, of course, even here there are exceptions. See C. N. L. Brooke on Walkelin, an incontinent (though unmarried) archdeacon of Suffolk described in a letter of John of Salisbury (1156), in *Medieval Church and Society* 90.

80. Barlow, *The English Church, 1066–1154* 311; Loyn, *The English Church, 940–1154* 96.

81. Bishop Eborard apparently realizes the potential of the corpse as a relic and pilgrimage destination when a visiting prior offers to purchase the remains, apparently to display them at his home foundation of Lewes, 1.18.

82. Another nearby and revenue-generating shrine was that to the royal virgin St. Etheldreda, whose uncorrupted body lay at Ely. As Diana Webb points out, the last miracle that Thomas added to the *vita* (in which a man from Canterbury is miraculously accompanied by saints Thomas Becket and Edmund to Norwich to be cured by William) is concession of these saints' "natural rights to the boy martyr: Thomas his patronage over a Canterbury man, and Edmund his suzerainty within the East Anglian sphere" (*Pilgrimage in Medieval England* 56).

83. There is something desperate about the erection of this statue, in that it must substitute for the real relics Norwich so painfully lacks (Felix's remains were kept at Ramsey).

84. " 'Racial' Minorities in the Anglo-Norman Realm" 49–50.

85. On the evolution of the idea that Jews were the enemies of Christians and the murderers of Christ, see Jeremy Cohen, "The Jews as the Killers of Christ." Thomas provides the first text to combine both traditions.

86. Thomas has the Jews refer to themselves as a unified *genus* in 1.6, one of the many sections of the text in which the Jews act as a united, undifferentiated group with a transnational homogeneity.

87. See Robert C. Stacey, "Crusades, Martyrdoms, and the Jews of Norman England" 247.

88. *De Expugnatione Lyxbonensi* 104–11; Gillingham, *The English in the Twelfth Century* 139.

89. Benedicta Ward enumerates the vengeance episodes and contextualizes them within the conventions of contemporary hagiography in *Miracles and the Medieval Mind* 68–69, quotation at 69.

90. Thomas, by his own admission, is rather like Godwin in that when William's corpse is transferred to the cathedral, he seizes two teeth that have fallen from the jaw (3.1). The translation of the now decomposed body, incidentally, contrasts with Thomas's earlier insistence that its flesh was resistant to decay.

91. Lipman, *Jews of Medieval Norwich* 157. Lipman also points out that several of the most powerful Jews in England—including Jurnet of Norwich, his son and two grandsons—were referred to as *HaNadib*, patron of scholarship ("Anatomy of Medieval Anglo-Jewry" 70).
92. "The Dynamics of Jewish Renaissance and Renewal in the Twelfth Century" 29.
93. Anthony Bale, "Fictions of Judaism in England before 1290" 131.
94. "Jews disappeared from England in 1290; 'the Jew' did not" (Colin Richmond, "Englishness and Medieval Anglo-Jewry" 56). See Tomasch's trenchant argument in "Postcolonial Chaucer and the Virtual Jew" and Stephen F. Kruger, "The Spectral Jew." A related phenomenon is what Jeremy Cohen calls the hermeneutic or theological Jew: *Living Letters of the Law* 2.

Epilogue: *In medias res*

1. Susan L. Einbinder has produced an excellent edition and translation of the poem, from which I quote: "Meir b. Elijah of Norwich."

BIBLIOGRAPHY

Primary Sources

Adomnan of Iona. *The Life of Saint Columba*, ed. and trans. Alan Orr Anderson and Marjorie Ogilvie Anderson (Oxford: Clarendon Press, 1991).

The Anglo-Saxon Chronicle: A Revised Edition, ed. Dorothy Whitelock, with David C. Douglas and Susie I. Tucker (New Brunswick: Rutgers University Press. 1962).

[*The Anglo-Saxon Chronicle*]. *Two of the Saxon Chronicles Parallel*, ed. Charles Plummer (Oxford: Clarendon Press, 1892).

Aristotle. *Politics*, trans. B. Jowett (New York: Random House, 1941).

Bede. *Bede's Ecclesiastical History of the English People*, ed. Bertram Colgrave and R. A. B. Mynors (Oxford: Clarendon Press, 1969).

———. *The Ecclesiastical History of the English People*, ed. Judith McClure and Roger Collins, trans. Bertram Colgrave (Oxford: Oxford University Press, 1994).

Beowulf, ed. Fr. Klaeber (Lexington: D. C. Heath, 1950).

———. trans. Seamus Heaney (New York: W. W. Norton and Company, 2000).

Brut y Tywysogyon, or the Chronicle of the Princes: Red Book of Hergest Version, ed. and trans. Thomas Jones (Cardiff: University of Wales Press, 1955).

The Carmen de Hastingae Proelio of Guy, Bishop of Amiens, ed. and trans. F. Barlow (Oxford: Oxford University Press,1999).

Chrétien de Troyes. *The Story of the Grail (Li Contes del Graal or Perceval)*, ed. Rupert Pickens, trans. William W. Kibler (New York: Garland, 1990).

Chronicle of the Abbey of Bury St Edmunds, ed. Diana Greenway and Jane Sayers (Oxford: Oxford University Press, 1989).

Councils and Synods, with other documents relating to the English Church, I: *A.D. 871–1204*, ed. D. Whitelock, M. Brett, and C. N. L. Brooke (Oxford: Clarendon Press, 1981).

De Expugnatione Lyxbonensi: The Conquest of Lisbon, ed. Charles Wendell David (New York: Columbia University Press,1936).

Dudo of St. Quentin. *The History of the Normans*, trans. Eric Christiansen (Woodbridge, Suffolk: Boydell & Brewer, 1998).

Eadmer of Canterbury. *Eadmeri historia novorum in anglia et opuscula duo de vita sancti anselmi et quibusdam miraculis eius*, ed. M. Rule. Rolls Series (1884).

———. *Eadmer's History of Recent Events in England*, trans. G. Bosanquet (London: Cresset Press, 1964)

Encomium Emmae Reginae, ed. A. Campbell. Camden Third Series 57 (London: Royal Historical Society, 1949).

English Episcopal Acta 6: Norwich 1070–1214, ed. Christopher Harper-Bill (Oxford: Oxford University Press, 1990).

English Historical Documents I c. 500–1042, 2nd ed., ed. Dorothy Whitelock (London: Eyre Methuen, 1979).

English Historical Documents II 1042–1189, 2nd ed., ed. David C. Douglas and George W. Greenaway (London: Eyre Methuen, 1981).

The First Register of Norwich Cathedral Priory, ed. H. W. Saunders. Norfolk Record Society 11 (1939).

Gaimar, Geoffrey. *L'estoire des Engleis*, ed. Alexander Bell (Oxford: Anglo-Norman Texts Society, 1960).

Garnier of Rouen. *Moriuh: A Norman Latin Poem from the Early Eleventh Century*, ed. and trans. Christopher J. McDonough (Toronto: Pontificial Institute of Medieval Studies, 1995).

Geoffrey of Monmouth. *The* Historia Regum Britannie *I: Bern, Bürgerbibliothek MS 568 (the 'Vulgate' Version)*, ed. Neil Wright (Cambridge: D. S. Brewer, 1984).

———. *The* Historia Regum Britannie *II: the First Variant Version*, ed. Neil Wright (Woodbridge: D. S. Brewer, 1988).

———. *The History of the Kings of Britain*, trans. Lewis Thorpe (London: Penguin Books, 1966).

Giraldus Cambrensis [Gerald of Wales]. *The Autobiography of Gerald of Wales*, ed. and trans. H. E. Butler (London: Jonathan Cape, 1937).

———. *De Principis Instructione* [*On the Instruction of Princes*], trans. Joseph Stevenson, *The Church Historians of England* (Seeleys: London, 1858).

———. *Descriptio Kambriae* [*Description of Wales*], v. 6 in *Giraldi Cambrensis Opera*; trans. Lewis Thorpe, *The Journey Through Wales and the Description of Wales* (London: Penguin Books, 1978).

———. *Expugnatio Hibernica: The Conquest of Ireland*, ed. and trans. A. B. Scott and F. X. Martin (Dublin: Royal Irish Academy, 1978).

———. *Gemma Ecclesiastica* [*Jewel of the Church*], trans. John J. Hagen (Leiden: Brill, 1979).

———. *Giraldi Cambrensis Opera*, ed. J. S. Brewer, J. F. Dimock, and G. F. Warner, 8 vols. *Rerum Britannicarum Medii Aevi Scriptores* ["Rolls Series"] 21 (London, 1861–1891).

———. *Invectiones*, ed. W. S. Davies. *Y Cymmrodor* 30 (1920).

———. *Itinerarium Kambriae* [*Journey Through Wales*], v. 6 in *Giraldi Cambrensis Opera*; trans. Lewis Thorpe, *The Journey Through Wales and the Description of Wales* (London: Penguin Books, 1978).

———. *Topographia Hibernica* [*History and Topography of Ireland*], v. 5 in *Giraldi Cambrensis Opera*; trans. John O'Meara (London: Penguin, 1951).

Gesta Stephani, ed. and trans. K. R. Potter, introduction and notes by R. H. C. Davis (Oxford: Oxford University Press, 1976).

Gildas. *De Excidio Britonum*, ed. and trans. Michael Winterbottom (London and Chichester: Phillimore, 1978).

Henry of Huntingdon. *Historia Anglorum*, ed. and trans. Diana Greenway (Oxford: Clarendon Press, 1996).

Herbert de Losinga. *The Life, Letters and Sermons of Bishop Herbert de Losinga*, 2 vols., ed. Edward Meyrick Goulburn and Henry Symonds (Oxford: James Parker and Co., 1878).

Isidore of Seville. *Isidori Hispalensis Episcopi Etymologiarum sive Originum*, ed. William Lindsay (Oxford: Oxford University Press, 1911; rpr. 1989).

John of Ford. *Wulfric of Haselbury by John, Abbot of Ford* (Somerset Record Society 47, 1933). Trans. Pauline Matarasso in *A Gathering of Friends: The Learning and Spirituality of Jon of Forde*, ed. Hilary Costello and Christopher Holdsworth (Kalamazo, MI: Cistercian Publications, 1995) 43–63.

John of Salisbury. *Letters of John of Salisbury I: The Early Letters (1153–1161)*, ed. W. J. Millor and H. E. Butler, rev. C. N. L. Brooke (London: Thomas Nelson and Sons, 1955).

John of Worcester. *The Chronicle of John of Worcester*, 3 vols., ed. and trans. R. R. Darlington and P. McGurk, trans. Jennifer Bray and P. McGurk (Oxford: Clarendon Press, 1995–1998).

Lanfranc. *The Letters of Lanfranc, Archbishop of Canterbury*, ed. Helen Clover and Margaret Gibson (Oxford: Oxford University Press, 1979).

Laȝamon. *Brut*, 2 vols., ed. G. L. Brook and R. F. Leslie (London: EETS OS 250, 277 1963, 1978).

———. *Brut*, trans. Rosamund Allen (London: J. M. Dent and Sons, 1992).

Nennius. *British History and the Welsh Annals*, ed. and trans. John Morris (London: Phillimore with Rowan and Littlefield, 1980).

Orderic Vitalis. *The Ecclesiastical History of Orderic Vitalis*, 6 vols., ed. Marjorie Chibnall, (Oxford: Oxford Medieval Texts, 1969–1980).

Paris, Matthew. *The Chronicle of Matthew Paris: Monastic Life in the Thirteenth Century*, trans. Richard Vaughan (Gloucester: A. Sutton, 1984).

The Peterborough Chronicle, 1070–1154, ed. Cecily Clark (Oxford: Clarendon Press, 1955).

Richard of Devizes. *The Chronicle of Richard of Devizes*, ed. and trans. J. T. Appleby (London: T. Nelson, 1963).

Richard fitzNigel, *Dialogus de scaccario [Course of the Exchequer]*, ed. and trans. Charles Johnson with, corrections by F. E. L. Carter and D. E. Greenway (Oxford: Clarendon Press, 1983).

Symeon of Durham. *Libellus de exordio atque procursu istius, hoc est Dunhelmensis, ecclesie [Tract on the Origins and Progress of this the Church of Durham]*, ed. David Rollason (Oxford: Clarendon Press, 2000).

Statutes, Ordinances and Acts of the Parliament of Ireland, King John to King Henry V, ed. Henry F. Berry (Dublin: Her Majesty's Stationery Office, 1907).

Tacitus, Cornelius. *The* Agricola *and the* Germania, trans. H. Mattingly, rev. S. A. Handford (London: Penguin, 1970).

Thomas of Monmouth. *The Life and Miracles of St William of Norwich*, ed. and trans. Augustus Jessopp and Montague Rhodes James (Cambridge: University of Cambridge Press, 1896).

The Travels of Sir John Mandeville, ed. and trans. C. W. R. D. Moseley (London: Penguin, 1983).

Wace. *Roman de Brut: A History of the English*, ed. and trans. Judith Weiss (Exeter: University of Exeter Press, 1999, revised 2002).

———. *Le Roman de Rou de Wace*, 3 vols ., ed. A. J. Holden (Paris: A. and J. Picard, 1970–1973).

William de Jumièges. *The "Gesta Normannorum Ducum" of William of Jumiegès, Orderic Vitalis, and Robert of Torigni*, 2 vols., ed. E. M. C. van Houts, (Oxford: Oxford Medieval Texts, 1992–1995).

William of Malmesbury. *The Deeds of the Bishops of England (Gesta Pontificum Anglorum)*, trans. David Preest (Woodbridge, Suffolk: Boydell Press, 2002).

———. *Gesta Regum Anglorum: The History of the English Kings*, 2 vols., ed. and trans. R. A. B. Mynors, completed by R. M. Thomson and M. Winterbottom (Clarendon Press; Oxford, 1998).

———. "Vita Dunstani" in *William of Malmesbury: Saints' Lives*, ed. and trans. M. Winterbottom and R. M. Thomson (Oxford: Clarendon Press, 2002) 159–303.

———. "Vita Wulfstani" in *William of Malmesbury: Saints' Lives*, ed. and trans. M. Winterbottom and R. M. Thomson (Oxford: Clarendon Press, 2002) 3–155.

William of Newburgh. *Historia rerum Anglicarum [The History of English Affairs]*, Book 1, ed. and trans. P. G. Walsh and M. J. Kennedy (Wilthsire: Aris and Phillips, 1988).

William of Poitiers. *The Gesta Guillelmi of William of Poitiers*, ed. and trans. R. H. C. Davis and Marjorie Chibnall (Oxford: Clarendon Press, 1998).

Secondary Sources

Abulafia, Anna Sapir. "Bodies in the Jewish-Christian Debate." *Framing Medieval Bodies*, ed. Sarah Kay and Miri Rubin (Manchester: Manchester University Press, 1994) 123–37.

———. "Theology and the Commercial Revolution: Guibert of Nogent, St Anselm and the Jews of Northern France." *Church and City, 1000–1500*, ed. David Abulafia, Michael Franklin, and Miri Rubin (Cambridge: Cambridge University Press, 1992) 23–40.

Akbari, Suzanne Conklin. "From Due East to True North: Orientalism and Orientation." *The Postcolonial Middle Ages*, ed. Jeffrey Jerome Cohen (New York: St Martin's Press, 2000) 19–34.

———. "Imagining Islam: The Role of Images in Medieval Depictions of Muslims." *Scripta Mediterranea* 19–20 (1998–1999) 9–27.

———. "The Rhetoric of Antichrist in Western Lives of Muhammad." *Islam and Christian-Muslim Relations* 8 (1997) 297–307.

Albu, Emily. *The Normans in their Histories: Propaganda, Myth and Subversion* (Woodbridge, Suffolk: Boydell Press, 2001).

Alexander, James W. "Herbert of Norwich, 1091–1119: Studies in the History of Norman England." *Studies in Medieval and Renaissance History* 6, ed. William M. Bowsky (Lincoln: University of Nebraska Press, 1969) 115–232.

Alsford, Stephen. "History of Medieval Norwich." Medieval English Towns, www.the-orb.net/encyclop/culture/towns.

Amory, Patrick. *People and Identity in Ostrogothic Italy, 489–554* (Cambridge: Cambridge University Press, 1997).

Anderson, Benedict. *Imagined Communities: Reflections on the Origin and Spread of Nationalism*, 2nd ed. (London: Verso, 1991).

Anderson, M. D. *A Saint at Stake: The Strange Death of William of Norwich* (London: Faber and Faber, 1964).

Anzaldúa, Gloria. *Borderlands / La Frontera: The New Mestiza* (San Francisco: Aunt Lute Books, 1987).

Anzaldúa, Gloria and Cherríe Moraga. *This Bridge Called My Back: Writings by Radical Women of Color* (Watertown, MA: Persephone Press, 1981).

Ashcroft, Bill, Gareth Griffiths, and Helen Tiffin. "Introduction: Hybridity." *The Post-Colonial Studies Reader* (New York: Routledge, 1995)183–84.

Ayers, Brian S. "The Cathedral Site before 1096." *Norwich Cathedral: Church, City and Diocese, 1096–1996*, ed. Ian Atherton, Eric Fernie, Christopher Harper-Bill, and Hassell Smith (London: Hambledon Press, 1996) 59–72.

———. *English Heritage Book of Norwich* (London: B. T. Batsford / English Heritage, 1994). Republished as *Norwich: "A Fine City"* (Charleston, SC: Tempus Publishing, 2003).

Bahri, Deepika. "Predicting the Past." *Modern Language Quarterly* 65 (2004) 481–503.

Bale, Anthony P. "Fictions of Judaism in England before 1290." *The Jews in Medieval Britain: Historical, Literary and Archaeological Perspectives*, ed. Patricia Skinner (Woodbridge, Suffolk: Boydell Press, 2003) 129–44.

———. "'House devil, town saint': Anti-Semitism and Hagiography in Medieval Suffolk." *Chaucer and the Jews: Sources, Contexts, Meanings*, ed. Sheila Delany (New York: Routledge, 2002) 185–210.

———. "Richard of Devizes and Fictions of Judaism." *Jewish Culture and History* 23 (2000) 55–72.

Balibar, Etienne and Immanuel Wallerstein. *Race, Nation, Class: Ambiguous Identities* (New York: Verso, 1991).

Balsdon, J. P. *Romans and Aliens* (Chapel Hill, NC: University of North Carolina Press, 1980).

Banks, Marcus. *Ethnicity: Anthropological Constructions* (London: Routledge, 1996).

Banton, Michael. *Racial Theories*, 2nd ed. (Cambridge: Cambridge University Press, 1998).

Barlow, Frank. "The Effects of the Norman Conquest." *The Norman Conquest: Its Setting and Impact*, ed. Dorothy Whitelock, David C. Douglas, Charles H. Lemmon, and Frank Barlow (New York: Charles Scribner's Sons, 1966) 125–61.

———. *The English Church 1000–1066: A History of the Later Anglo-Saxon Church*, 2nd ed. (London: Longman, 1979).

———. *The English Church, 1066–1154: A History of the Anglo-Norman Church* (London: Longman, 1979).

———. *The Godwins: The Rise and Fall of a Noble Dynasty* (Harlow: Pearson Education, 2002).

Barrett, Robert W. "Writing From the Marches: Cheshire Poetry and Drama, 1195–1645" (PhD thesis, University of Pennsylvania, 2001).

Bartlet, Suzanne. "Women in the Medieval Anglo-Jewish Community." *The Jews in Medieval Britain: Historical, Literary and Archaeological Perspectives*, ed. Patricia Skinner (Woodbridge, Suffolk: Boydell Press, 2003) 113–27.

Bartlett, Robert. *England Under the Norman and Angevin Kings, 1075–1225* (Oxford: Clarendon Press, 2000).

———. *Gerald of Wales, 1146–1223* (Oxford: Clarendon Press, 1982).

———. *The Making of Europe: Conquest, Colonization, and Cultural Change, 950–1350* (Princeton: Princeton University Press, 1993).

———. "Medieval and Modern Concepts of Race and Ethnicity." *JMEMS* 31.1 (2001) 39–56.

———. "Rewriting Saints' Lives: The Case of Gerald of Wales." *Speculum* 58 (1983) 598–613.

———. "Symbolic Meanings of Hair in the Middle Ages." *TRHS* 6th series 4 (1994) 43–60.

Batcock, Neil. "The Parish Church in Norfolk in the 11th and 12th Centuries." *Minsters and Parish Churches: The Local Church in Transition, 950–1200*, ed. John Blair (Oxford: Oxford University Committee for Archaeology, 1988).

Bate, A. K. "Walter Map and Giraldus Cambrensis." *Latomus* 31 (1972) 860–75.

Bates, David. "The Rise and Fall of Normandy, c. 911–1204." *England and Normandy in the Middle Ages*, ed. David Bates and Anne Curry (London: Hambledon Press, 1994) 19–35.

Beauroy, Jacques. "La conquête cléricale de l'Angleterre." *Cahiers de civilisation médiévale* 27 (1984) 35–48

Bennett, Matthew. "First Crusaders' Images of Muslims: The Influence of Vernacular Poetry?" *Forum for Modern Language Studies* 22 (1986) 101–22.

Beresford, Maurice. *New Towns of the Middle Ages: Town Plantation in England, Wales, and Gascony* (New York: Frederick A. Praeger, 1947).

Bhabha, Homi K. *The Location of Culture* (London and New York: Routledge, 1994).

Biddick, Kathleen. *The Shock of Medievalism* (Durham: Duke University Press, 1998).

Birns, Nicholas. "The Trojan Myth: Postmodern Reverberations." *Exemplaria* 5 (1993) 45–78.

Blair, John, ed. *Ministers and Parish Churches: The Local Church in Transition, 950–1200* (Oxford: Oxford University Committee for Archaeology, 1988).

Boswell, John. *Christianity, Social Tolerance, and Homosexuality: Gay People in Western Europe from the Beginning of the Christian Era to the Fourteenth Century* (Chicago: Chicago University Press, 1981).

Brand, Paul. "The Jewish Community of England in the Records of English Royal Government." *The Jews in Medieval Britain: Historical, Literary and Archaeological Perspectives*, ed. Patricia Skinner (Woodbridge, Suffolk: Boydell Press, 2003) 73–83.

Brannigan, John. " 'A Particular Vice of that People': Giraldus Cambrensis and the Discourse of English Colonialism." *Irish Studies Review* 6.2 (1998) 121–30.

Brathwaite, Edward Kamau. *The Development of Creole Society in Jamaica, 1770–1820* (Oxford: Clarendon Press, 1971).

Brett, M. *The English Church under Henry I* (Oxford: Oxford University Press, 1975).

Britton, John. *The History and Antiquities of the See and Cathedral Church of Norwich* (London: Longman, Hurst, Rees, Orme, and Brown, 1816).

Brooke, C. N. L. "The Churches of Medieval Cambridge." *History, Society and the Churches: Essays in Honor of Owen Chadwick*, ed. Derek Beales and Geoffrey Best (Cambridge: Cambridge University Press, 1985) 49–76.

———. "Geoffrey of Monmouth as a Historian." *Church and Government in the Middle Ages: Essays Presented to C. R. Cheney on His 70th Birthday*, ed. C. N. L. Brooke et al. (Cambridge: Cambridge University Press, 1976).

———. "Married Men among the English Higher Clergy, 1066–1200." *Cambridge Historical Journal* 12.2 (1956) 187–88.

———. *Medieval Church and Society: Collected Essays* (London: Sidgwick and Jackson, 1971).

Brooks, Nicholas P. and H. E. Walker, "The Authority and Interpretation of the Bayeux Tapestry." *Anglo-Norman Studies* 1 (1978) 1–34.

Broughton, Bradford B. *The Legends of King Richard I Coeur de Lion: A Study of Sources and Variations to the Year 1600* (The Hague: Mouton and Co., 1966).

Brown, Catherine. "In the Middle." *JMEMS* 30.3 (2000) 547–74.

Brown, George Hardin. *Bede the Venerable* (Boston: Twayne Publishers, 1987).

Brown, Peter. *The Rise of Western Christendom: Triumph and Diversity, A.D. 200–1000*, 2nd ed. (Oxford: Blackwell Publishing, 2003).

Brown, R. Allen. *Castles, Conquest and Charters: Collected Papers* (Woodbridge, Suffolk: Boydell Press, 1989).

———. *The Normans and the Norman Conquest*, 2nd ed. (Woodbridge, Suffolk: Boydell Press, 1985).

Burger, Glenn. *Chaucer's Queer Nation* (Minneapolis: University of Minnesota Press, 2003).

———. "Cilician Armenian Métissage and Hetoum's *La Fleur des histoires de la terre d'Orient*." *The Postcolonial Middle Ages*, ed. Jeffrey Jerome Cohen (New York: Palgrave, 2000) 67–83.

Burns, Robert I. "The Significance of the Frontier in the Middle Ages." *Medieval Frontier Societies*, ed. Robert Bartlett and Angus MacKay (Oxford: Clarendon Press, 1989) 307–30.

Butler, Judith. *Bodies That Matter: On the Discursive Limits of "Sex"* (New York: Routledge, 1993).

———. *Gender Trouble: Feminism and the Subversion of Identity* (New York: Routledge, 1990).

———. *Undoing Gender* (New York: Routledge, 2004).

Bynum, Caroline Walker. *Metamorphosis and Identity* (New York: Zone Books, 2001).

Cain, James D. "Unnatural History: Gender and Genealogy in Gerald of Wales's *Topographia* Hibernica." *Essays in Medieval Studies* 19 (2002) 29–43.

Campbell, James. "The East Anglian Sees before the Conquest." *Norwich Cathedral: Church, City and Diocese, 1096–1996*, ed. Ian Atherton, Eric Fernie, Christopher Harper-Bill, and Hassell Smith (London: Hambledon Press, 1996) 3–21.

Campbell, James. *Essays in Anglo-Saxon History* (London: Hambledon Press, 1986).
———. "The Late Anglo-Saxon State: A Maximum View." *Proceedings of the British Academy* 87 (1995) 37–65.
———. "Norwich." *Historic Towns*, 3 vols., ed. M. D. Lobel and W. H. Johns (Oxford: Historic Towns Trust, 1969–1989) vol. 2 (1975) 1–25.
———. "The United Kingdom of England: The Anglo-Saxon Achievement." *Uniting the Kingdom? The Making of British History*, ed. Alexander Grant and Keith J. Stringer (London: Routledge, 1995) 31–47.
———. "Was it Infancy in England? Some Questions of Comparison." *England and Her Neighbours, 1066–1453*, ed. Michael Jones and Malcolm Vale (London: Hambledon Press, 1989) 1–17.
Canclini, Néstor García. *Hybrid Cultures: Strategies for Entering and Leaving Modernity*, trans. Christopher L. Chiappari and Silvia L. López (Minneapolis: University of Minnesota Press, 1995).
Carr, A. D. *Medieval Wales* (New York: St. Martin's Press, 1995).
Carter, Alan. "The Anglo-Saxon Origins of Norwich: The Problems and Approaches." *Anglo-Saxon England* 7 (1978) 175–204.
Chadd, David. "The Medieval Customary of the Cathedral Priory." *Norwich Cathedral: Church, City and Diocese, 1096–1996*, ed. Ian Atherton, Eric Fernie, Christopher Harper-Bill, and Hassell Smith (London: Hambledon Press, 1996) 314–24.
Chazan, Robert. "The Conversion of Jews to Christianity in Thirteenth-Century England." *Speculum* 67 (1992) 263–83.
———. *European Jewry and the First Crusade* (Berkeley: University of California Press, 1987).
———. "From the First Crusade to the Second: Evolving Perceptions of the Christian-Jewish Conflict." *Jews and Christians in Twelfth-Century Europe*, ed. Michael A. Singer and John Van Engen (Notre Dame: University of Notre Dame Press, 2001) 46–62.
———. *God, Humanity, and History: The Hebrew First Crusade Narratives* (Berkeley: University of California Press, 2000).
———. *Medieval Stereotypes and Modern Antisemitism* (Berkeley: University of California Press, 1997).
Chibnall, Marjorie. *Anglo-Norman England, 1066–1166* (Oxford: Basil Blackwell, 1986).
———. *The Debate on the Norman Conquest* (Manchester: Manchester University Press, 1999).
———. "Monastic Foundations in England Normandy, 1066–1189." *England and Normandy in the Middle Ages*, ed. David Bates and Anne Curry (London: Hambledon Press, 1994) 37–49.
———. *The Normans* (London: Blackwell Publishers, 2000).
———. *Piety, Power and History in Medieval England and Normandy* (Aldershot: Ashgate, 2000).
———. " 'Racial' Minorities in the Anglo-Norman Realm." *Minorities and Barbarians in Medieval Life and Thought*, ed. Susan J. Ridyard and Robert G. Benson (Sewanee, TN: University of South Press, 1996) 49–61.

———. *The World of Orderic Vitalis* (Oxford: Clarendon Press, 1984).

Clanchy, M. T. *From Memory to Written Record: England, 1066–1307* (Cambridge: Harvard University Press, 1979).

Clarke, Cecily. "Battle c.1110: An Anthroponymist Looks at an Anglo-Norman New Town." *Anglo-Norman Studies* 2 (1980) 21–41.

———. "Women's Names in Post-Conquest England: Observations and Speculations." *Speculum* 53.2 (1978) 223–51.

Cohen, Jeffrey Jerome. "Introduction: Midcolonial," *The Postcolonial Middle Ages*, ed. Jeffrey Jerome Cohen (St. Martin's Press, 2000), 1–17.

———. "*Kyte oute yugilment*: An Introduction to Medieval Noise," *Exemplaria* 16.2 (2004): 267–76.

———. *Medieval Identity Machines* (Minneapolis: University of Minnesota Press, 2003).

———. "Monster Culture (Seven Theses)," *Monster Theory: Reading Culture*, ed. Jeffrey Jerome Cohen (University of Minnesota Press, 1996), 3–25.

———. *Of Giants: Sex, Monsters, and the Middle Ages* (Minneapolis: University of Minnesota Press, 1999).

———. "Postcolonial Theory." *Chaucer: An Oxford Guide*, ed. Steven Ellis (Oxford: Oxford University Press, 2004) 448–62.

———. "Race." *Dictionary of the Middle Ages*, Vol. 14: First Supplement, ed. William Chester Jordan (New York: Charles Scribner's Sons, 2004) 515–18.

Cohen, Jeremy. "A 1096 Complex? Constructing the First Crusade in Jewish Historical Memory, Medieval and Modern." *Jews and Christians in Twelfth-Century Europe*, ed. Michael A. Signer and John Van Engen (Notre Dame: University of Notre Dame Press, 2001) 9–26.

———. ed. *Essential Papers on Judaism and Christianity in Conflict, from Late Antiquity to the Reformation* (New York: New York University Press, 1999).

Corradini, Richard, Max Diesenberger, and Helmut Reimitz, *The Constitution of Communities in the Early Middle Ages: Texts, Resources and Artefacts* (Leiden: Brill, 2003).

Coulton, G. G. "Nationalism in the Middle Ages." *Cambridge Historical Journal* 5 (1935–1937) 15–40.

Crane, Susan. "Anglo-Norman Cultures in England, 1066–1460." *The Cambridge History of Medieval English Literature*, ed. David Wallace (Cambridge: Cambridge University Press, 1999) 35–60.

———. *The Performance of Self: Ritual, Clothing, and Identity During the Hundred Years War* (Philadelphia: University of Pennsylvania Press, 2002).

Crawford, T. D. "On the Linguistic Competence of Geoffrey of Monmouth." *Medium Ævum* 51 (1982) 152–62.

Crick, Julia C. "The British Past and the Welsh Future: Gerald of Wales, Geoffrey of Monmouth and Arthur of Britain." *Celtica* 23 (1999) 60–75.

———. *The* Historia Regum Britannie *of Geoffrey of Monmouth III: A Summary Catalogue of the Manuscripts* (Cambridge: D. S. Brewer, 1989).

———. *The* Historia Regum Britannie *of Geoffrey of Monmouth IV: Dissemination and Reception in the Middle Ages* (Cambridge: D. S. Brewer, 1991).

Crouch, David. *The Images of the Aristocracy in Britain, 1000–1300* (London: Routledge, 1992).

Crouch, David. "The March and the Welsh Kings." *The Anarchy in King Stephen's Reign*, ed. Edmund King (Oxford: Clarendon Press, 1994) 255–89.

———. "Normans and Anglo-Normans: A Divided Aristocracy?" *England and Normandy in the Middle Ages*, ed. David Bates and Anne Curry (London: Hambledon Press, 1994) 51–67.

———. *The Normans: The History of a Dynasty* (London: Hambledon and London, 2002).

———. *The Reign of King Stephen, 1135–1154* (Harlow: Pearson Education, 2000).

Curta, Florin. *The Making of the Slavs: History and Archaeology of the Lower Danube Region, c.500–700* (Cambridge: Cambridge University Press, 2001).

———. Review of *Medieval Europeans: Studies in Ethnic Identity and National Perspectives*, ed. Alfred Smyth. *The Medieval Review* 99.03.06

Cutts, Edward L. *Parish Priests and their People in the Middle Ages in England* (1898; rpr. New York: AMS Press, 1970).

Dalton, Paul. *Conquest, Anarchy and Lordship: Yorkshire, 1066–1154* (Cambridge: Cambridge University Press, 1994).

Daniel, Norman. *The Arabs and Mediaeval Europe* (London: Longman, 1975).

———. "Crusade Propaganda." *The Impact of the Crusades on Europe*, ed. Harry W. Hazard and Norman P. Zacour, 39-97. in the *A History of the Crusades*, ed. Kenneth M. Setton, v. 6. (Madison: University of Wisconsin Press, 1989).

———. *Heroes and Saracens: An Interpretation of the Chansons de Geste* (Edinburgh: Edinburgh University Press, 1984).

———. *Islam and the West: The Making of an Image* (Edinburgh: Edinburgh University Press, 1960 [rpr. 1980]).

Darby, H. C. *The Domesday Geography of Eastern England* (Cambridge: Cambridge University Press, 1952)

Davies, Rees R. *The Age of Conquest: Wales, 1065–1415* (Oxford: Oxford university Press, 1991).

———. *Conquest, Coexistence and Change: Wales 1063–1415* (Oxford: Oxford University Press, 1987).

———. *Domination and Conquest: The Experience of Ireland, Scotland, and Wales, 1100–1300* (Cambridge: Cambridge University Press, 1990).

———. *The First English Empire: Power and Identity in the British Isles, 1093–1343* (Oxford: Oxford University Press, 2000).

———. "Frontier Arrangements in Fragmented Societies: Ireland and Wales." *Medieval Frontier Societies*, ed. Robert Bartlett and Angus MacKay (Oxford: Clarendon Press, 1989) 77–100.

———. "In Praise of British History." *The British Isles 1100–1500: Comparisons, Contrasts and Connections*, ed. R. R. Davies (Edinburgh: John Donald Publishers, 1988) 9–26.

———. "Kings, Lords and Liberties in the March of Wales, 1066–1272." *TRHS* 5th series 29 (1979) 41–61.

———. "Kinsmen, Neighbours and Communities in Wales and the Western British Isles, c.1100–1400." *Law, Laity and Solidarities: Essays in Honour of Susan Reynolds*, ed. Pauline Stafford, Janet L. Nelson, and Jane Martindale (Manchester: Manchester University Press, 2001) 172–87.

———. "The Law of the March." *Welsh History Review* 5 (1970–1971) 1–30.

———. *Lordship and Society in the March of Wales* (Oxford: Oxford University Press, 1987).

———. *The Matter of Britain and the Matter of England* (Oxford: Clarendon Press, 1996).

———. "The Peoples of Britain and Ireland, 1100–1400: I. Identities." *Transactions of the Royal Historical Society* 6th series 4 (1994) 1–20.

———. "The Peoples of Britain and Ireland, 1100–1400: II. Names, Boundaries and Regnal Solidarities." *Transactions of the Royal Historical Society* 6th series 5 (1995) 1–20.

———. "The Peoples of Britain and Ireland, 1100–1400: III. Laws and Customs." *Transactions of the Royal Historical Society* 6th series VI (1996) 1–23.

———. "The Peoples of Britain and Ireland, 1100–1400: IV. Language and Historical Mythology." *Transactions of the Royal Historical Society* 6th series VII (1997) 1–24.

———. "Race Relations in Post-Conquest Wales: Confrontation and Compromise." *Transactions of the Honourable Society of Cymmrodorion* (1974–1975) 32–56.

Davies, Wendy. *Wales in the Early Middle Ages* (London: Leicester University Press, 1982).

Davis, Kathleen. "Nation Writing in the Ninth Century: A Reminder for Postcolonial Thinking about the Nation." *Journal of Medieval and Early Modern Studies* 28 (1998) 611–37.

Davis, R. H. C. *King Stephen, 1135–1154*, 3rd ed. (London: Longman, 1990).

———. *The Normans and Their Myth* (London: Thames and Hudson, 1976).

Delany, Sheila. "Chaucer's Prioress, the Jews, and the Muslims." *Chaucer and the Jews: Sources, Contexts, Meanings*, ed. Sheila Delany (New York: Routledge, 2002) 43–57.

———. " 'Turn It Again': Jewish Medieval Studies and Literary Theory." *Exemplaria* 12 (2000) 1–20.

Deleuze, Gilles and Félix Guattari. *L'Anti-Oedipe: Capitalisme et Schizophrénie* (Paris: Les Éditions de Minuit, 1972). Trans. Robert Hurley, Marke Seem, and Helen R. Lane, *Anti-Oedipus: Capitalism and Schizophrenia* (Minneapolis: University of Minnesota Press, 1983).

———. *Mille plateaux, v. 2 de Capitalisme et Schizophrénie* (Paris: Les Éditions de Minuit, 1980). Trans. Brian Massumi, *A Thousand Plateaus: Capitalism and Schizophrenia* (Minneapolis: University of Minnesota Press, 1987).

Dinshaw, Carolyn. "Pale Faces: Race, Religion, and Affect in Chaucer's Texts and Their Readers." *Studies in the Age of Chaucer* 23 (2001) 19–41.

Dobson, R. B. *The Jews of Medieval York and the Massacre of March 1190*, University of York Borthwick Papers 45 (1974, rev. 1996).

———. "The Medieval York Jewry Reconsidered." *The Jews in Medieval Britain: Historical, Literary and Archaeological Perspectives*, ed. Patricia Skinner (Woodbridge, Suffolk: Boydell Press, 2003) 145–56.

———. "A Minority Ascendant: The Benedictine Conquest of the North of England, 1066–1100." *Minorities and Barbarians in Medieval Life and Thought*, ed. Susan J. Ridyard and Robert G. Benson (Sewanee, TN: University of the South Press, 1996) 5–26.

Dobson, R. B. "A Minority Within a Minority: The Jewesses of Thirteenth-Century England." *Minorities and Barbarians in Medieval Life and Thought*, ed. Susan J. Ridyard and Robert G. Benson (Sewanee, TN: University of the South Press, 1996) 27–48.

Dodwell, Barbara. "Herbert de Losinga and the Foundation." *Norwich Cathedral: Church, City and Diocese, 1096–1996*, ed. Ian Atherton, Eric Fernie, Christopher Harper-Bill, and Hassell Smith (London: Hambledon Press, 1996) 36–43.

———. "The Monastic Community." *Norwich Cathedral: Church, City and Diocese, 1096–1996*, ed. Ian Atherton, Eric Fernie, Christopher Harper-Bill, and Hassell Smith (London: Hambledon Press, 1996) 231–54.

———. "The Muniments and the Library." *Norwich Cathedral: Church, City and Diocese, 1096–1996*, ed. Ian Atherton, Eric Fernie, Christopher Harper-Bill, and Hassell Smith (London: Hambledon Press, 1996) 325–38.

Dolan, Terence. "Writing in Ireland." *The Cambridge History of Medieval English Literature*, ed. David Wallace (Cambridge: Cambridge University Press, 1999) 208–29.

Donoghue, Daniel. "Laȝamon's Ambivalence." *Speculum* 65 (1990) 537–63.

Dundes, Alan, ed. *The Blood Libel legend: A Casebook in Anti-Semitic Folklore* (Madison: University of Wisconsin Press, 1991).

Dymond, David. *The Norfolk Landscape* (London: Hodder and Stoughton, 1985).

Eales, Richard. "Royal Power and Castles in Norman England." *The Ideals and Practice of Medieval Knighthood* III (1990) 49–78.

Edwards, John. "The Church and the Jews in Medieval England." *The Jews in Medieval Britain: Historical, Literary and Archaeological Perspectives*, ed. Patricia Skinner (Woodbridge, Suffolk: Boydell Press, 2003) 85–95.

Einbinder, Susan. *Beautiful Death: Jewish Poetry and Martyrdom in Medieval France* (Princeton: Princeton University Press, 2002).

———. "Meir b. Elijah of Norwich: Persecution and Poetry among Medieval English Jews." *Journal of Medieval History* 26 (2000) 145–62.

Elukin, Jonathan. "The Discovery of the Self: Jews and Conversion in the Twelfth Century." *Jews and Christians in Twelfth-Century Europe*, ed. Michael A. Signer and John Van Engen (Notre Dame: University of Notre Dame Press, 2001) 63–76.

Epstein, Steven A. *Speaking of Slavery: Color, Ethnicity, and Human Bondage in Italy* (Cornell: Cornell University Press, 2001).

Evans, M. Carey. *The Legend of St. William, Boy-Martyr of Norwich* (Norwich: F. Crowe and Sons, n.d.).

Faletra, Michael A. "Narrating the Matter of Britain: Geoffrey of Monmouth and the Norman Colonization of Wales." *Chaucer Review* 35.1 (2000) 60–85.

Faral, Edmond, ed. *La légende Arthurienne: études et documents*, 3 vols. (Paris: Honoré Champion, 1929).

Felsenstein, Frank. *Anti-Semitic Stereotypes: A Paradigm of Otherness in English Popular Culture, 1660–1830* (Baltimore: Johns Hopkins University Press, 1995).

Fernandez-Armesto, Felipe. *Before Columbus: Exploration and Colonization from the Mediterranean to the Atlantic, 1229–1492* (Philadelphia: University of Pennsylvania Press, 1987).

Fernie, Eric C. *An Architectural History of Norwich Cathedral* (Oxford: Clarendon Press, 1993).

———. "Architecture and the Effects of the Norman Conquest." *England and Normandy in the Middle Ages*, ed. David Bates and Anne Curry (London: Hambledon Press, 1994) 105–116.

———. *The Architecture of Norman England* (Oxford: Oxford University Press, 2000).

———. "The Building: An Introduction." *Norwich Cathedral: Church, City and Diocese, 1096–1996*, ed. Ian Atherton, Eric Fernie, Christopher Harper-Bill, and Hassell Smith (London: Hambledon Press, 1996) 47–58.

———. "Saxons, Normans and their Buildings." *Anglo-Norman Studies* 21 (1999) 1–9.

Finke, Laurie A. and Martin B. Shichtman. *King Arthur and the Myth of History* (Gainesville: University Press of Florida, 2004).

Finucane, Ronald C. *Miracles and Pilgrims: Popular Beliefs in Medieval England* (Totowa, NJ: Rowman and Littlefield, 1977).

Fleming, Robin. *Kings and Lords in Conquest England* (Cambridge: Cambridge University Press, 1991).

Flint, Valerie I. J. "The *Historia Regum Britanniae* of Geoffrey of Monmouth: Parody and its Purpose. A Suggestion." *Speculum* 54 (1979) 447–68.

Floyd-Wilson, Mary. *English Ethnicity and Race in Early Modern Drama* (Cambridge: Cambridge University Press, 2003).

Foot, Sarah. "The Making of *Angelcynn*: English Identity before the Norman Conquest." *Transactions of the Royal Historical Society*, 6th series 6 (1996) 25–49.

Fradenburg, L. O. Aranye. "Criticism, Anti-Semitism, and the Prioress's Tale." *Exemplaria* 1 (1989) 69–115.

Frankenberg, Ruth. *White Women, Race Matters: The Social Construction of Whiteness* (Minneapolis: University of Minnesota Press, 1993).

Franklin, Michael. "The Cathedral as Parish Church: The Case of Southern England." *Church and City, 1000–1500*, ed. David Abulafia, Michael Franklin and Miri Rubin (Cambridge: Cambridge University Press, 1992) 173–98.

Frazer, William O. "Introduction: Identities in Early Medieval Britain." *Social Identity in Early Medieval Britain*, ed. William O. Frazer and Andrew Tyrrell (London: Leicester University Press, 2000) 1–22.

Freedman, Paul. *Images of the Medieval Peasant* (Stanford: Stanford University Press, 1999).

Freeman, E. A. *The History of the Norman Conquest of England*, 6 vols. (Oxford: Clarendon Press, 1870–1879).

Friedman, John Block. *The Monstrous Races in Medieval Art and Thought* (Cambridge: Harvard University Press, 1981).

Fuchs, Barbara and David J. Baker. "The Postcolonial Past." *Modern Language Quarterly* 65 (2004) 329–40.

Gaimar, Geffrei. *Estoire des Engleis*, ed. A. Bell (Oxford: Basil Blackwell, 1960).

Galloway, Andrew. "Writing History in England." *The Cambridge History of Medieval English Literature*, ed. David Wallace (Cambridge: Cambridge University Press, 1999) 255–83.

Garnett, George. " 'Franci et Angli': The Legal Distinctions Between Peoples After the Conquest." *Anglo-Norman Studies* 8 (1986) 109–37.

Geary, Patrick. *Before France and Germany: The Creation and Transformation of the Merovingian World* (Oxford: Oxford University Press, 1988).

———. "Ethnic Identity as a Situational Construct in the Early Middle Ages." *Medieval Perspectives* 3 (1988) 1–17.

———. *The Myth of Nations: The Medieval Origins of Europe* (Princeton: Princeton University Press, 2002).

Gellner, Ernst. *Nations and Nationalism* (Ithaca: Cornell University Press, 1983).

Giffney, Noreen. "Que(e)rying Mongols." *Medieval Feminist Forum* 36 (2003) 15–21.

Gillett, Andrew, ed. *On Barbarian Identity: Critical Approaches to Ethnicity in the Early Middle Ages* (Turnhout, Belgium: Brepols, 2002).

Gillingham, John. *The English in the Twelfth Century: Imperialism, National Identity and Political Values* (Woodbridge, Suffolk: Boydell Press, 2000).

———. "'Slaves of the Normans'? Gerald de Barri and Regnal Solidarity in Early Thirteenth-Century England." *Law, Laity and Solidarities: Essays in Honour of Susan Reynolds*, ed. Pauline Stafford, Janet L. Nelson, and Jane Martindale (Manchester: Manchester University Press, 2001) 160–71.

Gilman, Sander L. *Jewish Self-Hatred: Anti-Semitism and the Hidden Language of the Jews* (Baltimore: Johns Hopkins University Press, 1986).

Given, James. "The Inquisitors of Languedoc and the Medieval Technology of Power." *The American Historical Review* 94.2 (1989) 336–59

Glick, Leonard B. *Abraham's Heirs: Jews and Christians in Medieval Europe* (Syracuse: Syracuse University Press, 1999).

Goffart, Walter. *Barbarians and Romans, A.D. 418–584: The Techniques of Accommodation* (Princeton: Princeton University Press, 1980).

———. *The Narrators of Barbarian History (A.D. 550–800): Jordanes, Gregory of Tours, Bede, and Paul the Deacon* (Princeton: Princeton University Press, 1988).

Goldenberg, David M. "The Development of the Idea of Race: Classical Paradigms and Medieval Elaborations" [review of Ivan Hannaford, *Race: The History of an Idea in the West*]. *International Journal of the Classical Tradition* 5 (1999) 561–70.

Goldstein, R. James. " 'Why calle ye hym crist, siflen Iewes called hym Iesus?': The Disavowal of Jewish Identification in Piers Plowman B Text." *Exemplaria* 13 (2001) 215–51.

———. "Writing in Scotland, 1058–1560." *The Cambridge History of Medieval English Literature*, ed. David Wallace (Cambridge: Cambridge University Press, 1999) 229–54.

Gransden, Antonia. *Historical Writing in England I, c. 550 to c. 1307* (London: Routledge, 1974).

———. "Realistic Observation in Twelfth-Century England." *Speculum* 47 (1972) 29–51.

Grant, Lindy. "Architectural Relationships between England and Normandy, 1100–1204." *England and Normandy in the Middle Ages*, ed. David Bates and Anne Curry (London: Hambledon Press, 1994) 117–29.

Green, Barbara and Rachel M. R. Young. *Norwich: The Growth of a City* (Norwich: Norfolk Museum Service, 1963), reprinted 1977.

Green, Judith A. *The Aristocracy of Norman England* (Cambridge: Cambridge University Press, 1997).

Griffiths, Ralph A. *Conquerors and Conquered in Medieval Wales* (New York: St. Martin's Press, 1994).

Hadley, Dawn. " 'Cockle amongst the Wheat': The Scandinavian Settlement of England." *Social Identity in Early Medieval England*, ed. William O. Frazer and Andrew Tyrrell (London: Leicester University Press, 2000) 111–35.

Hahn, Thomas. "The Difference the Middle Ages Makes: Color and Race before the Modern World." *Journal of Medieval and Early Modern Studies* 31 (2001) 1–37.

Hamil, F. C. "Presentment of Englishry and the Murder Fine." *Speculum* 12 (1937) 285–98.

Hannah, Ian C. *The Heart of East Anglia: The Story of Norwich from Earliest to Latest Times* (London: Heath, Cranton and Ouseley, 1913).

Hanning, Robert. *The Vision of History in Early Britain: From Gildas to Geoffrey of Monmouth* (New York: Columbia University Press, 1966).

Harper-Bill, Christopher. "Bishop William Turbe and the Diocese of Norwich, 1146–1174." *Anglo-Norman Studies* 7 (1985) 142–60.

———. "Introduction." *English Episcopal Acta 6: Norwich 1070–1214*, ed. Christopher Harper-Bill (Oxford: Oxford University Press, 1990) xxv–lxxxviii.

———. "The Medieval Church and the Wider World." *Norwich Cathedral: Church, City and Diocese, 1096–1996*, ed. Ian Atherton, Eric Fernie, Christopher Harper-Bill, and Hassell Smith (London: Hambledon Press, 1996) 281–313.

Harris, Stephen J. *Race and Ethnicity in Anglo-Saxon Literature* (New York: Routledge, 2003).

Harrison, Faye V. "Expanding the Discourse on 'Race.' " *American Anthropologist* 100 (1998) 609–31.

Hayman, Robert L. Jr., and Nancy Levit. "Un-Natural Things: Constructions of Race, Gender, and Disability." *Crossroads, Directions, and a New Critical Race Theory*, ed. Francisco Valdes, Jerome McCristal Culp, and Angela P. Harris (Philadelphia: Temple University Press, 2002) 159–86.

Heng, Geraldine. *Empire of Magic: Medieval Romance and the Politics of Cultural Fantasy* (New York: Columbia University Press, 2003).

Heywood, Stephen. "The Romanesque Building." *Norwich Cathedral: Church, City and Diocese, 1096–1996*, ed. Ian Atherton, Eric Fernie, Christopher Harper-Bill, and Hassell Smith (London: Hambledon, 1996).

Higham, N. J. *The Convert Kings: Power and Religious Affiliation in Early Anglo-Saxon England* (Manchester: Manchester University Press, 1997).

———. *The English Conquest: Gildas and Britain in the Fifth Century* (Manchester: Manchester University Press, 1994).

———. *An English Empire: Bede and the Early Anglo-Saxon Kings* (Manchester: Manchester University Press, 1995).

———. *The Kingdom of Northumbria, AD 350–1100* (Stroud, Gloucestershire: Alan Sutton Publishing, 1993).

Hillaby, Joe. "Jewish Colonisation in the Twelfth Century." *The Jews in Medieval Britain: Historical, Literary and Archaeological Perspectives*, ed. Patricia Skinner (Woodbridge, Suffolk: Boydell Press, 2003) 15–40.

———. "The Ritual-Child-Murder Accusation: Its Dissemination and Harold of Gloucester." *Jewish Historical Studies* 34 (1996) 69–109.

Hinton, David. "Medieval Anglo-Jewry: The Archaeological Evidence." *The Jews in Medieval Britain: Historical, Literary and Archaeological Perspectives*, ed. Patricia Skinner (Woodbridge, Suffolk: Boydell Press, 2003) 97–111.

Hobsbawm, E. J. *Nations and Nationalism since 1780* (Cambridge: Cambridge University Press, 1990).

Hoffmann, Richard C. "Outsiders by Birth and Blood: Racist Ideologies around the Periphery of Medieval European Culture." *Studies in Medieval and Renaissance History* 6 (1983) 1–36.

Holdsworth, Christopher. "The Church." *The Anarchy in King Stephen's Reign*, ed. Edmund King (Oxford: Clarendon Press, 1994) 207–29.

Hollister, C. Warren. *Henry I*. Ed. and completed by Amanda Clark Frost (New Haven: Yale University Press, 2001).

———. *Monarchy, Magnates and Institutions in the Anglo-Norman World* (London: Hambledon Press, 1986).

Holmes, Urban T. "Gerald the Naturalist." *Speculum* 11 (1936) 110–21.

Holsinger, Bruce. "Medieval Studies, Postcolonial Studies, and the Genealogies of Critique." *Speculum* 77 (2002) 1195–227.

Holt, J. C. *Colonial England, 1066–1232* (London: Hambledon Press, 1997).

Howe, Nicholas. *Migration and Mythmaking in Anglo-Saxon England* (New Haven: Yale University Press, 1989).

Hsia, R. Po-Chia. *The Myth of Ritual Murder: Jews and Magic in Reformation Germany* (New Haven: Yale University Press, 1988).

Huet, Marie-Hélène. *Monstrous Imagination* (Cambridge: Harvard University Press, 1993).

Hyams, Paul. "The Jewish Minority in Mediaeval England, 1066–1290." *Journal of Jewish Studies* 25 (1974) 270–93.

Ingham, Patricia Clare. *Sovereign Fantasies: Arthurian Romance and the Making of Britain* (Philadelphia: University of Pennsylvania Press, 2001).

Ingham, Patricia Clare and Michelle Warren, eds. *Postcolonial Moves: Medieval Through Modern* (New York: Palgrave Macmillan, 2003).

Ingledew, Francis. "The Book of Troy and the Genealogical Construction of History: The Case of Geoffrey of Monmouth's *Historia Regum Britanniae*." *Speculum* 69 (1994) 665–704.

Jacobs, Joseph. *The Jews of Angevin England: Documents and Records* (New York: Putnam and Sons, 1893).

———. "Little St. Hugh of Lincoln: Researches in History, Archeology, and Legend." *Transactions of the Jewish Historical Society of England* 1 (1893–1894) 89–135.

James, Simon. *The Atlantic Celts: Ancient People or Modern Invention?* (Madison: University of Wisconsin Press, 1999).

Jochens, Jenny. "Race and Ethnicity in the Old Norse World." *Viator* 30 (1999) 79–103.

Johnson, Lesley. "Imagining Communities: Medieval and Modern." *Concepts of National Identity in the Middle Ages*, ed. Simon Forde, Lesley Johnson, and Alan V. Murray (Leeds: School of English, University of Leeds, 1995) 1–19.

Johnson, Willis. "The Myth of Jewish Male Menses." *Journal of Medieval History* 24 (1998) 273–95.

Jones, Malcolm. *The Secret Middle Ages* (Stroud, UK: Sutton Publishing Limited, 2002).

Jones, Michael. " 'The Place of the Jews': Anti-Judaism and Theatricality in Medieval Culture." *Exemplaria* 12 (2000) 327–59.

Jones, W. R. "The Image of the Barbarian in Medieval Europe." *Comparative Studies in Society and History* 13 (1971) 376–407.

Jordan, William Chester. "Adolescence and Conversion in the Middle Ages: A Research Agenda." *Jews and Christians in Twelfth-Century Europe*, ed. Michael A. Signer and John Van Engen (Notre Dame: University of Notre Dame Press, 2001).

———. " 'Europe' in the Middle Ages." *The Idea of Europe: From Antiquity to the European Union*, ed. Anthony Pagden (Cambridge: Cambridge University Press, 2002) 72–90.

———. *The French Monarchy and the Jews: From Philip Augustus to the Last Capetians* (Philadelphia: University of Pennsylvania Press, 1989).

———. "Jewish Studies and the Medieval Historian." *Exemplaria* 12 (2000) 7–20.

———. "Why 'Race'?" *JMEMS* 31.1 (2001) 165–73.

Kapelle, William E. *The Norman Conquest of the North: The Region and its Transformation, 1100–1135* (Chapel Hill, NC: University of North Carolina Press, 1979).

Kaplan, Amy. " 'Left Alone with America': The Absence of Empire in the Study of American Culture." *Cultures of United States Imperialism*, ed. Kaplan and Donald E. Pease (Durham: Duke University Press, 1993) 3–21.

Kealey, Edward J. *Roger of Salisbury: Viceroy of England* (Berkeley: University of California Press, 1972).

Kersken, Norbert. "High and Late Medieval National Historiography." *Historiography in the Middle Ages*, ed. Deborah Mauskopf Deliyannis (Leiden: Brill, 2003) 181–215.

Keynes, Simon. "Regenbald the Chancellor *(sic)*." *Anglo-Norman Studies* 10 (1988) 185–222.

Keynes, Simon and Michael Lapidge. *Alfred the Great* (Harmondsworth: Penguin, 1983).

Kieckhefer, Richard. "Erotic Magic in Medieval Europe." *Sex in the Middle Ages: A Book of Essays*, ed. Joyce E. Salisbury (New York: Garland, 1991) 30–55.

King, Edmund, ed. *The Anarchy in King Stephen's Reign* (Oxford: Clarendon Press, 1994).

Kinoshita, Sharon. " 'Pagans are Wrong and Christians are Right': Alterity, Gender, and Nation in the *Chanson de Roland*." *Journal of Medieval and Early Modern Studies* 31 (2001) 79–111.

Knight, Rhonda. "Procreative Sodomy: Textuality and the Construction of Ethnicities in Gerald of Wales' *Descriptio Kambriae*." *Exemplaria* 14 (2002) 47–77.

———. "Werewolves, Monsters, and Miracles: Representing Colonial Fantasies in Gerald of Wales's *Topographia Hibernica*." *Studies in Iconography* 22 (2001) 55–86.

Knight, Stephen. *Arthurian Literature and Society* (New York: St Martin's Press, 1983).

Knowles, David. *The Monastic Order in England*, 2nd ed. (Cambridge: Cambridge University Press, 1963).

———. "Some Enemies of Gerald of Wales." *Studia Monastica* 1 (1959) 137–41.

Kowaleski, Maryanne. "Town and Country in Late Medieval England: The Hide and Leather Trade." *Work in Towns 850–1850*, ed. Penelope J. Corfield and Derek Keene (Leicester: Leicester University Press, 1990) 57–73.

Kruger, Steven F. "Becoming Christian, Becoming Male?" *Becoming Male in the Middle Ages*, ed. Jeffrey Jerome Cohen and Bonnie Wheeler (New York: Garland, 1997) 21–42.

———. "The Bodies of the Jews in the Late Middle Ages." *The Idea of Medieval Literature: New Essays on Chaucer and Medieval Culture in Honor of Donald R. Howard*, ed. James M. Dean and Christian K. Zacher (Newark: University of Delaware Press, 1992) 301–23.

———. "Conversion and Medieval Sexual, Religious, and Racial Categories." *Constructing Medieval Sexuality*, ed. Karma Lochrie, Peggy McCracken, and James A. Schultz (Minneapolis: University of Minnesota Press, 1997) 158–79.

———. "Medieval Christian (Dis)identifications: Muslims and Jews in Guibert of Nogent." *New Literary History* 28 (1997) 185–203.

———. "Racial/Religious and Sexual Queerness in the Middle Ages." *Medieval Feminist Newsletter* 16 (1993) 32–36.

———. Review of James Muldoon, *Varieties of Religious Conversion in the Middle Ages*. *Arthuriana* 9 (1999) 144–46.

———. "The Spectral Jew." *New Medieval Literatures*, ed. Rita Copeland, David Lawton, and Wendy Scase (Oxford: Clarendon Press, 1998) 9–35.

Kushner, Tony. "Heritage and Ethnicity: An Introduction." *The Jewish Heritage in British History: Englishness and Jewishness*, ed. Tony Kushner (London: Frank Cass, 1992) 1–28.

Lampert, Lisa. *Gender and Jewish Difference from Paul to Shakespeare* (Philadelphia: University of Pennsylvania Press, 2004).

———. "Race, Periodicity, and the (Neo-) Middle Ages." *Modern Language Quarterly* 65 (2004) 391–421.

Langfors, Arthur. " 'L'Anglais qui couve' dans l'imagination populaire au Moyen Age." *Mélanges de philologie romane et de littérature médiévale offerts à Ernest Hoepffner* (Paris: Publications de la Faculté des Lettres de l'Université de Strasbourg, 1949) 89–94.

Langmuir, Gavin I. *History, Religion, and Antisemitism* (Berkeley: University of California Press, 1990).

———. "Thomas of Monmouth: Detector of Ritual Murder." *Speculum* 59 (1984) 820–46.

———. *Toward a Definition of Antisemitism* (Berkeley: University of California Press, 1990).

Leckie, William. *The Passage of Dominion: Geoffrey of Monmouth and the Periodization of Insular History in the Twelfth Century* (Toronto: University of Toronto Press, 1981).

Lees, Clare A. "Engendering Religious Desire: Sex, Knowledge, and Christian Identity in Anglo-Saxon England." *Journal of Medieval and Early Modern Studies* 27 (1997) 17–45.

—————. *Tradition and Belief: Religious Writing in Late Anglo-Saxon England* (Minneapolis: University of Minnesota Press, 1999).

Lees, Clare A. and Gillian R. Overing. "Signifying Gender and Empire." *Journal of Medieval and Early Modern Studies* 34 (2004) 1–16.

Lefroy, W. *Norwich Cathedral* (London: Isbister and Co., 1896).

Lerer, Seth. "Old English and its Afterlife." *The Cambridge History of Medieval English Literature*, ed. David Wallace (Cambridge: Cambridge University Press, 1999) 7–34.

Lipman, Vivian D. "The Anatomy of Medieval Anglo-Jewry." *Transactions of the Jewish Historical Society of England* 21 (1967) 64–77.

—————. *The Jews of Medieval Norwich* (London: Jewish Historical Society of England, 1967).

Lloyd, John Edward. *A History of Wales From the Earliest Times to the Edwardian Conquest*, 2 vols. (London: Longmans, 1911 [rpr. 1967]).

Lotter, Friedrich. "*Innocens virgo et martyr*: Thomas von Monmouth und die Verbreitung der Ritualmordlegende im Hochmittelalter." *Die Legende vom Ritualmord*, ed. Rainer Erb (Berlin: Metropol, 1993) 25–72.

Loud, G. A. "The 'Gens Normannorum'—Myth or Reality?" *Anglo-Norman Studies* 4 (1981) 104–16.

Loyn, H. R. *Anglo-Saxon England and the Norman Conquest*, 2nd ed. (London: Longman, 1991).

—————. *The English Church, 940–1154* (Harlow, Essex: Pearson Education, 2000).

—————. *The Norman Conquest*, 3rd ed. (London: Hutchinson, 1982).

Maccoby, Hyam. *Judaism on Trial: Jewish-Christian Disputations in the Middle Ages* (Rutherford: Fairleigh Dickinson University Press, 1981).

MacDougall, Hugh. *Racial Myth in English History: Trojans, Teutons, and Anglo-Saxons* (Montreal: Harvest House, 1982).

Marcus, Ivan. "The Dynamics of Jewish Renaissance and Renewal in the Twelfth Century." *Jews and Christians in Twelfth-Century Europe*, ed. Michael A. Signer and John Van Engen (Notre Dame: University of Notre Dame Press, 2001) 27–45.

Matthew, D. J. A. "The English Cultivation of Norman History." *England and Normandy in the Middle Ages*, ed. David Bates and Anne Curry (London: Hambledon Press, 1994) 1–18.

Matthew, Donald. *King Stephen* (London: Hambledon Press, 2002).

Mayr-Harting, Henry. *The Coming of Christianity to Anglo-Saxon England*, 3rd ed. (University Park, PA: Pennsylvania State University Press, 1991).

McClintock, Anne. "The Angel of Progress: Pitfalls of the Term 'Post-Colonialism.' " *Social Text* 31–32 (1992) 84–98.

—————. *Imperial Leather: Race, Gender and Sexuality in the Colonial Contest* (New York: Routledge, 1995).

McCracken, Peggy. *The Curse of Eve, the Wound of the Hero: Blood, Gender, and Medieval Literature* (Philadelphia: University of Pennsylvania Press, 2003).

McCulloh, John M. "Jewish Ritual Murder: William of Norwich, Thomas of Monmouth. and the Early Dissemination of the Myth." *Speculum* 72 (1997) 698–740.

McNamara, Jo Ann. "The Herrenfrage: The Restructuring of the Gender System, 1050–1150." *Medieval Masculinities: Regarding Men in the Middle Ages*, ed. Clare A. Lees (Minneapolis: University of Minnesota Press, 1994) 3–29.

McRuer, Robert. *The Queer Renaissance: Contemporary American Literature and the Reinvention of Lesbian and Gay Identities* (New York: New York University Press, 1997).

Mehan, Uppinder and David Townsend. " 'Nation' and the Gaze of the Other in Eighth-Century Northumbria." *Comparative Literature* 53 (2001) 1–26.

Mellinkoff, Ruth. *The Mark of Cain* (Berkeley: University of California Press, 1981).

———. *Outcasts: Signs of Otherness in Northern European Art of the Late Middle Ages*, 2 vols. (Berkeley: University of California Press, 1993).

Meredith, Gwenn. "Henry I's Concubines." *Essays in Medieval Studies* 19 (2002) 14–28.

Metlitzki, Dorothee. *The Matter of Araby in Medieval England* (New Haven: Yale University Press, 1977).

Meyvaert, Paul. " 'Rainaldus est malus scriptor Francigenus': Voicing National Antipathy in the Middle Ages." *Speculum* 66 (1991) 743–63.

Michaelsen, Scott and David E. Johnson, eds. *Border Theory: The Limits of Cultural Politics* (Minneapolis: University of Minnesota Press, 1997).

Minh-ha, Trinh T. *Woman, Native, Other: Writing Postcoloniality and Feminism* (Bloomington: Indiana University Press, 1989).

Moore, R. I. *The Formation of a Persecuting Society: Power and Deviance in Western Europe, 950–1250* (Oxford: Blackwell, 1987).

Moreland, John. "Ethnicity, Power and the English." *Social Identity in Early Medieval England*, ed. William O. Frazer and Andrew Tyrrell (London: Leicester University Press, 2000) 23–51.

Morillo, Stephen. *Warfare under the Anglo-Norman Kings, 1066–1135* (Woodbridge, Suffolk: Boydell Press, 1994).

———, ed. *The Battle of Hastings: Sources and Interpretations* (Woodbridge, Suffolk: Boydell Press, 1996).

Muldoon, James. *Identity on the Medieval Irish Frontier: Degenerate Englishmen, Wild Irishmen, Middle Nations* (Gainesville: University of Florida Press, 2003).

Mundill, Robin R. "Christian and Jewish Lending Patterns and Financial Dealings During the Twelfth and Thirteenth Centuries." *Credit and Debt in Medieval England, c.1180–c.1350*, ed. P. R. Schofield and N. J. Mayhew (Oxford: Oxbow Books, 2002) 42–67.

Muñoz, José Esteban. *Disidentifications: Queers of Color and the Performance of Politics* (Minneapolis: University of Minnesota Press, 1999).

Nelson, Lynn H. *The Normans in South Wales, 1070–1171* (Austin: University of Texas Press, 1966).

Nichols, Stephen G. "Fission and Fusion: Mediations of Power in Medieval History and Literature." *Yale French Studies* 70 (1986) 21–41.

Nilson, Ben. *Cathedral Shrines of Medieval England* (Woodbridge, Suffolk: Boydell Press, 1998).

Nirenberg, David. *Communities of Violence: Persecution of Minorities in the Middle Ages* (Princeton: Princeton University Press, 1996).

Olender, Maurice. *The Languages of Paradise: Race, Religion and Philology in the Nineteenth Century.* Trans. Arthur Goldhammer (Cambridge: Harvard University Press, 1992).

Orchard, Andy. *A Critical Companion to* Beowulf (Cambridge: D. S. Brewer, 2003).

———. *Pride and Prodigies: Studies in the Monsters of the* Beowulf-*manuscript* (Cambridge: D. S. Brewer, 1995).

Otter, Monika. *Inventiones: Fiction and Referentiality in Twelfth-Century English Historical Writing* (Chapel Hill, NC: University of North Carolina Press, 1996).

———. "1066: The Moment of Transition in Two Narratives of the Norman Conquest." *Speculum* 74 (1999) 565–86.

Partner, Nancy F. *Serious Entertainments: The Writing of History in Twelfth-Century England* (Chicago: University of Chicago Press, 1977).

Paster, Gail Kern. *The Body Embarrassed: Drama and the Disciplines of Shame in Early Modern England* (Ithaca: Cornell University Press, 1993).

———. *Humoring the Body: Emotions and the Shakespearean Stage* (Chicago: University of Chicago Press, 2004).

Patterson, Lee. *Negotiating the Past: The Historical Understanding of Medieval Literature* (Madison: University of Wisconsin Press, 1987).

Pelteret, David A. E. *Slavery in Early Mediaeval England: From the Reign of Alfred until the Twelfth Century* (Woodbridge, Suffolk: Boydell Press, 1995).

Perloff, Marjorie. "Cultural Liminality / Aesthetic Closure? The 'Interstitial Perspective' of Homi Bhabha." http://wings.buffalo.edu/epc/authors/perloff/bhabha.html.

Pizarro, Joaquín Martínez. "Ethnic and National History Ca. 500–100." *Historiography in the Middle Ages*, ed. Deborah Mauskopf Deliyannis (Leiden: Brill, 2003) 43–87.

Platt, Colin. *The Abbeys and Priories of Medieval England* (New York: Fordham University Press, 1984).

———. *The English Medieval Town* (New York: David McKay Company, 1976).

Pohl, Walter. "The Construction of Communities and the Persistence of Paradox: An Introduction." *The Constitution of Communities in the Early Middle Ages: Texts, Resources and Artefacts*, ed. Richard Corradini, Max Diesenberger, and Helmut Reimitz (Leiden: Brill, 2003) 1–15.

———. "Ethnic Names and Identities in the British Isles: A Comparative Perspective." *The Anglo-Saxons from the Migration Period to the Eighth Century: An Ethnographic Perspective*, ed. John Hines (Woodbridge, Suffolk: Boydell Press, 1997) 7–31.

———. "Introduction: Strategies of Distinction." *Strategies of Distinction: The Construction of Ethnic Communities, 300–800*, ed. Walter Pohl (Leiden: Brill, 1998) 1–15.

———. "Telling the Difference: Signs of Ethnic Identity." *Strategies of Distinction: The Construction of Ethnic Communities, 300–800*, ed. Walter Pohl (Leiden: Brill, 1998) 17–69.

Potts, Cassandra. " '*Atque unum ex diversis gentibus populum effecit*': Historical Tradition and the Norman Identity." *Anglo-Norman Studies* 18 (1996) 139–52.

Pounds, N. J. G. *The Medieval Castle in England and Wales: A Social and Political History* (Cambridge: Cambridge University Press, 1990).

Powicke, F. M. "Gerald of Wales." *The Christian Life in the Middle Ages and Other Essays* (Oxford: Clarendon Press, 1935) 107–29.

Pratt, Mary Louise. "The Anticolonial Past." *Modern Language Quarterly* 65 (2004) 443–56.

Resnick, Irven M. "Medieval Roots of the Myth of Jewish Male Menses." *Harvard Theological Review* 93 (2000).

Reuter, Timothy. "The Making of England and Germany, 850–1050: Points of Comparison and Difference." *Medieval Europeans: Studies in Ethnic Identity and National Perspectives in Medieval Europe*, ed. Alfred P. Smyth (New York: St Martin's Press, 1998) 53–70.

Reynolds, Susan. *An Introduction to the History of Medieval Towns* (Oxford: Clarendon Press, 1977).

———. *Kingdoms and Communities in Western Europe, 900–1300*, 2nd ed. (Oxford: Clarendon Press, 1997).

———. "Medieval *Origines Gentium* and the Community of the Realm." *History* 68 (1983) 375–90.

———. "Our Forefathers? Tribes, Peoples, and Nations in the Historiography of the Age of Migrations." *After Rome's Fall: Narrators and Sources of Early Medieval History*, ed. Alexander Callander Murray (Toronto: University of Toronto Press, 1998) 17–36.

———. "What Do We Mean by 'Anglo-Saxon' and 'Anglo-Saxons'?" *Journal of British Studies* 24 (1985) 395–414.

Richardson, H. G. *The English Jewry under Angevin Kings* (London: Methuen, 1960).

Richmond, Colin. "Englishness and Medieval Anglo-Jewry." *The Jewish Heritage in British History: Englishness and Jewishness*, ed. Tony Kushner (London: Frank Cass, 1992) 42–59.

Richter, Michael. "Canterbury's Primacy in Wales and the First Stage of Bishop Bernard's Opposition." *Journal of Ecclesiastical History* 22 (1971) 177–89.

———. "Gerald of Wales: A Reassessment on the 750th Anniversary of His Death." *Traditio* 29 (1973) 379–90.

———. "Giraldus Cambrensis: The Growth of the Welsh Nation." *National Library of Wales Journal* 16 (1969–1970) 193–252; 17 (1971–1972) 1–50.

———. "National Identity in Medieval Wales." *Medieval Europeans: Studies in Ethnic Identity and National Perspectives in Medieval Europe*, ed. Alfred P. Smyth (New York: St Martin's Press, 1998) 71–84.

———. "The Political and Institutional Background to National Consciousness in Medieval Wales." *Nationality and the Pursuit of National Independence*, ed. T. W. Moody (Belfast: Appletree Press, 1978) 37–55.

Roberts, Brynley F. "Geoffrey of Monmouth and the Welsh Historical Tradition." *Nottingham Mediaeval Studies* 20 (1976) 29–40.

———. "Writing in Wales." *The Cambridge History of Medieval English Literature*, ed. David Wallace (Cambridge: Cambridge University Press, 1999) 182–207.

Robertson, Elizabeth. "The 'Elvyssh' Power of Constance: Christian Feminism in Geoffrey Chaucer's *The Man of Law's Tale.*" *Studies in the Age of Chaucer* 23 (2001) 143–80.

Robertson, Kellie. "Geoffrey of Monmouth and the Translation of Insular Historiography." *Arthuriana* 8.4 (1998) 42–68.

Roderick, A. J. "Marriage and Politics in Wales, 1066–1282." *Welsh History Review* 4 (1968–1969) 3–20.

Rollo, David. "Gerald of Wales' *Topographia Hibernica*: Sex and the Irish Nation." *The Romanic Review* 86.2 (1995) 169–90.

Rose, Emily. "The Cult of St. William of Norwich and the Accusation of Ritual Murder in Anglo-Norman England" (PhD thesis, Princeton University, 2001).

Rosser, Gervase. "Myth, Image and Social Process in the English Medieval Town." *Urban History* 23 (1996) 5–25.

Roth, Cecil. "The Feast of Purim and the Origins of the Blood Accusation." *Speculum* 8 (1933) 520–26.

———. *A History of the Jews in England*, 3rd ed. (Oxford: Clarendon Press, 1964).

Rubin, Miri. *Gentile Tales: The Narrative Assault on Late Medieval Jews* (New Haven: Yale University Press, 1999).

———. "Religious Culture in Town and Country: Reflections on a Great Divide." *Church and City, 1000–1500*, ed. David Abulafia, Michael Franklin, and Miri Rubin (Cambridge: Cambridge University Press, 1992) 3–22.

Salter, Elizabeth. *English and International: Studies in the Literature, Art and Patronage of Medieval England*, ed. Derek Pearsall and Nicolette Zeeman (Cambridge: Cambridge University Press, 1988).

Saperstein, Marc. "Jews and Christians: Some Positive Images." *Harvard Theological Review* 79 (1986) 236–46.

Searle, Eleanor. *Predatory Kinship and the Creation of Norman Power, 840–1066* (Berkeley: University of California Press, 1988).

Shinners, John R. "The Veneration of Saints at Norwich Cathedral in the Fourteenth Century." *Norfolk Archeology* 40 (1988) 133–44.

Shopkow, Leah. Review of Marjorie Chibnall, *The Normans* in *Speculum* 79 (2004) 466–67.

Short, Ian. "Patrons and Polyglots: French Literature in Twelfth-Century England." *Anglo-Norman Studies* 14 (1991) 229–49.

Siewers, Alfred K. "Landscapes of Conversion: Guthlac's Mound and Grendel's Mere as Expressions of Anglo-Saxon Nation-Building." *Viator* 34 (2003) 1–39.

Sims-Williams, Patrick. *Religion and Literature in the West of England, 600–800* (Cambridge: Cambridge University Press, 1990).

Skinner, Patricia. "Introduction: Jews in Medieval Britain and Europe." *The Jews in Medieval Britain: Historical, Literary and Archaeological Perspectives*, ed. Patricia Skinner (Woodbridge, Suffolk: Boydell Press, 2003) 1–11.

Smedley, Audrey. " 'Race' and the Construction of Human Identity." *American Anthropologist* 100 (1998) 690–702.

Smith, Anthony D. *The Ethnic Origins of Nations* (Oxford: Blackwell, 1986).

Snyder, Christopher A. *The Britons* (Oxford: Blackwell, 2003).

Southern, R. W. "Aspects of the European Tradition of Historical Writing 1. The Classical Tradition from Einhard to Geoffrey of Monmouth." *TRHS* 5th series 20 (1970) 173–96.

―――. "Aspects of the European Tradition of Historical Writing 4. The Sense of the Past." *TRHS* 5th series 23 (1973) 245–56.

―――. *Western Views of Islam in the Midde Ages* (Cambridge: Harvard University Press, 1962).

Stacey, Robert. "The Conversion of Jews to Christianity in Thirteenth-Century England." *Speculum* 67 (1992) 263–83.

―――. "Crusades, Martyrdoms, and the Jews of Norman England, 1096–1190." *Juden und Christen Zur Zeit der Kreuzzüge*, ed. Alfred Haverkamp (Sigmaringen: Jan Thorbecke, 1999) 233–51.

―――. "Edward I and the Final Phase of Anglo-Jewry." *The Jews in Medieval Britain: Historical, Literary and Archaeological Perspectives*, ed. Patricia Skinner (Woodbridge, Suffolk: Boydell Press, 2003) 55–70.

―――. "From Ritual Crucifixion to Host Desecration: Jews and the Body of Christ." *Jewish History* 12 (1998) 11–28.

―――. "Jews and Christians in Twelfth-Century England: Some Dynamics of a Changing Relationship." *Jews and Christians in Twelfth-Century Europe*, ed. Michael A. Signer and John Van Engen (Notre Dame: University of Notre Dame Press, 2001) 340–54.

―――. "Recent Work on Medieval English Jewish History." *Jewish History* 2 (1987) 61–72.

Stafford, Pauline. *Queen Emma and Queen Edith: Queenship and Women's Power in Eleventh-Century England* (Oxford: Blackwell, 1997).

―――. *Unification and Conquest: A Political and Social History of England in the Tenth and Eleventh Centuries* (London: Edward Arnold, 1989)

Stein, Robert M. "Making History English: Cultural Identity and Historical Explanation in William of Malmesbury and Laȝamon's *Brut*." *Text and Territory: Geographical Imagination in the Middle Ages*, ed. Sylvia Tomasch and Sealy Gilles (Philadelphia: University of Pennsylvania Press, 1998) 97–115

―――. "Signs and Things: The 'Vita Heinrici IV. Imperatoris' and the Crisis of Interpretation in Twelfth-Century History." *Traditio* 43 (1987) 105–119.

―――. "The Trouble with Harold: The Ideological Context of the *Vita Haroldi.*" *New Medieval Literatures* 2 (1998) 181–204.

Stenton, F. M. *Anglo-Saxon England*, 3rd ed. (Oxford: Clarendon Press, 1971).

Stenton, Frank. "Norman London: An Essay." *Norman London*, ed. William Fitz Stephen (New York: Italica Press, 1990) 1–45.

Stevens, Wallace. *The Collected Poems of Wallace Stevens* (New York: Vintage, 1982).

Strohm, Paul. *Theory and the Premodern Text* (Minneapolis: University of Minnesota Press, 2000).

Stow, Kenneth R. *Alienated Minority: The Jews of Medieval Latin Europe* (Cambridge: Harvard University Press, 1992).

Strickland, Debra Higgs. *Saracens, Demons, and Jews: Making Monsters in Medieval Art* (Princeton: Princeton University Press, 2003).

Sutherland, A. C. "The Imagery of Gildas's *De Excidio Britanniae.*" *Gildas: New Approaches*, ed. Michael Lapidge and David Dumville (Woodbridge, Suffolk: Boydell Press, 1984) 157–68.

Tait, James. *The Medieval English Borough: Studies on its Origins and Constitutional History* (Manchester: Manchester University Press, 1936).

Tanner, Norman. "The Cathedral and the City." *Norwich Cathedral: Church, City and Diocese, 1096–1996*, ed. Ian Atherton, Eric Fernie, Christopher Harper-Bill, and Hassell Smith (London: Hambledon Press, 1996) 255–80.

Tatlock, J. S. P. *The Legendary History of Britain: Geoffrey's "Historia Regum Britanniae" and its Early Vernacular Versions* (Berkeley: University of California Press, 1950).

Thomas, Hugh M. *The English and the Normans: Ethnic Hostility, Assimilation, and Identity, 1066-c.1220* (Oxford: Oxford University Press, 2003).

Thomson, Rodney. *William of Malmesbury* (Woodbridge, Suffolk: Boydell Press, 1987).

Tolan, John V. *Saracens: Islam in the Medieval European Imagination* (New York: Columbia University Press, 2002).

Tolhurst, Fiona. "The Britons as Hebrews, Romans, and Normans: Geoffrey of Monmouth's British Epic and Reflections of Empress Matilda." *Arthuriana* 8.4 (1998) 69–87.

Tomasch, Sylvia. "Judecca, Dante's Satan, and the *Dis*-placed Jew." *Text and Territory: Geographical Imagination in the Middle Ages*, ed. Sylvia Tomasch and Sealy Gilles (Philadelphia: University of Pennsylvania Press, 1998) 247–67.

———. "Postcolonial Chaucer and the Virtual Jew." *The Postcolonial Middle Ages*, ed. Jeffrey Jerome Cohen (New York: Palgrave, 2000) 243–60.

Townsend, David. "Anglo-Latin Hagiography and the Norman Transition." *Exemplaria* 3 (1991) 385–433.

Trachtenberg, Joshua. *The Devil and the Jews: The Medieval Conception of the Jew and its Relation to Modern Anti-Semitism* (Philadelphia: The Jewish Publication Society of America, 1983).

Turner, Frederick Jackson. *The Frontier in American History* (New York: Holt, 1947).

Turner, Norman. "The Cathedral and the City." *Norwich Cathedral: Church, City and Diocese, 1096–1996*, ed. Ian Atherton, Eric Fernie, Christopher Harper-Bill, and Hassell Smith (London: Hambledon Press, 1996) 255–80.

Tyerman, Christopher. *England and the Crusades, 1095–1588* (Chicago: University of Chicago Press, 1988)

Tyrrell, Andrew. "*Corpus Saxonum*: Early Medieval Bodies and Identity." *Social Identity in Early Medieval England*, ed. William O. Frazer and Andrew Tyrrell (London: Leicester University Press, 2000) 137–55.

Uebel, Michael. "Unthinking the Monster: Twelfth-Century Responses to Saracen Alterity." *Monster Theory: Reading Culture*, ed. Jeffrey Jerome Cohen (Minneapolis: University of Minnesota Press, 1996) 264–91.

Van Court, Elisa Narin. "Socially Marginal, Culturally Central: Representing Jews in Late Medieval English Literature." *Exemplaria* 12 (2000) 293–26.

Van Engen, John. "Introduction: Jews and Christians Together in the Twelfth Century." *Jews and Christians in Twelfth-Century Europe*, ed. Michael A. Signer and John Van Engen (Notre Dame: University of Notre Dame Press, 2001) 1–8.

van Houts, Elisabeth. "The Memory of 1066 in Written and Oral Traditions." *Anglo-Norman Studies* 19 (1996) 167–79.

Vélez-Ibáñez, Carlos G. *Border Visions: Mexican Cultures of the Southwest United States* (Tucson: University of Arizona Press, 1996).

Wada, Yoko. "Gerald on Gerald: Self-Presentation by Giraldus Cambernsis." *Anglo-Norman Studies* 20 (1998) 223–46.

Wald, Gayle. *Crossing the Line: Racial Passing in Twentieth-Century U. S. Literature and Culture* (Durham: Duke University Press, 2000).

Walker, David. *Medieval Wales* (Cambridge: Cambridge University Press, 1990).

Wallace, David. *Premodern Places: Calias to Surinam, Chaucer to Aphra Behn* (Oxford: Blackwell, 2004).

Wallace-Hadrill, J. M. *Bede's* Ecclesiastical History of the English People: *A Historical Commentary* (Oxford: Clarendon Press, 1988).

Ward, Benedicta. *Miracles and the Medieval Mind: Theory, Record and Event, 1000–1215* (Philadelphia: University of Pennsylvania Press, 1982).

Warren, Michelle. *History on the Edge: Excalibur and the Borders of Britain, 1100–1300* (Minneapolis: University of Minnesota Press, 2000).

———. "Making Contact: Postcolonial Perspectives Through Geoffrey of Monmouth's *Historia regum Britannie*." *Arthuriana* 8 (1998) 115–34.

———. "The Noise of Roland." *Exemplaria* 16 (2004) 277–304.

Waswo, Richard. "The History that Literature Makes." *New Literary History* 19 (1988) 541–64.

———. "Our Ancestors, The Trojans: Inventing Cultural Identity in the Middle Ages." *Exemplaria* 7 (1995) 269–90.

Webb, Diana. *Pilgrimage in Medieval England* (London: Hambledon Press, 2000).

Wells, Peter S. *The Barbarians Speak: How the Conquered Peoples Shaped Roman Europe* (Princeton: Princeton University Press, 1999).

Webster, Bruce. "John of Fordum and the Independent Identity of the Scots." *Medieval Europeans: Studies in Ethnic Identity and National Perspectives in Medieval Europe*, ed. Alfred P. Smyth (New York: St Martin's Press, 1998) 85–102.

West, Francis James. "The Colonial History of the Norman Conquest?" *History* 84 (1999) 219–36.

Westrem, Scott D. "Against Gog and Magog." *Text and Territory: Geographical Imagination in the Middle Ages*, ed. Sylvia Tomasch and Sealy Gilles (Philadelphia: University of Pennsylvania Press, 1998) 54–75.

Whitelock, Dorothy. "The Pre-Viking Age Church in East Anglia." *Anglo-Saxon England* 1 (1972) 1–22.

Williams, Ann. *The English and the Norman Conquest* (Woodbridge, Suffolk: Boydell Press, 1995).

Williamson, Tom. *The Origins of Norfolk* (Manchester: Manchester University Press, 1993).

Wolfe, Cary. *Animal Rites: American Culture, the Discourse of Species, and Posthumanist Theory* (Chicago: University of Chicago Press, 2003).

———. "Introduction." *Zootologies: The Question of the Animal*, ed. Cary Wolfe (Minneapolis: University of Minnesota Press, 2003) ix–xxiii.

Wollaston, Deirdre. "Herbert de Losinga." *Norwich Cathedral: Church, City and Diocese, 1096–1996*, ed. Ian Atherton, Eric Fernie, Christopher Harper-Bill, and Hassell Smith (London: Hambledon Press, 1996) 22–35.

Wood, Ian. "Conclusion: Strategies of Distinction." *Strategies of Distinction: The Construction of Ethnic Communities, 300–800*, ed. Walter Pohl (Leiden: Brill, 1998) 297–303.

Woolf, Alex. "Community, Identity and Kingship in Early England." *Social Identity in Early Medieval England*, ed. William O. Frazer and Andrew Tyrrell (London: Leicester University Press, 2000) 91–109.

Wormald, Patrick. "Bede, Beowulf and the Conversion of the Anglo-Saxon Aristocracy." *Bede and Anglo-Saxon England*, ed. Robert T. Farrell. British Archeological Reports 46 (1978) 32–90.

———. "Bede, the *Bretwaldas* and the Origin of the *gens Anglorum*." *Ideal and Reality in Frankish and Anglo-Saxon Society*, ed. Patrick Wormald, Donald Bullough, and Roger Collins (Oxford: Blackwell, 1983) 99–129.

———. "*Engla Land*: The Making of an Allegiance." *Journal of Historical Sociology* 7 (1994) 1–24.

Wright, Neil. "Geoffrey of Monmouth and Gildas." *Arthurian Literature* 2 (1982) 1–40.

Yntema, H. E. "The *lex murdrorum*: An Episode in the History of English Criminal Law." *Harvard Law Review* 36 (1922–1923) 146–79.

Yorke, Barbara. "Political and Ethnic Identity: A Case Study of Anglo-Saxon Practice." *Social Identity in Early Medieval England*, ed. William O. Frazer and Andrew Tyrrell (London: Leicester University Press, 2000) 69–89.

Young, Robert J. C. *Colonial Desire: Hybridity in Theory, Culture and Race* (London: Routledge, 1995).

Yuval, Israel Jacob. " 'Vengeance and Damnation, Blood and Defamation': From Jewish Martyrdom to Blood Libel Accusations." *Zion* 58 (1993) 33–90.

INDEX